Advertising Self-Regulation and Outside Participation

Advertising Self-Regulation and Outside Participation

A *Multinational Comparison*

J. J. Boddewyn

Quorum Books

New York • Westport, Connecticut • London

Library of Congress Cataloging-in-Publication Data

Boddewyn, J. J. (Jean J.)
Advertising self-regulation and outside participation : a
multinational comparison / J. J. Boddewyn.
p.   cm.
Bibliography: p.
Includes index.
ISBN 0–89930–295–5 (lib. bdg. : alk. paper)
1. Advertising—Self-regulation—Case studies. I. Title.
HF5834.B63   1988
659.1'1—dc19   87–24939

British Library Cataloguing in Publication Data is available.

Library of Congress Catalog Card Number: 87–24939
ISBN: 0–89930–295–5

First published in 1988 by Quorum Books

Greenwood Press, Inc.
88 Post Road West, Westport, Connecticut 06881

Printed in the United States of America

The paper used in this book complies with the
Permanent Paper Standard issued by the National
Information Standards Organization (Z39.48–1984).

10 9 8 7 6 5 4 3 2 1

To Marilyn

Contents

Part II. Country Analyses

Figure and Tables

Introduction

Purpose and Significance

That advertising behavior must be controlled is generally acknowledged. However, there is also increasing recognition—at least in more developed countries—that this control task need not, and even should not, be left entirely to regulation. Instead, the development and application of voluntary industry standards provides a complement to regulation—even a necessary one. For that matter, advertising self-regulation (ASR) already functions in quite a few countries, including less developed ones (Neelankavil and Stridsberg 1980), and it is quite advanced in a score of them (Boddewyn 1986).

Some of these ASR systems have been extensively studied—particularly, in Canada, the United Kingdom and the United States—so that much is already known about their major features such as overall structure, standards applied and number and types of cases handled. However, with a few exceptions (Brandmair 1978; Buell 1977; Miracle and Nevett 1987), most ASR analyses have been uninational rather than comparative. This study, however, deals with twelve countries and even borrows from a related survey of sixteen nations (Boddewyn 1986) in order to identify and compare major national differences.

Besides, other studies generally ignore or make only brief references to the participation of nonindustry members in the structure and functioning of ASR systems. Yet, such "outside participation" exists in some form in all of them, and plays a major role in some. While it may violate the principle of "pure" self-regulation by one's peers, outside participation is not only part of the spirit of our times, but is becoming necessary in some form(s) as the tasks of advertising self-regulation have grown and its credibility has been questioned. By focusing on this increasingly important dimension of ASR systems, the present study expands our knowledge of advertising self-regulation as it adjusts to new environmental situations and demands. In particular, this study analyzes and compares the factors facilitating and hindering outside participation in advertising self-regulation.

Finally, regulation and self-regulation are not just complementary forms of advertising control that coexist in autonomous and separated spheres. Instead, they interact in various ways, with governmental threat or prodding often needed for the creation and improvement of advertising self-regulation. Again, this interaction has usually been underanalyzed in other ASR studies, while this one emphasizes it as a form of outside participation. As such, the present study provides an opportunity to explore the political-science concept of neo-corporatism, which deals with certain forms of industry representation in social control (cf. Streeck and Schmitter 1985).

Scope and Limitations

Since advertising self-regulation exists in about thirty-five nations (Neelankavil and Stridsberg 1980), the twelve country studies in this volume do not cover the whole range of national experiences, and only two less developed nations (Brazil and the Philippines) are included. However, most of the "pilot" countries that have well-developed ASR systems are analyzed. Argentina, Australia, Hong Kong, Ireland, Singapore, Spain, South Africa and Switzerland are probably the single most important omissions (but see Chapter 15 for some information about them). Besides, the entire range of outside participation is present, from countries with practically none (Belgium and Germany) to those with much of it (Italy and the United Kingdom).

The country studies focus on the central ASR organization, which typically deals only with national advertising, the major media and key metropolitan areas. This leaves out other self-regulatory bodies: (1) focusing on advertising self-regulation in particular industries (e.g., pharmaceuticals and tobacco); (2) dealing with intraindustry ethics (e.g., advertiser, advertising agency and media associations), and (3) handling consumer complaints only at the local level (e.g., Better Business Bureaus in the United States). Such a complete analysis of all the forms assumed by advertising self-regulation in each country was out of the question for lack of time and financial resources (but see the LaBarbera 1983 survey of advertising self-regulation by numerous U.S. associations as well as the various studies conducted by this author for the International Advertising Association on the regulation and self-regulation of advertising in specific industries around the world).

Finally, this study stresses the use of advertising self-regulation in the context of consumer protection rather than for handling conflicts among competitors— the traditional fair-competition issue. Advertising is defined here as the use of paid communication through the mass and/or specialized media.

Methodology

In many countries, the available literature is scanty and usually written in languages unfamiliar to this author. Consequently, most of the information had to be gathered through personal and telephone interviews with seven to forty practitioners, regulators and experts in each country, over a week's time in 1981–1987. However, drafts of all the country studies were circulated to the respondents and to other people familiar with the local advertising self-regulatory system, so that gross errors of fact and interpretation could be avoided and further insights obtained. This supplementary checking also helped reduce the bias created by interviewers being suggested and/or selected in many cases by the local ASR body.

Each country study briefly describes the national ASR system and its inter-action with government and the consumerist movement. Particular emphasis is then put on the extent of outside participation and the contributions of outsiders—that is, nonindustry members—to the ASR system's functioning. The following list used in the Philippines illustrates the general thrust of the questions asked in each country.

1. To what extent are "outsiders" (that is, nondustry members) involved in the activities of the Philippine Board of Advertising (PBA) and other advertising self-regulatory bodies in the Philippines?

1. What proportion of the total PBA membership do they represent?
2. How are they selected? Whom do they represent?
3. What are they expected to contribute to the PBA process?
4. Does their participation vary according to the nature of the problem (for example, advertising to children, comparison advertising, premiums, feminine-hygiene products)?

2. How do the outside members, government officials and consumer organizations as well as academic and other experts feel about the need for, and effectiveness of, outside participation in advertising self-regulation? Does it work? Is more of it needed? How can it be improved if necessary?

3. What factors explain the present state of outside participation in Philippine self-regulatory bodies, and are likely to affect its development?

These descriptive questions and the resulting answers were progressively informed by a review of the general and national literatures in a "grounded theory" framework. Glaser and Strauss (1967) have emphasized the evolutionary nature of research, particularly during the fieldwork phase, as categories and properties emerge, develop, become interrelated and gradually begin to form an integrated theoretical framework. In other words, original theoretical insights are progressively developed into a larger and more coherent theory (that is, an explanation) as data and understanding become available through fieldwork. Consequently, the hypotheses presented at the end of chapters 1 and 2 were not fully developed a priori, but progressively emerged and were refined as research progressed.

Even in this form, they are not intended as precise and rigorous statements to be tested through the collection of quantitative data, but as guides to the interpretation of the country analyses and as broad statements of the explanations to be advanced and argued regarding advertising self-regulation as well as about the presence and effectiveness of outside participation in it.

Plan of Study

Chapter 1 conceptualizes and theorizes about advertising self-regulation in order to provide a background for a comparable study of outside participation in Chapter 2. The twelve country analyses of Belgium, Brazil, Canada, France, The Federal Republic of Germany, Italy, Japan, the Netherlands, the Philippines, Sweden, the United Kingdom and the United States blend these two topics, with particular emphasis on what has prompted, facilitated or hindered outside participation in the light of each nation's environment. In Chapter 15, the results of a 1986 survey conducted by this author for the International Advertising Association are presented for sixteen major ASR systems, thereby broadening the international scope of this analysis, and providing some comparative data. Chapter 16 provides an integrative proto-theory of advertising self-regulation and outside participation, together with some recommendations for further research and policy development.

The general chapters and the country studies include their own bibliographies while the references used in chapters 1, 2, 15, and 16 appear at the end of this book.

Acknowledgments

The country chapters mention most of the people who assisted as interviewees, experts, interpreters and draft reviewers. This research was mainly financed by Grant No. B19793 from the PSC-CUNY Research Award Program of the City University of New York, but the moral support of the International Advertising Association—particularly of Sylvan M. Barnet, Jr.—was also very important. I deeply thank all of them but particularly Maurizio Fusi (Italy), Raymond Haas (France), Robert Oliver (Canada), Sten Tengelin (Sweden) and Peter Thomson (United Kingdom), from whom I learned much about the essence, inner workings and external relations of ASR systems. The word–processing staff of Baruch College deserves unbound praise and gratitude for working over this text for several years.

Advertising Self-Regulation and Outside Participation

I

General Analysis

1

Advertising Self-Regulation: Concept, Rationale, Forms and Evolution

There is an abundant, if scattered, literature on the nature, history, advantages and disadvantages, legal standing, functioning and effectiveness of self-regulation—in general and as applied to advertising.[1] This chapter, therefore, provides only the overview needed to understand its principles and functioning as well as to develop hypotheses about its existence and evolution.

Key Concepts

Fair competition, consumer protection and other public policies require that advertising not be false, misleading, unfair, unwholesome or otherwise contrary to prevailing standards—legal, social and moral—even though the precise meaning of such norms differs from place to place and evolves over time. Thus, the International Code of Advertising Practice of the International Chamber of Commerce—the bible of advertising self-regulation—starts by stating that: "All advertising should be legal, decent, honest and truthful. Every advertisement should be prepared with a due sense of social responsibility, and should conform to the principles of fair competition as generally accepted in business. No advertisement should be such as to impair public confidence in advertising (ICC 1973 and 1987)."

Ensuring such "good" advertising behavior requires that the following control tasks be performed: (1) developing standards; (2) making them widely known and accepted by advertising professionals; (3) advising advertisers and agencies beforehand on a voluntary or mandatory basis; (4) monitoring compliance with the norms; (5) handling complaints from consumers, competitors and other interested parties; and (6) penalizing "bad" behavior in violation of the standards.

The performance of these control tasks can be achieved through a variety of means ranging from laissez-faire to regulation, with self-regulation and various hybrid forms in between. As Gupta and Lad (1983) point out, too many people assume that if the market system fails, only governmental regulation can correct its shortcomings: "It appears that researchers have focussed primarily on the alternative *substantive* forms that regulation can take and have ignored the alternative *institutional* arrangements through which rules and standards are/might be set, performance monitored, and correction of deviation from the set rules and standards enforced [p. 416]." Actually, several forms of advertising control usually coexist and complement each other.

Laissez-faire and Self-discipline

Under laissez-faire, the control of advertising behavior is left to individual firms and customers—not to associations or the government: "If competition alone would effectively regulate the market in all circumstances, both laws and self-regulation would be superfluous (Rosden and Rosden 1982, p. 40.3)." Business's temptation to fool the clientele or abuse competitors is also tempered by self-discipline[2] based on personal moral principles, current notions of fair/ethical business behavior, and/or on self-interest since advertisers fear consumer defection as well as regulatory restrictions. Consequently, a number of advertisers and agencies as well as most media have developed their own code or internal rules for the production and acceptance of advertisements. This approach to advertising control (not further discussed here)[3] has been endlessly challenged on the grounds that: (1) there is no necessary correspondence between private and public interests, and (2) abuses are inevitable but will not always be redressed through the working of the market or of people's conscience.

Regulation

Here, all or part of advertising behavior is mandated and/or circumscribed by various government rules backed by the use of legal penalties, on the ground that the public interest is best served through statutory controls because: (1) business cannot be trusted to self-discipline and/or self-regulate itself well, and (2) many consumers and even competitors lack the will or the means to countervail bad business behavior.[4] Its major advantages lie in universal reach and compulsion—compared to laissez-faire, self-discipline and self-regulation, where only those who care enough do apply standards of good advertising behavior. However, the regulatory approach has been criticized for being oppressive, ineffectual, confused, conflictual, costly, rigid, weakly enforced (recent budget-cutting is not helping here), amenable to capture by its targets, and the like. In other words, the regulation designed to correct "market failures" often results in "regulatory failures" of its own (Carman and Harris 1986). The recent deregulatory movement aimed at retrenching the State, applying cost-benefit analysis to regulation and restoring greater scope to private initiative rests, of course, on such philosophical and practical arguments (cf. Thompson and Jones 1982).

Self-Regulation

This system refers to "the control of business conduct and performance by business itself rather than by government or by market forces (Pickering and Cousins 1980, p. 17)." In its pure form, industry assumes full responsibility for the six control tasks previously outlined. Control is exercised by one's peers so that "outsiders" such as consumer representatives and/or government officials are kept out of the development, use and enforcement of an industry's code of practice and/or guidelines. This pure approach does not preclude informal consultations with outsiders but it excludes a formal decision-making role for them. More hybrid forms involving outsiders are growing, however (see below).[5]

The notion of self-regulation as a fully "voluntary" process is an ambiguous one since it is seldom administered only to "members" who have explicitly subscribed to agreed-upon rules of conduct, but is applied instead to all or most advertising participants. When governments mandate self-regulation or intervene in its functioning, its voluntary character also becomes tenuous.[6] Still, it relies mainly on various forms of moral suasion to obtain compliance, and is "voluntary" to the extent that its sanction are not legally binding but are freely accepted by most advertisers found to have erred.

Forms and Evolution of Self-Regulation

This classification of achieving control of advertising behavior through either laissez-faire, self-discipline, self-regulation and regulation should not suggest an "either-or" situation nor a static one (Garvin 1983, p. 48). For one thing, these four systems coexist in various mixtures throughout most of the world where there are at least thirty-five fairly sophisticated self-regulatory systems—particularly in developed countries but also in Brazil, Hong Kong, the Philippines and Singapore, among developing nations (Boddewyn 1986; Burleton 1982; Neelankavil and Stridsberg 1980). Elsewhere, regulation, self-discipline or laissez-faire predominates. More generally, as Streeck and Schmitter (1985) have pointed out, even where a large share of public policy is made by, and implemented through, intermediary industry associations, these are always to some extent dependent on community values and cohesion (that is, they must reflect current social concerns), are kept in check by economic and political market forces and are subject to hierarchical control, political design and the pressure of potential direct state intervention. Therefore, there is always interrelatedness among the various forms of advertising control.

Second, "pure" advertising self-regulation administered only by industry members is being progressively replaced by hybrid forms, where a variety of "outsiders"—whether consumer representatives (as in Canada and the Netherlands) or public members (as in Brazil, Italy, the United Kingdom and the United States)—are *co-opted* to participate to varying degrees in the implementation of codes and guidelines. While most of these outsiders are in a minority position, the British Advertising Standards Authority includes a two-third majority while the Italian Advertising Jury is made up entirely of independents. Even relatively pure self-regulatory bodies (e.g., in France) involve outsiders (including government representatives) as advisers or experts. Consequently, external representatives have acquired "voice" and even developed "loyalty" within the self-regulatory system (Hirschman 1970) through what Hondius (1984, p. 140) calls "concerted action."

Third, further down the road are *codes of practice voluntarily negotiated* between self-regulatory and consumer associations and/or the government (European Advertising Tripartite [EAT] 1983; European Communities [EC] 1981; European Consumer Law Group [ECLG] 1983). Thus, the European Advertising Tripartite (of advertiser, agency and media associations) and COFACE (EEC Committee of Family Associations) are jointly developing guidelines for toy advertising as well as an enforcement system. The guidelines issued by the Swedish Consumer Policies Board (to which the Ombudsman is related) provide another example of rules negotiated among business, government and consumer representatives. This approach helps reduce the criticism that codes only reflect the industry's interests, but such negotiations are difficult to handle and seldom satisfy consumerists.

Fourth, negotiated agreements can be *sanctioned by government* and become "collective conventions" applying to an entire industry, including nonmembers of the self-regulatory system. This "corporatist" stage has not been fully reached in advertising, as far as is known, although there are elements of it in Brazil, the Philippines and even the United Kingdom. Some agreements between governments and local tobacco and pharmaceutical industries about the promotion of their products also belong here. The advertising industry, however, is generally opposed to it because a corporatist approach tends to "freeze" codes and guidelines, which cannot be changed without government approval, thereby reducing their crucial flexibility.

Fifth, codes like the World Health Organization's Code of Marketing of Breast-milk Substitutes (which bears on their advertising) are being *morally imposed* on business from the outside. They often lack clear instructions and procedures for monitoring advertising practices and adjudicating complaints although they are being translated into laws and industry codes by some countries. Commenting on such codes, the European Advertising Tripartite remarked that: "Industry should not be expected to enter into agreements against its own interests or better judgment. In such cases, national legislation fought through the democratic process may be the most effective means of establishing controversial controls (EAT 1983, p. 10)."

Figure 1.1 recapitulates these various forms of advertising controls and their characteristics (see also ICC [1984] for a similar classification).

Figure 1.1
Types of Advertising Controls

SELF-DISCIPLINE: Norms are developed, used and enforced by the <u>firm</u> itself.

    TYPE A: The norms apply only to members of the organization.

    TYPE B: The norms apply to everybody (e.g., the acceptance codes of
           broadcasting stations, newspapers and magazines that are
           applied to advertisers using their services).

PURE SELF-REGULATION: Norms are developed, used and enforced by the <u>industry</u>
    itself ("one's peers").

    TYPE A: The norms apply only to members of the association.

    TYPE B: The norms apply to everybody, even to nonmembers.

COOPTED SELF-REGULATION: The industry, on its own volition, involves
    nonindustry people (e.g., consumer and government representatives,
    independent members of the public, experts) in the development, application
    and/or enforcement of its norms. These "outsiders" are thereby "internalized."

    TYPE A: Same as above.

    TYPE B: Same as above.

NEGOTIATED SELF-REGULATION: The industry voluntarily negotiates the development,
    application and/or enforcement of norms with some outside body (e.g., a
    government department or a consumer association). In this case, "outsiders"
    remain "outside."

    TYPE A: Same as above.

    TYPE B: Same as above.

MANDATED SELF-REGULATION: An industry is ordered or designated by the government
    to develop, apply and/or enforce norms - whether alone or in concert with
    other bodies. This system is akin to "corporatism."

    TYPE B: The norms apply to everybody.

PURE REGULATION: The government monopolizes the development, application and/or
    enforcement of norms.

    TYPE B: The norms apply to everybody.

These various approaches involving outsiders are not without problems, both philosophical and practical, since they violate the principle of *self*-regulation and require able, willing and credible outside participants, who are not always readily available (see Chapter 2). Concern has also been expressed by some advertising-industry members (e.g., in Canada) that self-regulation may become onerous in terms of assumed assignments and quasiregulatory tasks (e.g., the required pre-clearance of certain types of advertisements). Better then to leave such functions to government and/or to lobby against regulatory restrictions. Besides, self-regulatory systems may be "captured" by government once a code has been developed and found to be operational—in other words, self-regulation can serve as the "pilot" for ultimate regulation by proving what is acceptable and feasible.

However, the present deregulatory climate as well as the cost of governmental assumption of self-regulatory tasks militates against such a capture, which has not taken place to date so far as advertising self-regulation is concerned even though its threat concerns some industry leaders and members.

The Pros and Cons of Self-Regulation

Advantages

To its proponents, self-regulation presents many advantages over regulation (cf. Bourgoignie 1984; Grumbly 1982; Hondius 1984; ICC 1984; Jones and Pickering 1985; LaBarbera 1980a and b; Lad 1985; Maitland 1985; Pickering and Cousins 1980; Rosden and Rosden 1982; and Thomson 1983).

1. Self-regulation is faster and cheaper[7] as well as more efficient and effective (flexible, on target, up to date, etc.) than government regulation because industry knows better what the problems and their realistic remedies are.[8] While obsolete government regulations tend to remain on the books, voluntary rules are subject to a market test since no one will follow them when they become unnecessary. Should the industry lack information or expertise about certain matters (e.g., to what extent are consumers misled by certain advertisements), they can be obtained by tapping experts or by commissioning studies.

2. Self-regulation does not require that injury to a consumer or competitor be proven—as is usually required by law, except when class actions are allowed to waive that requirement. Instead, it is in the industry's and the public's interest that ads be true and not misleading so that such proof of individual injury is not necessary. Besides, complainants can remain anonymous and free to pursue their case through other means (e.g., by publicizing their case to the media), while legal processes usually preclude such ''publicity'' approaches while the case is being investigated and handled in court.

3. Self-regulation constitutes an essential line of defense against excessive advertising regulation, whose limits are often boundless since freedom of ''commercial speech'' is protected in very few countries.[9]

4. It does not replace regulation but complements the latter, going beyond the minimum prescribed by the law. Actually, in Belgium, Canada and France, the self-regulatory system also applies legal standards—besides its own codes and guidelines—in appraising apparent violations of good advertising behavior. In particular, codes can deal with matters that the law finds difficult to handle (e.g., taste, decency and sexism), and be even more stringent than regulation (e.g., the prohibited broadcasting of hard-liquor commercials by the U.S. distilled-spirits industry) when the law itself does not forbid a particular practice (LaBarbera 1980a and b, Wyckham 1987). Self-regulation may even serve as a testing ground for rules to be ultimately incorporated into the law once their effectiveness has been proven. Conversely, self-regulation allows government to focus on more important matters such as fraud and trade restraints, and on

those problems where solutions are clear-cut and consensus has developed (e.g., direct-mail advertisers should always include a full mailing address rather than a mere postal-box number in their ads). As has been observed, courts do not choose cases, do not deal with a representative sample of issues, and see only the tips of icebergs and the bottoms of barrels.

5. Self-regulation generates greater moral adhesion than the law because codes and guidelines are voluntarily developed and adopted by industry members who must obey not only the letter but also the spirit of self-imposed rules, and must abide by the decisions of their peers — at least in principle. As one commentator put it: "The idea is to develop the feeling among those who subscribe to the voluntary standards that the latter are really compulsory although they are not." In this perspective, self-regulation represents a continuation or resurgence of an old type of norm, namely, customs or mores (Bureau de Vérification de la Publicité [BVP] 1985, pp. 17–18).

6. The self-regulatory approach helps minimize the frictions between business and consumers as well as among businessmen, which regulation tends to encourage by stressing compulsion, conflict (e.g., suing) and penalization instead of persuasion, mediation and negotiation.[10]

7. Compared with self-regulation in other industries, advertising self-regulation benefits from one major element: *the intermediary position of the media.*[11] The latter, in most countries where a self-regulatory system exists, usually agree to suspend the publication or broadcasting of advertisements found deficient (this is not true in the United States, where antitrust considerations make such an agreement problematic). Besides, most media have their own acceptance rules, which provide some additional screening if not censorship of advertising;[12] and they react on their own to consumer and competitor complaints about what they publish or broadcast. Only nonmedia promotions (such as direct-mail) escape this further scrutiny although there are self-regulatory direct-mail associations in quite a few countries, and post-office systems generally control the fraudulent use of the mails.

Disadvantages

Conversely, self-regulation has been *criticized* for the following reasons.

1. Impairing business competition and innovation because of self-serving restraints on the part of associations (e.g., many advertising bodies have opposed comparison advertising).

2. Representing a transparent device to subvert the setting of more rigorous government standards by pretending that business will do the job when, in fact, voluntary standards are set at minimal levels (to avoid low membership or schism) and/or enforcement is lax: "Why would they accept strict voluntary codes if they oppose strict mandatory rules (ECLG 1983)?"

3. Being ineffective whenever antitrust and other laws (e.g., freedom of association): (a) forbid compulsory membership so that the worst offenders stay

out (the "free-rider" problem), and/or (b) preclude extreme penalties for offenders such as fines, expulsion and boycott.

4. Lacking the proper judicial tools (e.g., subpoena power and other discovery procedures), rules (e.g., of evidence, due process and adversary hearings) and penalties (restitution, corrective advertising, etc.) (cf. Lad 1985, pp. 30–37 and 76–78).

5. Being insufficiently financed, publicized (e.g., investigations and decisions are often kept secret) and promoted (e.g., consumer complaints are not actively solicited) (Zanot 1977).

6. Including too few consumer and public-interest representatives who are, in any case, selected by the industry, and may thus be "token" outsiders. Besides, negotiations with outside groups can be lengthy and difficult, and consumer organizations often lack sufficient bargaining power (ECLG 1983).

Altogether, such criticisms have led one group of consumerist experts to conclude that: "Where there is very little, or even no prospect of legislation at all, where the choice is clearly a [voluntary] code or nothing else, then codes should be given careful consideration as a possible means of improving consumer protection. One should, however, keep in mind that the mere existence of a code can seriously undermine the case for future legislative reform (ECLG 1983, p. 211)." Besides, some critics point out that the preemption of regulation may result in inferior standards since self-regulation need only elevate the performance of the industry to the point where it no longer represents a relatively attractive target to the resource-constrained regulatory agency (Garvin 1983, p. 42). Moreover, consensus-building for new self-regulatory norms is not necessarily faster than in the case of regulation.

If anything, these pessimistic conclusions suggest that industry self-regulation cannot by itself establish a balance in the relative bargaining powers of buyers and sellers, but must be considered as only one of several means of achieving advertising control (Pickering and Cousins 1980, p. 7).[13] As Thomas (1984, p. 202) put it:

There is not a stark choice between "hard law" or "soft law;" between "regulation" or "deregulation." So far as the United Kingdom is concerned, there are many stopping points along the broad spectrum between completely unilateral self-regulation and precise, specific statutory control. It is the nature of the problem, the desired policy objectives and the political-economic background that will largely determine the most appropriate approach. This is summed up in the phrase "horses for courses" coined by the Director General of Fair Trading in his 1982 Annual Report.

Table 1.1 highlights the respective advantages and disadvantages of regulation and self-regulation (self-discipline is not covered here), although each country presents special characteristics that require different control mixes. It also confirms that neither approach can satisfactorily control advertising behavior by itself, but that a multiple approach must be used for that purpose. In any case,

Table 1.1
Respective Strengths and Weaknesses of Advertising Regulation and Self-Regulation

ADVERTISING-CONTROL TASKS	REGULATION	SELF-REGULATION
DEVELOPING STANDARDS	+ Greater sensitivity and faster response to emerging public concerns - Difficulty in elaborating standards in areas of taste, opinion and public decency - Difficulty in amending standards	- Greater lag in responding to emerging concerns + Greater ability to develop and amend standards in areas of taste, opinion and public decency
MAKING STANDARDS WIDELY KNOWN AND ACCEPTED	+ Everybody is supposed to know the law - Compulsory nature of the law generates more hostility and evasion	- Difficulty in making the public aware of the industry's standards and consumer-redress mechanisms + Greater ability to make industry members respect both the letter and the spirit of voluntarily adhered to codes and guidelines
ADVISING ADVERTISERS ABOUT GREY AREAS BEFORE THEY ADVERTISE	- This service is usually not provided by government	+ This service is increasingly being promoted and provided by industry - sometimes for a fee
MONITORING COMPLIANCE	± Routinely done but often with limited and even relatively declining resources	± Increasingly done by the industry although restricted by available financial resources
HANDLING COMPLAINTS	+ Impartial treatment + Extensive capability to handle many complaints - Slower and more expensive - Cannot put the burden of proof on advertisers in criminal cases	- Treatment may be perceived as partial - Limited capability to handle many complaints + Faster and cheaper + Usually puts the burden of proof on the incriminated advertiser
PENALIZING BAD BEHAVIOR, INCLUDING THE PUBLICITY OF WRONGDOINGS AND WRONGDOERS	+ Can force compliance - Generates hostility, foot-dragging, appeals, etc. - Limited publicity of judgments unless picked up by the press	- Problem of the noncomplier but the media will usually refuse to print or broadcast incriminated ads or commercials + More likely to obtain adherence to decisions based on voluntarily accepted standards + Greater publicity of wrongdoings and - to a lesser extent - of wrongdoers

some advertisers will remain beyond the reach of both the law and self-regulation because they are hard to reach, convince and/or prosecute; and some harm may have been done in any case before a legal or self-regulatory remedy is found (Wyckham 1987).

The Limits of Self-Regulation

It is doubtful that self-regulation, in whatever form, will ever fully satisfy consumerists and regulators because of what Streeck and Schmitter (1985, p. 16) call the counterintuitiveness of the idea that organized special interests can be turned into promoters of the public interest. Besides, consumerists and regulators have a vested interest in protecting their turf and livelihood, irrespective of their attitudes—favorable or unfavorable, strong or mild—toward business and self-regulation (cf. Vogel 1979).

A good part of the skepticism expressed toward self-regulation centers on the "free-rider" problem, namely, that not all members of an industry will accept and apply voluntary standards and bear their costs (LaBarbera 1980c, Maitland 1985)—a criticism that can also be addressed to the law whose reach and application is always incomplete and even seriously deficient (cf. Carman and Harris [1986], and the next chapter's discussion of the complaints expressed by consumerists regarding consumer-protection legislation). In this context, one must examine why people join industry associations and/or accept industry standards. The vast literature on interest groups (e.g., Moe 1981) offers various explanations centering on political objectives (e.g., obtaining legitimacy and checking the spread of regulation), economic advantages (e.g., information and advice provided by the association) and solidary goals (e.g., feeling of unity, confirmation of societal worth and personal self-respect). Some people remain impervious to these appeals and benefits, and there will always be deviants under any control system—whether mandatory or voluntary.

Therefore, the question is really whether advertising self-regulation can minimize the problem of the "free rider." In this respect, advertising benefits from the fact that *it practically always requires a medium*—the press, the postal service, electronic media, etc., and even the advertising agencies whose services are used by larger companies. Since most media have their own acceptance standards (cf. the earlier discussion of self-discipline) and accept to cooperate with ASR systems, self-regulation truly minimizes the free-rider problem in advertising. When the ASR system is financed by an automatic levy on most advertising expenditures (as in the United Kingdom), even the deviants cannot escape bearing the cost of self-regulation.

Yet, the advertising industry appears reluctant in most countries to expand self-regulation past a certain point whose exact position is hard to determine (see Chapter 15 for a discussion of this issue on the basis of a 1986 survey). Considering the endless business proclamations against the burden, inappropriateness and ineffectiveness of regulation, and the extolling of the benefits of self-regulation, one would expect the latter to receive ample and even growing resources. In fact, few systems (e.g., the British Advertising Standards Authority [ASA]) have a large staff as well as sizable and steady finances, and do engage in wide publicity efforts designed to elicit more consumer complaints. Is it then a matter of "tokenism," with business only willing to display some concern and commitment as a way of placating the public, defusing consumerist demands and warding off the threat of more regulation? For sure, some people, firms and associations hold such a view. However, the promoters and leaders of ASR systems are usually interested in their genuine development, and in making them more responsive to emerging concerns and threats. In any case, the development of self-regulation depends on such variables as the strength of the external threats, the quality of the leadership and the cohesion of the industry (Lad 1985; Provan 1983).

Besides, one significant variable limits the scope and effectiveness of advertising self-regulation, namely, the unwillingness of many ASR supporters (principally, the advertisers who ultimately foot the bill of these systems) to make self-regulation as burdensome—financially, technically and morally—as regulation itself. If industry were to cope with every problem, to issue elaborate and ever-growing standards, to develop extensive preclearance and monitoring procedures, to solicit more complaints (which ultimately require advertisers to justify their behavior), to publicize the wrongdoings of too many firms *and* to require that such a burden be willingly assumed by practitioners, then a breaking point is likely to develop somewhere along the line. Since regulation is always incomplete and often poorly enforced, and new regulatory proposals can be opposed, defeated, postponed and watered down, business might as well learn to live with governmental control and private litigation, past that elusive breaking point. A comment by the Chairman of the Association of Canadian Advertisers is very instructive in this regard:

Self-regulation must be kept in perspective—its value understood, but also its limitations and its potential for the creation of misunderstanding. We regulate our industry, in part at least, in order to maintain responsibility for our own performance—to keep the intrusive and often heavy hand of government at a reasonable distance. To do so intelligently, we anticipate government policies in many fields—from public health to cultural diversity— and work to reflect such policy before being forced into doing so. And yet, there is a danger point. If, for example, government were to formulate a policy for purely political and self-serving ends, how wise would we be to unwittingly comply with it in advance? Were the industry to sense such a possibility on the horizon, it would be far wiser and far more ethical to exert its point of view than to simply comply and congratulate itself on how efficient it is at self-regulation (Association of Canadian Advertisers [ACA] Newsletter 1985).

Furthermore, some problematic areas are relatively intractable by both regulation and self-regulation. When is the use of fear, violence, sex, humor, greed, etc. excessive? When and where should ads for feminine-hygiene products, contraceptives, handguns, liquor, tobacco, casinos, etc. be displayed—if at all? Are there too many ads, are they boring, annoying, insulting, overaggressive, disruptive of broadcast programs, and so on? National self-regulatory systems tend to shun such issues and complaints because of their subjectivity; they accept only certain types of complaints; and/or they leave them to other bodies such as media acceptance committees and specific industry associations (e.g., for liquor and cigarettes).[14] Government agencies are equally reluctant or unable to cope with such problems, apart from issuing some specific bans (against contraceptives advertising, for example) and general prohibitions against sex or ethnic discrimination, which are often very difficult to enforce.

Finally, evergrowing restrictions and requirements—whether statutory or voluntary—may simply result in more "puffery" and "image" advertising, with no increase in the informative content of advertisements (Jones and Pickering 1985, p. 67). Chapter 16 returns to these issues which keep plaguing the understanding and effectiveness of advertising self-regulation.

Government Policy toward ASR

Industry self-regulation constitutes a form of private government to the extent that peers, rather than outsiders, formally control or at least dominate the establishment and enforcement of self-imposed and voluntarily accepted behavior rules. However, there is growing interest in the actual and potential functions of private intermediary organizations as agents of public policy (Streeck and Schmitter 1985). The underlying idea is that public-policy functions may be performed and the public interest safeguarded not just by the State, but also by social groups such as business associations, trade unions, community-action groups and the like, provided they are properly institutionalized and supervised. Self-regulation by an industry such as advertising fits into this scheme.

For one thing, the limits of regulation are evident even if not static nor remediable to some extent (Thompson and Jones 1982). Hence, there is always a need for complementary forms of behavior control (cf. Gupta and Lad 1983; Streeck and Schmitter 1985). Actually, courts in a number of countries use the International Code of Advertising Practice of the International Chamber of Commerce, as well as national voluntary codes, as expressions of fair commercial practice: "The distinction and preference between the rules of self-regulation and statutory regulation is too simplistic. There is a large category of rules of self-regulation which are applied by the courts as rules of law, and there are statutory rules which the self-regulation bodies use as professional recommendations. It is also a mistake to think that professional rules are less restrictive than laws: they affect the freedom of business quite as much, and sometimes more (ICC 1978, p. 35)." The only cases where self-regulation is deemed to be inappropriate from a public-policy viewpoint are where the consequences of its failure are too large (e.g., the approval of new drugs) or the dangers of collusion are too great (Lad 1985, p. 48).

Second, discussions of the control of economic systems have generally ignored or underplayed what might be called the "meso" level between the "micro" (the firm or consumer) and "macro" (the government) levels. A good part of this ignorance can be ascribed to overreaction against the corporatism often associated with restrictive medieval guilds, the puppet corporations of the fascist State, and even the U.S. National Recovery Administration of the 1930s and its proposed industry-wide cartels (Streeck and Schmitter 1985). Yet, the industry level has first-hand expertise about problems and possible solutions within its own domain. Such expertise is not complete nor impartial—but whose is? The industry's conception of the public interest is bound to be partial and limited, but whose is not, even though the government is more likely to provide a better forum for the expression, however imperfect, of the public interest. In advertising, self-regulatory codes and guidelines are frequently being refined and expanded on the basis of such expertise while governments tend to under- or overreact with various lags to new issues (cf. Carman and Harris 1986). Still, the advertising industry normally reacts rather than proacts in the face of new issues.

Third, public policy in most developed countries has encouraged the development and use of associations for various purposes, including the elaboration and application of technical and ethical standards, although not unaware of the real and constant danger of anticompetitive behavior on their part—as with the U.S. Department of Justice's successful court case against some features of the National Association of Broadcasters' television code.[15] Hence, governments frequently support the existence of a self-regulatory system that complements the law because: (1) it relieves the administration and the courts of some burdensome, costly and/or complex tasks, and (2) it even applies statutory rules since "the first principle of ethical behavior is respect of the law."[16] As mentioned before, it can also serve as a "pilot" or trial balloon for future regulation once the voluntary norms have been tested, refined and broadly accepted; and self-regulation is considered more flexible in dealing with such "soft" issues as taste and decency although some systems (e.g., in the United States) refuse to deal with them.

Supranational bodies such as the European Communities, the European Parliament, the Council of Europe, and, to a lesser extent, the United Nations have also encouraged the development of self-regulation for similar reasons although they tend to prefer negotiated codes (see above and next chapter). Some governments (e.g., Australia, Canada, Singapore and the United Kingdom) are already actively involved in the development of ASR systems through such means as consultation, initiation, approval of codes, lodging of complaints by agencies, and the threat of further regulation.

In this context, the implicit or explicit obligation of business to "trade fairly" is very relevant. It may be argued that compliance with a voluntary code is evidence that a company is trading fairly (Jones and Pickering 1985, p. 59). This is, of course, a complex issue linked to codes being sufficiently elaborate, explicit, enforceable, not anticompetitive, and adequately supervised by government. Still, it reveals the potential interest of public policy in the development of self-regulation. The true challenges in this area lie in governmental support and oversight of self-regulation. Some nations already have effective ASR systems, but the latter are largely missing in less developed countries at a time when the United Nations is urging the expansion of bureaucratic systems of consumer protection, which would include major consumerist inputs but relatively little industry participation (United Nations [UN] 1985).

Besides, new important issues are beginning to define the agenda for advertising control. They transcend the traditional concerns about false, misleading and unfair advertising and raise more subjective but no less crucial questions about taste, decency, privacy, sexism, violence and the advertising of objectionable products such as tobacco and liquor. It is likely that the resolution of such "social-responsibility" issues will require new structures for self-regulation, including greater outside participation in it (see next chapter). As such, "pure" self-regulation is an endangered species, although one likely to keep evolving in order to cope with these issues.

Altogether, self-regulation is increasingly being integrated into public policy while retaining most features of a private government whenever it has reached an advanced stage of development and encounters an environment favorable to private initiatives. This conclusion, however, overlooks the problem of whether public policy toward self-regulation is truly autonomous. Private interest groups have their own views about what constitutes adequate control in the public interest; they foster such views through lobbying and public-opinion campaigns, and they try to control or at least neutralize other control agencies such as bureaucracies and governmental commissions (cf. McConnell [1966]; and Moe 1981). Consequently, the ties between advertising self-regulatory bodies (and the associations that back them up) and state agencies must be considered in terms of relative power, including the support that government derives from, and imparts to, other interest groups such as consumerists (see next chapter).

ASR Functioning and Effectiveness

Scanning for Problem Areas

Principles, codes and/or guidelines about advertising behavior are not created in a vacuum but reflect, to some extent, real and legitimate areas of criticisms expressed by consumers and their associations, government bodies, expert observers and the like. LaBarbera (1983, p. 58) has classified the criticisms of advertising as dealing with: (1) the truthfulness of advertising; (2) the amount of advertising, which includes such issues as clutter, waste and omnipresence; (3) the cultural effects of advertising such as impacted social values and media control; (4) the function of advertising, specifically, the information versus persuasion issue, and (5) the "good taste" and "social-responsibility" dimensions of advertising such as moral concern over the product itself (e.g., liquor) or objections to the appeals employed (e.g., use of sex). Various public-opinion surveys (e.g., Barksdale et al. 1982; Burleton 1982; and Ogilvy & Mather 1985) broadly confirm the validity of this classification.

In the context of this study, the main issue is the manner in which, and extent to which, ASR systems monitor and tap expressions of public dissatisfaction in selecting the problem areas with which they deal. Advisory boards, specially commissioned studies, and institutionalized interaction with outside bodies (including formal outside participation in ASR systems) are some of the means used for that purpose.

Standards

The distinction between principles, codes, guidelines and recommendations revolves around the strength of the obligations imposed on the industry. General principles are like incontrovertible axioms that all advertisers should accept as self-evident, for example: ''All advertising should respect the law,'' ''Advertising should not be deceptive,'' and ''The special psychological characteristics of children should be considered when preparing advertisements addressed to them.'' Codes, however, usually refer to fairly explicit rules, whose violation is most likely to trigger some admonition or disciplining (e.g., ''All direct-mail advertisements should include the full address of the advertiser rather than a mere post-office box number''). Guidelines and recommendations are often of a less binding nature because the problems are novel, fluid and/or hard to clearly circumscribe so that precise rules are not possible. Decency, sexism, the use of humor, ethnic discrimination and the like are typically amenable to only such looser treatment. A few self-regulatory systems (e.g., in the Federal Republic of Germany) are increasingly issuing recommendations rather than firm and clear rules for fear that too much explicitness increases the danger of voluntary codes being transformed into laws and regulations.

The norms applied by ASR systems vary considerably. Some organizations have their own extensive principles, codes, guidelines and/or recommendations (e.g., in Brazil, France and the United Kingdom); others rely on a few general principles and borrow more specific norms from other associations and the law (e.g., in Japan and the United States).[17] Most apply the law to the extent that ''the first principle of ethical behavior is respect of the law.'' However, the U.K. Advertising Standards Association declines to do so on the ground that self-regulation does not provide enough procedural safeguards comparable to what would prevail in a court of justice (ASA 1980). In any case, most ASR bodies are not equipped to give legal advice or interpret the law.

A major although imprecise distinction between the standards applied by ASR bodies revolves around their ''hard'' vs. ''soft'' nature. Hard standards center on the deceptive character of advertisements as well as on the proper substantiation of advertising claims. There are still important disagreements about such matters as the omission of important information in advertisements, the nature of what constitutes a "reasonable consumer" who could be deceived, and the validity of tests used to support a claim (cf. Preston [1983]). Still, there is at least consensus that advertising should be truthful and accurate so that ASR systems are comfortable with the development and application of "hard" standards.

Implementing the general principles that advertising behavior be "decent . . . prepared with a due sense of social responsibility . . . [and] not be such as to impair public confidence in advertising [ICC Code]" is another matter. Translating such "soft" principles into rules or guidelines that practitioners can understand and follow and that ASR adjudicating bodies can apply is a very difficult task. Yet, it is an important issue because soft standards reach beyond the relations between sellers and buyers by including those who are exposed to advertising even if not buyers or would-be buyers (e.g., men exposed to feminine sanitary-protection advertisements). Many criticisms of advertising focus precisely on such problems of its being overpervasive, materialistic and promoting socially undesirable or "embarrassing" products.

Self-regulatory consensus has emerged about a few soft areas, for example, that advertisements should not show a disregard for safety by presenting dangerous practices or situations, and should not exploit the natural credibility of children. However, many other issues related to fairness,[18] taste, opinion, unconscionable practices and social responsibility remain vague in terms of desirable goals and acceptable means, for example: in the matters of threats to the legitimate interests of others, the exploitation of the vulnerable, the infliction of emotional shock, the occasioning of moral offense, the destruction of the means of communication through the devaluing of common symbols, or the weakening of trust (Advertising Standards Authority, Annual Report 1983–1984, p. 5).

In any case, ASR bodies refuse to consider the legitimacy of advertising controversial products and services on the ground that if these goods can be legally made, sold and consumed, they can also be advertised unless the law specifically prohibits or restricts their advertising (e.g., in the case of cigarettes and prescription drugs). Similarly, political advertising is not covered because it is too fraught with ideology and subjectivity; while personal classified ads for used cars, real estate, personal services, etc., are too numerous, local and transient to warrant attention in most cases.

One can deplore such exclusions because: (1) they affect the overall acceptability and effectiveness of advertising, and (2) they jeopardize the credibility of advertising self-regulation, which claims to be concerned with upholding and improving the quality of all advertising. The excuse that the limited resources of ASR systems prevent them from coping with all problems may be realistic, but the proliferation of "new media" (e.g., videotex, private broadcasting, direct satellite broadcasting, international editions of newspapers and magazines, direct marketing by mail and telephone) will force an increase in self-regulatory coverage and resources anyway. While government agencies themselves are often equally reluctant to address "soft" issues and prefer to leave such matters to legislative bodies, self-regulation's claim that it is a more flexible tool of advertising control is damaged by its reluctance or inability to develop soft standards, leaving it largely to the "Community" (public opinion) and the "State" to rule on these matters (Streeck and Schmitter 1985).

In the main thrust of this study, the central question is whether nonindustry members participate *directly* in the development of hard and soft standards as distinct from the indirect impact of consumerist, governmental and public complaints, requests and demands.

Advising

Most ASR organizations assist their members who inquire about what is permissible; and they answer a variety of queries—general and/or specific—coming from practitioners, consumers, government agencies, scholars, etc., at least to the extent allowed by their resources, which are rather meager in most cases. These services are usually free or set at nominal prices, and they are rendered by the in-house staff. A few organizations, however, provide or even require the advance preclearance of ads—a task also automatically performed by all media, which can refuse those found unacceptable in the light of their own or more general acceptance criteria. (This is done for all commercials in the Philippines, but only for certain types in Canada and the United Kingdom.)

The central question again is whether outsiders are involved in ad preclearance (or prevetting) by ASR organizations' prescreening committees, where they exist.

Monitoring

Complaints may miss important violations, or people may not bother to complain at all—hence the need to monitor all or certain media and product categories. However, sampling various media to detect possible violations of the standards is performed systematically and extensively by very few ASR systems (e.g., in France and the United Kingdom)—the others simply lack the necessary resources. When performed, ASR secretariats handle this monitoring task, which never involves outsiders. Industry, however, sometimes assists government agencies in conducting surveys about advertising problems (e.g., in the United Kingdom).

Complaint Acceptance and Handling

The extent to which ASR bodies accept and handle complaints is related to: (1) their domain definition; (2) the publicity they give to their standards and services, and (3) consumer/competitor perception and evaluation of alternative ways of complaining.

Domain Definition. Most ASR systems limit themselves to national media, leaving complaints about ads appearing in local newspapers, etc., to ASR branches (for example, in Canada), other business organizations (e.g., the U.S. Better Business Bureaus) or simply to oblivion because the necessary resources are lacking. Advertisements in newspapers and magazines are always covered, but some ASR systems do not handle complaints about radio and television commercials (e.g., in the United Kingdom, such complaints are handled by the Independent Broadcasting Authority) or about direct-mail ads (where nondelivery and refunding are often problematic, with complaints handled by special industry bodies). Political, religious and "opinion" ("controversy" or "advocacy") advertising are also generally excluded, and so are personal classified ads.

Complaints are accepted from any source but quarrels among advertisers and/or agencies about fair-competition practices (e.g., whether an ad copied another, or one advertiser denigrated another) are typically referred to the appropriate associations (e.g., of advertisers) that have codes of conduct about such matters. However, if a competitor's complaint bears on matters of interest to consumers (truth, accuracy, good taste, etc.), it is handled as any other complaint.

Moyer and Banks (1977, p. 189) have concluded that complaints, in Canada at least, are more likely to be sustained if they originate with organizations (e.g., consumer associations and government agencies) rather than with individuals, because the former have more expertise and do screen complaints before submitting them to ASR bodies, requiring or obtaining substantial documentation before accepting to act as "champion" for an individual complainant.

ASR bodies that "apply the law" refuse to handle some legally based complaints when the government itself is lax about enforcing the law (e.g., the ban against the use of foreign languages and the use of imagery in cigarette advertising in France). Some ASR bodies (e.g., in Japan) handle complaints "as is," that is, they focus on finding out whether the complainant has a valid gripe, while others (e.g., the U.S. NAD/NARB system) assume the complaints as their own and handle them in terms of the public and industry interests in achieving "truth and accuracy" in advertising.

Some ASR systems accept "taste and opinion" complaints—even specialize in them as in The Federal Republic of Germany—while others by far emphasize the hard cases of "truth and accuracy in advertising" (see the previous discussion of "hard" vs. "soft" issues). Three tentative explanations can be provided for this situation.

First, ASR systems have no particular expertise in soft areas (nobody does, really) while what constitutes advertising deception and even unfairness (at least in the case of competitive behavior) can rely on extensive precedents derived from regulatory standards, court decisions and self-regulatory experience.

Second, ASR bodies and supporters fear that "taste and opinion" has no true boundaries or limits. Some issues are fairly manageable and are already incorporated in international, national and industry standards: for example, do not exploit fear, do not encourage violence, avoid ethnic slurs, keep in mind that children are differently affected by advertising, etc. Such principles took time to be recognized and accepted by the advertising industry and they still present problems of implementation, but they have become manageable on the basis of experience and precedent-setting decisions. However, newer issues such as sexism are still at an early stage, so that it is difficult to discern where prevailing and changing societal standards lie exactly between the complaints of vocal feminists and the silence of most women. Several ASR systems have set up investigative committees, dialogued with concerned groups, and issued reports and general guidelines about such issues, but the latter have not yet been fully operationalized so that they cannot be readily used by complaint-handling panels.

Even more unmanageable are those complaints about advertising in general—it is boring, too pervasive, emphasizes the wrong societal values, increases the cost of products, etc.—or about the advertising of certain products (cigarettes, feminine-hygiene products, contraceptives, etc.). ASR systems intend to improve the quality of advertising, but refuse to evaluate its raison d'être and overall effectiveness even though some taste-and-opinion issues straddle both of these objectives (e.g., offensive ads are likely to alienate people against advertising and thus impair its reach and influence). Consequently, ASR bodies only accept taste-and-opinion complaints when their handling can be operationalized, with much reluctance in most cases. In general, they refer to prevailing public attitudes and values rather than to emerging or ideal ones; and they concern themselves only with the content of an advertisement (is it truthful, etc.) rather than with whether the product itself (e.g., cigarettes) or advertising in general may cause offense (see the Canadian chapter for a more extensive discussion of this problem).

Third, accepting taste-and-opinion complaints complicates the functioning of ASR systems and increases their cost. Most "hard" complaints can be handled in a fairly routine manner by ASR secretariats and adjudicating panels, but "soft" ones increase the latter's load and the overall cost of the system by requiring more study and consultation, often prove divisive within the industry, and/or expose self-regulation to renewed criticism for either hesitating to assume new responsibilities or coming up with vague guidelines. As is discussed in the next chapter, soft issues also bring up and frequently require the inclusion of non-industry members ("outsiders") in order to broaden perspectives.

On the one hand, a few ASR systems simply refuse to handle "soft" complaints and limit themselves to matters of "truth and accuracy" (e.g., in the United States); the Canadians, on the other hand, have bravely, if reluctantly, accepted to cope with "taste, opinion and decency" in such matters as the advertising of feminine sanitary-protection products and the treatment of women, sex and violence in advertisements. Most ASR bodies stand in between, sometimes accepting soft cases on the basis of the general principles they apply—particularly when gross breaches of societal standards are involved as in matters of pornography, racism and denigration (cf. Cranston 1984, p. 61).

Publicity. All ASR systems provide some publicity about their standards and the availability of their complaint-handling mechanisms, but its extent, frequency and quality vary considerably. This situation reflects their limited resources but also a deliberate choice. Intensive soliciting may generate too many complaints—whether valid or frivolous—which the system may not be able to handle or handle well, at great cost to its effectiveness and credibility (see Moyer and Banks [1977] for comments to that effect). Besides, mild solicitation may offer a better gauge of "true" dissatisfaction with advertisements than more numerous complaints "churned up" through intensive and sustained publicity campaigns. Linked to the function of monitoring (see above) is the notion that a professional Secretariat can better spot important violations and precedent-setting cases than the general public that may, for lack of expertise, report violations where none exists or raise marginal issues. Finally, a high or increasing number of complaints may imply that there are many problems with advertising when, in some sense, their true intensity is low and/or stable. Thus, can one truly conclude that the British system with its 8,000-plus "contacts" is superior to that of the United States, which handles only 100-plus "cases" a year, simply because the former is more active in publicizing itself and in inviting consumer inquiries? The answer has to be negative because the philosophy and resources of the two systems are different.

In any case, there is no simple or accurate way of determining the optimum number of complaints under any system—whether regulatory or self-regulatory—as is amply revealed by the literature on consumer satisfaction and dissatisfaction (e.g., Hunt and Day 1980).[19] While inviting more complaints may appear to be the honest way of implementing a self-regulatory system and of providing a better indicator of what concerns the public, it is largely unmanageable by most ASR organizations for the reasons stated above—even governments are not that eager to invite too many complaints. This observation, however, does not exonerate ASR bodies from developing a workable system to identify important problem areas and spot significant violations.[20] Whether outside participation can improve this process is, of course, the focus of this study.

Alternative Complaint Channels. While this topic was not systematically analyzed, the country studies in this book revealed various national and even cultural differences. The Japanese trust their governmental agencies and dislike direct confrontations with business so that they lodge most of their complaints with the former. The United States and The Federal Republic of Germany, however, are very litigious societies, which witness many suits, at least from competitors; while the Dutch have a strong corporatist tradition, which facilitates recourse to industry bodies. Obviously, these are broad observations in need of further research but some aspects of them are discussed in the country chapters.

The central question again is whether outsiders are involved in selecting and adjudicating the cases chosen for review—whether obtained through complaints or internal monitoring—once the Secretariat has gathered the necessary information about the incriminated advertisement.

Applying Sanctions

Besides requiring that the offending ad be discontinued or modified, typical sanctions applied by self-regulatory bodies include: (1) denial of access to member media (frequently); (2) publicizing the names of violators and/or recalcitrant advertisers (occasionally); (3) denunciation to the authorities (rarely); (4) expulsion from the association (very rarely);[21] and (5) suing to protect the interests of the profession (very rarely). Most of these sanctions are applied to both formal members and nonmembers of the self-regulatory system on the ground that the industry and public interests require that bad advertising behavior be penalized wherever it is found. Appeals to such decisions are often allowed, however.

Some ASR systems close the case once an advertiser complies with the request to discontinue or modify the incriminated ad, but others carry on the investigative and publicity processes because they want to set a precedent. Most systems do not reveal the name of the implicated advertiser and agency in their press releases for fear of offending members when the ASR body is directly financed by them. However, the media are often notified about the identity of the former in order to allow them to refuse accepting such ads; and more publicity is usually given to the cases of advertisers refusing to comply with ASR decisions.

The use of sanctions is tricky. On the one hand, a code or guidelines without significant penalties usually turn out to be fraudulent, or perceived as such by members and outsiders alike; on the other hand, antitrust legislation in some countries looks suspiciously at heavy sanctions on account of their possible anticompetitive effects (cf. Lad 1985; Levin 1967). At the limit, it is argued that ''discipline'' is a government monopoly: ''The question then arises as to whether an industry is privileged to crack the whip on the illegal few within it . . . [If persuasion fails], it is not your privilege to discipline them. Such is the sole responsibility of governmental authority (Carretta 1968, p. 16).'' Similarly, a FTC Commissioner voiced strong reservations about the Code of Ethics of the Magazine Publishers' Association and its implementation:

It is one thing to encourage business to promote voluntary compliance with the law. It is something else to approve a private scheme of law enforcement, where investigations are conducted by private ''policemen'' and where violations of privately-decreed ''law'' are punished by fines and penalties imposed by private ''judges'' after privately-conducted ''trials.'' The Code's Administrator and his staff will apparently function like a small version of the Federal Trade Commission. But there is a big difference between an administrator and the Commission, which is a public agency of government, with powers and duties that are defined and circumscribed by specific statutory provisions enacted by Congress. The decisions and orders of the Commission are subject to judicial review. Commission proceedings are public and must be conducted in conformity with the requirements of due process, the Administrative Procedures Act, and other applicable provisions of law. Findings of fact must be supported by substantial evidence on the record. In short, all our actions are subject, substantively and procedurally, to the basic safeguards and restraints established by law. It is fundamental that the regulatory powers of government are too awesome to be turned over to private policemen, prosecutors and judges—no matter how well-intentioned. Regulation of business—at least when it involves the imposition of fines and penalties for violations of prescribed standards of conduct— is the job of government agencies and officials bound by the limitations of due process and the rule of law. It runs against the basic grain of American society to permit private "vigilantes" to act as policemen and to allow private judges to hold "kangaroo courts" where punishment is imposed. The fundamental safeguards and restraints which protect the public against arbitrary or lawless official action are absent when the powers of government are sought to be exercised by private individuals or groups (File No. 6737038, 23 May 1967, Federal Trade Commission Decisions).

Besides, strict sanctioning discourages membership, generates resignations, and/or reduces interest in voluntary compliance, unless the government has specifically delegated regulatory power to an association in a corporativist manner so that industry members cannot avoid its reach. Consequently, most ASR bodies emphasize informal persuasion and publicity (with or without names), and rely on recommendations or "requests" (rather than orders) to the alerted media (whether "members" or not) to turn down incriminated ads. However, not all media cooperate; and some ASR systems do not even include the media as members (e.g., in the United States). Therefore, Thomson's (1983, p. 4) claim that "the most characteristic sanction of self-regulation is exclusion from participation in the activity regulated" is not uniformly true.

The central question in this study is, once more, whether outsiders are involved in the meting out of sanctions.

Effectiveness

There is hardly any consensus on the effectiveness of government regulation on account of different and ideologically driven answers to such key questions as "effectiveness from whose perspective; effectiveness over what period of time, and effectiveness of regulation as compared to what?" (Gupta and Lad 1983, p. 419). Unfortunately, the same problems plague any investigation of ASR effectiveness:[22] "Are the codes relevant in the light of current concerns? Do practitioners adhere to them? Does advertising self-regulation improve the credibility of advertising? Is it faster and cheaper, and does it deal with issues not covered by law? Does it result in better behavior on the part of advertisers, agencies and media? Does it bring about greater consumer protection and satisfaction? Does it lighten the government's task in advertising control and reduce the threat of regulation? Is the system readily publicized and accessible to complainants? Are its modes of operation and decisions properly explained to the public? Are sufficient resources devoted to generating the proper number and types of complaints? Are outsiders involved in code development and application?" (Adapted from LaBarbera 1980b and 1983; Moyer and Banks 1977).

There are no simple answers to these questions because of their interrelatedness, and for lack of sufficient studies that would be difficult in any case (cf. Lad 1985). Yet, partial evidence is available. On the positive side, there are the present pause in advertising regulation, laudatory governmental statements in many countries, a few favorable public-opinion polls, and complimentary appraisals by some independent observers and scholars (e.g., Moyer and Banks [1977]; Wyckham [1987]). On the negative side, most consumerist bodies remain skeptical if not unconvinced (ECLG 1983); some governments display indifference toward self-regulation; and the overall reputation of advertising is still low in many countries (Burleton 1982). In between, one finds measurements that are ambiguous to interpret—such as the number of complaints received and decisions rendered—since their size is largely a function of the resources and efforts of ASR systems and of competing redress systems (see above).

As Garvin (1983, p. 46) noted: "Virtually all critiques of the voluntary standards system have paid far more attention to the process of standards setting than to its actual results" because the former are easier to scrutinize than the latter. Wyckham (1987), however, compared the respective costs of self-regulation vs. regulation in Canada, and concluded that the former is by far the least expensive control activity although that is not to say that it is the most cost-effective one from a social perspective. It is also faster in practically all cases. Yet, even if advertising self-regulation were more effective, there would still be consumerists, jurists and bureaucrats to argue that it undermines the case for necessary legislative reform (ECLG 1983, p. 211).

In any case, the central question of this study is whether outside participation does increase ASR effectiveness because it results in greater credibility, better standards and stronger implementation—a topic addressed in the next chapter and in the country studies.

The Theory of Advertising Self-Regulation

Previous sections have already introduced relevant factors explaining the generation, operation, effectiveness and relative dominance of advertising self-regulation vis-à-vis regulation. However, several literatures are relevant to develop a "condition-motivation-precipitating circumstances" framework after a review of interorganizational-relations and interdependence theories in a cultural context.

Interorganizational Relations

Self-regulation represents a collective response to: (1) threats and opportunities in the industry's environment, and (2) problems within the industry (in this case, among advertisers, agencies and media). Of course, firms can also resort to individual responses such as self-discipline, the operation of consumer-affairs departments to handle consumer complaints, suing competitors for deceptive or unfair advertising, public-relations campaigns, and the like. The problematic issue revolves around determining when collective action becomes possible, necessary and effective, beyond what firms can do singly (Lad 1985).

At a high level of abstraction, it is easy to answer that it is a matter of costs and benefits, namely, that self-regulation must offer advantages over laissez-faire, self-discipline and regulation in the handling of problems amenable to the various types of advertising control. In practice, however, there are: (1) national differences (economic, political, social, cultural, etc.); (2) firm and industry characteristics, and (3) personal factors (e.g., quality of leadership) that do affect the possibility, necessity and effectiveness of collective action through self-regulation.

Astley and Fombrun's classification of collective responses would position advertising self-regulation closer to the "confederate collective type [which] is comprised of organizations from the same species that directly associate with each other for the purpose of concerting their actions toward joint ends (Astley and Fombrun 1983, pp. 580ff)." This type applies to ASR systems because they are characterized by: (1) ease of keeping the activities of other members under close surveillance since advertisements are highly visible; (2) important personnel flows since ASR systems rely mainly on industry participation in its activities; (3) the greater use of social (rather than economic, legal and political) sanctions, and (4) some degree of collusion within what antitrust laws allow.

Provan has provided an even more detailed analysis of "federations" that allow members' organizations (associations, firms, etc.) to reduce both the uncertainty and complexity of their external environments, although elements in the general environment (e.g., government) may also pressure interdependent organizations to serve the need of external publics better: "Overall, then, federations tend to form when a relatively large number of interdependent organizations exist, when there is a relatively large discrepancy between the prime expertise and goal orientation of the interdependent organizations and the anticipated role of the federation's management, and when there are substantial external pressures to form a federation (Provan, 1983, p. 81)." He then proceeded to identify three types of federations, besides other types of systems used to manage organizational interdependence. The ASR systems analyzed in this volume generally correspond to his "participatory, independent and mandated federations," which are detailed in Table 1.2.

The resources provided by federations include information, legitimacy, credibility and clients (that is, complainants in the case of ASR systems); and their strength derives from whether they provide essential and nonsubstitutable resources (Provan 1983, pp. 85–86). It is appropriate to observe that a "participatory federation" is more representative of those ASR systems where: (1) a strong Secretariat and leadership have not yet developed, and (2) third-party influences (including government and consumerist pressures as well as the participation of outsiders) are less strong than in "independent" and "mandated" (that is, corporativist) federations.

Table 1.2
Three Types of Federations

Network Characteristics	Coalition	Voluntary Federations		Mandated Federation	Owned Systems (Intraorganizational)
		Participatory Federation	Independent Federation		
Basis for affiliation	mutual benefit and stability	previous plus complexity reduction	previous plus legitimacy	legal mandate or strong external pressures	ownership
Participation of affiliates in network management	high	moderate	low	low	low
Number of organizations in network	few to moderate	moderate	moderate to many	few to many	few to many
Primary source of FMO power	N/A	affiliates	affiliates	third party	owners
Importance of network for legitimacy	low	low to moderate	moderate to high	high	low to high
Essentiality (importance/ pervasiveness of issues/ resources mediated by FMO)	N/A	high	low to high	moderate to high	moderate to high
Substitutability of FMO (capacity to obtain services elsewhere)	N/A	moderate to moderately high	moderate to low	low	low
Examples	joint programs joint purchase decisions interlocking boards	social service exchanges some multihospital systems some cartels (O.P.E.C.)	United Way N.C.A.A. trade associations some multi-hospital systems	professional sports leagues county welfare boards	holding company conglomerate divisionalized firm
Network structure					varies depending on control exercised by the systems' management (generally similar to an independent federation)

N/A = not applicable
O = organizations in the network
□ = federation management organization (FMO)
△ = third party attempting to monitor the activities and decisions of affiliates
— = strong relationship
-- = moderate strength relationship

Source: Provan (1983), p. 83. Reprinted with permission of the publisher.

Private-Public Interdependences

It has already been argued that regulation and self-regulation are complementary forms of advertising control, but are they competing or cooperating ones? Regulatory bureaucracies and ASR organizations compete for scarce resources (financial, moral, etc.) and for clients (business and consumer complainants). However, if self-regulation performs well, the need for governmental regulations, agencies and bureaucrats will be minimized—and vice versa. In that sense, regulation and self-regulation are ''interdependent organizations'' whose behaviors are mutually contingent (Pennings 1981, p. 433; see also Molnar 1978). However, interdependence can take various forms: horizontal (as among firms competing in the same market), vertical (as successive levels in a channel of distribution) and/or symbiotic:

Symbiotic interdependence exists among organizations that complement each other in the rendering of services to individual clients. Such organizations have a functional relationship analogous to the interplay between organizational subunits. [Their] outputs . . . are complementary in much the same way as the pieces of a jigsaw puzzle . . . Symbiotically interdependent organizations, oriented toward complementary resources or outputs, generally do not manipulate each other to optimize their growth and survival. Each may have competed with other similar organizations . . . but as soon as the complementary relationships have crystallized, they rely on collaboration (Pennings 1981, p. 434).

Which form of interdependence prevails between governmental agencies and ASR organizations? The alternatives are many. At both ends of the spectrum, one system eclipses the other on account of having effectively preempted the field of advertising control: the Japanese case illustrates to some extent this situation of governmental preemption. In between, one finds various forms of accommodation: (1) joint ventures, as between the Swedish Consumer Ombudsman system and business interests; (2) delegation of quasiregulatory "corporatist" powers to an ASR organization, as in the Philippines; (3) capture (or merger) of one system by the other (no example was found in this study), and (4) governmental supervision of the ASR system, which becomes an explicit "agent of public policy" although retaining its autonomy as a "private government" (Streeck and Schmitter 1985), as in the British case. In still other countries, the interdependent relationships are less well articulated—as in Belgium and Italy, where a horizontal type of plain competition exists between the regulatory and self-regulatory systems of advertising control.

The factors determining the predominance of one form over another are multiple. For example, a centralized and unitary government, compared to one with many decision-making levels and agencies, tends to favor bureaucratic dominance, but other historical, cultural and organizational conditions are also important, for example, a long tradition of associationism (as in the Netherlands), basic trust in the law (as in The Federal Republic of Germany) or in government agencies (as in Japan), and strong industry associations (as in Canada). Besides, interdependences fluctuate on account of external and internal developments ("precipitating factors") as political parties with different ideologies come into power; the consumer movement waxes and wanes; innovations (e.g., the "new media"), scandals or crises alter the agenda; new leaders enter the public or private scene; deregulation becomes popular; new ASR leaders expand their role and influence—and so on.

Cultural Perspectives

The plain observation that national industry-wide ASR systems exist in only some thirty-five countries and are well developed in only about twenty of them suggests that a multiplicity of factors affect their creation, operation and effectiveness. For example, Lad (1985, p. 48) has referred to "industry capability" in terms of economic criteria such as the magnitude of advertising expenditures in a particular country serving as an index of resources available for the development of an ASR system. Political factors such as the strength of the consumerist movement (see next chapter) are also relevant, as are personal elements such as the quality of ASR leaders.

The cultural dimension cannot be overlooked either. Why is the mix among the "Market, Community, State and Private-Interest Government" forms of advertising control different from country to country? (cf. Streeck and Schmitter 1985.) More generally, why do "federations" (Provan 1983) to which advertising self-regulation is related exist at all? In this respect, Boisot (1986) provides an interesting cultural interpretation of transactions among firms, that can be applied to advertising self-regulation.

Cultural patterns are the product of individual and collective communication strategies through which knowledge (including norms about advertising behavior, in our case) is created, codified and diffused within a given population: "In effect, codification and diffusion are two key dimensions of a cultural space in which meaning gets created and shared (Boisot 1986, p. 140)." In this context, well-codified norms are more conducive to "market" and "hierarchical-bureaucratic" (= State) approaches—as with contract laws and regulations that apply to advertising. Less-well-codified norms, however, favor "federative" and "hierarchical-feudal" solutions (cf. Provan [1983]).[23]

Two factors are particularly important regarding the latter two solutions in those cases where transactions are more personalized. First, uncodified information is generally more difficult to transmit in other than face-to-face situations, so that the number of parties that can effectively participate is necessarily limited. Second, the lack of codified information increases the uncertainty and risks associated with the transactions, so that there is a need for trust and an ability for the parties to get on the same "wavelength." Such transactions are generally only possible among people who share common values or have a common outlook—a requirement that may call for substantial time investments by the parties in getting to know each other prior to serious dealing (Boisot 1986, p. 144). These "clan" transactions, which Boisot prefers to call "federative," can be observed in professional associations where there is information parity among the members, that is, a general diffusion of the relevant information.[24]

Boisot's framework is applicable to advertising self-regulation to the extent that the knowledge of some of the control norms applying to advertising are located within the industry itself because of its members' experience, constant interaction and isolation vis-à-vis the rest of society. This is, in fact, the basis of the self-regulatory claim that practitioners "know better" what the problems and their realistic solutions are. Once this knowledge can be codified and broadly diffused, the Market and the State can take over—as when self-regulation has served as the "trial chamber" for new standards. This perspective also helps explain why regulation and self-regulation can coexist, complement each other and even grow apace without one replacing the other.

The fact that many self-regulatory standards remain in the form of general principles—"semicodified" in Boisot's terminology (Boisot 1986, p. 146)—

reflects the need for face-to-face personal interaction for full transmission and understanding, particularly in the matter of "soft" cases of decency, taste and opinion. Such knowledge cannot be readily codified and diffused but "can only be learned by 'doing it,' that is by a process of watching, inferring, trying out and adapting (Boisot 1986, p. 147)."

Boisot's analysis also explains why self-regulatory systems prefer to remain "pure" and exclude "outsiders" in their functioning (see next chapter). While complaint-adjudicating bodies now often include some outsiders, the elaboration of "voluntary" principles, guidelines and codes is, for all practical purposes, still an "inside" project. While external outputs (advisory panels, consultations, consumer complaints, etc.) are used to some extent, the industry insists on being the sole "codifier" of the norms to which it will freely adhere because it "knows best" what is realistic and acceptable (the "user-friendly" argument developed in Chapter 2). In some cases, the industry even refuses to diffuse its standards among the public but retains them as "industry-specific knowledge (Boisot 1986, p. 146)" because, among other reasons, it fears they will be misunderstood and lead to frivolous complaints.

Boisot's cultural analysis also helps understand why there are national differences in the development of ASR systems. He briefly argues that different cultures exhibit different preferences for codifying and diffusing information (Boisot 1986, pp. 153–155) so that the existence and effectiveness of "federative" arrangements are likely to vary from nation to nation. The country studies do, in fact, illustrate the importance of such cultural factors as political culture, individualism vs. associationism and trust as key variables explaining the importance but also the varieties of advertising self-regulation and of outside participation in its functioning.[25] As R. E. Oliver, former president of the [Canadian] Advertising Standards Council put it, there are too many local variables to permit the establishment of a formula that would have wide international application in answering the question: "What is the right mix between government controls . . . and self-regulation by the business community (Boddewyn 1986, p. 81)."

Conditions, Motivations and Precipitating Circumstances

According to Webster's dictionary, a condition is something essential to the existence or occurrence of something else; a prerequisite. In this context, what is required for the development and success of advertising self-regulation? Motivation refers to an inner drive, impulse, intention, incentive, goal, etc., that causes a person to do something or act in a certain way—Aristotle called it the "final cause" (finis means end or goal in Latin), meaning the purpose or end toward which an act tends. Why then is ASR promoted and supported? A precipitating circumstance is a hastening element that causes something to happen before it is expected, needed or desired—Aristotle's "efficient cause." In our context, what brings ASR about? While these three types of explanation are not completely separate and do overlap to some extent, they are useful in organizing and interpreting relevant theories (Boddewyn, "Theories," 1985). The following theoretical analysis relies considerably on Gupta and Lad's (1983) propositions about industry self-regulation, but related analyses were also used.

ASR Conditions

Hypothesis C1: The existence of an industry-wide decision-making system (such as a capstone trade association)
increases the probability of industry self-regulation
(Streeck and Schmitter 1985).

One would expect ASR to be more developed in those countries where advertisers, agencies and major media are already well organized in autonomous associations capped by a peak organization (e.g., the British Advertising Association). In other words, "industry capability" is necessary (cf. Lad 1985, p. 48)—a condition which itself is linked to some minimum size of advertising expenditures as a measure of industry size (Neelankavil and Stridsberg 1980, pp. 12, 45).

Hypothesis C2: Industry self-regulation is more effective
when it involves all interrelated levels.

Advertising expenditures are paid by advertisers, with the large ones typically relying on advertising agencies and other production-support firms (printers, filmmakers, etc.) to prepare their advertisements. What distinguishes advertising from other industries, however, is that most advertisements are issued through media (press, television, radio, billboards, etc.)—only handbills and direct-mail advertising can bypass media, although even here there may be dependence on a postal system. Therefore, the effectiveness of ASR is greatly enhanced when the media support the self-regulatory system by refusing advertisements that do not comply with industry and/or media codes and guidelines. To the extent that advertising agencies and, particularly, the media wholeheartedly participate in the ASR system, the "free-rider" problem is minimized since the noncomplying advertiser cannot readily gain access to the services needed to advertise effectively.

Hypothesis C3: The development and effectiveness of an
industry self-regulatory system are enhanced by government threat and oversight.

To achieve its full potential, advertising self-regulation requires a strong State that promotes its development as a matter of public policy, and stands ready to substitute for it if industry does not comply and perform (Garvin 1983, p. 48; Streeck and Schmitter 1985).

Hypothesis C4: The strength and effectiveness of an industry self-regulatory system are enhanced by its essentiality and non-substitutability (Provan 1983).

Self-regulation is more likely to succeed where it focuses on problems not readily amenable to regulatory solutions, and/or where it clearly complements other forms of advertising control.

Hypothesis C5: The existence and effectiveness of industry self-regulation are affected by cultural factors
(Boisot 1986).

Although economic and political factors are also important, various cultural elements such as political culture and associative propensity definitely affect the development of ASR systems.

ASR Motivations

Hypothesis M1: Industry self-regulation is more likely in
those situations where it can increase the overall demand
for the industry's product.

ASR can be expected to be more developed where advertising has come under greater criticism from consumerists and government officials so that its overall legitimacy and credibility have been challenged and even harmed. The development of self-regulation is then motivated by the desire to restore public confidence in advertising, without which the latter's effectiveness is greatly impaired.

Hypothesis M2: Industry self-regulation is more likely in
those situations where the externally imposed costs from
not undertaking such self-regulation would be greater than
the cost of undertaking such self-regulation.

One would expect ASR to be more developed where the burden of regulation—in terms of compliance and litigation costs—is perceived as more onerous than that of self-regulation. Avoiding burdensome regulation is, thus, a primary motive for ASR. This proposition emphasizes a proactive view of ASR in contrast to reaction to activist threats for more regulation. However, the fear of government regulation is not necessarily the main explanatory variable. The achievement of status and a desire to professionalize the advertising community are also potential motivators based on financial self-interest (noncredible advertising is a waste) and individual self-respect (the self-discipline element discussed above).

ASR Precipitating Circumstances (Precipitators)

Hypothesis PC1: The creation and improvement of an
industry self-regulatory system are precipitated by the
threat of governmental regulation.

One would expect ASR to exist and be more effective following demands and/or threats for greater control of advertising behavior by government—often at the request of consumerist groups (Garvin 1983, p. 42; Neelankavil and Stridsberg 1980, p. 12; Zanot 1977, p. 326; and Zanot 1979, pp. 35–37).

> *Hypothesis PC2*: Encouragement and support of industry
> self-regulation as an instrument of public policy is more
> likely when the limits of government intervention have
> become apparent.

In other words, ASR would receive more public-policy encouragement and support when budgetary constraints, a deregulatory mood and novel problems not readily amenable to regulatory solutions have become more urgent.

Conditions, motivations and precipitating circumstances are typically inter-related—notice, for example, how government regulation (actual or threatened) is associated with all three types of explanations. In principle, these three types are each "necessary" but not "sufficient" to explain the development and effectiveness of advertising self-regulation, although one of them can in fact reach a high enough intensity and thus become the single "cause." The threat of government regulation is often presented as such a predominant if not over-whelming factor.

Chapter 16 compares the evidence from this book's twelve country studies regarding these hypotheses. However, a historical dimension must be added to these rather static categories. Once an advertising self-regulatory system is in place and functions well under capable leadership, it becomes an actor of its own, which interacts with its sponsors, other trade associations, the government, consumer organizations, public opinion, and so forth. Consequently, the total "organization set" changes, and new interdependent relationships develop with their own conditions, motivations and precipitating circumstances.

NOTES

1. The U.S. literature was particularly used in this study because of its greater scope and readier accessibility, but foreign sources were also relied upon—particularly for the country chapters. (See also Brandmair [1977] for a general and multicountry study of advertising self-regulation as well as Business International [1980] and Rijkens and Miracle [1986] for comments about the European situation.)

2. "Self-regulation is a concept distinct from self-discipline. The latter describes the individual's control, or attempts to control, his own actions; the former entails control by the individual's peers, subjection to whose judgment is central to the description of such systems as regulatory. Self-discipline's only sanction is the individual conscience. The most characteristic sanction of self-regulation is exclusion from participation in the activity regulated (Thomson 1983, p. 4)."

3. That self-discipline is still insufficiently developed was mentioned by Virginia Knauer, President Reagan's consumer adviser, who challenged U.S. media to more carefully screen the ads they accept for weight-loss schemes, arthritis, cancer and baldness cures, and even car sales. "Media Must Screen out Fraudulent Advertising," *AMA Marketing News* (December 6, 1985), p. 5.

4. "Economic regulation may be defined as the imposition of rules by a government,

backed by the use of penalties, that are intended specifically to modify the economic behavior of individuals and firms in the private sector. This definition distinguishes economic regulation as an instrument of public policy from others such as exhortation, direct expenditure, taxation, tax expenditures, and public ownership (Thompson and Jones 1982, p. 17).''

5. ''Soft law'' (Hondius 1984, p. 142) encompasses both ''pure'' self-regulation and various forms of ''concerted action'' with outside groups, and is generally characterized by public-policy support and by its nonbinding legal nature. Another term is ''non-legislative means'' of achieving desirable economic and social goals (ECLG 1983).

6. An interesting comment about voluntarism is provided by Mitchell (1978, p. 147) in the British context of the Office of Fair Trading's promotion of self-regulatory codes: ''While a code of practice may be 'voluntary' in the sense that it is open to a trade association to adopt one or not, OFT approval is conditional on member firms of the association undertaking to abide by the provisions of the code. It is not open to a member firm to accept some provisions and not others. This . . . distinguishes a code of practice as such from the many recommendations or guidelines which trade associations produce.''

7. The regulatory process is usually lengthy and costly since it involves research, drafting, hearings, debates, investigation, prosecution, etc., while industry and consumerists spend much time and money on lobbying, public-relations efforts and the like. However, the development of new ASR norms is not necessarily faster than that of regulation because a broad consensus must be achieved. Nevertheless, the application of ASR standards may be faster than that of regulations. For further discussion of such costs and benefits, see Darvall (1980), Hondius (1984) and Wyckham (1987).

8. The newsletter of the French ASR body provides an illuminating example of the flexibility and realism offered by self-regulation in its comparison of the ineffective French law against tobacco advertising and of the more effective guidelines developed by the alcoholic-beverage industry (*BVP Echos*, no. 81, September 1986, p. 3).

9. For a discussion of this growing issue in the United States and Europe, see: R. R. Bruce, B. P. Keller, and J. P. Cunnard, *Worldwide Restrictions on Advertising: An Outline of Principles, Problems and Solutions* (New York: International Advertising Association, 1985); and Anthony Lester and David Pannick, *Advertising and Freedom of Expression in Europe* (Paris: International Chamber of Commerce, Marketing Commission, October 1984).

10. A five-country survey in 1979–1980 indicated that about half of the general-public respondents agreed that: ''In general, self-regulation by business itself is preferable to stricter control of business by the government (Barksdale et al. 1982, pp. 83–85).''

11. Further differences between self-regulation in advertising and other industries are discussed by Jones and Pickering (1985, pp. 23–24). In particular, they mention that breaches are more likely to be picked up in the case of advertising because of its high visibility.

12. In some countries (e.g., Australia), the media are liable for publishing false, deceptive and/or unfair advertisements. This situation encourages them to develop their preclearance activities—singly or as a group.

13. A related issue not discussed here is where consumers prefer to complain: directly to manufacturers and distributors or to industry bodies and government agencies (including the courts)? Competitors, for that matter, face the same choices (Stridsberg 1976, p. 7).

14. Self-discipline is already mandated by various legislations requiring firms to set up control systems for such matters as safety, equal-employment opportunity and fraud.

While delegations of this sort help firms avoid externally imposed standards, they often result in internal procedural requirements from government, which can make self-discipline as burdensome as regulation itself (Bardach and Kagan 1982).

15. Levin (1967) has commented on the legality and desirability of self-regulation under U.S. antitrust laws: "The conditions which bona fide self-regulatory programs must meet include: (a) clear, socially meritorious standards widely accepted in the community; (b) adequate internal safeguards against self-serving policies and procedures; (c) the need for joint action to forestall product deterioration, (d) non-availability of less restrictive remedies. However, the conflicting interests of code members often make for an uneasy alliance at best. Short of some unusual community of fear, a general disparity in the members' economic positions and their divergent goals may impair conditions (a) and (b), producing a program that favors dominant members at the expense of others, including outsiders. In that case, competition could be impaired with no satisfactory enhancement of other dimensions of business performance. Alternative remedies [such as government regulation] may then become more attractive (Levin 1967, p. 643)." (See also Lad [1985], pp. 30–37).

16. The International Chamber of Commerce's International Code of Advertising Practice starts by saying that "All advertising should be legal." Most national ASR codes include the same principle (see Chapter 15). An emerging problem concerns what laws—national, foreign, regional (e.g., European Economic Community [EEC] directives) or supranational—do apply, for example, in the case of satellite advertising and other forms of "international" advertising.

17. Industry codes (e.g., for pharmaceuticals) dealing with advertising are often more detailed than those used by national ASR bodies, which have to cope with a very heterogeneous set of goods and issues.

18. The concept of "unfairness" is a difficult one to develop in law and to apply in the courts. See the forthcoming *Proceedings of the Fifth European Workshop on Consumer Law (Unfair and Comparative Advertising)*, held in Louvain-la-Neuve, Belgium, September 1986, for recent discussions of unfairness.

19. Various studies have estimated that from 2 to 16 percent of people do complain when something bothers them, and that from 4 to 7 percent of advertisements could be considered to be false, misleading or contrary to voluntary guidelines. In any case, advertising has a low salience for most people, with only 2 to 8 percent expressing spontaneous concern about it.

20. The problem is similar to that of determining the optimum amount of advertising for a particular product—an issue far from resolution for advertisers, their agencies and advertising scholars. Besides, advertising for complaints generates costs, not revenues, so that profit-maximization tools of analysis are inappropriate.

21. Membership in a self-regulatory body and/or adherence to its rules is mandated in a few countries (e.g., Australia, where the accreditation of an advertising agency may be suspended), but this requirement is used more to force moral adherence than as the basis for using the possible sanction of expulsion.

22. Three-fourths of thirty-two U.S. association executives said that their organizations did not have a way of measuring their code's effectiveness (Opinion Research Corporation 1980, p. 225).

23. The "hierarchical-feudal" mode is not further analyzed here although it may apply to situations where there is a lack of information parity—as when one segment of the

advertising industry (e.g., the media) is more knowledgeable and dominates private-interest government.

24. As has been observed about ''corporate cultures,'' their guiding concepts, values and aspirations are often unwritten, expressed at high levels of abstraction, and may mean very little to outsiders while, for insiders, they are rich with significance.

25. The conceptual framework developed by Hofstede (1980) in his cross-cultural study of work-related values is also very relevant: power distance, uncertainty avoidance, individualism/collectivism and masculinity/femininity.

2

Outside Participation in Advertising Self-Regulation: A General Analysis

If advertising self-regulation is an effective complement to regulation, is it desirable or even imperative to include "outsiders"—that is, nonmembers of the advertising industry—in the functioning of ASR systems? Since such outsiders are already involved in several countries,[1] this is not a hypothetical question. Besides, outside participation has been advocated by a number of observers, researchers and policymakers. Consequently, its rationale, functioning and effectiveness deserve examination in conceptual, theoretical and empirical terms.

This chapter: (1) defines outside participation (OP) and points out some precedents; (2) discusses its advantages and disadvantages; (3) theorizes about its conditions, motivations and precipitating circumstances; (4) reviews the encouragement and opposition it has encountered, and (5) analyzes its forms and functioning in the context of advertising self-regulation.

OP Definition and Precedents

Participation can be understood to mean that those affected are involved in the setting of rules as well as in their application. This century has witnessed numerous propositions and some embodiments of such participation—particularly, the various schemes involving employees in company policymaking and application. In the field of consumer policy, this development has often taken the form of consumer representation on consultative bodies that advise governments. Thus, the Belgian government-sponsored Consumers Council is usually consulted about new legislative proposals bearing on consumer affairs, and it can suggest new laws or amendments to the government. Similarly, the European Economic Community Commission has a Consumers Consultative Committee to advise it on EEC activities. In a more active manner, Swedish consumer and business representatives participate in developing the Ombudsman-system's guidelines on marketing practices; while "public" members of various kinds sit on licensing, standard-setting and product-certifying bodies in quite a few countries (cf. Thain et al. 1979).

In this study, "outside participation" (OP) refers to what in the previous chapter is called "coopted" self-regulation where industry, on its own volition, involves nonindustry people in the development, application and enforcement of its voluntary norms, although Hondius (1984, p. 140) prefers the term "concerted action" to refer to self-regulation with the participation of consumers and other relevant constituencies.

OP Rationale

Outside participation is generally rationalized in terms of greater legitimacy and effectiveness—two goals that are not always compatible. In the context of advertising self-regulation, it presents a number of advantages and disadvantages for the advertising industry and for consumers.

Advantages for Advertising

Greater Legitimacy and Credibility. Legitimacy rests either on a status granted by the State—as in the case of private bodies given some monopoly of rule-making in a corporativist manner[2]—or on societal contributions recognized by an institution's publics. Since ASR systems are practically never granted a monopolistic status, they depend on credible performance as perceived by their publics. However, as Streeck and Schmitter (1985, pp. 13–14) point out in their study of private-interest government to which self-regulation is related, its credible performance usually rests on second-best compromised solutions, which are often difficult to justify. Opening their deliberations to outsiders can help ASR systems alleviate criticisms of being self-serving bodies, or of amounting to a pretense of coping with public dissatisfaction in the matter of advertising.[3] In other words, a change in structure and process—outside participation—may improve the credibility of ASR systems, or at least its perception (Neelankavil and Stridsberg 1980, pp. 19–21; Thain et al. 1979, pp. 4–5).

Greater Expertise. Private-interest governments must be rooted in the values and interest perceptions of existing social collectivities (Streeck and Schmitter 1985, p. 27). Industry members on ASR bodies bring in technical expertise and can be considered apt judges in matters of "truth and accuracy" in advertising. After all, 'it takes a crook to catch a crook,' and, if advertising practitioners are as devious as their critics imagine them to be, then a jury made up exclusively of insiders can readily detect false, misleading and denigrating ads, and is unlikely to accept such ads from competitors. Consequently, outside expertise is not truly needed for detecting "hard" violations of good advertising practice unless one assumes some industry conspiracy to condone such misbehavior. In any case, various experts are routinely or occasionally used by self-regulatory bodies to examine controversial technical claims (e.g., one toothpaste does or does not remove tartar, is or is not superior to another brand).

Even more relevant for the expertise issue is the fact that advertising is increasingly being criticized on "soft" grounds such as good taste, decency, sexism, privacy, objectionable products (e.g., cigarettes and alcohol) and audiences (e.g., children and uneducated women in developing countries). (See Chapter 1, and Boddewyn 1982.) There are no real experts in such moral matters unless one wants to rely on opinion polls, but the latter are too expensive and time-consuming to use in connection with hundreds of consumer complaints. This situation led one French observer to comment that:

Self-regulation resembles judiciary institutions more than administrative ones because the former are based on the notion of the "sage" rather than that of the "expert," or their expertise belongs more to the "judgment" category than that of "technical competence." What would the laws be without mores? If there is an institution which illustrates well the interdependence of laws and mores as well as the complementarity of the "rule" and of "adhesion," it is self-regulation (*BVP* 1985, p. 36).

For example, are pictures in a catalog for men's clothing, showing a daughter wearing her father's shirt while sitting on his lap next to his bare torso, too suggestive of incestuous behavior? (This was a real case discussed by an ASR panel including outsiders.) Nobody can definitely answer such a question, but outsiders can help widen opinions beyond what advertising practitioners may simply see as a new attention-getting technique in a highly competitive environment. This represents a situation where the moral expertise of insiders is questionable: while they are people like everybody else—neither superior nor inferior beings—they can be suspected of bringing an industry-specific perspective on what constitutes community standards, particularly in the matter of vague, fluid and sometimes contradictory values in modern societies.[4] Although this judgment is disputed by those advertising practitioners who consider themselves to be as good judges of community standards as the next person, or who argue that public-opinion surveys can help them gauge social trends, it constitutes another major rationale for bringing in outsiders from the Community and/or the State, who are expected to contribute additional information and viewpoints to the deliberations of self-regulatory bodies.

Antitrust Antidote. Although probably a minor consideration, the inclusion of outsiders helps alleviate the legal problems associated with peers judging and disciplining peers. What may be judged to be "fair" or "unfair" on the part of competitors may not be so regarded by outsiders, who are also likely to consider the consumer and public interests—as with comparison advertising, which names competitors and is thus abhorred by them, although such a practice may well serve consumers (Boddewyn and Marton 1978). Outsiders can thus help dispel the fears of anticompetitive behavior on the part of inside members.[5]

Greater Publicity for Self-Regulation. Outsiders—particularly, well placed and visible ones—help diffuse information about the existence, availability and performance of ASR bodies via their membership in other important organizations (consumer associations, government agencies, professional societies, etc.)—hopefully, in a favorable manner.

Advantages for Consumers

Participating in ASR activities increases the possibility and even the probability that the development and application of voluntary standards will improve consumer protection by enhancing their rights to be heard and to obtain redress. This expectation can be related to fundamental principles of action for affected but interdependent parties. Consumers and producers—like labor and management in another context—have different interests, yet need each other so that they should acknowledge their interdependence. This "pluralistic model" recognizes the legitimacy of inherently competing and divergent interests, but considers that negotiated compromises can be achieved for mutual benefits: "[The] pluralistic conception . . . consists of these key elements: competing *and* cooperative interests, joint decision-making, the expandability of organizational benefits, and procedural as well as substantive norms (King and van de Vall 1978, p. 133)."

This perspective can be related to Hirschman's (1970) analysis of how individuals, organizations and states cope with lapses from efficient, rational, law-abiding, virtuous or otherwise functional behavior. Briefly stated, there are three major options that can be used sequentially or concurrently in the context of advertising deficiencies:

1. *Exit*: Consumers "tune out" and refuse to hear or heed those advertising messages they find objectionable—whether singly or collectively (as through boycotts).
2. *Voice*: Consumers "speak up" by complaining to advertisers, agencies, media, government bureaus, advertising self-regulatory bodies and other professional associations by suing, by publicity campaigns,[6] by lobbying, etc.,—again, either singly or collectively.
3. *Loyalty*: Instead of "staying out," consumers and/or their representative organizations "get inside" the ASR system in order to express "voice."

Outside participation is related to the "loyalty" option as a way of operationalizing the pluralistic model outlined above: "If you can't beat them, join them!" Alternatively, outsiders can "join them to beat them" since becoming an insider provides a complementary way of expressing and securing consumer rights without fully sacrificing the "exit" and "voice" alternatives (Olander and Lindhoff 1975). Besides, the loyalty approach is attractive in view of its relatively successful use in industrial relations and other contexts. It may not be a panacea, but what is—so why not use it? (See below for further evidence of support for dialogue and concerted action between producers and consumers.)

Disadvantages for Advertising

Explicit and significant outside participation in ASR systems is resisted on both philosophical and practical grounds.

Philosophical Objections. The inclusion of outsiders in ASR structures and processes violates the very principle of *self*-regulation. Other forms of social control via the Market, the State and the Community already allow for the confrontation and reconciliation of consumer and producer interests so that there is no point in duplicating such processes within private-interest governments. Besides, outside participation is likely to undermine the acceptance of self-imposed rules by industry members. One of the major attractions of the self-regulatory system is precisely that members voluntarily subscribe to both the letter and the spirit of the self-regulatory principles and rules, while such moral commitment is not required so far as the law is concerned. In this context, the fact that ASR norms have to be "user-friendly" usually requires that they be developed by the industry itself, without outside participation.

Practical Objections. In the first place, inexpert (at least as far as the technical aspects of advertising control are concerned) and antagonistic outsiders can create dissensus, complicate the delicate weighing of factors, slow down a process that prides itself on its relative simplicity and speed, and generate potential leaks about its deliberations. In particular, will the speed of self-regulation, which constitutes one of its main assets, be slowed down by the inclusion of outsiders who have to learn how advertising really works—not a small task, considering commonly held prejudices and misinformation—and to familiarize themselves with advertising regulations and voluntary standards? Besides, will the decisional consensus required for the smooth functioning of ASR systems be hampered or shattered by the presence of possibly hostile outsiders with other values and attitudes, when there should be no major division of opinions regarding what constitutes "truth and accuracy" in advertising, nor about what is "right and fitting"? Dissensus could even deter industry members from joining and staying, since they may view themselves as "responsible people of action" and abhor "philosophical" discussions of advertising.

Boisot's (1986) discussion of the "uncodified" nature of some norms also helps explain the advertising industry's reluctance to include outsiders. Practitioners tend to feel that only they "know" what the problems and their "realistic solutions" are in some cases. However, such uncodified information is difficult to transmit in other than face-to-face transactions involving only a limited number of "understanding" participants. Transactions of the sort are generally only possible among people who share common values, thereby militating against the inclusion of outsiders.

Second, outside participation increases the direct cost of self-regulation, since outsiders must usually be subsidized—at least for their out-of-pocket costs—while insiders' time and expenses (travel, etc.) are usually provided freely by their sponsoring organizations.[7] Thereby, outside participation reduces self-regulation's comparative advantage of being less expensive than regulation unless outsiders finance their own participation, a rare occurrence (see Netherlands chapter).

Third, how will outsiders be chosen so that legitimacy and effectiveness may be obtained without appearing to have coopted unrepresentative "tokens" or "stooges"? (See below for further discussion of this selection problem.)

Fourth, there is the potential loss of control as well as the risk of failure. How can one guard against outsiders imposing their own standards, especially if they are in a majority position on the ASR body? Is it not better to bargain in the forum of politics if "alien" notions of good advertising practice are going to be proposed (see comments to that effect in Chapter 1)? How can outsiders be dropped if outside participation turns out to be a failure, without appearing to revert to a closed and self-centered formula for self-regulation? Will not advertising standards developed in concerted action with outsiders be more likely to be transformed into law since they represent a consensus between producers and consumers? And where will it end since the same rationale could be used for putting outsiders on the board of directors of companies, on their consumer-affairs staffs, on media acceptance committees that prescreen submitted advertisements, and so on?

Disadvantages for Consumers

Since outside participation is likely to increase the legitimacy and credibility of advertising self-regulation, it may undermine the effectiveness of "voice" on the part of consumers and consumerists—particularly their demands for further regulation (ECLG 1983, p. 211; Business International 1980, p. I–31). Even though the "loyalty" route does not exclude simultaneous recourse to "exit" and "voice" (see above), it constrains these alternatives because outside participation implies that it will be given a fair try by outsiders. This is a matter of weighing the costs and benefits of outside participation—as is true for business too. However, as an "upstart" interest group with weaker political legitimacy, fewer resources and lesser cohesiveness than business and government (see below), consumerists may feel that they are in a weak bargaining position to be heard and heeded on the inside so that they will look like fools for having granted legitimacy to an imperfect or even useless ASR system.

Consumerists also know that some topics will always be off limits. Advertising is related to such values as materialism, individualism, commercialism, hedonism and acquisitiveness; and advertisers adhere to such principles as "Legal to make and sell, legal to advertise." Most consumerist organizations find these values and principles unacceptable, but advertisers are very unlikely to abandon them, so that compromise is improbable in such matters. It is one thing to discuss whether cigarette advertising should be directed at children or should encourage smoking in general—here, both producers and consumers can negotiate and reach some understanding. It is another for outsiders to demand that self-regulation ban all cigarette advertising.

Altogether, both the advertising industry and the consumer movement are divided about the benefits of outside participation, a situation that explains why its practice is limited. Consequently, it will function only when certain conditions, motivations and precipitating circumstances are present—as will be argued in a subsequent section. Before turning to this theoretical analysis, it is necessary to discuss: (1) the respective political powers of business and consumers; (2) public policy toward outside participation, and (3) the forms that can be assumed by the latter.

Business and Consumerist Powers

A full analysis of the respective political powers of business and consumers cannot be provided here. However, in the context of explaining why outsiders— including consumer representatives—are asked to participate in advertising self-regulation and accept, a few general observations will be presented.[8]

Growing Consumerist Power

It is widely acknowledged that consumer interests have not always been adequately considered in corporate and public policies. Such a realization has led to the articulation and promotion of general "consumer rights" to be informed, to choose, to get safe products, to be heard, and to obtain redress. This development was both promoted and accompanied by a social movement (made up of individuals, public-interest and special-purpose organizations) seeking to protect and extend these newly recognized rights and to increase the power of buyers in relation to sellers. Consequently, both on their own initiative and with the prompting and support of consumer-interest groups, governments—particularly in developed countries—have enacted laws, regulations and other measures (e.g., subsidization) designed to protect and promote consumers or, at least, to provide for a fairer balance of power between producers and consumers. That this task is still incomplete and will always remain so in view of changing values, economic resources and political powers does not gainsay the progress made along these lines.

The organization of consumerist power is an important variable in negotiating with business and government. Five broadly defined situations can be identified: (1) consumer associations are practically nonexistent or very weak, leading to an absence of valid spokesmen; (2) consumer associations are multiple but divided along various lines, precluding unified representative action; (3) a few activist consumerist bodies, while relatively small, are able to alter the agenda of government agencies and self-regulatory bodies through the skillful use of lobbying activities, the media, the courts and industry complaint-handling mechanisms (including ASR systems); (4) government-created consumers councils provide a locus for the airing and partial reconciliation of business and consumerist interests through concerted action and even the negotiation of collective agreements, and (5) a powerful capstone consumer organization (sometimes a couple of them, as in the Netherlands) is accepted as a valid representative of consumer interests by business and government (cf. Koopman [1986]). The country studies illustrate these various situations, revealing that consumerist outside participation in ASR systems is more likely under options 3 and 5.

Greater Business Power

Apart from those few who truly believe that consumerists and regulators are omnipotent, invincible and in total control of business, most qualified observers would agree that business power is still greater than consumer power. Speaking of public-interest groups in Canada, Goldstein (1979) reached a conclusion that can probably be extended, *mutatis mutandis*, to consumer movements around the world (see also Nadel 1971 and Vogel 1979):

[As] nonprofit agencies, [public-interest groups] lack any vital economic role within the system [unlike business]. Since they represent no special interests, they are unlikely to possess any automatic source of financial support and must scramble for money where they can. Nor do they possess the kind of legitimacy available to both private enterprises and government. Few people challenge the mandate of General Motors to represent its stockholders, or of Parliament to represent the citizens of Canada. But it may not be immediately clear whether a public-interest group performs a function not performed by government: on what grounds, for example, can any consumer group claim to represent the Canadian public more effectively than the federal Department of Consumer and Corporate Affairs? And even if consumer groups *can* claim a special role, how do we know that any one consumers' group, like the Consumers' Association of Canada, speaks for *the* Canadian consumer (Goldstein 1979, p. 140)?

These are strong words, even fighting words. Goldstein himself acknowledges that some public-interest groups are influential under certain conditions; and the successes of consumer organizations around the world attest to their occasional or intermittent power. Still, consumerists would not be asking for more recognition, access, regulations, subsidies and the like if they already felt that consumer power is now equal to that of business—unless one chooses to equate these demands with an appetite for even more power after parity or better has already been achieved.

The literatures reviewed and the interviews conducted for the twelve country studies included in this volume consistently revealed a relatively weak and often divided consumer movement as well as feeble or vacillating public policies toward consumer protection. The recent discussions generated within and around the European Economic Community in connection with its consumer-protection policies also disclosed much dissatisfaction with what has been achieved since 1972–1975.[9] Business, of course, has its own problems since it does not always agree and cohere about such matters as the harmonization of national advertising regulations; and it has to wage incessant battles on various fronts (e.g., medicine, cigarette, food, children and satellite advertising). Still, it can be adjudged to be generally stronger than the consumerist side even though the latter has strong "nuisance" value.

Power and Participation

This brief discussion of consumerist power is intended to gauge the likelihood of consumer participation in advertising self-regulation. In terms of conditions, a united, competent, strong and confident consumer movement or consumerist organization is more likely to participate. Since this condition is seldom present, formal consumer participation in advertising self-regulation is unlikely, although the advertising industry can enlist other types of "public" members and use other ways of incorporating "voice" or "loyalty" (see below). Besides, interest groups more concerned about "solidary" purposes—that is, to generate ideological unity—are less likely to engage in dialogue with other groups (Moe 1981), and this characteristic can be applied to many small consumer organizations and to the International Organization of Consumers Unions.

Regarding motivation, participation promises access as well as "inside" information and influence, which can benefit consumerism. Yet, success is not guaranteed as is evident from various aborted relationships between ASR bodies and consumer representatives (e.g., in the Federal Republic of Germany and the Philippines). Failure often results from mixed motives since both sides talk of "dialogue"—probably sincerely—but also want to "win." As Vogel put it in the context of the demands of U.S. public-interest groups to participate in policymaking: "They want a foothold within the public bureaucracy through 'participation' designed to strengthen the regulatory process. Of course, consumer advocates—like business representatives—do not want participation for its own sake but for concrete victories over business; they do not simply want to 'balance' the consideration of various interests in the regulatory process but to dominate it (Vogel 1979, p. 33; 1980–1981, p. 626)." For Vogel, this explains why consumerists are more inclined to participate in regulation-making than in negotiation with business, because they are more confident of winning in the former than in the latter. Since business represents a strong pressure group in policymaking, it too prefers to avoid outside participation within its own councils. This broad conclusion naturally requires various national qualifications.

Besides, consumerists' refusal to participate in self-regulation gives them some leverage, since those who know their acquiescence is needed will find it in their interest to hold out for better from the other side. Even a weak consumer movement can withhold its participation and make it appear as if it is done from strength, to the detriment of advertising self-regulation.

Even if the conditions and motivations present are not always conducive to participation, the latter may still receive impetus from precipitating or facilitating circumstances, as is explained in the next section.

Dialogue and Participation: Support and Disenchantment

Precedents for outside participation have provided some impetus in the context of advertising self-regulation. Besides, reputed ASR bodies, such as the British Advertising Standards Authority, which includes a majority of outsiders on its Council, have demonstrated that outside participation does work (under certain conditions, for sure) and that the principle of pure self-regulation is not sacrosanct. Besides, various students of ASR systems (e.g., Brandmair 1978; La-Barbera 1980b; and Zanot 1979) have repeatedly urged the inclusion of outsiders. Probably more influential still have been various governmental initiatives.

National and Supranational Encouragement

The Swedish government has consistently encouraged concertation between business and consumers in the implementation of its Consumer-Ombudsman system, and Sweden is considered a "pilot nation" in the field of consumer protection. More generally, the encouragement of advertising self-regulation by various governments (e.g., in the United Kingdom, another pilot nation) and the hard-won reference to ASR bodies in the 1984 EEC Directive on Misleading Advertising have made ASR systems more attractive as an alternative or complement to regulation.[10] In Europe, at least, various supranational bodies have spoken out in favor of dialogue, concertation, negotiated agreements and the like between producers and consumers.

- A Resolution (16 October 1980) of the European Parliament "considers that the [EEC] Commission must encourage industrial codes of conduct which take account of the interests of consumers, and that it should also promote consultation between the consumers, industry and traders with a view to the conclusion of agreements; legislative provisions are necessary only when voluntary agreements do not suffice or do not work (Par. 3)." It also "requests that efforts should be stepped up to achieve better dialogue and consultation between representatives of consumers, producers and traders (Par. 11)."

- The First Consumer Program (1975) of the European Communities had focused on legislative and regulatory remedies—an initial position that may have raised consumerist expectations and hampered dialogue with business. The Second Program (1981), however, while acknowledging that consumer protection still required regulatory measures, also spoke of creating the right conditions for better dialogue and greater consultation between consumer and producer representatives. It also mentioned that, even when certain commercial practices appear suitable for legislation, it may be advisable to test the effectiveness of voluntary agreements:

> The purpose of this program is to enable the Community to continue and intensify its measures in this field and to help establish conditions for improved consultation between consumers on the one hand and manufacturers and retailers on the other (Par. 2). The Commission will endeavor to facilitate

the elaboration and conclusion of [specific agreements between the various interests] on an experimental basis (Par. 5).

• In its Recommendation No. 947 of 1982, the Parliamentary Assembly of the Council of Europe (a twenty-one-country deliberative body) encouraged negotiations between consumer associations and trade bodies (Par. 12). Already in 1973 it had issued Resolution 543 on a Consumer Protection Charter, which stated that:

> Responsible associations of manufacturers and traders, nationally and collectively in Western Europe, shall be encouraged to formulate their own codes of trading practices which, while basically conforming to national laws, shall seek to promote higher standards, and shall be submitted— together with proposals for a private and objective enforcement of such codes in collaboration with the consumers—to national consumer authorities for approval. The authorities shall give public support and backing to approved codes.

• The Organization for Economic Cooperation and Development (OECD) issued a Note on Consumer Policy by its Secretary General on 26 August 1982, which refers to consumer representation:

> The growing importance of consumer representation in governmental and non-governmental institutions as well as the involvement of consumers in the development of voluntary codes of conduct dealing with consumer policy not only represents a general recognition of the consumer interest, but also reflects the increasing desire of policy-makers to transform the spirit of confrontation which formerly often characterized the relations between consumers' and suppliers' interests into a more cooperative approach (Par. 35).

• Even the International Chamber of Commerce, a private business body, referred to outside participation in a Report of its Commission on Marketing, Advertising and Distribution (No. 240/166 of 30 March 1984):

> Experience shows that self-regulatory bodies are sensitive to the criticism that they are not independent. In practice, they go to very considerable lengths to make sure that they take an objective stance in assessing cases. The independence of a self-regulation control body and its decision-making can be increased over time in a number of ways: appointing an independent chairman and some independent members; nominating members in their personal capacity (p. 17).

These various recommendations reflect recent acknowledgments that regulation has its limits, that governmental resources had started to dwindle in the 1970s, and that public opinion was turning against some regulatory measures seen as costly and overly restrictive for consumers (Business International 1980). The resulting "deregulatory" or "antiregulatory" climate was thus conducive to considering and trying other control alternatives such as self-regulation. Since consumerists wanted to participate in the development and application of advertising controls, why would they not do it also in the context of self-regulation?

Disenchantments

This perspective was reasonable but it has not worked out too well to date. The preceding analyses of advantages and disadvantages of participation as well as of the respective powers of business and consumers have already revealed numerous philosophical and practical obstacles, which remain operative, but additional considerations are in order.

First, participation assumes a generally "symbiotic interdependence" between producers and consumers (Pennings 1981; Yuchtman and Seashore 1967), that is, that they share common goals (e.g., consumer satisfaction) and will derive high mutual benefits from cooperation. However, this situation prevails only under certain conditions (see below) and, as Vogel (1979) has argued, both business and consumerists ultimately prefer domination over participation—in other words, "political" rationality (what is good for *one* sector or movement) often dominates "economic" rationality (what is good for *both* producers and consumers).

Second, the EEC, Council of Europe and OECD proposals were vague, and wisely so since it was a novel initiative that would need some experimentation. The references to "dialogue" could mean anything; those to "negotiated codes" were more specific but did not seriously consider the conditions necessary for successful negotiation; and there were no mentions of participation within self-regulatory bodies (the "loyalty" route). There are instances of negotiated codes between producers and consumers—particularly in the Netherlands and Sweden (see country chapters)—but not through advertising self-regulatory bodies. As was mentioned earlier, the advertising industry is concerned about the difficulty of revising such negotiated codes, and about the danger of their being incorporated into law. Consumerist advocates, in any case, remain divided about this approach and generally prefer regulation (ECLG 1983).

Dialogue is superficially cheap—hence, its appeal—but has hidden costs. Both sides want to be heard and understood; and better information and access to the other side can be conducive to more realistic demands for effective regulation and self-regulation. However, there are usually alternative ways to "know and understand" the other side through the use of experts, informal contacts[11] and surveys, unless one is prepared to argue that it is essential to bring the antagonists formally together, as is done in industrial relations. A stronger objection to dialogue is that the parties expect not only to be "heard" but also to be "heeded." As many studies of personnel and consumer relations have proven, it is dangerous to ask people what they feel and want, if one is not ready to deliver on the expectations generated by the dialogue. Hence, "dialogue" often turns out to be a disguised form of "negotiation" but, then, the conditions for effective negotiation have to be present. Besides, the contentious nature of some issues and the adversarial relationships that have sometimes developed between an industry and its critics may preclude or protract any productive dialogue (Business International 1980, p. I–79).

A 1983 conference at the University of Bremen on "Implementing the Consumer-Supplier Dialogue through Soft Law" revealed serious reservations about the use of dialogue and negotiation.[12] As was later echoed by the discussions regarding new directions for consumer policy on the part of the European Communities (EEC), consumerists concluded that such attempts were bound to fail for lack of incentives to negotiate at the EEC level, and of an adequate institutional framework. The prerequisites for a dialogue resulting in an effective voluntary consumer-protection system are that the parties have equal status and equal access to information, that the terms be applicable to the entire sector, and that there be effective sanctions for noncompliance—all conditions that are still lacking. Thus, the EEC Commission has refused to be a party to the producer-consumer dialogue and has limited its role to facilitating it. More important, it has failed to make credible the threat of further EEC regulation, should the dialogue fail or the agreements lack adequate enforcement. In any case, there is nothing equivalent at the European and international levels to the national self-regulatory systems to draw up and monitor codes; and difference in national market and regulatory situations may preclude easy international solutions (Business International 1980, p. I–68).[13]

Last but not least, consumerists still prefer regulation; they fear that their participation in self-regulatory schemes will weaken their demands and supports for regulation, and they consider "soft law" only as a preliminary, temporary or minor complement to regulation. As one consumerist spokesman put it:

There is no necessary link between "dialogue" and "codes." It was hoped that a voluntary approach would somehow choose the right subjects—from the [EEC] Commission's point of view. Codes would then emerge like Venus from the waves. However, industry representatives in several meetings ruled out European Codes, and no one spoke in favor of the Commission's approach. The meetings have tended to end with a last-minute search for something positive to say about the discussions which "next time" must be more precise and based on an inventory of common problems. Not only is there no link between "dialogue" and "codes" [but] trying to make one has even made dialogue more difficult, and our [European Bureau of Consumer Unions, BEUC] relations with different European industry associations have hardly improved (Venables 1984, p. 297).[14]

Consequently, Bourgoignie spelled out the conditions for accepting "soft law" as a valid alternative strategy for consumers:

1. The existence of imperative norms or of a legislative framework within which voluntary initiatives can take place.
2. The existence of a public or administrative institutional structure charged with initiating soft-law mechanisms where necessary, and with monitoring the voluntary system;

failures and violations of soft law have to be corrected not only by soft-law remedies but also by effective administrative and court actions.

3. The direct participation of consumers in the functioning of soft-law mechanisms has to be ensured; in particular, the legislative framework which is called for has to provide for the right of consumer groups to denounce the violations of soft law before the courts through collective redress mechanisms (Bourgoignie 1984, pp. 317–18).

These are very strong requirements, which would drastically alter the nature and erode the business support of most current forms of advertising self-regulation. In any case, the advertising industry is equally dubious about the desirability and feasibility of negotiated codes, although it feels more positive about dialogue and outside participation, provided it can remain in control of its ASR systems[15] (but see the chapter on Italy for information about loss of control).

The next section analyzes: (1) the forms that outside participation can assume in ASR systems, and (2) the conditions under which such participation can be effective.

OP Forms and Functioning

The advertising industry and its various publics regularly engage in informal dialogues and even occasional negotiations, but this section focuses on the *formal* inclusion of nonindustry "outsiders" in all or part of an ASR system's functioning—from scanning the environment for issues to the development and application of standards.[16] How is it being worked out in practice? King and van de Vall (1978) have suggested five analytical dimensions: (1) the "horizontal span" of participation, which refers to the number of topics and issues under consideration; (2) the "vertical range" of participation, from consultation to decisionmaking; (3) the "timing" of participation, from issue-spotting to the setting of standards and to their implementation; (4) the "representativeness" of outside participants, and (5) the "comprehensiveness" of participation in the organization's structure (board of directors, executive committee, investigative and deliberative committees, etc.). These criteria are loosely used in the following analyses.

Selection Criteria for Outsiders

It was seen earlier that the main rationales for including nonindustry members have been the needs for: (1) legitimacy or credibility based on the outsiders' independence; (2) expertise about "soft" issues; (3) protection against antitrust charges of industry collusion, and (4) greater publicity for ASR activities. Since the last two considerations follow more or less automatically from satisfying the first two requirements, only the former will now be analyzed.

The legitimacy/credibility criterion dictates recruiting people whose independence is undisputable on account of: (1) membership and even leadership in "other-side" organizations (e.g., consumer associations); (2) professional status

(e.g., physicians, jurists and academic experts) or government affiliation, and/or
(3) high social visibility (e.g., "Establishment" types). The ideal candidate is
one who: (1) really does not need to serve on an ASR body for either monetary
or prestige reasons since he or she already satisfies these prerequisites in other
ways, and (2) would even suffer if affiliation with self-regulation were to tarnish
his or her reputation on account of being perceived as a captured or token outsider.

The expertise criterion usually takes care of itself if legitimate/credible outsiders are chosen, because they usually learn rather quickly what the issues and
relevant standards are, especially when a competent ASR Secretariat sorts out
and prepares the cases for consideration. Even when staff assistance is missing
or deficient, members tend to instruct and socialize each other about what is
relevant and problematic (Thain et al. 1979). Besides, inappropriate complaints
and clear-cut violations are usually handled by the Secretariat so that only "judgmental" cases are brought up for the full consideration of decisionmaking bodies.
It is mostly in such "soft" areas or borderline "hard" cases that the joint
"moral" expertise of insiders and outsiders can fruitfully complement each other.
Still, outsiders can ultimately become so socialized into considering business
viewpoints that they can lose their original freshness of viewpoint and familiarity
with the grassroots (Business International 1980, pp. II–148–49).

Needless to say, the selection process both of insiders and outsiders involves
considering personality factors. Ideal candidates must not only be independent,[17]
intelligent and diligent but also consensus- and action-oriented as well as constructive participants. This requirement holds particularly for complaint-handling
bodies, because other ASR phases—scanning the environment for emerging
issues, developing standards and monitoring advertising practice—can take place
at a more leisurely pace and even involve separate consultative, deliberative
and/or auditing panels that include a broader variety of insiders and outsiders
(including experts). The rest of this analysis therefore focuses on complaint-
handling panels.

Availability of Outsiders

Can credible and otherwise qualified outsiders be found and retained in sufficient numbers, and will they accept to serve? While ASR panels do not exceed
twelve members (but there can be several smaller panels), they have to be
regularly renewed on account of fatigue, personal reasons (geographical move,
illness, dissatisfaction, etc.) and the often benevolent nature of this unsalaried
service. Active participation may—as in the United Kingdom—require exam-
ining and even deliberating about hundreds of cases a year. This amounts to a
sizable amount of constant and frequently underpaid or unpaid work with relatively little prestige—it is not a presidential or royal commission after all. The
novelty wears thin after a while, except for the most dedicated outsiders, who
may not be ideal members on account of their professional interest in consumer
issues.

Besides, as was previously argued, qualified outsiders may be unwilling to serve for fear of being used or perceived as token ASR participants without any real power, and of granting legitimacy to self-regulation when the main task should be to strengthen regulation. Furthermore, they may prefer to remain independent of any involvement with advertising self-regulation in order to stay free to engage in "exit" and "voice" actions such as lobbying, exposing malpractices and organizing boycotts. Such watchdog, gadfly and antagonist roles are largely incompatible with serving as "loyal" ASR participants. As Moyer points out in the context of a Canadian retail-industry experiment involving public participation: "Altogether, while it is understandable that businessmen should wish that their public advisors could commit the organizations of which they are members, this is not a *quid pro quo* that can be met . . . Desirous of having an influential role, but wary of being co-opted in the process, delegates from non-industry organizations may insist that it be made clear from the beginning that their personal advice is not equivalent to their organization's consent (Moyer 1979, p. 66)."[18] Business must accept this ambivalent or dual role of outsiders representing other organizations, or they must minimize this conflictual situation by selecting independent members who do not represent any particular constituency.

Finally, there may not be any ready way of finding qualified outsiders in countries lacking an "Establishment," or in those that are so divided along ethnic, political, ideological and other lines that nobody can be considered as independent or as representative of outside interests (e.g., in Belgium). The frequent fragmentation of the consumerist movement has already been mentioned in this respect, but some nations also lack a tradition of dialogue and compromise between business and other sectors. The absence of governmental encouragement and prodding also hampers the participation of outsiders.

Types of Outsiders

While often overlapping in practice, four major types of formal outside participants can be distinguished.

Public members (also called "independents") are mainly chosen on account of the legitimacy/credibility they contribute to self-regulation. The key criterion is perceived independence, but a variety of representational criteria (occupation, geography, sex, etc.) are used to achieve some subtle and flexible dosage. This approach works best in countries such as the United Kingdom, where there is a tradition of respected independent commissions and a readily available Establishment of "notables" with a developed sense of public service. Expertise is typically of minor importance or is broadly defined in terms of bringing in different perspectives.

Consumer representatives constitute a second category, which clearly depends on the existence of a relatively unified, nonideological, middle-of-the-road and cooperative consumer movement. Canada and the Netherlands benefit from the presence of such conditions. Again, they mainly contribute legitimacy, but the expertise criterion is more evident because ASR consumer members can and do serve as a channel for bringing in specific complaints documented by their associations, and for contributing greater knowledge of relevant regulations as well as of current and emerging consumer issues.

True experts are rarely used, except in Italy, where jurists and social scientists are used on adjudicatory panels. In countries where the consumer movement is fragmented and other pronounced cleavages exist, current or former magistrates and jurists as well as academic experts may constitute the only body from which credible and otherwise qualified outsiders can be drawn.

ASR staff people are not true outsiders once they join an ASR body as their chairperson of the board, chief executive officer or Secretariat employee. Still, some of them constitute what may be called "expert boundary spanners." ASR chairpersons are often drawn from outside the advertising industry; and some ASR executives and their staff are or become true professionals who bring in perspectives and stances somewhat distinct from those of the advertising associations that sponsor self-regulation. For sure, this is a delicate balancing act for which such line-and-staff people are not always suited on account of lack of status, visibility, personality, adequate personal finances, etc. However, some of them do achieve a reasonable measure of independence, because their firing or quitting would cause serious legitimacy/credibility problems for self-regulation.

In practice, ASR systems use some mixture of all four types of outsiders, especially when all ASR functions are considered and not just complaint-adjudication. For example, the French ASR body (BVP) has a president who is typically a former judge; its current executive director came from the government-sponsored National Consumer Institute, where he served as an expert; its Secretariat include several lawyers; its board of directors has a few members from outside the advertising industry; and the BVP uses technical committees where government experts collaborate with industry representatives in drafting industry-specific ASR standards. However, no consumer-association representatives serve on the BVP because of the fragmentation and other problems of the French consumer movement.

Silent Partners

Finally, one can identify a fifth category of outsiders—namely, "silent partners"—who do not officially participate in ASR structures and operations but informally guide, monitor, assist, prod and even threaten them. In this context, Streeck and Schmitter (1985) have observed that the State and the Community always inform what happens in private-interest associations. Government agencies and officials are often the most evident silent partners in this regard. The U.S. Federal Trade Commission and the U.K. Office of Fair Trading have played such a role, which is also present when there exists some "corporatist" delegation of control power to a self-regulatory body, as in the Philippines.

Less important but occasionally significant are those individuals, small groups and broad-based organizations, who observe and comment upon regulation and self-regulation: academics, journalists, public-interest groups, expert commissions and freelance commentators. Most of the time, they remain unheeded and even unheard, being ignored or dismissed for lack of practical experience, prestige or power. However, they offer a latent reservoir of data, opinions and visions, which sometimes become relevant—as when deregulation gained support, long after the limits of regulation had been studied and argued in hitherto marginal academic circles.

In a few countries (e.g., Brazil), there are miscellaneous outsiders that are hard to categorize: journalists, editors of women's magazines, housewives, university professors, etc. This situation often reflects an inability to tap outside constituencies in any systematic manner, but it helps alleviate, in a rather haphazard way, the fundamental problem of the representativeness of outsiders.

The Problem of Representativeness

Outside of democratic political systems, the task of designing a true representation of the various producer, consumer, and public interests affected by advertising is practically insuperable—and even political systems encounter problems of representing all economic and social interests since parliamentarians and other elected officials are principally voted in on the basis of geography (states, districts, cities, etc.). Only government-created consultative bodies try to truly represent all affected interests although they usually turn out to be large cumbersome assemblies whose function is more to clarify and express a variety of positions than to reconcile them. Advertising self-regulation encounters the same insuperable problems of defining what outside interests are relevant and of achieving some reasonable representation among them (Business International 1980, pp. II–142ff), so that they typically take some "satisficing" shortcut rather than try to "optimize" outside participation—hence, the mixture of approaches analyzed above.

Consequently, the underrepresentation of outside interests is endemic to ASR systems. Some of it is unavoidable because of the complexity of the task and the unavailability of some types of outsiders. However, outside participation to date has unaccountably failed to include large segments of the population who often are the major consumers of advertising: young affluent urbanites, the lower bourgeoisie, and even the working class. Instead, all ASR outsiders in the countries analyzed in this study are solid middle-class and upper-class people. Their choice is readily understandable since they have more to offer in terms of education, time availability, relative financial independence, visibility, contacts, prestige and other resources related to the legitimacy, expertise and personality criteria previously discussed. In some sense, their social standing has to match that of the industry representatives on ASR bodies.

Nevertheless, such an "Establishment" or "elitist" bias is bound to warp the perception of current issues and values. When ethnic slurs in advertising are examined, where are the ethnic representatives? When sexy ads are criticized, are young consumers to whom they are often addressed involved in their scrutiny? When sexism-in-advertising issues are at stake, who are the experts? In practically all cases, middle-age or golden-age bourgeois who may not be avid watchers of television nor readers of the more popular tabloids or lurid magazines are the arbiters of what constitutes "good taste" in advertising. Clearly, the inclusion of a few random housewives, journalists or professors is not going to resolve the problem of representativeness, which is bound to remain elusive and even fundamentally insoluble, but they provide a nice touch of *vox populi*, which ASR systems should further acknowledge and incorporate.

Number and Choice of Outsiders

The proportion of formal outside representation falls into recognizable categories—from nil to 100 percent, with 50–50 or minority-majority representations in between. Both extremes are very rare because they create either a severe problem of legitimacy or of lack of control by the industry. In fact, there is almost always some formal outside representation in the form of an independent chairperson, combined with occasional and/or informal means such as consultative bodies, technical committees and independent experts. Why outsiders have obtained minority, majority or parity representation was not readily ascertainable from this study, which focused on the present situation rather than on the precise historical circumstances that informed these choices. Still, a few factors emerged from the country studies.

First, the decision to include any outsider(s) at all appears to be related to a legitimacy/credibility crisis rather than to any lack of expertise. However, ASR sponsors and leaders must believe that outside participation will alleviate or eliminate such a crisis without also jeopardizing broad industry support, because self-regulation depends on voluntary adherence to the system and its standards. As was argued before, abandoning a "pure" system represents a wrenching departure from the very principle of self-regulation. Besides, there is uncertainty about how the inclusion of outsiders will work out, since even the successful experience of other ASR systems is no sure guarantee because national conditions vary considerably in terms of favorable and unfavorable circumstances. Finally, outside participation has to be operationalized but the desirable type(s) of outsiders to include may not be obvious or even available. Therefore, outside participation usually follows some fairly predictable progression, keeping in mind that more recent systems have more readily accepted outside participation from their very inception, now that successful foreign experiences as well as assistance from older systems can be tapped.

The appointment of an independent chairperson is the simplest and typically the first step. Retired judges, former government officials and the like can easily be recruited. This innovation rarely encounters significant opposition since, at the limit, it seems like a token or minimal gesture, which does not threaten industry control. However, the camel's nose is now under the tent, and this creates an irreversible precedent. It may even generate some momentum if the "camel" and the permanent staff he controls are or become relatively independent of the industry—but this is a hypothesis greatly in need of explicit verification.

When the inclusion of outsiders on complaint-handling panels and other functions is decided—usually on account of some mixture of legitimacy and expertise problems not systematically explored in this study—some credible degree of outside participation must be attained. Where the acceptable minimum lies defies scientific precision, but 20 percent seems to be the lowest limit. Besides, having two outsiders is clearly better than one because a single outsider creates an enormous burden of proving any degree of tolerable representativeness: who is that single man or woman who alone can express outside interests? Besides, what if that single outsider is absent from a particular meeting? Past the "significant-minority" point, it is really a matter of choice, rather than of necessity, if the original experience has proved successful and no further crisis of public confidence in the ASR system has developed. Still, it takes a confident industry and ASR leadership to move to outsider parity or majority.

In any case, the industry and/or the ASR leaders retain control of what outsiders will be appointed.[19] Outside groups are rarely granted a permanent seat except when there are strong or at least unified and middle-of-the-road consumer associations—as in Canada, the Netherlands and the United Kingdom. Even then, these consumer associations do not "appoint" their representative(s); instead, a subtle consultation and negotiation process takes place outside of public view. Again, this should be the subject of further research, which could draw from related studies of how "representative" members are selected for special commissions, consultative bodies, appointive positions in sensitive domains, etc.

Operationalizing the Roles of Outsiders

The legitimizer and expert roles of outsiders can be operationalized in at least three ways: (1) consultative, (2) deliberative and decision-making, and (3) auditing. As was argued in a previous section, consultation (dialogue) has its limits and has even received some bad press lately. It appears necessary if the industry wants to keep abreast of broad issues and of what transpires in the consumer movement, government and other relevant publics. However, talk is cheap, and seldom if ever confers legitimacy by itself. Besides, there are many ways of obtaining the necessary access and information so that it is not necessary to institutionalize consultation as part of a self-regulatory system. There may even be undesirable consequences if consultation/dialogue results in unfulfilled expectations on one or both sides. Therefore, one finds few ongoing formal consultative schemes in ASR systems (see the chapter on France for a rare example). Special committees including outsiders are occasionally appointed when some major revisions of ASR standards, structures and processes are initiated. However, little publicity is usually given to them unless some major crisis has developed: "Better to sound them off quietly and informally" seems to be the operating principle.

Although recommended by some academic experts (e.g, Lazer and LaBarbera 1975, pp. 119–21), the regular and systematic external auditing of ASR systems at the initiative of the industry was only detected in the U.K. case. Government bodies (parliamentary committees, regulatory agencies, etc.) occasionally study self-regulation, but these are really external initiatives. In practically all cases, the advertising industry wants to retain control of its present and future courses of action, so that it "self-audits" through annual reports and rare systematic and comprehensive studies. Most of this introspection takes place quietly behind closed doors, if not without acrimonious internal debate at times. The resulting lack of outside participation in such auditing experiences has not affected the legitimacy of ASR systems to date. However, one can anticipate that this situation will become less acceptable as other self-regulatory bodies in the legal and medical professions, among others, come to broaden membership on their auditing committees in order to quell criticisms of self-serving behavior. At the limit, such outside involvement may lead to negotiated codes, which industry abhors by and large.

This leaves deliberation and decision-making on complaint-handling ASR panels as the only prevalent forms of outside participation at the present time, as a source of legitimacy and—to a lesser extent—expertise. However, significant outside participation is sometimes restricted to special situations, where it is difficult to justify leaving outsiders out. Thus, the U.S. NAD/NARB system uses outsiders to a greater extent in the matter of advertising to children through its specialist CARU unit. In Canada, there are special committees to prescreen advertisements for feminine-hygiene products and to investigate sexist complaints. These are "taste-and-opinion" topics, where concern has reached a fairly high pitch, where some consensus has emerged or is emerging about specific standards, and where the "experts"—mainly women and psychologists—can be readily obtained.

Television advertising is another special arena where outsiders and insiders frequently cohabit and even cooperate—at least when the State monopolizes the airwaves or has mandated some supervisory body charged with setting acceptance standards for programs, commercials and sponsorships, and even with pre-screening commercials. This situation reflects the original monopolistic or oligopolistic characteristics of this medium with only a few networks or stations, and with a widely feared "cultural" impact. However, the proliferation of the "new media" (satellite broadcasting, pay TV, videocassettes with or without commercials, videotext, etc.) is likely to relax some of these "mixed" controls on advertising, although it will be difficult if not impossible to reduce the role of outsiders—that is, nonadvertising and nonmedia representatives—because of the precedents already set and the persistent fears, justified or not, about the cultural influence of these omnipresent, popular and still fast-growing media.

OP Effectiveness

The previous chapter has already argued that the overall effectiveness of advertising self-regulation is difficult to determine; *a fortiori*, that of outside participation in ASR systems is even harder to isolate and measure in terms of: (1) better standards; (2) more effective implementation of the standards, and (3) improved legitimacy/credibility.

The few public-opinion surveys that have focused on the notoriety, reputation and effectiveness of advertising self-regulation have not isolated the contribution of outside participation to its functioning. The interviews used for the country studies in this volume, however, strongly suggest that outside participation has helped achieve these goals, where it has been implemented (e.g., in Canada and the United Kingdom). Yet, some ASR systems (e.g., in France and the United States) are considered to be effective even without significant formal outside participation. Consequently, outside participation is neither a generally necessary nor sufficient condition for ASR effectiveness, although it facilitates it under certain circumstances and is even imperative under others. The organization-theory literature suggests that ill-specified objectives for outside participation, inappropriate outside members, and poor behavior on the part of the interacting outsiders and insiders will impede its functioning (e.g., Stumpf et al. 1979, p. 590). The next section hypothesizes about these and other factors.

The Theory of Outside Participation

Previous sections as well as more general analyses of participation (e.g., Dachler and Wilpert 1978) suggest the following hypotheses built around conditions, motivations and precipitating circumstances (see the previous chapter for a definition of these terms).

OP Conditions

Hypothesis C1. Outside participation is a function of the relative unavailability and ineffectiveness of other ways of obtaining consumer protection and of participating in policymaking, as far as outsiders are concerned.

Hypothesis C2. Outside participation is associated with cultures emphasizing cooperation and trust rather than conflict and distrust.

Hypothesis C3. Outside participation depends on the existence of a cohesive, middle-of-the-road and well-resourced consumer movement, or of a truly independent elite.

Hypothesis C4. Self-regulatory bodies accept outsiders only if they can control or neutralize them.

OP Motivations

Hypothesis M1. Outsiders—individually or collectively—accept to participate only when outside participation provides an effective way of achieving ''voice.''

Hypothesis M2. Self-regulatory bodies accept outsiders only when they provide legitimacy and/or expertise.

OP Precipitating Circumstances

Hypothesis PC1. Outside participation is linked to the emergence and salience of ''soft'' issues of taste and opinion and the related need for new expertise about them.

Hypothesis PC2. Outside participation is precipitated by legitimacy crises.

Hypothesis PC3. Outside participation is more likely when public policy encourages and facilitates it.

These propositions as well as those about advertising self-regulation (see Chapter 1) are loosely tested in a ''grounded-theory'' perspective (see the Introduction) in the country chapters that follow as well as in the last chapter. It is worth noting that the updating of the country studies, which originated in 1981, revealed how fast some conditions, motivations and precipitating circumstances can change—even over a mere six-year period, which has not been particularly marked by great regulatory and consumerist fervor in the twelve countries studied.

NOTES

1. An analysis of their 1979 structures and processes in twenty U.S. self-regulatory associations handling consumer complaints about advertising revealed that 45 percent of them provided for some ''public'' participation in their deliberations—meaning full or partial recourse to nonstaff or nonindustry members in handling complaints; but, only two had codes entirely administered by an independent body (LaBarbera 1980b, p. 30).

2. See chapters 1 and 16 for discussions of corporatism and neocorporatism.

3. The perceived independence of ASR systems is also linked to the source of their financing, but this dimension, which also affects their credibility, was not analyzed in this study.

4. There is some tension between advertiser and advertising-agency representatives on ASR bodies to the extent that advertisers tend to be more conservative than agency people who "live" advertising in a more intense and secluded manner—the "Madison Avenue type"—to use the industry's lingo. Media people are different still.

5. The Dutch ASR system has a 60 percent amount of outside participation at the appeal level (versus 40 percent at the first level) in order to satisfy the procompetition requirement of the law.

6. Consumerists often gain access to the media, which may be able to demonstrate thereby the independence of their editorial side from their commercial department, which solicits and accepts advertisements.

7. "Insiders" refers here to industry representatives sitting on ASR boards and panels—not to the permanent ASR secretariats whose salaries and other expenses are financed by the industry in one way or another.

8. There is an abundant literature on the issue of consumerism, the consumer organizations that promote it, and the public policies that embody it. See, for example, Business International (1980); Rijkens and Miracle (1986); Weiss and Chirouze (1984); the special issue on consumerism of the *European Journal of Marketing* 12, no. 4 (1978); Philip Kotler's "What Consumerism Means for Marketers," *Harvard Business Review*, (May–June 1972), 48–57; the research of Nadel (1971), and Vogel (1979), and the country studies published by Van Nostrand Reinhold (London and New York) on consumer legislation in various European nations and the European Community. The country chapters include further bibliographical references on national consumer movements.

9. Useful documentation can be found in a special issue of *Consumer Affairs* 77 (September–October 1985) a publication of J. Walter Thompson in London, as well as in a report of the Commission of the European Communities, "A New Impetus for Consumer Protection Policy" (1985), Brussels, Belgium.

10. However, Article 4.3 of the Directive requires that bodies involved in its implementation "be composed so as not to cast doubt on their impartiality"—a requirement that bears on the representativeness of ASR bodies when they are used by national governments. The country studies provide further evidence of government encouragement and support of outside participation (or lack thereof) at the national level.

11. "In Brussels, where there are some 2,000 EEC watchers, 'dialogue' hardly needed inventing to bring both sides together (Venables 1984, p. 297)."

12. The *Journal of Consumer Policy* 7, no. 2 (June 1984) reports extensively on this conference, but only a few of the presentations will be cited here. See also the previously mentioned issue of *Consumer Affairs* (September–October 1985) in note 9, and the European Communities' paper on "A New Impetus for Consumer Protection Policy," 1985.

13. The toy-advertising code being negotiated between the European Advertising Tripartite (of advertiser, agency and media associations) and COFACE (EEC Committee of Family Associations) has not yet come to life, and will largely depend on national voluntary organizations for implementation, thereby not affecting outside participation at the national level. The International Chamber of Commerce has considered greater outside involvement in the handling of complaints related to its International Code of Advertising Practice, but this organization lacks the resources to conduct such a worldwide exercise.

14. Tony Venables is the Director of BEUC (Bureau Européen des Unions de Consommateurs) and a member of the EEC-financed Consumers Consultative Committee (CCC). Another consumerist advocate asked: "What is to be deregulated when there is no regulation? (Bourgoignie 1984, p. 318)."

15. It is well to observe that consumer associations themselves have not been eager to include outsiders—particularly, industry representatives—in their own councils.

16. The literature on industrial democracy provides useful models of analysis for participation, which have been partially incorporated in this section (e.g., King and van de Vall 1978; and Dachler and Wilpert 1978). Stumpf et al. (1979) offer a pertinent analysis of how to structure groups for judgmental decisions of the types frequently made by ASR bodies.

17. Even industry members are typically defined in ASR manuals as "appointed in their independent capacity" rather than as representatives of advertisers, agencies and media.

18. Moyer's (1979) analysis of the conditions required for effective outside participation is very relevant: the right people must be chosen, additional costs must be incurred, etc. See also Thain et al. (1979).

19. LaBarbera (1980a, p. 62) has recommended that "consumer leaders" appoint outside members, but such a situation was not encountered. See her study of U.S. self-regulatory bodies in a variety of industries for an analysis of the extent and manner of outside participation (LaBarbera 1980b).

II

Country Analyses

3

Belgium: Jury d'Éthique Publicitaire

The Belgian Advertising Ethics Jury (Jury d'Éthique Publicitaire; Jury voor Eerlijke Praktijken inzake Reclame, JEP) excludes nonindustry members, except for its independent president. As such, it almost represents a case in pure self-regulation. This situation reflects various Belgian institutional and ideological factors: conflicting views about advertising, self-regulation and outside participation; the fragmentation of the consumerist movement; the relative weakness of consumer-protection legislation; the ambiguity of government policy toward self-regulation; the underrepresentation of advertising on government councils, and the shortage of independent personalities in a highly polarized society. The following sections analyze these factors after highlighting the JEP's purpose, structure and functioning as well as industry and consumerist positions for and against the inclusion of outsiders in the JEP's activities. It is based on secondary sources, interviews (mainly in 1981–1983) and subsequent correspondence with major actors and observers of the Belgian scene.

This analysis, by focusing on JEP's difficult relations with outside organizations, underplays its positive contributions, which should not be overlooked: it has evolved to cope with new problems; a sizable number of relevant complaints have been handled in comparison with the government's relative inactivity or slowness; member media accept its recommendations, and it has been acknowledged by several qualified observers as a useful complement to regulation. Thus, Stuyck (1986) has concluded that: "I believe it is fair to say that the impact of the JEP in the protection of the consumer against misleading and unfair advertising is greater than that of the courts . . . Not only the frequency and flexibility of the JEP interventions but also the relative importance of consumer complaints in the initiation of JEP interventions (37 percent of the cases from 1975 to 1984)

as well as the wider range of consumer-protection rules it enforces . . . justify
this assessment.''

The JEP Self-Regulatory System

The Advertising Ethics Jury (JEP) was set up in 1974 by the Advertising
Council (Conseil de la Publicité, dating of 1967), following a less successful
body dating of 1968 (Brandmair 1978; Neelankavil and Stridsberg 1980).[1] This
council groups all major associations representing advertisers, agencies and media; and its membership is estimated to represent some 75 to 80 percent of
Belgian advertising. The Council's purpose is to promote and defend advertising's role in economic development in the spirit of the International Advertising
Code of the International Chamber of Commerce (ICC) and its principles of
truthfulness, fairness and good taste in advertising.

The JEP's seventeen members are appointed by the Advertising Council and
drawn from industry: four from advertisers, three from agencies and ten from
the media, plus the president of the Jury who is an ''independent'' person
(currently a university professor of business administration while his predecessor
was the honorary president of the Brussels Commercial Court).

Source of Cases

JEP handles complaints emanating from consumers and consumer associations
as well as from industry. While competitor complaints dealing with unfair practices (e.g., plagiarism and denigration) are left to their respective trade associations and to the courts, the JEP accepts such complaints if they deal with ads
likely to mislead consumers. In contrast with the first couple of years of JEP's
existence, very few complaints now come directly from consumer groups, although one of them, the Consumers' Association, used to invite its members to
complain to the JEP. It appears that these groups were originally testing the
JEP's willingness to accept consumer-organization complaints. However, complaints emanating directly from consumers still represent the major source (45
percent) of JEP actions.

JEP itself initiates investigations on the basis of its own limited monitoring
of cosmetics and nonprescription-drug advertisements as well as of occasional
''hot'' areas such as phony job offers, financial services and diamond advertising.
Besides, advertiser, agency and media members can and do ask for the Jury's
advice, prior to publication. In fact, this preadvice has grown in recent years
(between a fourth and a fifth of the cases handled)—a situation that reflects the
industry's increasing acceptance of advertising ethics. It also distinguishes self-
regulation from the regulatory and judiciary systems, which do not provide such
preadvertising advice.

Case Handling

Both advices and complaints are handled on the basis of the ICC International Code of Advertising Practice and of special codes developed by the Belgian pharmaceuticals, cosmetics and hygiene-products, and electrical-appliances industries since JEP does not have its own code. However, the Jury has issued several "rules" (*règles d'éthique publicitaire*) pertaining to credit, weight-loss schemes and references to people. Besides, member media regularly carry "warnings" (*avis de mise en garde*) drawing the readers' attention to dubious financial schemes, and inviting them to complain to JEP if dissatisfied.

JEP checks the conformity of advertisements not only with the above codes and rules but also with legal prescriptions ("The first principle of ethical behavior is respect of the law [JEP 1980, p. 9])" and with its own conception of sound professional practice and of what constitutes good taste in advertising (Articles 1 and 4 of the JEP Bylaws). However, JEP is more prudent in matters of good taste since it only provides advice and recommendations in this area, instead of requesting that media members stop publishing the incriminated advertisement, as is true with more objective types of violations.

JEP's handling of complaints is largely shielded from public view. If a complaint falls within JEP's jurisdiction, a file is opened and the author of the criticized advertisement is invited to defend himself. If necessary, the Jury takes the advice of experts. Where the Jury considers the advertisement to be contrary to the law or to the voluntary codes and rules it applies, the advertiser receives a written, reasoned opinion whereby he is requested to modify the advertisement. The interested parties (including the consumer who complained) get a copy of this opinion. If the request is refused or ignored, the Jury addresses a personal and confidential letter to the media, who are asked to use their "discretionary right to refuse any advertisement." JEP's members, who include the most important media, have signed a contractual obligation to respect JEP recommendations to refuse an advertisement. The intervention of the Jury, in most cases, leads to a voluntary modification or withdrawal by the advertiser. While brief anonymous synopses of JEP's major opinions are regularly reported, its actual recommendations are not published in order not to "pillory" incriminated advertisers and to avoid the risk of being sued for damaging someone else's reputation.

The Jury applies the law to the extent that it checks the conformity of ads with the provisions against misleading advertising of the 1971 Commercial Practices Act, and of special statutes relating to tobacco, health products, foods, cosmetics, credit and investment, lotteries and games, etc. However, JEP does not act as a judge or even arbiter between the affected parties, but rather as the guardian of the fairness and correctness of advertising practice in order to protect the public's interest and its confidence in advertising on the basis of the advertiser's and media's self-discipline (Article 2 of the JEP Bylaws). Therefore, it draws the advertiser's attention to the pertinent voluntary codes, laws and regulations, and tries to have the incriminated advertisement voluntarily modified or withdrawn.

During its first ten years of operations (1975–1984), the JEP handled 2,088 valid cases: 494 (24 percent) were preadvices; 946 (45 percent) were consumer and consumer-association complaints; 335 (16 percent) were business complaints; and 313 (15 percent) were monitoring cases. There were 459 complaints turned down for being outside of JEP's competence (Conseil de la Publicité 1986, p. 51). There were 259 valid cases in 1985 and 241 in 1986, although JEP's caseload has generally increased from year to year.

These activities have been conducted without any significant outside participation on the part of nonindustry members. The following sections analyze the factors explaining this rather unique situation among advanced advertising self-regulatory systems.

The Industry's Case Against Outside Participation

The Belgian advertising industry remains suspicious of outside participation, and has been frustrated in its attempts to open up dialogue with outside bodies.

True Self-Regulation Precludes Outside Representation

It is axiomatic that self-regulation implies that this policing is done by insiders. Consequently, the Advertising Council created JEP in the classical tradition of the "professional orders" in law and medicine. The latter monitor and discipline their own members on the ground that one's peers can best judge what constitutes fair and ethical business behavior: "[The JEP's] collegial deliberations allow it to come up with reasonable albeit rigorous solutions which, under the prodding of its supporting industry associations and of the challenge of public opinion, are neither corporatist solutions nor forms of censure or of externally imposed constraints (JEP 1979, p. 19)."

The industry has been anxious to prove that it can assume responsibility for the behavior of its members—or most of them anyway—in order to justify its opposition to unnecessary or overrestrictive government regulations, and to protect public confidence in advertising. It also points out that the exclusion of outsiders from the JEP does not preclude dissatisfied people from using the court system where a more balanced consideration of the interests of consumers and advertisers can be provided if the law has been broken. In other words, self-regulation is not the only avenue for redress, although it provides a readily available, fast and inexpensive first line of correction, whereby professionals prove their social responsibility.

Unsuccessful Offers of Dialogue and Participation

Still, the advertising industry did not completely rule out some form of consumerist involvement in the JEP's activities. From 1976 to 1977, the government as well as consumer associations were invited to send in observers—not full-fledged members—to sit on the JEP's complaint-handling sessions in order to evaluate its functioning and consider further forms of collaboration (Actes du Colloque 1977, p. 186; JEP 1980, p. 13).

While these attempts have failed for various reasons analyzed below, they have been largely motivated by the encouragement provided by the European Economic Community, the Council of Europe and the European Parliament for voluntary codes and industry-consumer dialogue and cooperation (see Chapter 2). Besides, the Belgian advertising industry had been criticized by the press as well as various observers, opinion-leaders and consumerist organizations for excluding outsiders from the JEP's activities, since such outsiders sit as full-fledged members on advertising self-regulatory bodies in the Netherlands and France—two major "pilot" nations as far as Belgium is concerned. Inviting observers seemed like a right first step along these lines. Outside participation could also have increased JEP's credibility by providing greater transparency, since it does not publicize the names of the advertisers ruled against.

The advertising industry, however, was not convinced that its expertise would be increased by consumer representation, since JEP members are well informed about advertising principles and practices; and outside technical experts are often consulted. Besides, the presence of possibly antagonistic consumerist representatives would probably slow down the deliberative process typically speedily resolved (six to eight weeks) on a consensual basis. Still, in 1982, the Advertising Council renewed its offer to open up a dialogue through JEP with consumer-association and government representatives in order to discuss JEP's activities and other problems concerning advertising. Since no dialogue ensued, this effort has been discontinued.[2]

Consumerist Positions

Belgian consumer associations have turned down invitations for dialogue and cooperation on account of various fears and objections.

Tokenism

The JEP's offer to have consumer-association representatives sit in as observers on its sessions is considered to amount to a minor "jump-seat" position. That is, the "dialogue" and "observation" offered by the JEP do not go far enough in that they do not provide for "parity" representation and influence by consumerists in the matters of norm development, behavior-sanctioning and publicizing of the incriminated advertisers (cf. Bourgoignie [1984], pp. 317–18).

Unwarranted Backdoor Legitimacy

Consumerists feel strongly that participation in the JEP's activities would grant it legitimacy when some leaders of the Belgian consumer movement consider the JEP to be a "corporatist and medieval" relic no longer appropriate for the handling of modern conflicts between consumers and advertisers (Actes du Colloque 1977, p. 183).[3] Most consumerist organizations can conceive of negotiated "collective agreements" between industry and consumer representatives—paralleling those between management and labor—but they refuse to sanction the validity of an industry-based body that preempts their relationships with consumers and ignores their claims of exclusive representation of the latter. As one interviewee put it: "Consumer associations cling to their virginity which they do not want to compromise, nor do they want to appear as betraying their high principles."

Shortcomings of Self-Regulation

Consumerists consider the JEP as a rather weak and ineffective organism (Fontaine and Bourgoignie 1982, p. 74). For one thing, critics contend that the small number of valid consumer complaints resolved by the JEP (131 in 1984 and 109 in 1985) does not vouch for its seriousness but represents an alibi or window dressing to oppose the need for further regulation of advertising. This criticism, however, overlooks the fact that JEP also engages in prepublication advisement and in some postpublication monitoring; that some 76 percent of consumer complaints were upheld in 1985 (versus 60 percent in 1984), and that the growing number and proportion of consumer complaints vouches for JEP's notoriety and credibility as far as the public is concerned (cf. Stuyck 1986).

Furthermore, these critics point out that JEP's resources are quite limited since only three full-time people (shared with the Advertising Council) handle all of its advising, monitoring, complaint-handling and publicizing activities, although outside experts are tapped whenever necessary to complement in-house technical competence. Such limited resources are perceived as a lack of commitment to serious self-regulation.

The secrecy surrounding JEP deliberations also bothers its critics. Even JEP members do not receive advance information about the cases that are only presented, discussed and settled at the meetings proper in order to achieve maximum confidentiality and to develop on-the-spot collegial decisions. Besides, when notified of the JEP's decision, complainants are asked not to publicize it.[4] Such a secretive system is hardly acceptable to consumerist representatives who like to use any information they can get to make their case against business. Still, the Jury conducted a 1985 public-opinion survey, which revealed that, despite its limited publicity efforts, 19 percent of the respondents were aware of its existence.

The classical claim that self-regulation works faster than the court system and is cheaper than litigation is dismissed by consumerists on the ground that one necessary reform is precisely the creation of quick and inexpensive forms of legal recourse (Bourgoignie et al. 1981; Association des Consommateurs 1981). As one interviewee put it: "Justice must be neutral, and consumers should not, in the name of efficiency, have to settle for a second-rate, unilateral and non-enforceable type of justice.''

In the way of sanctions, the JEP can only recommend that its media members abstain from publishing incriminated ads (but they usually do since they have committed themselves in writing to doing so); it can exclude individual members from the JEP but has not done so; it can report to the government illegal practices but seldom has; the Advertising Council, as a professional association, can apply for cease-and-desist injunctions against law-breaking advertisers but has rarely done it;[5] and the JEP does not publicize the names of offending advertisers. Moreover, when confronted with tough issues such as violations of cigarette-advertising restrictions, the JEP has reacted too slowly or referred the problem to the Advertising Council. As one consumerist interviewee put it: ''They finger out a few notorious black sheep but handle the more significant cases in secrecy.''

Of course, this is precisely why the JEP invited outsiders to attend its sessions in order to dispel such an impression. Besides, the JEP and the Advertising Council negotiate with criticized industries in order to eliminate or alleviate such problems even though these maneuvers remain hidden from public view. Furthermore, the press has given much publicity to JEP's annual reports and its warnings. Still, the Jury is not considered by consumerists as very effective nor as a force with which to reckon. Why deal with an ''enemy'' whose role and power most consumerists consider to be minimal if not passé, and whose effectiveness they rank as low?

Self-Regulation as an Obstacle to Further Regulation

Consumerists feel that Belgian laws and regulations bearing on advertising fail to provide adequate protection and redress for consumers and their associations (see below). Therefore, they are convinced that the first task is to strengthen the law. Any participation in self-regulation would, in their opinion, weaken the drive for new regulations by making it appear that proper legal remedies already exist or are unnecessary because of the complementary or preemptive role of the JEP. For them, dialogue and cooperation can come only after the law has been reinforced, as Roger Ramaekers, the former president of the Consumers Council, stressed:

I think that Belgian consumers will be more open to dialogue [with the advertising industry] when the atmosphere will have changed and their demand to have advertising legislation become more precise and effective will have been better acknowledged because they fear the maneuver which consists of substituting self-regulation for legislation . . . Consumer representatives [on the Consumers Council] are the only ones to ask for more severe [advertising] laws: this creates a malaise (Actes du Colloque 1977, pp. 190–191).

Belgian Institutional Factors

The positions of the advertising industry and of consumer advocates reflect major legal, ideological and institutional factors, which constrain a ready resolution of the conflicts between these two groups as well as hamper cooperation in the elaboration and application of rules of advertising practice.

Inadequate Legal Remedies

While there is still plenty of disagreement between consumers and advertisers about the matter, one could conclude on the basis of various legal studies (Stuyck 1978, 1981 and 1982; Fontaine and Bourgoignie 1982) that Belgian advertising laws and regulations have been relatively weak in protecting consumer interests and providing for redress; and that they suffer in comparison with those of France, the Netherlands, Sweden, the United Kingdom and the United States, among others. Still, the fact that the 1984 EEC Directive on Misleading Advertising has required only minor adaptations of Belgian laws reveals that it is up to par with European standards in this area.[6]

Thus, the key 1971 Law on Commercial Practices (whose revision has been constantly postponed due to frequent government changes and higher priorities) is designed more to protect competitors against unfair practices than consumers against false and misleading advertisements (Stuyck 1978 and 1982). For example: (1) the burden of proof still rests mainly on the complainant in court cases (this is not true in the case of self-regulation where the advertiser must be able to substantiate his claims when challenged);[7] (2) except in the case of foods, drugs and cigarettes, for which special regulations exist, there is no obligation to provide consumers with objective information; and comparison advertising is generally prohibited; (3) individual consumers cannot petition for a cease-and-desist order, nor can they be readily granted damages if a misleading ad caused them to buy a deficient product; (4) a recognized consumer association can petition for cease-and-desist orders (a kind of class action) and even sue for damages but, in the latter case, the association itself must have suffered a prejudice owing to the incriminated ad; and (5) penalties have been nil until recently, unless the advertiser ignored the court order; and corrective advertising cannot be imposed.[8] (Consumerists have many more regulatory demands beyond those pertaining to advertising, but they are not considered here.)

Moreover, consumerists feel that both the courts and executive departments (mainly, the Ministry of Economic Affairs) charged with the application of consumer-protection legislation are not terribly interested in this branch of the law, that they lack adequate resources, and/or that they have failed to vigorously apply existing rules (Association des Consommateurs 1981; Bourgoignie et al. 1981; Conseil de la Consommation 1979; Centre de Recherche et d'Information Socio-politiques [CRISP] 1978). This helps explain why Belgian consumer organizations are reluctant to endorse and facilitate the use of self-regulatory devices as a vehicle for consumer redress as long as the government does not get its act together.

While the Belgian advertising industry supports some regulatory reform, it has essentially assumed a defensive/reactive position in the face of demands deemed to be often excessive on the part of consumer representatives. This situation cultivates the malaise mentioned before.

Governmental Attitudes

Interviews with government officials revealed that they are aware of the Council of Europe's 1972 resolution in support of self-regulation, but they pointed out that ''1982 is not 1972''—meaning that demands for consumer protection have escalated since then. While willing to acknowledge the complementary role of self-regulation (Actes du Colloque 1977, pp. 192–193), they also share many of the criticisms of the JEP voiced by consumer advocates. Besides, they are not quite happy with the JEP's application of government laws and regulations as parts of the standards it uses, which they see as impinging on the proper role of the courts. Instead, they would prefer to see JEP expand its prepublication advising activities, and stick to the application of voluntary codes.

In any case, they stress that the 1971 Law on Commercial Practices needs strengthening in the light of domestic, EEC and foreign experiences and initiatives. Actually, a new government bill (*projet de loi*) on Commercial Practices and Consumer Information and Protection was first proposed in 1982 and introduced in Parliament in 1985, providing for greater restrictions and penalties as far as advertising is concerned (Bill No. 947/1), and it will soon be enacted.

More fundamentally, the government entertains a proregulatory philosophy. While Belgium is definitely a capitalistic country, the French government-intervention (*étatiste*) influence has never been absent. Hence, the government always welcomes greater powers, whether it uses them or not. Particularly in the twentieth century, regulation has been favorably embraced as a solution to socioeconomic problems. The principle that ''The law frees people while freedom [=laissez-faire] oppresses them'' has been generally accepted—meaning that, in the face of various dominant positions exercised by certain types of employers, industrialists and traders, the government must step in and restore some equilibrium by granting the aggrieved minorities (e.g., consumers) some absolute legal rights and protections. Advertising represents such a conflictual arena where the law can countervail business interests considered to be dominant. In this interventionist context, self-regulation can only assume a complementary and relatively minor role.

Yet, the government itself provides limited consumer protection, because its laws are not matched with sufficient enforcement resources. This allows it to play a double game by telling consumers: ''We have strengthened the law,'' while reassuring businessmen: ''Don't worry, the law will not be strenuously applied.'' Faced with divided opinions emanating from the Consumers Council where consumerists usually oppose business and vice versa, the government feels free to do what it wants or to do nothing (CRISP 1978).

Hence, consumerists consider government departments to be probusiness or neutral at best, often divided, lacking leadership from most recent Economic

Affairs Ministers, and in need of major prodding to achieve proconsumer reforms (CRISP 1978, pp. 15, 20–22). In this context, a survey revealed that consumers expect the executive branch to give them more information but do not trust it with providing redress through the administrative system: the courts, however imperfect, are preferred for that purpose (Bourgoignie et al. 1981). According to one respondent, this largely precludes the adoption of an administrative consumer-ombudsman system in Belgium.

Still, the forthcoming Law on Commercial Practices and Consumer Information and Protection represents a definite increase in regulatory controls. A business respondent commented that the revision of the 1971 law started when the regulatory mood was still high, and that further restrictions were added all along as its proponents—mainly, consumerist and small-business representatives afraid of large firms—traded support with each other (cf. Conseil de la Consommation, Avis No. 61 and 64, 1986). He added that Belgium likes to be ahead of other EEC countries in terms of regulation so that it may have something to bargain away when EEC regulatory harmonization is negotiated. Consequently, as one consumerist interviewee put it: "The government went ahead with more advertising regulation, despite the deregulatory mood, and no mention was made of increasing the role of the JEP as an adequate substitute—an option allowed under the 1984 EEC Directive on Misleading Advertising." As the preamble to that forthcoming Belgian law comments about its Section 5 on advertising, it "now constitutes a real advertising code."

Antiadvertising Positions

Consumerist spokespersons tend to hold negative views about advertising—particularly the Socialist trade-union and cooperative movements. For example, to the repeated remarks by Roger Ramaekers (former president of the government-sponsored Consumers Council, and president of the Socialist cooperative association FEBECOOP) that "Consumers are not against advertising [and] not in principle hostile to it," a business participant retorted that: "While you're not against advertising, you're certainly not for it (Actes du Colloque 1977, pp. 183–85)."

Similarly, the government-subsidized Consumer Organizations' Information and Research Center (Centre de Recherche et d'Information des Organisations de Consommateurs, CRIOC), charged by the consumer representatives on the Consumers Council with studying the proposition to legalize commercials on the government-owned radio and television network, wrote a 145-page report (CRIOC 1981), which relentlessly criticized advertising in general and TV commercials in particular in terms of their negative impact on the other media, children, junk-food consumption and the portrayal of women and values, while giving short shrift to the proadvertising arguments equally available. While commercials have not been allowed on Belgian television and radio,[9] they will soon be. In this regard, consumerists are no longer opposed to them but they favor heavy restrictions that continue to reflect their fundamentally negative views of advertising (cf. Conseil de la Consommation, Avis No. 64 and 65, 1986).

Discussions within the Consumers Council[10] concerning the revision of the 1971 Law on Commercial Practices reveal the consumer representatives to be consistently in favor of: (1) banning certain types of advertising (e.g., alcohol, tobacco, nonprescription drugs and medical products, firearms, endorsements, and the "unnecessary use of people in ads"); (2) reversing the burden of proof on the advertiser even in the case of subjective or emotional claims, and (3) imposing more drastic criminal penalties on offenders, including corrective advertising (Conseil de la Consommation, Avis No. 40, 64 and 65, 1979 and 1986). Even the more ideologically neutral Consumers' Association is in general very dissatisfied with advertising, and lists many criticisms as well as suggestions for consumers redress, without even mentioning the JEP (Association des Consommateurs 1981). Of course, such negative views are commonly found among consumerists around the world. Still, one finds fewer balanced opinions among Belgian consumerist spokespersons than is the case in the United Kingdom and even in France.

Advertising's Lack of Official Status

Linked to these negative views of a more ideological character, are the facts that: (1) advertising is not generally perceived as an important economic activity in Belgium, and (2) there is limited recognition of the Advertising Council (which sponsors the JEP) as a bona fide professional association.

For one thing, Belgium ranks relatively low in Western Europe in terms of advertising expenditures on a per-capita basis and as a percentage of the Gross National Product—only Greece, Ireland, Portugal, Spain and Turkey rank lower among major European countries (Starch INRA Hooper 1985; Conseil de la Publicité 1986). This situation is largely explained by the fact that the Belgian state-monopoly radio and television stations do not carry commercials, although some Belgian commercials are routed via Radio Télévision Luxembourg (which broadcasts only in French). The division of the country into linguistic groups— Flemish, French and some German—further fragments the potential audience, and makes it more attractive to reach customers via foreign media—mainly French, Dutch and Luxemburger. Under these conditions, Belgian advertising agencies are not very large. These elements help explain why the Advertising Council, which is a duly incorporated professional association, does not have its own representatives on important government-sponsored consultative bodies, such as the Central Economic Council and the Consumers Council (where advertising "experts" may appear if necessary, however).

Another pertinent factor is that business representation on various Belgian consultative bodies is organized along broad sectoral (agriculture, manufacturing, distribution, etc.) and socioeconomic (small-business, big-business, labor, etc.) lines. The proper representation of these sectoral and socioeconomic segments amounts to a delicate exercise in socio-politico-economic proportioning (*dosage*) so that it has been difficult to introduce advertising as a new professional sector without upsetting the equilibrium. Consequently, advertising agencies, advertisers and the media are represented through various professional and interprofessional bodies but not as a profession or industry *sui generis*; and production and distribution representatives on these councils (and on other government commissions) are expected to speak up for advertising in their role as advertisers.

This situation is even perpetuated in the proposed committees that would supervise the development of a code for television and radio advertising, prescreen commercials and handle complaints, after such broadcast advertising becomes legal. A 1981 government bill on this subject refers only to advertisers but not to the Advertising Council or JEP, and neither does a government proposal to set up a Commercial Advertising Council to control commercials, although the JEP's competence would seem obvious. This reveals that Belgian advertising and its self-regulatory body have not been taken seriously enough by the government and by consumer advocates.

The Fragmented Consumer Movement

The consumer movement is rather strong in Belgium (CRISP 1978, p. 13), but it is fragmented into no fewer than fourteen officially acknowledged consumer associations, which are represented on the legislatively mandated advisory Consumers Council (Conseil de la Consommation) and on the government-subsidized Consumer Organizations' Information and Research Center (CRIOC).

As is common in Western Europe, they originate from heterogeneous and often rival quarters. Some of them emanate from unions (syndicates) who claim that their broad socioeconomic mandate includes the representation of their members' interests as consumers. Others come from the cooperative movement, which is of relatively minor economic importance, but maintains significant symbolic value as an alternative to capitalistic forms of marketing. There are also family associations considered to have their own angle on consumerist matters. Finally, there are "pure"—that is, nonpolitical and nonconfessional (= nonreligious)— associations, which aim at providing various services such as consumer information, education and assistance as well as comparative product-testing of the U.S. Consumers Union type.

These divisions are further multiplied by very significant political, religious and linguistic cleavages. Historically, Belgium has been divided along "Leftist/Centrist/Rightist" lines, along "Catholic/anti-Catholic" lines, and along "French-speaking/Flemish-speaking" lines—sometimes with overlapping loyalties. Thus, the labor movement has affiliations with all three major political wings; the cooperative movement is mainly Socialist in orientation; the family movement is largely of Catholic inspiration; while the main product-testing organization (Association des Consommateurs) is fairly nonideological and independent.

The fourteen officially representative consumer organizations cooperate in various matters and on the Consumers Council, where they have set up a consumer group. Still, they remain jealous of one another and lack a capstone organization. This fragmentation discourages rather than facilitates cooperation with the advertising industry because there is no obvious valid spokesperson (*interlocuteur valable*) for consumers, and the rest of the consumerist movement stands ready to denounce any segment inclined to dialogue with or assist the advertising industry. Thus, the Consumers' Association, which considers itself a "pure" consumerist body and has been critical of advertising abuses, has been criticized by more leftist consumer organizations for being too elitist, bourgeois and nonideological, and would become even more suspect if it were to cooperate with JEP.

One could add that the tendency of consumer associations in such a competitive environment is to act aggressively. Like trade unions, they always want "more." Besides, in the relatively young state of development of consumerism, they prefer hit-and-run tactics to more deliberate and compromising approaches. They are more inclined to dramatize and lambaste business shortcomings and wrong-doings than to try for some quiet settlement of problems (CRISP 1978, p. 21)—just the opposite of JEP's policy. Clearly, such consumerist behavior is not conducive to sage and discreet dialogue and cooperation.

Institutionalization and Parity

Political science readily acknowledges that major socioeconomic issues are the focus of interest-group pressures. The U.S. tradition is rather flexible in this respect, allowing for various coalitions (parties, movements, etc.) to group and regroup for lobbying and opinion-manipulation purposes. European traditions, however, are different and date back to the pre-French Revolution corporations or guilds. Any existent or nascent interest group wants to have its existence legitimized through official representation on consultative and/or bargaining bodies, irrespective of its actual size and/or effectiveness. Consequently, the individual "voice in the desert," the "Mr. Smith Goes to Washington" syndrome or the "Ralph Nader" phenomenon are rare in Western Europe for all its intellectual individualism. If one wants to be heard, one must organize (this is true in the United States too, of course) *and* obtain official government recognition (which is less true in the Anglo-Saxon tradition, which recognizes political power, however constituted). In Belgium, the central question is not "How big or powerful is your constituency?" but rather, "Did the government formally acknowledge your existence?" Once an association has been acknowledged as representative, it is supposed to be equal in importance to any other acknowledged (*agréée*) association, irrespective of size.

A corollary of this parity-representation principle is that all subtendencies have to be acknowledged and represented. Hence, the consumer movement is supposed to be equally represented by its fourteen components, without any attempt to provide for any true proportional representation in terms of membership and other size or influence criteria. In general, whatever associations existed at the time of the creation of a *paritaire* (equal representation) body have usually been equally acknowledged by the government, in order to avoid territorial quarrels about who is "more" representative (CRISP 1978, p. 12).

Clearly, this situation does not facilitate the process of obtaining outside representation on the JEP since there are too many "equal" claimants for such representation. Fourteen representatives with somewhat divergent philosophies would be out of the question on a small body bound to the speedy and consensual resolution of consumer complaints. However, should only the largest associations be represented, this would lead to the predominance of "socialist" antiadvertising representatives, although somewhat counterbalanced by the largest and less ideological Consumers' Association.

While consumerist associations have been able to agree about which representatives sit on special government commissions (e.g., about prices, insurance and food), such a surmounting of ideological cleavages would be harder to achieve for representation on the JEP's board, where most associations would like to have a voice. Even one or two "ideological" representatives could turn the decisionmaking JEP into a debating society—at least until more experience has been gained in dialogue and cooperation.

Lack of an Independent Tradition

The preceding analysis makes it clear that in a relatively small country such as Belgium (about ten million people) with strong traditions of cleavage and institutionalization, there are practically no acknowledged "independent" persons who could be considered to be unassociated with special professional, linguistic, religious, political, ideological and other interests. Everybody is tagged as belonging to one side or another on any particular issue, so that mediation or arbitration is very difficult to achieve except through the bureaucracy and the judiciary, which are supposed to be neutral — a situation which reinforces the government-interventionist tendencies mentioned above. There is also an antielitist reaction against anyone who would claim to be above factions. These factors help explain why the JEP, in considering outside participation (except for the president's position), could not contemplate the inclusion of "independent" members (as in the United Kingdom), but focused instinctively on consumer associations since the latter are formally recognized as representing consumer interests in all their variety.

Evaluation and Possible Outcomes

The above analysis explains why the advertising industry and consumer associations remain suspicious of, and opposed to, one another in the matter of outside representation on the JEP. Neither side is accustomed or ready to compromise on ideological grounds; the government has not chosen to bring the parties together, benefiting instead from its role as arbiter; the consumerist movement fears acknowledging its division and missing out on bigger and better things—mainly, stronger legislation—if it grants legitimacy and credibility to self-regulation at this point. As J.–C. Dastot, Director of the Advertising Council and of the JEP, put it this way some years ago: "A dialogue between consumers, producers, distributors and the government is hard to initiate and conduct because it requires new mentalities, some equilibrium among the partners, and acknowledging the limits of what can be achieved (Actes du Colloque 1977, p. 181)." Most of these prerequisites are still missing. While it is difficult to predict any outcome, which would take years to fashion and implement in any case, alternative and nonmutually exclusive solutions will now be outlined and weighed.

A Stronger and more Active JEP

Undeniably, the JEP needs greater financial and human resources to make it a more active, better known, more credible, politically stronger and more effective instrument for self-regulation. Increased size and activity would also assist its acknowledgment—via the Advertising Council—as a bona fide institution worthy of official recognition by the government. In any case, larger resources is a *sine-qua-non* for most of the other recommendations discussed here.

1. As a bona fide professional organization, the Advertising Council could increasingly denounce apparent law violators to the authorities, and petition the courts for more cease-and-desist injunctions on the ground that its standing is being hurt by unethical behavior on the part of the incriminated advertisers (Stuyck 1981, p. 101). Such aggressiveness in the pursuit of wrongdoers would probably contribute to the JEP's credibility. However, suing in the name of the profession is costly and risky (Stuyck 1984, pp. 130–31), and the rather conservative Advertising Council is likely to shy away from such a "repressive" posture, emphasizing instead JEP's "constructive" and educational roles (Conseil de la Publicité 1986, p. 48).

2. Prepublication advice to advertisers is sizable, but the monitoring of published advertisements remains limited. Both JEP activities deserve expansion because they would reinforce the industry's ethical stand, preempt later complaints, and/or complement the trickle of consumer complaints.

3. More radical yet is a clearer public pronouncement of what the industry is willing to support in the way of revision of the 1971 Law on Commercial Practices and other relevant advertising regulations. Consumerists and the government both see the industry as acting reactively and defensively in this area. Such a perception and position only helps perpetuate the image of self-regulation as an alibi against regulation when most experts agree that such a revision is both necessary and inevitable. Taking the initiative may prove to be the best defense in this case, although the imminent enactment of a revised Law on

Commercial Practices and Consumer Information and Protection makes this a moot point.

More "Independent" JEP Members

The inclusion on the JEP's body of more members not affiliated with the advertising industry nor with consumer associations would help remove the stigmas of "medieval corporatism" and secrecy. Of course, such a solution would be difficult to implement in Belgium, where "one is always associated with one side or another." However, such a solution is not impossible since only a handful of people are at stake, and JEP has already been able to obtain an independent president.

Negotiated Advertising Codes

When the European Economic Community and Parliament as well as the Council of Europe have come out in favor of voluntary codes, they have often had in mind guidelines developed in common by industry and consumer associations, rather than those exclusively elaborated by industry itself. There are major precedents for such two-sided agreements (*conventions collectives*) in Belgium—particularly in the industrial-relations field, where fundamentally antagonistic but representative groups of employers and workers have agreed about various labor-practice rules, which the government may then impose on the entire industrial sector. Besides, the Consumers' Association has negotiated agreements about various contractual and conflict-resolution matters in the furniture, dry-cleaning and travel industries, including the principle that promises or claims made in an advertisement constitute an implicit part of the contract between buyer and seller (Association des Consommateurs 1981; Bourgoignie et al. 1981; Stuyck 1984).

1. Such an approach could be extended to other sectors (e.g., liquor) or even generalized to the entire advertising industry. For that matter, family and advertising associations at the European level have been negotiating a code about toy advertising. Should this endeavor succeed, national self-regulatory bodies such as the JEP would have to get involved with Belgian family associations to enforce such a code. This avenue is fraught with major difficulties because of the ideological and institutional obstacles previously analyzed. Yet, it may be worth gambling on the willingness of some major and less ideological consumer organizations to enter into such negotiations.

2. Barring such a solution, the JEP could borrow from the French experience and set up "technical commissions" where consumerist and government experts help develop advertising guidelines. The JEP relies mostly on other bodies' codes subscribed to by its members, but the time may well have come for integrating them into a JEP document. In this process, "outsiders" could be associated as ad hoc advisers without having to integrate them in the JEP struc-

ture, thereby sidestepping the trickier problem of determining who should sit on the JEP board.

3. The advertising industry could also initiate more discussion with consumerists through the Consumers Council. (This would have to be done through production and distribution representatives on that body, as was seen earlier). This council meets mostly at the government's request to discuss new bills and other state initiatives. Such a focus on proposed regulations tends to polarize both sides who simply reaffirm their traditional ideologies and positions for the government's benefit. This tired charade and pointless routine need not be the only role of the Consumers Council that could reassert its function as a discussion and negotiation rather than confrontation locus. Such concertation has already taken place regarding consumer thefts in large stores, and could be extended to advertising problems, since advertising experts are already invited to participate in relevant committee meetings.

4. The imminent creation by the government of a Commercial Advertising Council to develop a code for soon-to-be-authorized broadcast commercials, to prescreen such ads and to handle audience complaints will also provide an opportunity for concerted action about advertising standards—both legal and voluntary. This chance should not be missed, but the advertising industry will have to stand behind the JEP and promote it as its expert in the field, instead of letting the government and consumer advocates ignore or isolate it.

Conclusions

Advertising self-regulation is well developed and plays a useful role in complementing Belgian law—in fact, the codes and rules that JEP applies are more elaborate than present legal and regulatory provisions. Yet, as an expression of Belgian "soft law" (Stuyck 1984), it is poorly acknowledged by the government and the consumerist movement. In other words, the JEP has few if any "silent partners" interested in its existence and effectiveness.

Part of this problem lies in the JEP's tradition and policy of "pure" self-regulation, which largely excludes the explicit and active participation of outsiders. However, even a willing JEP would encounter many ideological and institutional obstacles to surmount. Various alternatives to overcome such obstacles have been discussed above, but the ultimate outcome of JEP's relations with government and consumer organizations will depend on personal reactions and initiatives as well as on environmental developments.

In this context, the imminent revision of the 1971 law whose new Section 5 has been labeled as a "true advertising code" could well introduce a more conciliatory posture on the part of the consumer movement. Not all of their battles have been won—for that matter, a Commission has just been appointed to study "the reform of consumer law."[11] However, it will be harder for consumer organizations to argue that consumer-protection regulation is still grossly inadequate in Belgium, and must be reinforced before "soft law" of the self-regulatory type can be seriously considered.

Besides, consumerist representatives are likely to acquire a powerful voice on the future Commercial Advertising Council—a situation that will give them real (if shared) decision-making power, compared to the more academic deliberations of the Consumers Council. The lessons to be learned in this sharing of power with business representatives may also foster a more cooperative stance that will spill over into the functioning of JEP. The government, by selecting cooperative consumer representatives, could play a most useful role in fostering a renewed dialogue.

In any case, it is safe to predict that JEP's fairly unique approach of almost pure self-regulation will not survive intact, and that some form of outside participation will come to be incorporated in its structure and/or operations.

NOTES

1. For further details about JEP's structure, functioning and activities, see its annual reports (Rapport d'Activité) and its 10th Anniversary issue (Conseil de la Publicité 1986).

2. The cosmetics industry, however, has recently proposed to discuss its code with consumer organizations.

3. This remark was made by Roger Ramaekers, who heads the Socialist cooperative organization (FEBECOOP), and was president of the government-appointed consultative Consumers Council (Conseil de la Consommation) for many years.

4. In a recent incident, a complainant violated this secrecy requirement and generated some unfavorable publicity for JEP.

5. Stuyck (1984, pp. 130–31) recounts a case where the Advertising Council (which sponsors JEP) tried unsuccessfully to obtain injunctive relief against a misleading direct-mail advertisement. Unlike JEP, which puts the burden of proof on the advertiser, the court concluded that the Council (and JEP) had not brought sufficient proof that the ad was misleading. Stuyck adds that any measure taken by JEP may be considered by the courts to be an unfair trade practice, especially when it leads to media boycotts.

6. The government issued several royal decrees regarding cosmetics, foods and cigarettes during the 1970s, following EEC directives about various products. This piecemeal approach is somewhat controversial, because such decrees do not involve so much consultation of the industry or of the Consumers Council as in the case of a law, and they are difficult to amend.

7. The draft Law on Commercial Practices and Consumer Information and Protection would put the burden of proof on the advertiser when a legal action is initiated by the Minister of Economic Affairs.

8. Since 1983, the courts are allowed to impose substantial penalties (*astreintes*) in order to obtain compliance with injunctions issued in connection with trade-practice cases (Stuyck 1986).

9. Many ads and commercials reaching Belgian audiences come from abroad (mainly France, Luxembourg and the Netherlands) and are thus largely outside of JEP's reach, although the private Luxemburger network (RTL) adheres to Belgian (JEP) and French (BVP) norms, while Belgian-originated commercials, broadcast from France and the Netherlands, are precleared there.

10. This Council includes a slight majority of consumer representatives, with the consumer-goods industry, distribution, agriculture, small- and medium-business, public services and experts also represented on this body.

11. This topic is more concerned with the speedy resolution of consumer problems through small-claim courts, etc., than with advertising per se. See Conseil de la Consommation, Avis No. 61 (1986) for a presentation of consumerist and business positions about reforming consumer law.

REFERENCES

"Actes du Colloque de 1976 consacré à la publicité face aux consommateurs." *Bulletin de l'Institut International de Concurrence Commerciale* [Bulletin of the International Institute for Commercial Competition] (April 1977): 172–93.

Association des Consommateurs. *Vers une nouvelle position juridique du consommateur: Les propositions de Test-Achats* [Toward a New Legal Status for Consumers]. Brussels: 1981.

Bourgoignie, Thierry. "The Need to Reformulate Consumer Protection Policy." *Journal of Consumer Policy* 7, no. 2 (June 1984): 307–21.

Bourgoignie, Thierry et al., *L'Aide juridique au consommateur* [Legal Help for Consumers]. Brussels: Bruylant, 1981.

Bourgoignie, Thierry, and Stuyck, Jules. "La représentation juridictionnelle des intérêts collectifs" [Jurisdictional Representation of Collective Interests]. In *L'Evolution du droit judiciaire; Actes des XIèmes Journées d'Études Juridiques Jean Dabin*, Bourgoignie and Stuyck, eds. Brussels: Bruylant, 1984, pp. 597–632.

Brandmair, Lothar. *Die freiwillige Selbstkontrolle der Werbung* [The Voluntary Self-Control of Advertising]. Cologne, Germany: Carl Heymans, 1978.

Centre de Recherche et d'Information des Organisations de Consommateurs (CRIOC). *La Publicité télévisée en Belgique* [Television Advertising in Belgium]. Brussels: April 1981.

Centre de Recherche et d'Information Socio-politiques (CRISP). *Les consommateurs en Belgique: Protection-information-représentation*. Brussels: November, 1978.

Conseil de la Consommation. *Avis No. 27 sur la proposition de loi Degroeve instituant un ombudsman des consommateurs*. Brussels: November 26, 1975.

Conseil de la Consommation. *Avis No. 40; Avant-projet de loi modifiant la loi du 14 juillet 1971 sur les pratiques du commerce*. Brussels: September 28, 1979; *Avis No. 61 concernant le projet de loi sur les Pratiques du Commerce et sur l'Information et la Protection du Consommateur*. Brussels: June 25, 1986; *Avis No. 64 relatif au problème de l'introduction de la publicité commerciale dans les médias audio-visuels*. Brussels: June 25, 1986; and *Avis No. 65 relatif à l'introduction de la publicité commerciale dans les médias audio-visuels*. Brussels: November 28, 1986.

Conseil de la Publicité. *La publicité: Mythes et réalités d'aujourdhui* [Advertising; Today's Myths and Realities]. White paper published on the occasion of the 10th Anniversary of the Advertising Concil and the JEP. Brussels: 1986.

Council of Europe. "Resolution No. 72/8 on Consumer Protection against Misleading Advertising." Strasbourg: February 13, 1972.

Dastot, J.–C. "L'autodiscipline en Matière de Publicité" [Advertising Self-regulation].

Bulletin de l'Institut International de Concurrence Commerciale (April 1977): 173–83.

Fontaine, M., and Thierry Bourgoignie. *Consumer Legislation in Belgium and Luxembourg*. New York: Van Nostrand Reinhold, 1982.

Jury d'Éthique Publicitaire [JEP]. *Rapport d'Activité* [Annual Report]. Brussels: 1979, 1980.

Neelankavil, J. P., and A. B. Stridsberg. *Advertising Self-regulation: A Global Perspective*. New York: Hastings House, 1980.

Starch INRA Hooper. *World Advertising Expenditures*. Mamaroneck, New York: distributed by the International Advertising Association, 1985.

Stuyck, Jules. "Consumer Soft Law in Belgium." *Journal of Consumer Policy*, 7, no. 2 (June 1984): 125–35.

———. "La loi du 14 juillet 1971 sur les pratiques du commerce: Applications et perspectives dans l'intérêt du consommateur." In: *Droit des consommateurs* [Consumer Law], Thierry Bourgoignie and Jean Gillardin, eds. Brussels: Facultés Universitaires Saint-Louis, 1982, pp. 171–244.

———. "National Legal Controls on Unfair Advertising: Belgian Report." Paper presented at the Fifth European Workshop on Consumer Law, Centre de Droit de la Consommation, Université Catholique de Louvain. Belgium: Louvain-la-Neuve, September 25–26, 1986, to be published by this Center in 1988.

———. "Six Years of Experience with Some Aspects of the Belgian Trade Practices Act of 1971 as An Instrument of Consumer Protection." In *Law and Economics*, edited by Göran Suogh. Lund, Sweden: 1978, pp. 133–51.

———. "Zelfdiscipline inzake reclame: Kritische evaluatie van de belgische praktijk [Advertising Self-regulation: A Critical Evaluation of Belgian Practice]. *Sociaal en Economische Wetgeving* 29 (February 1981): 91–108.

ACKNOWLEDGMENTS

The assistance of the following people is gratefully acknowledged: Thierry Bourgoignie (Louvain University), J.-C. Dastot (Director of JEP), Paul de Bruyne (Louvain University, and president of JEP), Paul de Win (President of the Advertising Council and of the World Federation of Advertisers), P. Dejemette (CRIOC), Charles Godart (Ministry of Economic Affairs), Jean Goebel (Ministry of Economic Affairs), Marc Goossens (CRIOC), Fernand Henet (Grey Belgium), P. Hilgers (CRIOC), Walter Hilgers (Test-Achats/Association des Consommateurs), Luc Joossens (CRIOC), Herman Koppen (CRIOC), André Lacroix (CACP), Dr. Martine Martel, F. Ruelle (Test-Achats/Association des Consommateurs), and Jules Stuyck (Leuven University).

4

Brazil: Conselho Nacional de Auto-Regulamentaçâo Publicitaria (CONAR)

Brazil has a well-developed advertising self-regulatory system. This situation is extraordinary, considering that some developed nations with longer commercial and associative traditions have not achieved a comparable feat. Besides, none of its immediate rivals among ''newly industrializing countries'' such as India, Mexico, South Korea and Taiwan, has achieved so much scope, sophistication and relative autonomy vis-à-vis government regulation. What factors account for this exceptional achievement?

The answers to this question can only be preliminary and tentative because of the lack of corroborating and multisided evidence. They are based mainly on 1983–1984 interviews with people connected with CONAR, the National Council for Advertising Self-Regulation. These respondents were responsible people who readily answered all questions, but it remains unfortunate that it was not possible to interview government officials and consumerists on this subject. Very little secondary information about CONAR as well as about the state of Brazilian consumerism and governmental consumer-protection policy could be found in the English language.[1] Several scholars in the United States and Brazil were queried but to little avail. Still, it was possible to piece together various shreds of information and analysis to interpret the development of advertising self-regulation in the context of Brazil's developing economy and authoritarian public policy.

Stimuli

Business views of the Brazilian government's involvement in the economy emphasize its interventionism through broad economic planning, a rather large

state-enterprise system, and numerous controls exercised by multiple bureaucracies and special agencies (Business International 1981).

Weak Consumer-Protection Concerns

In most developing countries, consumer protection assumes a relatively low
importance. A number of scholars have argued that consumerism is more a
reflection and a product of affluence and high-level development than a normal
policy ingredient at all levels of economic development: "First get the goods
out, then worry about the consumer, the physical environment and the like (cf.
Boddewyn and Hollander 1972)."

It appears that consumerism is underdeveloped in Brazil. Consumer associations—private and public—are found only at the state and local levels, with no
national coordination. While those associations are quite active, Brazilians are
generally perceived as uncomplaining consumers. For that matter, about half of
the cases handled by the self-regulatory body result from its own monitoring of
advertisements; and true consumerist inputs are absent in its functioning (see
below).

Consumers are protected in a general way through various provisions of the
civil, commercial and criminal codes in such matters as contract and fraud. Thus,
the Criminal Code forbids advertisements containing false statements detrimental
to a competitor, employing fraudulent means to divert customers from other
firms, using false indications of origin, designating merchandise as similar to
another seller's goods, claiming awards or honors that were not received, and
so on. More recently, Brazil's Supreme Court has ruled that promises made in
an advertisement constitute an implicit part of the contract. However, there is
little in the way of specific consumer-protection legislation, apart from a 1977
Act (Federal Law No. 6463) dealing mainly with abuses by retailers concerning
credit conditions, unit pricing and adherence to publicized prices. There have
been repeated congressional proposals to remedy this situation (see below), but
none has gathered momentum yet.

Still, a number of Brazilian federal ministries handle some aspects of consumer
protection as related to advertising: Justice deals with obscenity and censorship
(one of the exceptions to the Constitution's guarantee of free speech) and the
defense of consumer interests through a recent (1985) National Consumer Defense Council (see below); Telecommunications' DENTEL with the licensing
of broadcasting stations (violation of family and public morals or of "good
customs" is punishable); Health with pharmaceutical advertising; and Agriculture
with food advertising. For example, the Agriculture Ministry has a rule specifying
that a claim about a food being "natural" can only be made if the food has been
so classified by the technical-standards bureau. The Health Ministry forbids the
advertising through mass media of prescription drugs to the public; and it monitors
to some extent the quality of over-the-counter drug advertising without requiring
any preclearance, except in the case of chronic violators. However, these min-

istries' direct day-to-day involvement with advertising appears to be quite limited for lack of priority. The state and municipal levels are even less involved in these matters—largely because they have been denied much regulatory power by the central government (Business International 1981, p. 5).

Following the presidential election of 1985, a National Consumer Defense Council was created on the basis of electoral promises made during the campaign that led to the replacement of the 1964–1985 military regime by a civilian one (*Conselho Nacional de Defesa do Consumidor*; Decree No. 91469 of 24 July 1985). It includes representatives of the Agriculture, Health, Industry and Trade, Treasury and Justice ministries; the Executive Secretary of the National Debureaucratization Program; a member of the Attorney General's Office; 2 delegates from public and 3 from private consumer organizations; one "well-reputed citizen" connected with consumer protection, and the president of the advertising self-regulatory body, CONAR. Although this Council (now administered by the Ministry of Justice) is supposed to meet monthly, only four organizational and agenda-setting meetings were held at the outset. Its functions center on research, coordination and advisement in matters related to consumer protection. It is too early to tell whether the creation of this council presages stronger governmental interest in this matter.

Reaction against Government Interventionism

Brazil had a military government from 1964 to March 1985 in order to shore up a tottering economy and remove the Left from the political scene. While Brazilian advertising benefited tremendously from the ensuing "economic miracle," it also suffered from various censorship measures. Thus, television, radio and cinema commercials had to be approved in advance by the Ministry of Justice until 1978, based on the Law on Public Entertainment (dating of the Vargas era, 1937–1945) and on other enactments. More generally, Brazil lacks a democratic tradition. Its political system, over a long period of time and under a variety of regimes, has been characterized as elitist, patrimonial, centralized, bureaucratic and authoritarian, with a low level of national integration (e.g., Roett 1984). Since the mid–1970s, however, there have been growing business, labor and public-opinion pressures to reduce this autocratic yoke and instill more participation by the civilian sector in economic decisionmaking (Business International 1981, p. 13; Roett 1984, p. 20).

Subsequently, the military government—now endowed with fewer resources because of slower economic growth, and faced by sizable opposition to its meddling—started relaxing some political and economic controls. This novel situation created an opportunity for various business sectors to argue that they could handle some of the tasks assumed by government. Advertising was one of them, and that industry assumed such tasks at the urging and with the tolerance of the central administration (see below). The threat posed by various late–1970s proposals in the Senate and House of Deputies to set up a federal office to prescreen all commercials and to monitor and control television advertising—among others—also played an important role in prompting the industry to expand and restructure the relatively weak self-regulatory system that existed then ("Introduction to the Brazilian Advertising Self-Regulation Code," 1978).

Such congressional pressures have remained alive. According to a 1984 tabulation, sixty-seven different bills were presented to the Brazilian Congress over the past decade. They have included everything from the prohibition of "foreign music" in radio and TV commercials to the depiction of automobiles in unsafe situations, the use of models under forty-five in cigarette and alcohol advertising, and the use of company names on athletes' uniforms. There were seventeen bills to forbid the advertising of pharmaceutical products, eight to prohibit alcoholic-beverage ads, seven to ban cigarette advertising, and nine to ban both alcohol and cigarette ads. In most of these cases, CONAR's insistence that it was both able and willing to deal with these situations, together with pressure from the Brazilian Association of Radio and Television Stations (ABERT) and much of the press, has been effective in blocking the proposed legislation (Civita 1984, p. 8). However, it is premature to forecast what current governments will attempt in the areas of consumer protection and advertising regulation.

Corporatist Elements

Corporatism, in the Brazilian context, has usually meant government intermediation and adjudication between potentially conflicting socioeconomic groups—mainly in labor-management relations through the institutions of mandated "syndicates" to represent workers (e.g., Erickson 1977; Malloy 1977; Pike and Stritch 1974; Schmitter and Lehmbruch 1979, Wiarda 1981). Iberian corporatism, however, coexists with hierarchy, elitism, authoritarianism, bureaucracy and patrimonialism so that it has not resulted in the creation of Brazilian state-mandated industry associations where control of an industry's behavior is explicitly delegated by government to an accredited monopolistic association as a form of "private government." Instead, the national administration has retained direct bureaucratic control over many economic activities, although, as was seen before, it has exhibited limited interest in consumer protection and advertising regulation, and relaxed some of its controls after the mid–1970s.

Still, the limited Brazilian corporatist experience helped develop and nurture the practice and acceptance of business associations assuming various self-control tasks in the public interest. Besides, the government acted along corporatist lines when, at the urging of industry itself, it included as an appendix to the Standard Rules for the Rendering of Services by Advertising Agencies (Law No. 4680 of 18 June 1965, and its implementing Decree No. 57690 of 1966) the Code of Ethics for Advertising Professionals that had been approved in 1957 at the First Brazilian Advertising Congress organized by the Brazilian Association of Advertising Agencies (ABAP), the Association of Brazilian Advertising (ABP) and by the Sao Paulo Advertising Association (APP). Hence, this code has the force of law and can be used as a basis for government regulation or civil suits (Neelankavil and Stridsberg 1980, p. 63).[2]

In the 1970s, however, advertising self-regulation was developed in a voluntary rather than mandatory context, with the tolerance of a national government anxious to reduce the cost and burden of authoritarian state corporatism in favor of a more consensual and voluntary type (Erickson 1977, p. 190). Thus, the "Exposé of Reasons" for the development of the new 1978 self-regulatory code ("Introduction" 1978) as well as the preamble to the Code itself refers to recommendations and challenges expressed by legislators and high-level government officials in 1975 and 1976 "to set up a disciplinary action, which we had promised a long time ago but which was slow in acquiring substance and materializing."

It is also worth noting that the 1978 self-regulatory code anticipated in its Article 71 that its provisions would be incorporated into a new law—as had been done with the 1957 Code of Ethics (see above). Later versions of this Code as well as the CONAR Bylaws (1980) revoked such a corporatist inclusion as the industry came to realize that it would make subsequent code amendments very difficult, and would probably result in the creation of a new government agency to supervise it. It also appears that the central government was unwilling to allow the creation of a code and body with powers similar to those delegated to the law profession—as had been originally contemplated by the advertising industry.

Therefore, CONAR is not a corporatist institution. Instead, the initiative came from the advertising industry itself, if under the threat of further regulation and at the urging of the government; no enabling legislation was enacted to grant it particular powers, and there is no compulsory membership in CONAR, which cannot impose compliance on all advertising firms.

Responses

New Code Development

The 1957 Code of Ethics for Advertising Professionals was modeled by the ABAP agency association after the International Chamber of Commerce's (ICC) International Code of Advertising Practice, with special modifications for the Brazilian market (Neelankavil and Stridsberg 1980, pp. 63–65; and "Introduction" 1978). Consequently, the ABAP Committee on Ethics became the forum for inquiries and complaints, both from competitors and in the public interest. However, this first code never really worked because it was too brief and general to elicit specific action. Besides, the ABAP Committee on Ethics did not become operational because very few complaints or inquiries reached it. This has been ascribed to the lack of publicity given to these developments and to an advertising industry too busy with its fast expansion to bother about complaining or about improving the quality of its advertisements.

The relaxation of central executive controls and threats of restrictive congressional legislation, together with the urgings of foreign advertising associations expressed at International Advertising Association (IAA) World congresses (e.g., in Buenos Aires in 1976) prompted the Brazilian advertising industry to try again and do it better this time (Stridsberg 1974 and 1976). Work on a new code began in November 1976 when ABAP appointed a Special Commission for Self-Regulation, which held several meetings and circulated a first draft in May 1977. Simultaneously, ABAP formed an Inter-Associative Commission on Brazilian Advertising, composed of advertiser, agency and media representatives, plus members of the Confederation of Commerce and the Confederation of Industry. The codes of many other nations (e.g., Argentina, Belgium, France, Japan, United Kingdom and United States) were studied as well as various ICC and IAA publications on self-regulation. Afterward, ABAP as well as the Sao Paulo Advertising Association (APP) contacted organizations all over the country to discuss the draft code and suggest improvements. From all these associational inputs and general press airings resulted the Brazilian Code of Advertising Self-Regulation (*Codigo Brasileiro de Auto-regulamentaçâo Publicitária*), which was approved by acclamation at the Third Brazilian Advertising Congress in April 1978.

It is worth noting that the government and consumer associations were not formally consulted in the development of this code, although the Securities and Exchange Commission (CVM) and PROCON (the consumer-protection unit within the Sao Paulo State Secretariat for Industry and Commerce) commented on the original draft.

Overall Philosophy

The new 1978 self-regulatory Code contained no fewer than six chapters, sixteen sections and nineteen appendices in contrast to the rather brief 1957 ABAP Code of Ethics, which is still ruling agency behavior vis-à-vis clients and competitors; and it has been amended and expanded several times since then (the 5th edition is November 1985).[3]

The 1978 "Exposé of Reasons" presented self-regulation as the traditional "middle-of-the-road way" between "the absolute absence of any regulation, giving margin to disorderly practices which are detrimental to healthy competition among advertisers, and causes the consumer's lawful rights to be trampled on [and] the total and complete delegation of the regulatory function to government authorities, whose executive and legal structures do not always grasp the function, value and subtleties of advertising ("Introduction" 1978)." In this view, the public authorities' role is limited to "basic" legislation defining "general principles," while self-regulation fills in the details and keeps them up-to-date in the light of changing circumstances. However, the law must be obeyed. Thus, the Code's "Introduction" (Chapter 1) states that "advertising material and, in general, advertising activity, are naturally subject to the law and must be governed by the principle of legality," while Article 1 starts by saying that: "All advertisements must respect and comply with the laws of the country." Conversely, Article 16 mentions that: "Although this Code has been conceived essentially as an instrument of self-discipline for advertising activity, it is also intended for use by the authorities and the courts as a document of reference and a subsidiary source."

The main emphasis is put on ethical behavior based on the Code and grounded in voluntary moral commitment. In fact, the 1978 "Exposé of Reasons" stressed the positive and nonpunitive spirit of the new Code: "Prohibitions are not imposed; recommendations are made, measures and necessary action are taken but punishment and sanctions are never mentioned ["Introduction" 1978]." However, the Code has become sterner in successive versions, and now includes a Chapter 5 on "Infractions and Penalties" even though the penalties have not fundamentally changed since 1978 (see below). Adhesion to the CONAR Code is achieved automatically through membership in an association adhering to it. However, nobody is obliged to join such an organization, and CONAR also has individual members.

The New Self-Regulatory Body: CONAR

The 1978 Code provided for the creation of the National Council for Advertising Self-Regulation (*O Conselho Nacional de Auto-regulamentaçâo Publicitária*, CONAR), which was founded and operationalized in May 1980 although, between 1978 and 1980, CONAR had functioned on an informal and experimental basis, without a legal personality. Two operational organs are particularly relevant: the Superior Council and the Ethics Council.[4]

The Superior Council has thirteen members representing the six founding bodies: two from the advertising agencies' association ABAP; two from the advertisers' association ABA: two from the newspapers' association ANJ; four from the television and radio broadcasters' association ABERT; two from the magazines' association ANER, and one from Central de Outdoor (advertising) association. This Council is vested with both executive and normative functions. As to the first, it appoints a five-member Executive Directorate: a president (also Chairman of the Board of CONAR), a vice-president, a secretary and a treasurer as well as a full-time executive director (who has a legal background).

The executive director is assisted by a five-member staff who take care of all the administrative details, including the monitoring of advertisements, the preliminary handling of complaints to be adjudicated by the Ethics Council, correspondence with the parties involved in a complaint, and the like. The Executive Directorate handles broad policy matters; government, public and association relations; legal representation (as when CONAR is involved in a suit); the budget, and the overall supervision of CONAR's functioning. The executive director, with the assistance of his staff, prepares and presents cases before the Ethics Council.

The Superior Council performs the normative functions of improving and amending the Code (by a two-third majority vote) and of approving the Ethics Council's bylaws. It is worth noting that the Superior Council does not include any outside representatives from government, consumer associations or the public at large, although the original 1978 Code (Article 52) provided for one consumer representative on it. Code amendments are usually based on various investigations of its scope and effectiveness, but do not involve any formal solicitation of suggestions and comments from outsiders. Still, communications emanating from outside the industry are duly considered by the Superior Council (e.g., the government has passed on to CONAR various complaints originating with it or received from consumers about such matters as decency, safety and over-the-counter drugs).

The Ethics Council, however, includes outside representation although in a minority position (less than 20 percent). It is in fact divided into three chambers—two in Sao Paulo and one in Rio de Janeiro (more may be created in the future)—with one chamber meeting about every week throughout the year, outside of January. In 1986, there were thirty-three meetings of the three Ethics-Council chambers, seven of the Special Appeal Chamber, and five of the Plenarium (all three chambers) appeal group. Each Chamber has eleven members (with an equal number of alternates): seven from the founding associations, one advertising professional from state advertising associations, another from advertising creative professionals, and two "consumer representatives," plus a president with no vote, who is a member of the Superior Council.[5]

The consumer representatives (*representantes de consumidores*) should more properly be called "nonindustry" or "general public" representatives, although Paragraph 5 of Article 40 of the Bylaws of CONAR provides that such representatives, invited by CONAR's Superior Council to sit on the Ethics Council, "shall belong to national legally constituted private entities for consumer protection, with no political, religious or racial ties, and with a good reputation—the participation of representatives coming from public, party-affiliated or religious entities being excluded." However, Paragraph 6 of Article 40 provides that, in the absence of any such entities or impossibility of designating one of their representatives, "persons with good reputation" will be chosen by the Superior Council. Consequently, "consumer representatives" have usually been physicians, lawyers, nutritionists, engineers and journalists because there are no Brazilian private national consumer associations—only private state and local ones as well as federal and state (e.g., PROCON) government-connected bodies. Such formalistic restrictions on consumerist participation seem almost designed to prevent it.

The absence of a unified and middle-of-the-road consumerism has militated against involving some of its representatives in advertising self-regulatory activities (this is also the case in Belgium and France). Besides, one can guess that the elitist tradition in Brazilian culture favors the use of "bourgeois" rather than "popular" elements as outside representatives (Roett 1984; Malloy 1977, pp. 71 and 78).

CONAR's Functioning

Complaints are first handled by the executive director's staff who also monitor press and broadcast advertisements on their own. Typically, the CONAR staff request the broadcast media to submit samples of commercials shown on a particular day, and it regularly examines a variety of publications. This applies mostly to the South/Southeast regions (Sao Paulo, Rio de Janeiro), where the economy is more developed, but it is being extended to less-developed parts of the country. Some problematic industries (e.g., over-the-counter drugs) are particularly monitored. Subsequently, the executive director selects those controversial ads worth pursuing, gathers the necessary information from advertisers and agencies (supporting evidence for the claims made, etc.) and even from the government; and he presents their case before one of the Ethics Council's three chambers, where an incriminated advertiser, agency or medium can defend himself.

Complaints are accepted from any source: competitors, governmental units (e.g., PROCON, which sent in eight complaints in 1986), congressmen, consumers and their associations, but CONAR's own monitoring generates the majority—about half of the cases in 1981–1986 (see Appendix). If after discussion by one of the Ethics Council's chambers, an advertisement is found to be in violation of the Code, the advertiser can be subjected to: (1) a warning; (2) a recommendation to have the questioned advertisement changed or corrected; (3) a recommendation to the media to suspend its publication or broadcasting or (4) a public announcement by CONAR of its position regarding an advertiser's, agency's and/or medium's noncompliance, together with its recommendation (names are cited). This last and most drastic penalty has been applied very rarely, and the majority of them have dealt with direct mailings, which bypass the media. Decisions usually take a couple of months after a case is initiated—a rather slow process, which allows most delinquent campaigns to run their course.

CONAR's Superior Council can also request that a noncomplying party be expelled from or denied membership in member associations. When the fault or negligence constitutes a misdemeanor or crime, CONAR must communicate that fact to the proper authorities. Any decision of the Ethics Council can be appealed to the Special Appeal Chamber (which met seven times in 1986) and, further, to the Plenarium of all three chambers meeting together. In addition, CONAR maintains regular contacts with federal ministries and congressional consumer-protection committees through its Executive Directorate and its president. Legislative bills are monitored by CONAR but also by member associations (e.g., for television and outdoor advertising) particularly interested in them.

CONAR's Effectiveness

Coverage. The CONAR Code is very comprehensive and compares favorably to that of its British, Canadian and French counterparts. Like them, however, it remains weak or indecisive about some issues such as decency and sexism. Thus, Article 20 opposes ads offensive or discriminatory in terms of race, social or political affiliation, religion or nationality but not on the basis of sex. An amendment to strengthen this article in terms of "good taste and respect" was defeated. It seems that most Brazilians are tolerant of sexy and even sexist ads, and that there is too much cultural diversity within Brazil to come up with more specific norms about good taste.[6] Besides, the demise of the military regime appears to have led to some relaxation of moral and ethical standards so that more controversial ads have appeared (frontal nudity, sexual innuendoes, etc.) and have generated stronger reactions from both feminist and conservative groups.

Reach. In 1986, 190 associations and firms financed CONAR, which reaches about 75 percent of Brazilian advertising because most of the networks and the four major print groups subscribe to the CONAR code.[7] Most financial support comes from the advertiser side while leadership has traditionally originated from the agency side, although the media are becoming more influential.

The "noncomplier" problem is inevitable in any voluntary system. CONAR deals with it by having its media members mention on their tariff lists that they subscribe to the Code. Hence, agencies and advertisers have to abide by the code's rules to advertise in these media, and will usually have their advertisements withdrawn in the case of a negative CONAR ruling. This setup was challenged by an advertiser, but a court in 1981 upheld CONAR's decision because the Constitution guarantees freedom of association, and the Code's provisions were not in violation of the law, since CONAR did not issue an order, but only recommended withdrawal to the medium who, as a member, simply abided by voluntarily accepted rules.

One of CONAR's major members, Globo TV, which is the market leader, is pressuring independent regional and local networks to join CONAR and abide by its rules because it sells programs to them. Still, some financially strapped media accept questionable advertisements, although they usually stop publishing or broadcasting them after being challenged by CONAR—too late, of course.

Cases Handled. In 1986, a total of 109 externally and internally generated complaints were investigated (there were 139 of them in 1985; see Appendix). Over the years, CONAR has looked at 856 advertisements and suggested that 265 of them be withdrawn from the media. Particularly troublesome are exaggerated claims about over-the-counter drugs as well as misleading retail installment-credit and direct-mail ads. The latter usually do not use an advertising agency and do bypass the media, thereby avoiding the checkpoints set up by CONAR. Most of the cases involve small firms, since large advertisers are more likely to behave according to the Code and to respond quickly to CONAR admonitions.

The number of cases handled is relatively low.[8] This may be interpreted as evidence of: (1) very good behavior on the part of advertisers; (2) a very weak code; (3) limited knowledge of the CONAR Code; (4) disinterest in complaining;

(5) limited monitoring by CONAR, and/or (6) more effective alternative remedies (e.g., through the courts). On the basis of the available evidence, it is impossible to reach a definite conclusion. The uncomplaining behavior of Brazilians as well as the youth of CONAR are pertinent factors, but the absence of publicity campaigns since 1984 and the reluctance of CONAR to act until several complaints are received about a particular advertisement have probably contributed to this situation. Still, the number of suspensions decreed by CONAR increased in 1986, and advertisers and agencies have been advised to air more controversial sexy ads after 10 PM.

No Prior Approval System. CONAR receives a growing number of calls (some five a day) from members seeking advice or inquiring about ads that may have encountered problems in some other medium. The executive director can only point to the relevant code articles without granting any formal prior approval, since CONAR does not have a preclearance system for advertisements. Most media, however, apply the CONAR Code when screening proposed advertisements, besides using any other internal acceptance rules they may have.

Publicity. CONAR engaged (until 1984) in annual promotion campaigns to publicize the existence of the Code and to instruct professionals as well as the general public on how to complain. Thus, newspapers, magazines, radio and television have shown CONAR commercials ridiculing excessive claims (e.g., "How I became Miss Universe after using cosmetic X"; "How I became president of my company after taking a correspondence course"). Copies of the CONAR Code are sent to local, state and federal authorities when new officials are appointed or a new edition has been issued. However, very little publicity is given to CONAR decisions (see Appendix).

Credibility. It is not known how public opinion feels toward CONAR since no survey has been conducted to that effect, but it has probably benefited from the central government's declining moral authority, from growing revulsion against excessive controls, and from the resurging interest in private enterprise guaranteed by the Constitution of the Federative Republic of Brazil and vigorously promoted by business.[9] However, CONAR's reluctance to act aggressively against more blatantly sexual advertisements weakens self-regulatory claims that it can better handle such problems than government.

Conclusions

What happens in Brazil is important because it is a large (130 million people) and fast-developing country with the seventh largest advertising budget in the world in 1981, some 130 television stations (most of them private) and hundreds of radio stations as well as a sizable press (Levi 1983). the Brazilian experience is particularly significant because it is unusual to find a well-developed advertising self-regulatory system in a developing nation. As such, it provides a much needed example to the advertising industry around the world if business is to go beyond

pious declarations in favor of free enterprise and against excessive state intervention in economic affairs.

Barring continuing economic decline, which would affect its financing, the
Brazilian self-regulatory system appears likely to expand and improve. However,
this beneficial development is unlikely to prevent the development of consumer-
protection legislation if only because: (1) some problems are more amenable to
statutory treatment, and (2) economic development usually generates stronger
consumer, feminist and other movements, which press for further protection and
promotion measures.[10] Such a development is not necessarily inimical to advertising self-regulation, whose best and well-tested guidelines can safely be
incorporated into law, leaving to self-regulation novel and ill-defined problems
such as decency and sexism where fast-changing values are not conducive to
rigid rules.

The Brazilian CONAR is weak in terms of soliciting and integrating "outside"
inputs in its code development and application since few consumer, government
and even general-public representatives participate in them. This is largely a
consequence of Brazilian conditions, which are likely to prevail until more
democratic voices can be heard (a new Brazilian Constitution is expected in
1988) and/or local, state and national governments decide to pay more attention
to consumer-protection issues, possibly at the urging of the recent National
Consumer Defense Council.

Appendix

Complaints Handled by CONAR, 1980–1986

ORIGIN	NUMBER OF COMPLAINTS						
	1980	1981	1982	1983	1984	1985	1986
Executive Director (monitoring)	6	104	150	80	51	62	67
Superior Council (*)	14	12	13	25	25	45	28
Members of the Public	1	5	8	17	54	20	6
Members of CONAR	2	9	4	8	20	12	8
T O T A L	23	130	175	130	150	139	109

(*) These are complaints originating from or transmitted by public bodies and governmental authorities (Article 32, VII of the CONAR Bylaws) and media (Article 45, c. 1 of CONAR Code).

Sanctions Applied by CONAR, 1980–1986

	SUSPENSIONS (*)	PUBLIC ANNOUNCEMENTS (**)
1980	7	2
1981	36	2
1982	23	2
1983	40	2
1984	57	2
1985	33	4
1986	69	4

(*) "Suspensions" refers to recommendations to the media to suspend an advertisement's publication or broadcasting.

(**) "Public announcements" refers to CONAR's announcing its position regarding an advertiser's, agency's and/or medium's noncompliance with its recommendations (the names of the offenders are cited).

NOTES

1. This author does not read Portuguese and had to rely on an interpreter to obtain most of his information during two visits to Brazil in November 1983 and January 1984. The CONAR staff, under the leadership of its then executive director, Gilberto Carlos Leifert, was most helpful in making the research trip possible and in providing most of the necessary information through the translating efforts of Berenice Malta.

2. The 1957 code was included in the law at the request of the industry itself because the 1965–1966 legislation was passed at the time of the onset of Brazilian-owned advertising agencies (foreigners had dominated the field until then).

3. Later editions removed organizational and administrative details from the Code and moved them to a new Bylaws section (*Estatutos Sociais*) so that the present Code contains fifty articles distributed over five chapters, sixteen sections and nineteen appendices.

4. There is also a General Assembly and a Fiscal Council, which supervise and audit CONAR's operational bodies. For details, see CONAR's *Estatutos Sociais* (Bylaws).

5. The president of the Ethics Council is also president of the Superior Council. All members serve two-year terms, which are renewable.

6. This topic was extensively discussed at the International Advertising Symposium organized by the Sao Paulo Advertising Association (APP) from November 7–10, 1983, with the cooperation of CONAR.

7. As of 31 December 1986, CONAR had as members: seventy advertisers, fifty-eight advertising agencies, fifty-two media, four suppliers and six founding associations. There is no particular profile of the nonmembers; some are large, others are small and try to avoid membership expenses. In 1986, investments and costs amounted to about $100,000, while dues and other revenues added up to $146,000 so that dues remained below the maximum allowed by the CONAR Bylaws.

8. "Relative" is the appropriate term to use since there are no conclusive measures of consumer dissatisfaction nor of advertising misbehavior. Still, the British, Canadian

and French experiences suggest that 109 to 175 cases a year is on the low side although the U.S. NAD handles only about 100 cases a year.

9. See, among others, the efforts of Hector Brener through the National Movement for Free Enterprise: *Movimento Nacional pela Livre Iniciativa* (Sao Paulo: Conselho Nacional de Propaganda, 1982).

10. During 1987 discussions of a new Constitution, the industry succeeded in getting the Brazilian Congress to reject proposals banning the advertising of alcohol, tobacco and pharmaceutical products.

REFERENCES

Boddewyn, J. J., and S. C. Hollander, eds. *Public Policy toward Retailing: An International Symposium*. Lexington, Mass.: D. C. Heath, 1972.

Business International Corporation. *Managing Successfully in a Brazil under Pressure; A Balanced Perspective on Problems and Opportunities*. New York: September 1981.

Civita, Roberto. "Self-Regulation of Advertising in Brazil; Speech before the 32nd International Union of Advertisers Associations." Mimeographed. Rio de Janeiro, Brazil: May 29, 1984.

Erickson, K. P. *The Brazilian Corporative State and Working-Class Politics*. Berkeley, Calif.: University of California Press, 1977.

"Introduction to the Brazilian Advertising Self-Regulation Code to Be Presented at the XXVI International Advertising Association World Congress, Copenhagen, 1978." (No source or pagination given.)

Levi, P. L. "A Giant Awakens to Hard Times." *International Advertiser* (November–December 1983): 6–8.

Malloy, J. M., ed. *Authoritarianism and Corporatism in Latin America*. Pittsburgh, Pa.: University of Pittsburgh Press, 1977.

Neelankavil, J. P., and A. B. Stridsberg. *Advertising Self-Regulation: A Global Perspective*. New York: Hastings House, 1980.

Pike, F. B., and Thomas Stritch, eds. *The New Corporatism; Social-Political Structures in the Iberian World*. Notre Dame, Ind.: University of Notre Dame Press, 1974.

Roett, Riordan. *Brazil; Politics in a Patrimonial Society*. New York: Praeger, 1984.

Schmitter, P. C., and G. Lehmbruch, eds. *Trends toward Corporatist Intermediation*. Beverly Hills, Calif.: Sage, 1979.

Stridsberg, A. B. *Effective Advertising Self-Regulation*. New York: International Advertising Association, November 1974.

———. *Progress in Effective Advertising Self-Regulation*. New York: International Advertising Association, 1976.

Wiarda, H. J. *Corporatism and National Development in Latin America*. Boulder, Colo.: Westview Press, 1981.

ACKNOWLEDGMENTS

The assistance of the following people is gratefully acknowledged: Professor Maria Cecilia Countinho de Arruda (Faculdades Oswaldo Cruz), J. Ray Kennedy (Johns Hopkins University), Marilena Igreja Lazzarini (Executive Director of PROCON), Gilberto Carlos Leifert (former Executive Director of CONAR), Berenice R. de Salles Oliveira Malta (lawyer and translator), and Edney G. Narchi (Executive Director of CONAR). Professor Arruda's doctoral dissertation ("Etica na administração de Marketing"; University of Sao Paulo, Faculty of Economics and Administration, 1986) includes survey data on CONAR (pp. 156–171).

5

Canada: The Canadian Advertising Foundation's Standards Division and Conseil National de la Publicité

Canada's advertising self-regulatory system has been very innovative. It has pioneered the use of nonindustry members in its structure and functioning, the invitation of consumer complaints through multimedia campaigns, the preclearance of children and feminine-hygiene commercials, the application of guidelines about sex-role stereotyping and the handling of multiculturalism in advertising. Compared to other countries, it developed earlier as well as more explicit and elaborate responses to some of the "soft" areas in advertising behavior, where matters of "taste, public opinion and public decency" are at issue. These responses, in turn, have necessitated the involvement of nonindustry "public members." This chapter focuses on these soft issues and novel responses.[1] It is based on secondary sources, personal and telephone interviews, and correspondence in 1981–1987 (see Acknowledgments).

The Canadian Self-Regulatory System

The Canadian advertising industry has recently (1980–1982 and 1985–1987) restructured its defense, promotion and self-disciplining systems.

Dual Mission

The Canadian Advertising Foundation (CAF)-Fondation Canadienne de la Publicité (FCP)—oversees and finances four separate bodies (two English, two French) charged with two distinct responsibilities: (1) two advocacy bodies, the Advisory Division (AD) and the Confédération Générale de la Publicité (COGEP) to address the social and economic issues related to advertising, and (2) two self-regulatory mechanisms, the Standards Division (SD) and the Conseil des Normes de la Publicité (CNP) to administer standards and codes of ethics.[2]

In other words, the Advisory Division (AD) and COGEP are the promoters and defenders of a "disciplined industry" but not its "judiciary [administrative] arm"—a task left to the Standards Division (SD) and CNP. In practice, this dichotomy is not perfect because the AD and COGEP have handled the sex-role stereotyping guidelines (see below).

The two Canadian cultures—English and French—do not share exactly the same problems. For example, advertising to children below the age of thirteen has been banned in the Province of Quebec so that its self-regulation applies only to the other nine provinces. In the latter, the advertising of feminine-hygiene products and multiculturalism are sensitive matters, but less of an issue in the French part of the country, which was originally much more concerned about sex-stereotyping and pornography in advertising than was English Canada.[3]

The norms applied by the Advertising Standards Division/Conseil des Normes de la Publicité (SD/CNP) are found mainly in the Canadian Code of Advertising Standards with its relatively short sixteen clauses loosely based on the International Chamber of Commerce's International Code of Advertising Practice. However, the SD and CNP also apply six additional codes issued by particular industries (e.g., horticulture, ethical and over-the-counter drugs, and cosmetics) or in cooperation with government and pressure groups (e.g., advertising to children and feminine-hygiene products).[4] The Advisory Division (formerly, AAB) and the Confédération Générale de la Publicité (until recently) have handled the Guidelines on Sex-Role Stereotyping in Advertising.

The distinction between voluntary codes and guidelines is that the former represent voluntary "must" while the latter allow leeway for judgment and are more like strong recommendations ("should"), which the industry as a whole supports and hopes members will voluntarily embrace. However, the Guidelines for the Use of Comparative Advertising in Food Commercials are handled by the SD/CNP as if they were part of a code because they have received widespread industry endorsement.[5]

Compliance with a SD/CNP ruling is usually obtained from the offending advertiser. When advertiser cooperation is not forthcoming, the media are notified, but this is a rare occurrence (about twice a year). Since all national media associations have endorsed the codes, they no longer consider the offending ad as acceptable. In effect, the media act as the SD/CNP's ultimate enforcement arm; and only direct-mail advertising, which does not rely on the media, presents serious problems in this regard. In the case of deliberately and persistently fraudulent ads, the appropriate government department may be notified.

The "Taste, Opinion and Public Decency" Issue

The codes administered by the Standards Division and the Conseil des Normes de la Publicité have been, with a few exceptions, developed and amended by the industry itself through the CAF's Copy Standards Committee. However, their content is not immune to public-opinion pressure nor to the threat of government intervention; and recent years have witnessed code amendments and the development of guidelines resulting explicitly from negotiations with outside groups.[6] Five related cases illustrate this interaction process and the problems they generate when "taste, opinion and public decency" are at issue.

Advertising to Children

In the late 1960s, members of Parliament received numerous letters complaining that commercials aimed at children were putting undue pressure on parents. The Advertising Standards Council was asked by the Canadian Radio-Television and Telecommunications Commission (CRTC, the federal regulatory body responsible for administering the Broadcasting Act) and by the Canadian Association of Broadcasters to develop a code as an alternative to government regulation. The ASC consulted with industry, government (the CRTC and the Ministry of Consumer and Corporate Affairs) and the Consumers' Association of Canada, and subsequently issued the first voluntary Broadcast Code for Advertising to Children in 1971 (Goldberg 1982). Although this development resulted in a sharp drop in the number of complaints, the ASC felt that the Code should be strengthened by requiring ASC approval prior to station acceptance of commercials aimed at children in order to ensure conformity with the Code's provisions. The amended code of 1973 included that requirement agreed upon by the broadcasters, and a special preclearance committee was set up.

As a result of a parliamentary bill proposing a ban on broadcast advertising to children, several hearings were held. Ultimately, the CRTC decided to endorse the self-regulatory approach, and the code was further strengthened. The CRTC also indicated that adherence to the code would be made part of a station's broadcasting license; and the number of representatives on the ASC (now SD) preclearance committee, which approves commercials directed to children, was expanded to include one from the CRTC (there are also three public representatives sitting on that committee). Further code revisions have since taken place after consultation with industry, government and consumer representatives (Boddewyn 1984).

The effectiveness of the Broadcast Code for Advertising to Children and of its mandatory preclearance system is attested by the fact that the 776 final commercials and scripts/storyboards reviewed in 1985 led to no complaints about them in that year, versus four in 1984. (There were 938 reviews in 1986, and 5 complaints—still quite a record.) Meanwhile, in Quebec Province, the legal ban on advertising to children was found to be unconstitutional by a court of appeals in September 1986 (this decision is being challenged in the Supreme Court and the law is still in effect, pending appeal), so that the reintroduction of such commercials may happen—at least on private stations. Company-sponsored "societal messages" linked to health or safety are already allowed, with the name of the firm mentioned (Pulse, August 1986, p. 6). The French-Canadian CNP is reactivating its Children's Committee in anticipation of a relaxation of the ban.

Taste and Opinion

The Canadian Code of Advertising Standards remained silent about matters of "taste, opinion and public decency" until 1980. The president of the [Canadian] Advertising Advisory Board typically remarked in 1975 that: "We acknowledge and often discuss but rarely deal with matters of taste and opinion, because these are personal, regional and fluctuating. Where good taste seems distressingly lacking, we will write the advertiser and/or the media expressing our points of view, and pointing out the negative response in the marketplace (Oliver 1975, p. 21)." Moyer and Banks (1977) however, made a pertinent observation about this ASC reluctance to handle such matters:

It is difficult to believe that the Council can make "an objective appraisal" as to whether an ad "would result in . . . moral damage to children," this being in the Code, but cannot judge whether a commercial for a personal product is being aired at an inappropriate hour, this being "an entry into the subjective area of taste." It seems more accurate to say that judgments of most advertising must be subjective to some extent, and that some of the issues that the Code still sidesteps are no more subjective than others that it already tackles.

The ASC hesitated because standards of taste are in fact subjective, changing and, therefore, hard to handle. It also wanted to avoid getting embroiled in discussing the morality of advertising such controversial products as tobacco and liquor. Still, the ASC was getting several hundred complaints a year about taste, opinion and public decency; the industry did not want government to regulate such matters (CRTC 1982, p. 168), and the government was not anxious to handle them either. Consequently, Clause 15 was added to the Code in 1980 to deal with advertisements containing "anything likely, in the light of generally prevailing standards, to cause deep or widespread offence. It is recognized, of course, that standards of taste are subjective and vary widely from person to person and community to community, and are, indeed, subject to constant change." Subsequently, the number of complaints handled under the "taste, opinion and public decency" clause has varied considerably; for example, twenty-three were upheld in 1984, none in 1985, and four in 1986. The 1984 upsurge was largely linked to the sex-stereotyping issue (see later discussion, below).

The Tobacco Issue

The new Clause 15 of 1980 was prompted by a variety of social concerns including the depiction of women in advertisements and the advertising of tobacco and alcohol. Regarding the latter, the ASC/CNP have consistently emphasized that their concern and mandate is with *how* goods are advertised, not with *what* may be advertised:

From the beginning, we had made it clear to the regulatory authorities in Ottawa that we did not have, nor did we seek to have, the authority to debar any advertiser from having access to the media. We are empowered only to tell an advertiser that a particular advertisement in a certain format does not meet ethical standards established by the industry and is therefore unacceptable. That principle was so well understood at the operating level that it was not even spelled out in the Code. But, with the addition of a "taste and opinion" clause, we realized there would be those who would say: "Well, now I can get rid of any advertising I dislike." So, we added a sub-clause [to Clause 15] which reads in part: "The authority of the Code and the jurisdiction of the Council are over the content of advertisements. The Code is not meant to impede in any way the sale of products which some people, for one reason or another, may find offensive... (Oliver, 1986)."

The inclusion of this caveat in Clause 15 turned out to be unfortunate.[7] In the fall of 1984, the Non-Smokers' Rights League chose to interpret the clause as applying only to "taste and opinion" issues, and demanded that the ASC/CNP prohibit all tobacco advertising under Safety Clause 11 which reads: "Advertisements shall not display a disregard for public safety or depict situations which might encourage inappropriate, unsafe or dangerous practices." Together with the Coalition of Health Interests, the League felt that the SD was violating the Code by permitting tobacco advertising that depicted an unsafe or dangerous product. Subsequently, the Consumers' Association of Canada asked that the Code be amended to ban all tobacco advertising and promotion. The advertising industry responded that: (1) such a ban was beyond its mandate of focusing on the content of advertisements, and (2) the government could readily challenge the right of any voluntary body to decide what sector has the right to advertise its legal products through the media.

The outcome of this dispute was that: (1) the Consumers' Association of Canada withdrew its participation in ASC/CNP activities for one-and-a-half years (until early 1986); (2) the number and origin of outside (nonindustry) members on the ASC/CNP was expanded, and (3) the "authority and scope of the Code" was clarified, removed from Clause 15, and put in the introduction to the Canadian Code of Advertising Standards: "The Code deals with *how* products or services may be advertised, *not* with *what* may be advertised. Thus, the authority of the Code and the jurisdiction of the Council are over the content of advertisements and do not include, in any way, the right to prohibit the promotion of legal products or services or their portrayal in circumstances of normal use (CAF 1986, p. 7)."

A related issue concerned the appearance and demeanor of models in cigarette advertisements whose messages were widely perceived as being directed to the teenager market. Critics were also convinced that so-called "lifestyle" commercials for beer encouraged alcoholic consumption among high-school students. Since the Code did not deal with this issue, a new Clause 15 was developed in concertation with the tobacco and alcoholic-beverage industries in early 1986:

Advertising to Minors. Products prohibited from sale to minors must not be advertised in such a way as to appeal particularly to persons under legal age; and people featured in advertisements for such products must be seen, and clearly seen to be, adults under the law.[8]

Feminine Sanitary-Protection Products

In the late 1970s, the television advertising of feminine-hygiene products became a hot issue. The ASC reports for 1978 and 1979 listed this product category as the one with the largest number of complaints. Several newspaper stories by consumerist columnists criticized the existence, style and tone of the commercials; and they urged readers with similar views to complain to the Canadian Radio-Television and Telecommunications Commission (CRTC). The Consumers' Association of Canada also became involved. As a result, thousands of petitions and letters from individuals and groups were sent to the ASC (1,200) and to the CRTC (83,000) in 1979.

Industry representatives had mixed feelings about the protests. Some were unsure they should be advertising these products on television but were engaged in the practice because their competitors were. Others felt that only a very small minority of women objected. Still, in response to the protest and to ease the pressure from the government, the ASC—in cooperation with the Canadian Association of Broadcasters (CAB), the Telecaster Committee and various advertisers and agencies—developed a 1979 self-regulatory Television Code of Standards for the Advertising of Feminine Sanitary Protection Products and provided for the prebroadcast approval of TV commercials by an ASC special preclearance committee (Courtney and Whipple 1983, p. 173). This Code was then adopted by the CAB, and it has been administered by the ASC (now SD). Since then, the number of complaints about these commercials has declined considerably. For that matter, the SD is now allowing the airing of feminine-hygiene products during prime time, and their more graphic depiction — after proper preclearance, of course.[9]

Sex-Role Stereotyping

Another facet of the "taste, opinion and public decency" issue emerged in the form of reactions to the way girls and women are portrayed in advertising. This time, however, the industry was unable to cope with it in a purely internal manner, but had to engage in direct negotiations with outside groups (the following account relies mostly on CRTC [1982 and 1986], Courtney and Whipple [1983, pp. 172–83] and Wyckham [1986]).

Original Industry Reaction. Faced with growing pressures from feminist groups, the Canadian Advertising Advisory Board (CAAB, the predecessor of the CAF) set up in 1976 a Task Force on Women and Advertising, which included a few outside members (Task Force 1977). While acknowledging that improvements were needed, its report noted that the most serious problems arose from the cumulative impact of numerous advertisements taking the same approach and being somewhat off in their portrayals of women. Such a cumulative effect defied easy regulatory remedies because no single advertiser was guilty, although all should be encouraged to change. Consequently, a checklist of positive and negative portrayals was included in the Task Force's report, but no new Code clauses were proposed. This report was just a position paper, and little was done beyond its initial introduction at an annual meeting of the CAAB in order to generate industry attention and response. However, many members were not ready to concede the importance of the issue (CRTC 1982, pp. 8 and 54–55), and a major stumbling block to further action was the stand taken by the CAAB, that issues concerning the portrayal of women fell into the category of taste and opinion.

Government Reaction. Still, protests and complaints continued about sex-role stereotypes. In 1978, the Federal Advisory Council on the Status of Women published a lengthy position paper reviewing relevant research data and recommending government intervention if industry did not respond more favorably. Despite this pressure, government reaction was limited—mainly on account of the difficulty of determining what would be an effective response and because the authorities favored a self-regulatory approach in this matter, as opposed to direct controls over advertising. The Quebec government, however, did act in August 1978 when it established a committee to probe sexism in advertising, which produced 1979 guidelines developed in consultation with industry and women's groups—an embodiment of the then ruling Parti Québecois' platform in favor of improving the "status of women."

In 1979, the federal Minister of Communications suggested that some action be taken on sex-role stereotyping, and a Task Force was set up by the Canadian Radio-Television and Telecommunications Commission (CRTC). It was composed of representatives from the advertising and broadcasting industries, the CRTC and the public, and its purpose was to develop policy recommendations and guidelines for a more positive and realistic portrayal of women in both programs and commercials nationwide. This CRTC Task Force had a stormy history (Courtney and Whipple 1983; Heslop and Courtney 1982). Unlike the more understanding atmosphere of a self-regulatory group whose members are chosen by the industry, this government-established committee included feminists not necessarily sympathetic to the advertising-effectiveness issues (e.g., "Should women be depicted in their present roles or in emerging ones?") that concerned industry.

Industry claimed that it had set up a number of committees to investigate the problem and develop positive-action statements designed to take the place of guidelines, although it had not activated their implementation. It also argued that some stereotyping was inevitable in short commercials, that time and education were needed to change attitudes and practices, and that a vocal minority or government committee should not use the advertising industry as a tool to reshape society according to its beliefs. As Courtney and Whipple put it:

Despite these vocalizations of righteous indignation from the industry, many of its leaders recognized that the CRTC Task Force would not quietly disappear and that, in fact, it had government support and evidence which would strongly support its case against advertising. Consequently, industry representatives began slowly to revise their positions. . . . Rather than allow that change to be imposed by government, proposals were developed for industry self-regulation to help alleviate the problem. In July 1980, the industry presented its own brief to the CRTC Task Force, [which] stated, in part, that: "Recognizing that self-imposed regulation is a difficult and serious matter, the associations submitting this brief have undertaken: (1) to communicate to advertisers and the agencies preparing advertising, concerns over the portrayal of women in broadcast advertising; and (2) to develop guidelines to help the industry present a more realistic portrayal of women in broadcast advertising (Courtney and Whipple 1983, pp. 178–79)."

Compromise. The battle was resolved—if not won by either side—by a series of compromises during the summer and fall of 1980. First, despite previous statements that the industry could not and should not attempt to rule in the areas of taste and opinion, the 1980 revision of the Canadian Code of Advertising Standards had added Clause 15 (see above) stating in part that: "As a public communication process, advertising should not present demeaning or derogatory portrayals of individuals or groups . . . " Second, nine "positive action statements" were developed and adopted by the Task Force as guidelines (but not as an addition to the Canadian Code of Advertising Standards) to encourage a more positive and realistic portrayal of men and women in commercials. These statements were prepared by the industry and ultimately accepted by the public members of the Task Force in exchange for a promise to review progress two years later (CRTC 1982, pp. 56–58). Third, both the CAAB (now, Advisory Division) and the Conseil des Normes de la Publicité (CNP) established an Advisory Committee on Sex-Role Stereotyping to: (1) receive and process complaints arising from the guidelines; (2) develop a public-information program about the Committee's activities; and (3) undertake research on public perceptions about issues affecting advertising, including sex-role stereotyping. In January 1983, the COGEP took on the responsibility of administering the sex-role stereotyping guidelines in French-language advertisements, but this task reverted to the CNP in March 1987 after the COGEP became largely dormant.

It is worth noting that the Task Force's compromise had agreed to a mutually acceptable version of the industry-suggested guidelines; and it had conceded that self-regulation, if done properly, could contribute to changed attitudes on the part of advertisers, agencies and media, which would ultimately provide the real solution to the problem. At the urging of the Task Force's public members, the industry accepted to "review [in 1984] and where appropriate modify industry codes relating to the portrayal of individuals, notably women, in advertising (CRTC 1982, p. 70)" after it had gained experience with the voluntary guidelines and the self-regulatory process.

Implementation. However, financial difficulties (see below) have hampered the full implementation of these commitments by the self-regulatory system. Courtney and Whipple (1983) have commented as follows on the early results:

The [CAAB, then AAB and now Advisory Division] began its efforts under the guidelines with the production of an eighteen-minute film dealing with advertising sex-role ster-eotyping. . . . As promised, the AAB [and COGEP] established a committee comprised of industry and public members to oversee compliance with the guidelines. . . . Most complaints come from members of feminist groups who are participating in a national effort to oversee advertising. . . . When the committee receives a complaint, members of the staff inform the advertisers of it, and of the committee members' deliberations concerning it. Of course, the committee cannot force advertiser compliance with its ruling because it administers guidelines, rather than a self-regulatory code. Nevertheless, the process of informing advertisers about complaints serves as an effective re-education effort. . . . As yet, the [committees] have not made major efforts to publicize the sex-stereotyping guidelines outside the advertising industry. Thus, public awareness of the guidelines is low, except among organized feminist groups. Despite that, the guidelines exist, and there is growing industry support for them, and that in itself makes the Canadian advertising industry the world leader in attempting to eliminate sex stereotyping in advertising (Courtney and Whipple 1983, pp. 182–83).

It is worth noting that these guidelines have been administered by the CAF's AAB (now Advisory Division) and COGEP rather than through the ASC (now SD) and CNP because they are guidelines rather than part of the Canadian Code of Advertising Standards.[10] They are only enforced through exhortations addressed to the advertiser, since the AAB and COGEP, acting as advisory committees, have had no power to order changes or withdrawals. Unfortunately, very few advertisers and agencies have asked for assistance in reviewing creative ideas and executions in order to determine their conformity with the guidelines (Wyckham 1983, pp. 8–9); and a sizable proportion of advertisers have ignored the Advisory Committees when approached by the latter (Wyckham 1986, p. 13).

The Committee for Non-Sexist Advertising (Comité pour la Publicité Non-sexiste), which was established by the Status of Women Council to administer the Quebec government's antidiscrimination guidelines, started forwarding the complaints it received about sex-role stereotyping to the COGEP committee for processing (CRTC 1982, p. 58). The COGEP, however, referred to the Conseil des Normes de la Publicité all complaints having to do with pornographic depictions since Clause 15 (now 16) of the Canadian Code of Advertising Standards is relevant here. The first AAB and COGEP Advisory Committees' reports to the CRTC came out in September 1983, with a final one issued in the fall of 1984.[11] The Media Watch group[12] issued its own report to the CRTC, and hearings were held across the country in April 1986, with a CRTC report issued in December 1986.

Industry Conclusions. The Advertising Advisory Board, in its 1984 report to the CRTC, concluded that "notable progress" had been made toward the sensitization and education of the industry about the portrayal of women in advertising even though "this is a long-term process." About 20 percent of the commercials brought to its attention over a two-year period had been found to contravene the guidelines, as were 40 percent of print ads (mostly in newspapers). While the responsiveness of advertisers had been excellent, there were problems of enforcement because "there is no requirement for cooperation, and no punitive 'clout' attached to the Advisory Committee's decisions." The vast majority of the complaints (see Wyckham [1986] for details) had come through the Media Watch group (and its Quebec counterpart, Evaluation-Médias) but many were not relevant in light of the guidelines:

This input has been of mixed value—certainly it has contributed to the educational process, but it also had definite drawbacks. Many of the advertisements commented upon, while they may have had other faults, were messages which simply did not contravene the sex-role stereotyping guidelines. Some of the messages originated from outdated sources, and some were of U.S. or other foreign origin. Some individuals complained more than once about the same message; others perceived various secondary messages—perceptions not shared by the committee and staff. Such complaints tend to trivialize and undermine the credibility of the whole process (Wyckham 1986, p. 10).

The AAB and COGEP advisory committees had developed and distributed a bibliography and "interpretive comments" to those creating and approving ads. However, the promised public-attitude survey had to be postponed for lack of adequate funding (some research was funded, however), and the general public was not broadly informed about the existence of the guidelines, nor about the availability of a complaint process. Still, the advertising industry chose to interpret the low number (42 in 1985) of comments from the general public (versus 310 from Media Watch) as revealing that "the public at large had a much reduced level of concern with the portrayal of the sexes in advertising as compared to 1979 or 1980 (Pulse, May 1986, p. 1)." Broadcasters and advertisers thought that self-regulation had been effective "if only to the extent of 'sensitizing' those involved to the existence of the issue . . . the most important first step (CRTC 1986, p. 15)."

In March 1985, the Canadian Advertising Foundation announced the creation of two new committees: (1) the Advisory Panel on Sex-Role Stereotyping, designed to replace the Advisory Committee and to place more emphasis on educating small advertisers and agencies (the 1982–1984 efforts had focused on national advertisers, agencies and media), and (2) a separate Committee on Sexuality and Violence in Canadian Advertising to explore these issues and their implications, and "to defuse them in a positive, proactive manner before they become full-blown ugly issues (Pulse, August 1986, p. 2).'' These panels are preparing new guidelines and other initiatives to be submitted for ''acceptance'' by the CRTC. Meanwhile, complaints are handled by the AD and CNP.

Feminist Conclusions. Media Watch is a national volunteer organization whose members monitor the media for advertisements offensive to women. In its report to the CRTC, it cast a rather negative perspective on the industry's performance, reporting that very little progress had been made toward eliminating negative and traditional stereotypes from radio and television advertising. It resented that many of its complaints were not found to be justified by the AAB/COGEP advisory committees, or were referred to the ASC/CNP (under its ''taste, opinion, and public decency'' clause), to the Canadian Broadcasting Corporation and to advertisers for further consideration (Wyckham 1986, p. 14).

CRTC Conclusions. After listening to all sides and reviewing various research findings, the CRTC challenged the limited interpretation given by the advertising industry to the 1982 goals by emphasizing only ''the first step . . . to educate and sensitize, gradually changing attitudes and thus eventually improving women's portrayal in Canadian Broadcasting (CRTC 1986, p. 15).'' Besides, after 1984, industry effort and commitment had dwindled; representatives from the public had been dropped from AAB and COGEP advisory committees; complaint handling had progressively received less attention and publicity, and no effective penalties could be imposed. Consequently, the CRTC report concluded that: ''Considerable work has been done to sensitize and educate the industry and the public to the issue of sex-role stereotyping, and a significant effort has been made both by broadcasters and advertisers alike, as well as by members of the public to make self-regulation work. Notwithstanding this effort, however, the Commission concludes from all of the foregoing that self-regulation has been only partially successful and that further action is necessary (CRTC 1986, p. 46).''

The Canadian Advertising Foundation subsequently committed itself to renewed and expanded efforts: (1) to activate the Committee on Sexuality and Violence in Canadian Advertising, to explore this issue and its implications with committee members from the public sector as well as the advertising community, and to adjudicate complaints related to the presence of sexuality and violence in Canadian advertising; (2) to continue its work on sex-role stereotyping with a new, modified Advisory Panel on Sex-Role Stereotyping, made up of people from the industry who will screen and monitor complaints, and work with the industry to maintain the educational process; (3) to develop a program with advertisers and agencies to encourage voluntary consultation; (4) to develop education programs for advertisers and agencies—particularly, smaller ones; (5) to incorporate a statement with regard to the portrayal of women when codes of standards are revised or when new codes are developed; (6) to ensure that the sex-role stereotyping guidelines are considered whenever preclearance is required (that is, for children's and feminine-hygiene product commercials);[13] (7) to set firm and measurable objectives for the implementation of guidelines that may be identified as requiring particular attention (e.g., male/female voice-over ratio); (8) to monitor national and regional advertising for violations of the guidelines in order to initiate discussions with advertisers; (9) to develop a complaint-solicitation program to inform the general public more about its ability to register disapproval about specific commercials; (10) to provide for the staffing of a complaint-handling specialist, and (11) to report regularly to the CRTC on objectives, activities and results (CRTC 1986, pp. 28–30).

The sex-role stereotyping guidelines will ultimately be revised to make them more specific and measurable in terms of compliance, and to deal with sexuality, the sexualization of children, and violence; and they will have to be "accepted" by the CRTC prior to their adoption. (At first, interpretive comments will be provided until studies are completed.) "Members of the public knowledgeable about the issue" will be included on the Advisory Panel on Sex-Role Stereotyping as they already are on the Committee on Sexuality and Violence, which is expected to formulate guidelines regarding the use of sexuality in adult-directed advertising, and the use of violence in children-directed advertising.

The CRTC report stressed that: "There must be knowledgeable public representation chosen by industry to sit on the committees to maintain a fresh perspective on sex-role stereotyping when these committees view programs and commercials regarding complaints [because] the committees, in some cases, have been reduced to one or two persons who have total discretion to determine which complaints will be considered and upheld, as in the case of COGEP; and this, in the Commission's view, is too limited a review process (CRTC 1986, pp. 40–41)." The advertising industry has been reluctant to include "one-cause, single-minded" public members on these bodies, that is, feminists less able or willing to understand the advertiser's viewpoint. This contrasts with experience on the Advertising Standards Council, where public members are more seasoned, come from middle-of-the-road consumer associations, and deal with a large variety of issues. However, feminist representatives seem more willing lately to cooperate with the self-regulatory system and give it another chance.

Overall Appraisal. One can readily endorse Wyckham's conclusions about the 1982–1985 experience in the face of difficult demands by feminists, the intrinsic conservatism of the industry, the dearth of adequate research, and the lack of clout of the advisory committees:

The Canadian self-regulation of sex-role stereotypes in advertising should be considered a qualified success. Progress has been made. The industry has recognized the existence of a problem and has taken steps to adjust its behaviour. A self-regulatory body and process are in place. Increasingly, more advertising people are sensitive to the sex-role issue and doing something about it. However, there is still some distance to travel. The target distance depends on the perception of the ultimate objective. There is no question that, no matter how much is achieved, some individuals will be dissatisfied. Unfortunately because of a lack of research, it is not possible to say how much progress, in terms of public perceptions, has been made since 1982. Only a systematic tracking of public opinion will allow that determination. . . . The Canadian experiment with self-regulation of advertising sex stereotypes suggests that only significant, and likely ongoing, public pressure will cause the industry to adjust its portrayals of women. Change, after all, is risky. The level of risk to individual firms can be lessened by a process under which all companies must change together. Self-regulation, with some element of compulsion, can guide that change (Wyckham 1986, p. 15).

This "element of compulsion" is troublesome, however. The Canadian advertising industry can be justifiably criticized for its limited implementation of the 1982 goals to which it had subscribed—under threat, of course. Besides, it is perfectly appropriate for government bodies such as the CRTC to pressure the industry to do more and threaten it with more regulation. However, the industry is being dragged into helping solve a societal "problem of injustice and inequality" rather than one of mere "poor taste (CRTC 1986, p. 2)," with critics stressing that advertising is a powerful "socializer" rather than a mere business-communication tool (CRTC 1986, p. 33). Since there is truly no limit to "problems of injustice and inequality," the dragooning of the advertising industry into their solution promises to be endless, with no realistic anticipation that feminist organizations will ever be satisfied because, like other pressure groups, they are bound to keep expanding their demands—as with the recent shift to "sexuality and violence in advertising" beyond the earlier "sex-role stereotyping in advertising." The advertising industry is likely to comply with CRTC demands, but this evolution toward negotiated codes and quasidictating of self-regulatory structures raises questions about the limits of self-regulation—an issue addressed at the end of this chapter.

The Environment of Self-Regulation

Before analyzing outside participation in Canadian self-regulation, the key pressure groups that have affected the latter's development and operation will be briefly introduced.

Government

After 1960, the federal government enacted consumer-protection laws and regulations mainly administered by the Consumer and Corporate Affairs Canada Ministry. The Provinces have further elaborated on these measures, thereby complicating the advertisers' task of complying with the law (Belobaba 1985).

The federal government often invites business cooperation in the development of new standards and regulations, and encourages business self-regulation as a complement to the law—as is evidenced by the joint drafting by the ASC and the federal-level Consumer and Corporate Affairs Canada (with inputs from other groups) of guidelines for comparative food commercials, left to be administered by industry. Conversely, the SD and CNP invite inputs—formal or informal— from government when drawing up and revising codes and guidelines (Oliver

1975, p. 17). The federal government's generally positive attitude is evident in a 1983 press release:

Federal Consumer and Corporate Affairs Minister André Ouellet today commended the Advertising Standards Council for its initiative in publishing, for wide industry use, guidelines [for food commercials] . . . [and] added that the self-regulatory approach could be very useful in combatting [unfair commercials that are otherwise legal]. . . . The type of cooperation which took place is an example of how industry and government can work together to resolve problems through the creation of guidelines in lieu of legislation. . . . [The Minister] added that his officials would refer advertisers and advertising agencies to the [ASC] Council when proposed [food] commercials [which have to be precleared by his Ministry], otherwise in compliance with federal regulations, are considered to contravene the ASC Guidelines (Consumer and Corporate Affairs Canada, press release NR–83 of July 21, 1983, p. 2).

However, an official of Consumer and Corporate Affairs Canada commented in a letter to this author that:

Some reservations prevent [our] "endorsement" from being unconditional. There is a concern that there is at least the potential for some self-regulatory activity to be anticompetitive. In addition, there are obvious equity issues raised when practices, of the types which Parliament has prohibited as quasi-criminal, are dealt with by the relatively mild sanctions of a self-regulatory body when one of the body's members is involved; whereas similar practices (by a non-member, for example) referred to a government agency would probably result in convictions. Moreover, the relative weakness of the self-regulatory sanctions raises questions about effectiveness . . . [Still] the general government attitude towards self-regulation is positive [private communication].

The picture is more mixed in the Province of Quebec where: (1) there is broader acceptance of the regulatory approach; (2) consumerist and feminist organizations have been subsidized, and (3) the Consumer Protection Office is active and zealous. However, budgetary problems have led to government staff cuts and greater emphasis on the cost-benefit analysis of further regulation, although official doubts will linger about self-regulation until businessmen fully accept the recent consumerist legislation (for example, some firms have kept fighting the ban on advertising to children, as was seen before).

Altogether, the Canadian government has been an active and not-so-silent partner of advertising self-regulation by relying explicitly on it, by negotiating various standards with it, by linking other regulations to adherence to self-regulatory norms (e.g., in the case of CRTC licensing of broadcasters), and by subsidizing feminist organizations that have put pressure on the self-regulatory system.

The Consumer and Feminist Movements

The consumerist movement is dominated by the Consumers' Association of Canada (CAC), which is middle-of-the-road in orientation—in contrast to the feminist movement, which is more radical (Morningstar 1977; Goldstein 1979; Shapiro and Heslop 1982). The CAC is not hostile to business in general or to advertising in particular; it fosters dialogue and cooperation with them, and it supports self-regulation as a complement to the law. The CAC encourages its numerous volunteers to serve on governmental and business committees, councils and commissions such as the Advertising Standards Council and the Conseil des Normes de la Publicité, which have CAC representatives serving as public members; and other consumer associations have similar cooperating policies. However, the tobacco-advertising issue led to the temporary withdrawal of CAC public members in 1984–1986 (see above).

Some Quebec consumer associations have been very supportive of the Parti Québecois' socialistic and consumerist programs.[14] However, there is now some disenchantment with the interventionist approach—particularly following budget cuts and some broken promises (e.g., the 2 percent tax on commercials was to be used for counteradvertising, but just disappeared in the provincial government's coffers). Hence, self-regulation is looking more attractive to consumer associations as a free and fast complement to the law on account of the COGEP and CNP having succeeded in building up public visibility and credibility.

The federal and provincial governments grant subsidies to some consumer and feminist organizations, and they pay decent fees to public representatives sitting on government commissions and agencies. However, the advertising self-regulatory system only reimburses out-of-pocket expenses for transportation and babysitters. This has led to some refusals to serve on self-regulatory bodies as well as grumblings and resignations—particularly from feminist organizations—regarding their insufficient level of participation in the administration of the sex-stereotyping guidelines. Still, enough unpaid volunteers have been found to serve on the ASC, CNP and Advisory Committees.

Industry

Members of the advertising industry acknowledge that regulation is needed to curb excesses, while emphasizing the necessity and usefulness of self-regulation as a complement to the law. Yet, they are somewhat ambivalent about developing additional "quasilaws" through voluntary codes and guidelines. They are also somewhat divided about who should finance and control advertising self-regulation.

In connection with the 1981 restructuring of the whole system via the Canadian Advertising Foundation (CAF), a new financing system was introduced. Instead of relying on voluntary contributions from the Institute of Canadian Advertising (the agencies' organization) and from major advertisers and media, a levy (1/20 of 1 percent of media expenditures, to be collected by the media) was progressively phased in. This new financing system, administered by the CAF, did not work very well—mainly because of relatively weak economic conditions. Broadcasting-media members, in particular, were reluctant to collect the levy for fear that it would reduce their own revenues as some advertisers refused to increase their budgets accordingly. Consequently, the Foundation was forced to abandon the levy system in 1984, and it reverted to relying on its former sponsors.

However, the revenues obtained through the present system are insufficient to adequately finance four key bodies, seven regional councils,[15] and the administration of no fewer than eight codes and guidelines. Clearly, resources have not kept pace with responsibilities—a problem shared by most advertising self-regulatory systems around the world. The result is that the four parts of the system have to function with very small (although highly capable and dedicated) and even part-time staffs, particularly in Montreal.[16] Consequently, some of the plans to publicize self-regulation, to promote advertising and to research issues have definitely suffered—including the commitments made by the industry to government and feminist associations to monitor and study sex-stereotyping in advertising.

The advertisers argue that ultimately they are the ones who pay for self-regulation and, therefore, should call the shots. The media are afraid that any automatic levy on billings would only result in net smaller advertising budgets and revenues for them; while agency people think that advertisers have fought too many pointless battles against valid issues such as advertising to children, feminine-hygiene products and sexist stereotypes. These problems are currently hampering the expansion of the Canadian self-regulatory system at a time when its tasks and its commitments vis-à-vis government as well as consumerist and feminist associations have grown considerably. It is worth noting that Canada was one of the countries that checked the answer "Industry is willing to spend *some* money (and other resources) on advertising self-regulation but not too much" in the IAA survey (see Chapter 15).

Outside Participation

Code Development and Amendment

The Canadian Code of Advertising Standards was first developed in 1963 by the industry without outside participation, but this process has since been modified, as recounted by R. E. Oliver, who served for many years as president of the Advertising Standards Council:

Perhaps, at the time, our view of "self-regulation" was a little parochial—certainly it did not occur to us at the time to involve the government or the Consumers' Association of Canada. However, like so many other things in life, self-regulation is an evolutionary process. As time went by, the Council, whose function is to administer the Code, began to develop suggestions for updating the same and, of course, the Council by this time included public representatives. Certainly, when the [1982] edition was being drafted, some specific clauses were also checked with government authorities (private communication).

However, the 1986 edition of the Canadian Code of Advertising Standards does not list any nonindustry associations among those who reviewed and approved it (CAF, p. 15) although the national and regional councils, which include public members, were consulted.

Public Members on the ASC and CNP

The CAF's Standards Division administers eight codes and guidelines, and has a staff of four, including the CAF president. The new Advertising Standards Council, which sets direction and policy for the Standards Division, is headed by a volunteer chairperson coming from the industry, who votes only in the case of a tie, and has fourteen voting members:

The 14 voting members are selected by the President in consultation with the various sectors represented. Three members shall be persons whose principal affiliation is with an advertiser or an advertising trade association, and at least two of them shall be nominees of the Association of Canadian Advertisers; three members shall be persons whose principal affiliation is with an advertising agency or an advertising trade association, and at least two of them shall be nominees of the Institute of Canadian Advertising; three shall be nominees of media associations endorsing the Code of Advertising Standards; five members shall be public members, nominated by broadly-based community interest groups such as academics, the Better Business Bureau, Consumers' Association of Canada, Status of Women Groups, the "Y" [YMCA, YWCA], etc. At least two of the public representatives shall be members of the Consumers' Association of Canada. In addition the Council/Conseil and its committees, when special issues arise (e.g., portrayals of the aging, minority groups, etc.) may invite qualified individuals to act as resource personnel (Section 1.2).[17]

It is worth noting that, compared to the 1982 structure, the number of "public members" has been increased from three to five. However, the representation of the Consumers' Association of Canada has been proportionately reduced since its two members now represent only two-fifths, instead of two-thirds, of the public members. This change was proposed by the CAC during the discussions arising from the temporary withdrawal of CAC participation in ASC-CNP activities in 1984–1986, in connection with the tobacco-advertising issue mentioned before. (The CAC also reviewed its relationships with all other "outside" organizations to ensure that its autonomy was not being compromised.) Consequently, the new structure broadens outside participation, but also minimizes the possible interference of any single outside group.

The inclusion of public members was a Canadian pioneering innovation designed to add expertise to the system:

The addition of consumer representatives again was part of the evolutionary process. Since most of our complaints came from consumers, and most of them, at least in the consumer's mind, were quite justified, we felt it appropriate to add the public voice to

Council deliberations, and I believe we were the first advertising self-regulatory body in the world to do so. . . . In our experience, the consumers have added a valuable dimension to our discussions, particularly since our judgments regarding "accuracy [and] clarity" have to do with the message *as perceived*. Who can comment better than those who are doing the perceiving? I don't think anyone in our industry would now want to silence the consumer voices on the Council—and we have found their representatives to be intelligent, fair-minded, firm and constructive (private communication from R. E. Oliver).

Public Members on Preclearance Committees

The 1972–1973 Broadcast Code for Advertising to Children was developed under the aegis of the ASC, working with the Canadian Association of Broadcasters as well as with advertisers and agencies, in response to public criticism and pressure for legislation. Having adopted this Code, the broadcasters asked the ASC to administer it on their behalf, as a complement to the Canadian Code of Advertising Standards. (It has been inoperative in Quebec Province, where there has been a legal ban on such advertising.) All commercial messages directed to children or appearing on children's programs must conform to the Code; and all finished commercials must be precleared by the Standard Division's Children's Advertising Section, which also handles public complaints about such commercials. This Children's Section has nine members: a chairperson; three public representatives, at least two of whom are nominees of the Consumers' Association of Canada; and one member each nominated by the CRTC, the Canadian Broadcasting Corporation, and the broadcaster, advertiser and advertising associations.

A similar setup applies to the 1979 Television Code of Standards for the Advertising of Feminine Sanitary Protection Products. Such commercials must be precleared by an eight-member panel: a chairperson; three people representing the public, and one member each nominated by the private broadcaster, public broadcaster (CBC), advertiser and agency associations. (Preclearance, however, is not required for French-language commercials.)

Public Members on the AAB and COGEP

The 1981 CAAB (now AD) Advisory Committee on Sex-Role Stereotyping and the CNP (or COGEP) Comité Consultatif sur les Stéréotypes Sexistes were each made up of seven members: (1) four from advertisers, agencies, broadcast and print media, and (2) three "public members," two of whom represent "recognized feminist organizations." These Advisory Committees have been restructured into panels (see above) with a similar composition.

Public Members' Behavior and Influence

The bulk of complaint-handling is carried out by the permanent staff of the SD, CNP, AD and COGEP.[18] The ASC/CNP councils meet only every two months to hear and discuss reports about the staff's activities, and to decide a few "high-judgment" cases, often involving matters of taste, but also including appeals by the advertiser or complainant over a staff decision. (Similar meetings took place for the AAB-COGEP Advisory Committees on Sex-Role Stereotyping every three months.) The minority position of consumer and feminist representatives on these bodies has not meant, however, that they do not wield significant influence.

1. As in France and the United Kingdom, many cases handled by the self-regulatory system consist of either improperly addressed complaints (e.g., about a product's performance, which is not an advertising matter), excluded subjects (e.g., political advertising) and relatively simple "open-and-shut" cases about false, misleading and unfair advertisements—some 90 percent of them—whose resolution can be speedily handled by the staff who may, however, telephone Council members for advice between meetings. (It is well to remember that one major advantage of self-regulation is its speed, simplicity and relative cheapness so that asking the full Council to handle hundreds of cases a year would overwhelm the present system.)

The SD and CNP staffs have considerable discretion in deciding what is not an acceptable complaint, and in choosing what cases to bring before the full Council whose members have no detailed information about other cases since they only see general reports classifying complaints by product category, origin and types of violation (Moyer and Banks 1977). However, staff recommendations are not always followed; and Council members can spotcheck what the staff does, besides raising new problems at Council meetings.[19] Still, compared to the United Kingdom, where the Advertising Standards Authority Council's members see all relevant cases in abbreviated form, can freely overturn staff decisions, and do play a more significant role in code revision, the Canadian system looks relatively underdeveloped. But then, the French system relies practically entirely on staff work, with no outside participation in complaint handling.

2. The cases handled by the full ASC/CNP councils and by the AAB-COGEP Advisory Committees or panels have dealt mostly with "taste, opinion and public decency" and with the sex-role stereotyping guidelines. This is where the expertise of outside members lies, because industry representatives may be thought to have too narrow or self-interested a perspective on such issues. Consequently, industry members typically defer in such matters to outside members—particularly if the latter are unanimous in opposing a controversial advertisement. Consistent rejection of such unanimous views could lead to the resignation of outside members; and the resulting fracas would put into question the legitimacy and credibility of the system. Actually, most decisions are based on a consensus—sometimes a fragile one, as with the tobacco-advertising issue, which generated a breakdown whose impact was only minimized by the discreet silence maintained about it by both sides.

3. Such a consensual approach depends on the careful selection of both "inside" and "outside" members as well as on the skills of the presiding officers

in creating the right mix and chemistry; and much successful attention has been paid to these matters. Consumer and feminist associations are typically asked to nominate delegates and alternates. While there is no profile of the "right" candidate, interviewees generally stressed conviction without fanaticism, articulateness without logorrhea, independence ("not being subdued by so-called professionals") without unwillingness to hear and heed. The trick is to avoid the "professionals" and the "antis," as is also true in the case of industry members; and rotation is necessary to avoid fatigue and undue cooptation by the system.

It appears that consumer representatives have generally met these requirements—largely because of the middle-of-the-road philosophy of Canadian consumer organizations and of most of their volunteers. As one industry interviewee put it: "Sometimes, new consumer representatives at first use the new podium they have acquired to vent pet peeves, 'wave the flag' and 'let it out of their system.' Once purged of that pent-up stuff, they make marvelous participants. Like U.S. Presidents, they 'rise to the office'—and so do we." Feminist representatives on the AAB/COGEP (now AD and CNP) sex-stereotyping advisory committees are newer to the system and seemingly less accommodating, asking for changes in the guidelines and their stricter enforcement.

4. Outside members, although in a minority, can induce industry representatives to change their behavior. As one industry respondent put it:

Outsiders force advertising representatives on the ASC Council to focus on the content of the ads discussed rather than on defending advertising at large. This gives a sense of objectivity to the proceedings. I have to forget that I am an advertiser: I no longer just represent advertisers but the self-regulation of advertising. In theory, no outsiders are needed but they provide a leavening, a constant reminder to think of the consumer and to stay at arm's length of the industry. Because you are under scrutiny, you behave better than you thought possible. You do not want to look like an ass before smart people; and why win on some stupid point and have them retaliate on some other matter?

The minority public representatives are backed up by their organizations and the weight of consumerist and feminist public opinion. These outside forces are silently present at self-regulatory meetings, lending great moral and political conviction and even a threat to what the public members say and do. Even if defeated, they can fight their battles elsewhere and endlessly—and they can resign and damn the self-regulatory system. The tobacco-advertising and sex-stereotyping issues have revealed that consumer and feminist organizations are not mere "token" participants in the self-regulatory process.

5. The tobacco-advertising episode also involved some information leakage about ASC deliberations. This led to an addition to its operating rules:

Council Confidentiality. In assessing complaints, answering queries and in clearing scripts, storyboards and commercials, Council staff and Council members frequently are made privy to confidential company information and proprietary data such as product components, market data, future promotional plans, etc. So, if the Council is to function effectively, companies must be sure that information submitted to Council staff or members remains confidential. This confidentiality, of course, does not preclude Council members from reporting to their parent association on Council activities or from consulting with them on a confidential basis or with regulatory authorities on matters of principle. But Council participation does preclude members from discussing the specifics of Council deliberations with other outside organizations unless the Council has already made its position public. In order to maintain Council credibility and effectiveness, any member who breaks this rule of confidentiality will be asked to resign (ASC Organization and Procedures 1986, Section 4.0).

6. An interesting twist is that the French-Canadian Conseil des Normes de la Publicité is now run by the former founder and director (1973–1975) of the Quebec Government's Consumer Protection Office, who is still very active in consumer associations. Thus, the self-regulatory staff has its own in-house consumerist, an approach that provides greater legitimacy to the system and facilitates contact with consumer and feminist organizations.

Conclusions

Because it was the first to introduce the practices of outside representation, to publicize its code and invite the public to complain, and to explicitly handle difficult matters of ''taste, opinion and public decency,'' the Canadian advertising industry lays claim to being a world model in the self-regulatory field. This claim is essentially valid and, as such, provides a touchstone for some of the new issues facing self-regulation—particularly in developed countries. Still, without minimizing the value of its achievements, some important questions can be raised about: (1) the overall shape and evolution of Canadian advertising self-regulation, and (2) the participation of outsiders in its functioning (cf. Moyer and Banks [1977]; and Wyckham [May 1985] for further discussions of strengths and weaknesses).

1. Self-regulatory standards have been regularly expanded and revised to address new issues. Outsiders have usually played an indirect role in this process, except when formal negotiations took place (e.g., about sex-role stereotyping and comparative food commercials). As in other countries, the industry has typically reacted to government and other pressures rather than anticipated problems, although reaction time has shortened and forceful initiatives have been more evident lately. It felt ill at ease dealing with the ''softer'' issues revolving around ''taste, opinion and public decency'' (feminine-hygiene products and sex-stereotypes) and vulnerable groups (children), but it finally came to handle them on account of such outside pressures.

2. Relatively little publicity has been given to the self-regulatory system to make it better known and invite more complaints, although it is acknowledged that less promotion means fewer consumer complaints (Oliver 1976, p. 10). However, more efforts are evident lately, particularly at the regional level,

although no national survey has been conducted about what people know and think of it—as has been done in France and the United Kingdom—for lack of adequate funding in a country where bilingualism and regionalism make national surveys more expensive.

3. The SD and CNP provide prepublication advice to advertisers, sometimes for a fee, as in the case of comparative food commercials. Besides, the SD handles the mandatory preclearance of English feminine-hygiene and children advertisements. Less success, however, has been encountered in the matter of sex-role stereotyping in advertising, although Canada is doing much more than other countries in this regard.

4. The monitoring of ads and commercials is rather weak, compared to U.K. and French efforts. Part of this situation is because of the lack of adequate financial resources, but interviews with various industry members actively involved in self-regulation revealed some reluctance to let the SD and CNP assume a greater role in this respect:

Monitoring should not replace the role of consumers as a source of complaints. There is a danger of witch-hunting here; and it could lead to government funding because of the necessary scope and cost. I do not need to be policed except by the government [an advertiser]. Advertising has low visibility and generates relatively few complaints. If you jack up their number artificially through monitoring, complaints will stop being a touch-stone of what bothers consumers [an agency representative].

5. Complaint-handling has not been lax, what with some 19 to 24 percent of valid consumer complaints being upheld in recent years. Only twice a year must the SD-CNP notify the media about an uncooperative advertiser. While the enforcement system has been weaker in the case of sex-role stereotyping, Canada has probably done more than any other country to cope directly and explicitly with this difficult issue. The complaint-handling task will not become any simpler if the prediction that the SD-CNP caseload will triple within the next two years turns out to be true, with the Canadian respondent to the sixteen-country IAA survey referring to such "social concerns" as environment, health, sexuality, sex-role stereotyping, violence (especially in commercials directed to children) and advertiser-sponsored children programs" (see Chapter 15).

6. Regarding the publicizing of its sanctions, the SD and CNP only publish very general analyses of the cases they handle, by source and type, but the names of the wrongdoers are never publicized—as is done in the United Kingdom and the United States—because industry is strongly opposed to it: "Why give a black eye to advertisers?" If an advertiser agrees to withdraw or modify his ad, nobody else is notified.

7. The Canadian experience reveals broad acceptance of the complementarity of self-regulation by industry and regulation by government. The federal authorities and the Consumers' Association of Canada have long held such a view, but more radical entities such as the former Parti Québecois government and

feminist organizations have come to share it, if only tenuously. As Niquette Delage, head of the self-regulatory CNP and former director of Quebec's Consumer Protection Office put it: "Three years spent in government, implementing the law, have convinced me that regulation won't be sufficient even though it is necessary to deal with uncooperative businessmen [récalcitrants]." While the law reaches everybody, even recalcitrants, self-regulation's strengths lie in its accessibility, simplicity, speed and cheapness for complainants and its voluntary acceptance by business people.

Wyckham's analysis of the costs and benefits of Canadian advertising self-regulation is particularly revealing in this regard. He concluded that: (1) the federal and provincial governments handle more complaints at a lower cost per complaint, but that self-regulation resolves them more cheaply (Wyckham April 1985, pp. 27–28); (2) government offices investigate only a fraction of the complaints they receive while the SD and CNP process all complaints covered by the Code (Wyckham April 1985, p. 28); (3) regulators have the resources to seek out and deal with deceptive advertisements not likely to be easily detected by the public, while the SD/CNP rely only on the complaints they receive (Wyckham April 1985, p. 29); (4) regulatory penalties can be high but self-regulation can deny access to the necessary media (Wyckham April 1985, pp. 29–30); (5) the law is generally slower than self-regulation (six to seven weeks) but may have a stronger deterrent effect (Wyckham April 1985, pp. 30–32); (6) self-regulation tends to deal with isolated incidents rather than repeated patterns of behavior and constant violators, as the law can (Wyckham April 1985, pp. 33–34), and (7) self-regulation is a continuous force whose learning effect may be more influential than the deterrent effect of law (Wyckham April 1985, p. 30) because it emphasizes the spirit rather than the letter of voluntarily accepted standards. Wyckham concluded:

There is a variety of advertising problems for which self-regulation is ideally suited. Advertisements which mislead consumers but result from poor management practices, a lack of quality control of advertising copy, inappropriate behavior of employees and consumer misperceptions, rather than management intention to mislead, are best handled by the Advertising Standards Council [p. 44]. . . . Unfortunately, there is no mechanism to channel advertising problems to the most effective regulator [p. 43]. . . . Neither self-regulation nor government regulation of advertising has a monopoly on efficiently dealing with misleading advertising. Working side by side, they seem to be capable of providing a service badly needed by consumers and competitors (Wyckham April 1985, pp. 44–45).

He could have added that Canadian governments have shied away from various "taste and opinion" issues, and have encouraged their handling through self-regulation involving the participation of outsiders.

8. By and large, the leaders and supporters of the Canadian self-regulatory system have managed to tame regulatory fervors quickly by providing effective voluntary alternatives, although less so in Québec Province until recently. Most

of these initiatives have been reactive rather than proactive, but there is growing awareness that the advertising industry should get better at the latter. Business is usually slower in detecting emerging issues, appraising their worth, developing a consensus, and shaping up responses—good or bad—than the political system with its greater openness and sensitivity to pressure groups (but see Belobaba 1985 for a less positive conclusion). This is probably a fact of life that will continue to limit business to a reactive role, although the speed and quality of its responses can be improved. Here, the greater speed and openness in coping with the recent "multiculturalism" issue (showing all races in advertisements) contrasts favorably with the slowness in acknowledging and handling the sex-role stereotyping problem.

9. The "taste, opinion and public decency" issue reveals that Canadian self-regulation has gone beyond the handling of false, misleading and unfair advertising into softer and more controversial areas. This is where most of the future battles will be fought (e.g., tobacco and alcohol advertising, and sex-role stereotyping), with business acknowledging that: "It is essential to tread the often narrow line between reflecting society as it is and society as some may wish it to be (Advertising Advisory Board 1984, p. 2)."

In this context, the preclearance of children and feminine-hygiene commercials has cast the SD into the role of censor of business behavior (the self-regulatory Telecaster Committee funded by most major private broadcasters also plays a censoring role). Actually, the Broadcast Code for Advertising to Children has taken the character of a law since the Canadian Radio-Television Telecommunications Commission makes compliance with it a condition for station licensing—and the same requirement will apply to the guidelines on sex-role stereotyping as well as sex and violence in advertising. It is one thing for a self-regulatory system to provide advice to the industry before advertisements are finalized—most foreign systems do it too. It is another to assume a censor's role by handing out preclearance visas. Business may come to rebel against this practice (which could be extended to tobacco and liquor advertising and other sensitive areas) because it departs too much from the voluntary character of the other phases of self-regulation.

10. Even if the Canadian self-regulatory system is not overreaching itself, is it overburdening itself? As each new issue reaches a critical stage, the industry grabs it and develops some new mechanism to cope with it: children, feminine-hygiene products, sex-role stereotypes, comparison advertising, multiculturalism and—soon—sexuality and violence. New codes, clauses, guidelines, preclearance systems, advisory committees and the like multiply without any commensurate increase in resources—human and financial. There is a clear danger of loss of effectiveness and credibility, as has happened in many countries where governments pass all sorts of new regulations to prove they are aware, concerned and responsive, but without increasing enforcement budgets, which may even be cut in recessionary times.

The same trap threatens Canadian advertising self-regulation unless it can marshal new resources from industry or from the government. State grants, however, would jeopardize the autonomy of the system and move it toward corporatism. Some tasks such as the monitoring of compliance with codes and guidelines could be left to consumerist and feminist organizations, provided they are able and willing to do it—as is already the case with sex-role stereotyping. There is also some move toward codes negotiated between business, government and consumer associations—rather than pure industry ones—as with the sex-stereotyping and comparative-advertising guidelines. This may well be the modern price to pay to ward off regulation, but self-regulation will never be the same thereafter.

11. It may be flattering to industry to be approached by government to develop alternatives to regulation, but would it be better off using the lobbying process to fight off unfriendly legislation? This has been the U.S. approach—with the self-regulatory system (NAD-NARB) limiting itself to the relatively classical task of complaint handling, while letting the advertiser, agency and media associations as well as the American Advertising Federation handle the rest through lobbying. A recent statement by the Chairman of the Association of Canadian Advertisers echoes this opposition to endless accommodation:

Self-regulation must be kept in perspective—its value understood, but also its limitations and its potential for the creation of misunderstanding. We regulate our industry, in part at least, in order to maintain responsibility for our own performance—to keep the intrusive and often heavy hand of government at reasonable distance. To do so intelligently, we anticipate government policies in many fields—from public health to cultural diversity—and work to reflect such policy before being forced into doing so. And yet, there is a danger point. If, for example, government were to formulate a policy for purely political and self-serving ends, how wise would we be to unwittingly comply with it in advance? Were the industry to sense such a possibility on the horizon, it would be far wiser and far more ethical to exert its point of view than to simply comply and congratulate itself on how efficient it is at self-regulation (ACA Newsletter No. 1423, July 11 1985, p. 3).

There is an insidious but significant danger that, although no broad frontal attack against advertising is intended by government and/or pressure groups, this industry may progressively find itself sliced to pieces as it yields on one special topic after another. Advertising's role may be accepted in principle, but a chorus of criticisms has grown about "vulnerable groups" (e.g., children, smokers and drinkers), "good taste" and "sexism." Accommodating each one of these partial demands may make tactical sense—each battle has been successfully engaged and regulation avoided—but may ultimately lead to strategic disaster—the war has been lost because industry has come to entangle itself in endless self-imposed restrictions for shortcomings it acknowledges after some grumbling.

It is becoming obvious that there are limits to what advertising self-regulation can and should handle. Past an undefined point, which the Canadian system may be fast approaching, it becomes overburdened, overwhelmed and something else altogether. There is an old French proverb "Qui trop embrasse mal étreint" which can be translated into "Grab all, lose all." Both versions are well worth pondering in this bilingual country.

12. The inclusion of outsiders does not reduce outside pressures on the self-regulatory system. Consumerists and feminists keep demanding more regulations, code revisions and guidelines; and they monitor the behavior of advertisers to see if they adhere to the voluntary codes. If anything, pressure groups are now better informed about the functioning and effectiveness of self-regulation since they have been involved in its devising and functioning, and thus can make more relevant and realistic demands.

Altogether, these are positive developments, which support the use of outsiders in advertising self-regulation. By pioneering in this field and succeeding at it, Canada has helped other nations (e.g., the United Kingdom) move in that direction. More countries can also learn from its struggling with the soft issues that are likely to keep festering or burgeoning (depending on one's inclination) around the world, although the Canadian experience suggests that advertising self-regulation has to be careful about assuming too many responsibilities in this area.

NOTES

1. For further details about the Canadian system, see: ASC (1986); Canadian Advertising Foundation [CAF] (1986); Moyer and Banks (1977); Neelankavil and Stridsberg (1980); Oliver (1986); and Wyckham (April and May 1985, 1986 and 1987). The first Code was issued in 1963 but the Advertising Standards Council dates from 1967.

2. The nomenclature used in this chapter is complex because of several name changes in recent years. In 1986, the Advertising Advisory Board (AAB) was renamed the Advisory Division (of CAF) because it was not an advisory "board." The AD handles the "social development" issues of sex-role stereotyping, sexuality and violence, multiculturalism, and portrayal of the aged in advertising, through panels and committees. The Standards Division (SD) used to be known as the Advertising Standards Council (ASC) when, in fact, it is the SD staff that conduct day-to-day operations regarding complaints and other matters. The ASC remains, however, as a volunteer group of individuals headed by a volunteer chairperson, who set direction and policy for the Standards Division and handle most appeals to SD decisions.

3. The multiculturalism issue refers to the problem of white Anglo-Saxon types dominating Canadian advertisements and commercials in what is in fact a multicultural society (Equality Now 1984). This problem is being handled informally by the advertising industry through discussions within the industry, and with governments and ethnic groups, rather than through formal codes or guidelines.

4. There are other advertising codes and guidelines that have been developed by associations, firms and broadcasting stations, but they are not handled by the SD and CNP, nor are they discussed here.

5. Comparison advertising has been a controversial practice in Canada as much as elsewhere (Boddewyn and Marton 1978). A committee including industry, consumer and government representatives concluded that existing industry and government guidelines were too vague to give real direction to those who create food commercials and approve them (that is, the Consumer and Corporate Affairs Canada ministry). Consequently, Guidelines for the Use of Comparative Advertising in Food Commercials (and the use

of research and survey data in this matter) were developed in 1983, and they have been implemented by the SD/CNP in the same manner as the other industry codes it applies.

6. The 1986 Code revision also benefited from comments received from the national and regional councils, which include public (that is, nonindustry) members.

7. This section borrows from Oliver (1986) but was complemented by various telephone interviews with key protagonists.

8. The addition of this clause required renumbering the old "Taste, opinion, public decency" clause as No. 16, after removing its second part to the introductory part of the Code.

9. Scheduling restrictions were imposed in response to consumer demands. However, they led to an undue concentration of feminine-hygiene commercials after 9 PM, which, in turn, produced new consumer complaints. An experimental "open scheduling" of these commercials led to no complaints (Pulse May 1986, p. 2).

10. The Canadian Association of Broadcasters' Code of Ethics and the Canadian Broadcasting Corporation's commercial acceptance code now include clauses against sex-role stereotyping (Wyckham 1986, p. 14).

11. Besides various publicity efforts, this report mentioned that sex-stereotype guidelines are now considered when comparative food commercials and advertisements directed to children are reviewed, and that research is underway (Sex-Role Stereotyping 1983).

12. The Federal government gave $50,000 to the Media Watch group, whose members send in complaints regularly — particularly from British Columbia and Ontario. Feminist organizations are regularly subsidized by various governments.

13. CRTC licensing requirements now include broadcaster adherence to the CAB's "Broadcasting Industry Self-Regulatory Code on Sex-Role Stereotyping." The Media Watch organization has published several reports and statements on this topic.

14. This socialistic party was voted out of office in December 1985, and a more centrist (Liberal) government now rules Quebec Province.

15. The seven regional councils now handle more complaints (341 in 1986) than the national office in Toronto (291 complaints, including those from Ontario Province). Their structure and mode of operations differ somewhat from those of the national office (CAF 1986).

16. The Toronto Office, where the CAF, AD and SD are located, now has a staff of eight full-time people. In Montreal, COGEP had two full-timers and the CNP has three part-timers (plus several intermittent assistants), but their involvement is being expanded as the CNP assumes COGEP's tasks.

17. Like other ASC members, public members serve a two-year term, which is immediately renewable once, and again after being off the Council for a full term. They do not receive any fee but are reimbursed for out-of-pocket expenses. Alternate delegates are appointed to ensure that all sides are normally represented at meetings. The six English-region ASC councils have a similar structure, which is also found in the French-region Conseil des Normes de la Publicité, except that the Association des Consommateurs du Québec (ACQ), the Women's Education and Social Action Association (AFEAS) and the Quebec Consumer Advisers' Association (ACCQ) provide the "public representatives," together with the French branch of the Consumers' Association of Canada.

18. For an analysis of the CNP complaint-handling process, see *Publi-Normes*, 4, 3, September 1985.

19. Staffs and councils across Canada closed a total of 634 complaints in 1986 (versus 541 complaints in 1985, and 998 in 1984). Appeals to staff decisions are handled by the

full ASC Council. Only about 2 percent of the cases are referred to the full SD/CNP councils, but this proportion has been higher in the case of sex-stereotyping cases.

REFERENCES

Advertising Advisory Board. *Final Report; Advisory Committee on Sex-Role Stereotyping to the Canadian Radio-Television Telecommunications Commission.* Toronto: Fall 1984.

Advertising Standards Council (ASC). *Manual of General Guidelines for Advertising.* Toronto: 1975.

————. *Organization and Procedures of the Advertising Standards Council.* Toronto: October 1982 and January 1986.

Association of Canadian Advertisers (ACA). *Newsletter*, No. 1423 (July 11, 1985): 3.

Belobaba, E. P. "The Development of Consumer Protection Regulation: 1945 to 1984." In *Consumer Protection, Environmental Law and Corporate Power*, edited by Ivan Bernier, and Andrée Lajoie. Toronto: University of Toronto Press, 1985, 1–88.

Boddewyn, J. J. *Advertising to Children: An International Survey of Its Regulation and Self-Regulation.* New York: International Advertising Association, 1984.

————. *Decency and Sexism in Advertising: An International Survey of Their Regulation and Self-Regulation.* New York: International Advertising Association, 1979.

Boddewyn, J. J., and K. Marton. *Comparison Advertising: A Worldwide Study.* New York: Hastings House, 1978.

Canadian Advertising Foundation (CAF). *The Canadian Code of Advertising Standards.* Toronto: May 1986. The French version, *Le Code Canadien des Normes de la Publicité*, was published in July 1986 by the Fondation Canadienne de la Publicité (FCP, Montreal).

————. *Who Speaks for Advertising?* Toronto: 1982.

————. *Pulse; The Canadian Advertising Foundation Newsletter.* May 1986, August 1986.

Canadian Radio-Television and Telecommunications Commission (CRTC). *Images of Women; Report of the Task Force on Sex-Role Stereotyping in the Broadcast Media.* Ottawa: Minister of Supply and Services, 1982.

————. *Policy on Sex-Role Stereotyping in the Broadcast Media.* Ottawa: December 22, 1986.

Courtney, A. E., and T. W. Whipple. *Sex Stereotyping in Advertising.* Lexington, Mass.: D. C. Heath, 1983.

Equality Now! Minutes of Proceedings and Evidence of the Special Committee on Participation of Visible Minorities in Canadian Society. Ottawa: House of Commons, no. 4 (March 8, 1984).

Forbes, J. D. "Organizational/Political Dimensions of Consumer Pressure Groups." Mimeographed. Vancouver, BC: Faculty of Commerce and Business Administration, University of British Columbia, October 1983.

Goldberg, M. E. "TV Advertising Directed at Children; Inherently Unfair or Simply in Need of Regulation?" In *Marketplace Canada: Some Controversial Dimensions*, edited by S. J. Shapiro, and Louise Heslop. Toronto: McGraw-Hill Ryerson, 1982, pp. 1–31.

Goldstein, Jonah. "Public Interest Groups and Public Policy: The Case of the Consumers'

Association of Canada." *Canadian Journal of Sociology* 12, no. 1 (March 1979): 137–55.

Heslop, Louise, and A. E. Courtney. "Advertising and Women." In *Marketplace Canada: Some Controversial Dimensions*, edited by S. J. Shapiro, and Louise Heslop. Toronto: McGraw-Hill Ryerson, 1982, pp. 59–85.

Morningstar, H. J. "The Consumers' Association of Canada; The History of an Effective Organization." *Canadian Business Review* 4 (Autumn 1977): 30–33.

Moyer, M. S. "Public Participation in Making Marketing Policies: A Canadian Experiment." *The Business Quarterly* [Western Ontario] (Winter 1979): 63–72.

Moyer, M. S., and J. C. Banks. "Industry Self-Regulation: Some Lessons from the Canadian Advertising Industry." In *Problems in Canadian Marketing*, edited by D. N. Thompson. Chicago, Ill.: American Marketing Association, 1977, pp. 185–202.

Neelankavil, J. P., and A. B. Stridsberg. *Advertising Self-Regulation: A Global Perspective*. New York: Hastings House, 1980.

Oliver, R. E. "Ethics in Advertising — A Shared Responsibility." In J. J. Boddewyn. *Advertising Self-Regulation: 16 Advanced Systems*, New York: International Advertising Association, October 1986, pp. 81–91.

———. "Tuning in on the Turned-off." Mimeographed speeches. Toronto: Canadian Advertising Advisory Board, 1975 and 1976.

Olley, R. E. "The Canadian Consumer Movement: Basis and Objectives." *Canadian Business Review* (Autumn 1977): 26–29.

Publi-Normes. Montreal: Conseil des Normes de la Publicité 4, 3 (September 1985).

"Sex-Role Stereotyping Committee Presents Interim Progress Report." *Advisory* [AAB Newsletter] (November 1983): 1–2.

Shapiro, S. J., and Louise Heslop, eds. *Marketplace Canada: Some Controversial Dimensions*. Toronto: McGraw-Hill Ryerson, 1982.

Task Force on Women and Advertising. *Women and Advertising: Today's Messages—Yesterday's Images?* Toronto: Canadian Advertising Advisory Board, November 1979.

Wyckham, R. G. "Advertising Self-Regulation: An Analysis of Costs and Benefits." In *Proceedings of the Annual Conference 1985 of the European Marketing Academy; Bielefeld, Germany, April 1985*. Brussels, Belgium: European Marketing Academy, April 1985, pp. 225–47. The final version appears as: "Industry and Government Advertising Regulation: An Analysis of Relative Efficiency and Effectiveness." *Canadian Journal of Administrative Sciences* 4, no. 1 (March 1987): 31–51.

———. "The Advertising Standards Council: A Critical Examination." In *The Information Society: Its Implications for Marketing; Proceedings of the Annual Meeting*, edited by J. C. Chabot. Montreal: Administrative Sciences Association of Canada, Marketing Division, May 1985, pp. 343–50.

———. "Female Stereotyping in Advertising." Mimeographed. Burnaby, BC: Simon Fraser University, Faculty of Business Administration, Discussion Paper 83–01–02, 1983.

———. "Self-Regulation of Sex-Role Stereotyping in Advertising: The Canadian Experience." Mimeographed. Burnaby, BC: Simon Fraser University, January 1986. To appear in revised form in *Journal of Public Policy and Marketing* 6 (1987).

ACKNOWLEDGMENTS

The assistance of the following people is gratefully acknowledged: Sally Ackerman (Consumers' Association of Canada), Jean-Marie Allard (former president of COGEP), Gilberte Bechara (Office de la Protection du Consommateur, Québec), Susan Burke (CAF), Pat Beatty (Telecaster Committee of Canada), Jacques Dagenais (Office de la Protection du Consommateur, Québec), Donald H. Davis (Canada Starch), Niquette Delage (Managing Director, Conseil des Normes de la Publicité), J. D. Forbes (University of British Columbia), John Foss (President, Association of Canadian Advertisers), Bill Givens (Global Television Network; ASC), Ada Hill (Federation of Women Teachers' Association of Ontario), Louise A. Heslop (Carleton University; ASC), Louise Imbeault (Canadian Broadcasting Corporation), Suzanne Keeler (CAF), R. H. McKay (Consumer and Corporate Affairs Canada), Keith B. McKerracher (President, Institute of Canadian Advertising), Michael Kennerly (General Foods; CAF), Robert E. Oliver (former President, Advertising Standards Council), J. H. C. Penaligon (Outdoor Advertising Association of Canada), Alan Rae (President, CAF), Barbara J. Shand (Consumers' Association of Canada), Marc Alain Soucy (Bureau d'Éthique Commerciale), Robert Tamilia (University of Québec, Montreal), Pierre Valois (Office de la Protection du Consommateur, Québec), J. A. Walker (Consumer and Corporate Affairs Canada), R. G. Wyckham (Simon Fraser University), and Ronald G. Willoughby (Imperial Oil; ASC).

6

Federal Republic of Germany:
The Deutsche Werberat

Advertising self-regulation (ASR) assumes several forms in the Federal Republic of Germany but the German Advertising Council (Deutscher Werberat, DWR) is its main organ. This body is fairly unique among advertising self-regulatory systems because it deals predominantly with matters of "taste and opinion," which other national ASR systems either completely ignore or handle rather reluctantly or marginally. Besides, the Werberat includes no outsiders (that is, nonindustry members) at all, and thus represents the extreme case of pure self-regulation. This unique situation is linked to the ready availability of legal remedies for most advertising problems in Germany, and to the subordinated rather than autonomous role of the German Werberat within the German Advertising Federation (ZAW). Yet it has not prevented the Werberat from making valuable contributions to the improvement of German advertising behavior.

These conclusions were reached through a partial review of relevant literature as well as through interviews with nine industry, consumerist, academic and legal experts during a one-week research visit to Germany in August 1985, followed by correspondence with these people as well as other qualified observers of the German scene (see Acknowledgments).

German Law and Advertising

Relevant Regulations

While some twenty laws affect marketing and advertising, the most relevant one is the 1909 Law against Unfair Competition (*Gesetz gegen den unlauteren Wettbewerb*, UWG). Originally designed to protect the rights of merchants, its aim has been extended through amendments and court decisions also to consider the public and consumer interests in a more balanced manner, although it is generally concluded that the protection of trade interests still dominates the application of this law. More specific consumer-protection regulations have since been enacted, following the consumerist demands of the 1970s, which coincided with the more interventionist policies of the German Social-Democratic Party (SPD) then in power. However, a liberal concept has generally prevailed to restrict legal strictures to fairly general terms; and the advertising industry and its Werberat are now facing relatively benign circumstances as harsh criticisms have largely disappeared.

Article 1 of the 1909 law is a general clause that has been extensively used[1] to apply to a large variety of competitive acts, including advertising: "A person who, in the course of business for purposes of competition, commits acts contrary to honest practices may be enjoined from continuing such acts and held for damages." This first article is *civil* rather than penal in nature, since it is aimed at stopping undesirable business practices through the use of interim and permanent injunctions readily obtainable by firms and associations through the civil courts. Damages are rarely granted to successful complainants, but the latter can recover reasonable legal expenses.[2] Article 3 of the 1909 law is more specific and provides against "misleading statements about business circumstances," thereby prohibiting deceptive advertisements and requiring truth in advertising. Here again, contraveners can be pursued through injunctions.

This law also includes a few penal clauses conducive to fines and imprisonment (e.g., against intentional deception under Article 4), but they are rarely used because intent must be proven in most cases, and this is a difficult enterprise. In any case, acts defined as criminal in nature under the 1909 law and other business regulations are generally amenable to Article 1 treatment since they are also considered to be fundamentally against the public interest;[3] and the lack of a German federal agency comparable to the U.S. Federal Trade Commission hampers the application of criminal clauses and regulations.[4]

In general, whoever challenges an advertising message as being deceptive (Article 3) or contrary to honest practices (Article 1) under the 1909 law has to prove the correctness of his complaint; in other words, the burden of proof is on the complainant, unless the defendent advertiser can reasonably be expected to prove his claims (e.g., in the case of superiority statements made by him), or the plaintiff encounters major difficulties in furnishing the necessary proof (Reich and Micklitz 1981, pp. 83–84). However, the 1984 European Community Directive on Misleading Advertising will require German law to put the burden of proof on the advertiser—a change hitherto opposed by German industry for "amounting to a general verdict against advertising as being misleading, and for exposing advertisers to intolerable risks," as one industry respondent put it.

Using the Law

Recourse to the 1909 law is relatively simple, inexpensive and fast—at least, as far as competitors are concerned. The first step is for a competitor, a trade association or a consumer organization to issue a warning (*Abmahnung*) to the advertiser (and other types of erring practitioners), asking him to stop a particular advertisement because it infringes on the 1909 law, and to give assurance that he will not repeat the offense. The issuer of this warning is entitled to recover legal expenses or to charge a fee (about DM 180 or some $50 to $100 in the case of first warnings issued by an association) in lieu of the legal expenditures he incurred.

If the advertiser declines to withdraw or modify his advertisement, the plaintiff can ask a civil court to issue an interim cease-and-desist injunction (*einstweilige Verfügung*). Such an order can be obtained in a few days—even in a few hours and over the weekend and holidays in some cases. Judges specializing in unfair-competition law are usually available for that purpose and are, in principle, able to distinguish between frivolous and significant requests. Again, the complainant will be reimbursed for the reasonable legal expenses incurred in obtaining this order. In the case of noncompliance with interim cease-and-desist orders, a permanent court injunction (*Unterlassung*) can be obtained. Judges may contact the advertiser in order to hear his counterarguments and/or obtain his voluntary compliance, but he can appeal injunctions in higher courts, all the way to the highest federal court in some cases—but so can the turned-down plaintiff. To discourage frivolous complaints and appeals, the Civil Procedure Code (ZPO) allows the successful plaintiff or defendant to recover all reasonable legal expenses from the losing party.

Since 1965, consumer organizations, but not individual consumers, have been allowed to sue in cases of deceptive advertising or when consumer interests are at stake.[5] However, most legal actions emanate from business firms and associations because, for lack of adequate resources, consumer organizations tend to handle only clear-cut and winnable cases. In this relative vacuum some "fake consumer associations" flourished for a while, set up by enterprising lawyers and backed up by nominal housewives in order to grant them some legitimacy under the law. By issuing warnings to firms and demanding to be reimbursed for their legal expenses by the complying advertisers, these fake associations were able to build a lucrative business because of the numerous legal violations—often minor ones—that they contested. However, advertisers are now resisting such intimidations; and courts are increasingly challenging their legitimacy when these associations sue for an interim order against a noncomplying advertiser. Besides, there are proposals to make the first warning free of recoverable legal expenses in order to discourage abuses. Still, there are bona fide consumer associations that are active and successsful in warning and enjoining firms to stop undesirable business practices—for example, the Consumer Protection Association of West Berlin—although they are usually underfunded and lack sufficient advertising and legal expertise.

This brief review of the German legal system reveals its uniqueness in terms of the predominant use of civil-law remedies through warnings and preliminary cease-and-desist orders, which are readily available and frequently used—at least, by competitors—under the evolving meaning of the 1909 law.[6] In this context, German advertising self-regulation has had to cope with a strong proclivity to "start with the legal (Nickel 1979, p. S–32)." There are many opportunities to sue because the case law developed around the 1909 law is complex and therefore easily violated. Hence, large advertisers have an in-house staff of lawyers; and many firms avail themselves of legal-service organizations (such as the ZBUW analyzed below), which advise and assist them in obtaining compliance from competitors who themselves are eager to spot violations and use the law as a form of competitive strategy. Consequently, there has been no pressing need for an advertising self-regulatory system to complement or parallel the law in those matters already covered by the unfair-competition law and to arrange settlements between private parties—except that individual consumers cannot directly rely on that law, and their associations often lack the resources to use it. The German Advertising Council has therefore been faced with the difficult task of convincing people that "extra-legal" means of redress are essential and do work.

What the Law Does Not Cover

Reaching all the way back to German medieval guilds, there has been the notion of acts in which a "honorable merchant" (*ehrbarer Kaufmann*) does not engage, and against which he should be protected.[7] This concept, however, is an elastic one—especially when case law (jurisprudence), rather than code law (as in many systems derived from Napoleonic law), is used to define and refine the limits of "fair" and "unfair." Thus, German courts have ruled that business "statements" (*Angaben*) must have a factual content in order to come under Article 3 of the 1909 UWG law, which provides remedies against false and misleading advertisements. However, mere expressions of opinion, value judgments, puffery and the like are not generally considered to be "statements" unless a "factual core" can be identified. Therefore, advertising claims of a subjective nature and appealing primarily to the subconscious—as is common in matters of taste and opinion—do not fall readily under the purview of this Article (Reich and Micklitz 1981, p. 75).

Similarly, the issue of unfairness in the matter of trade practices has not been significantly applied to matters of "taste and opinion" (*Gesmack und Meinung*) as well as to some undesirable or unacceptable practices in advertising under Article 1 of the 1909 law. Certain types of advertisements exploiting fear (e.g., in insurance advertising) or sexuality, unduly appealing to children, abusing pity or exciting prejudice may raise issues of unfairness in the marketplace and be against the public interest under the balance-of-interests principle, but only complaints against gross abuses have been handled by the courts (Reich and Micklitz 1981, pp. 81 and 83). For example, the ZBUW (see below) was successful in obtaining that the Ott Brewery stop using the slogan "Give us our daily Ott" (a pun on "brot," the German word for bread) on the ground that it offended the basic beliefs of German people under Article 1 of the 1909 law. Consequently, there has been a relative legal vacuum about matters of taste and opinion and about various "gray zones at the limit of the law," where advertising self-regulation can play a useful role.

The German Advertising Self-Regulatory System

The German Advertising Council (Deutscher Werberat, DWR) does not have a monopoly on self-regulation. As is common in other countries, particular industries (e.g., tobacco and pharmaceuticals) have their codes of good advertising behavior, and they handle complaints from competitors and consumers. Besides, the state-mandated Chambers of Industry and Commerce have set up complaint boards in their districts. Some observers even go so far as saying that the application of the 1909 Law against Unfair Competition (UWG) amounts to self-regulation, since it is mostly used by competitors rather than by consumers and the State. Therefore, this section starts with an analysis of the application of this law by the ZBUW, which is extensively used by competitors.

The ZBUW

The Central Organization against Unfair Competition (*Zentrale zur Bekämpfung unlauteren Wettbewerbs*, ZBUW) is a private business-interest organization set up and financed by a very large number (some 12,200 in 1985) of trade and industry associations as well as individual firms. It provides them with legal advice (about one-fourth of the 12,000 annual cases handled recently), but mostly initiates class actions through warnings against firms suspected of engaging in unfair business practices—including deceptive and otherwise unacceptable advertising—on the basis of the 1909 UWG law and other relevant regulations.

This warning activity is of a class-action nature because: (1) the ZBUW can only act on the basis of outside complaints (mostly from competitors although consumers and even government agencies can refer cases to it), and (2) it does not reveal the name of the complainant in order to avoid unnecessary bad feelings among ZBUW members. Instead, the ZBUW assumes their complaints as its own in the impartial role of an organization promoting fair competition in business.[8] Its major objective is to obtain compliance from advertisers and other erring business practitioners, once a warning has been issued by it. A measure of its success is that only some 650 complaints emanating from the ZBUW (out of about 8,000 warnings) end up each year in court or before an arbitration body (such as those set up by Chambers of Industry and Commerce). In most cases, the advertiser simply withdraws or modifies his advertisement—which is precisely what the complainant wanted.

Clearly, the ZBUW's activities are based on the law's mandates—not on its own code (it does not have any) nor on those guidelines of other business organizations such as the German Advertising Council and the pharmaceutical-industry association. Besides, unlike self-regulatory bodies, it uses the threat of

litigation rather than relying on voluntary compliance, the cooperation of the
media, publicity, etc., as the ultimate sanction—while the latter means are
overwhelmingly used by advertising self-regulatory bodies. Both the ZBUW and
the Werberat use persuasion, but as one respondent put it: "The ZBUW has the
sword of prosecution under the 1909 UWG law to back up its warnings while
the Werberat can only use moral suasion and publicity." Besides, the ZBUW
recovers a fee for its legal expenses from the firms which comply with its warnings
or ultimately lose in court against it, while the Werberat cannot and does not.
As such, the ZBUW is not an organ of self-regulation in any traditional sense
of that concept.

In the German context, however, one can argue that it is part of German
advertising self-regulation because: (1) persuasion rather than litigation is attempted by the ZBUW, and (2) the main use of German legislation on unfair
competition is to have competitors settle disputes among themselves—whether
done individually by a firm or through the intermediation of business-interest
organizations (such as the ZBUW), which are financed by industry. This led
one respondent to argue that: "Everybody entitled by the 1909 UWG law to
attack unfair competition is part of the German advertising self-regulatory system,
which therefore includes, besides the Werberat, competitors as well as the ZBUW
and consumer associations." However, this is a notion that most students and
practitioners of self-regulation outside of Germany would reject as foreign to its
traditional spirit, structure, functioning and sanctions.

Expert Commissions

Expert commissions associated with the Chambers of Industry and Commerce,
have issued industry position papers vis-à-vis emerging issues (including advertising ones) at the request of industry. In a sense, they amount to another
form of industry self-regulation since these expert opinions are seriously considered by the executive government and the courts as well as by industry itself
as expressing current notions of good business behavior.

The ZAW and DWR

The German Advertising Council (Deutscher Werberat, DWR) is an integral
part of the Advertising Federation (or Central Advertising Committee, Zentralausschuss der Werbewirtschaft, ZAW), an industry organization founded in
1949 by numerous associations of advertisers, agencies, media and related advertising professionals (researchers, producers, etc.).[9] The ZAW promotes, defends and otherwise represents the advertising industry through research,
education, lobbying (at the state, federal, European and international levels),
concertation with other sectors such as the trade-union and consumerist movements, and self-regulation. The latter is carried out by the Werberat, which was

set up in 1972 at the initiative of the German advertising industry—particularly, of advertisers.

As in many other countries, the late 1960s and early 1970s marked a high point in consumerist concerns, demands and influence as well as state interventionism.[10] Business and advertising were frequently criticized, and many proposals were made to increase their regulation—some of which were enacted through new laws pertaining to cigarettes, foodstuffs, medicines and cosmetics, among other topics. There were even discussions of creating a Consumer Ombudsman agency à la Sweden and of expanding the role of the Federal Cartel Office into a consumer-protection agency. Furthermore, both the International Chamber of Commerce and the Council of Europe had urged the expansion of business self-regulation as well as greater cooperation between self-regulatory bodies, government agencies and consumer organizations to combat deceptive and unfair business practices (see chapters 1 and 2). These developments prompted the ZAW to activate what was already contemplated in its statutes, namely, the creation of an advertising self-regulatory body to complement its other efforts to improve business's and advertising's images and to curtail generally acknowledged abuses in the field. This was achieved in 1972 when the Werberat was launched.

Standards. The ZAW and DWR subscribe to the broad principles and general guidelines issued by the International Chamber of Commerce, but they have also chosen to specialize in particular areas of advertising behavior. As was seen before, the German legal situation minimizes the need for traditional self-regulation. Consequently, it was decided from the beginning that the DWR would deal with: (1) subjective matters of "taste and opinion" not readily amenable to legal treatment; (2) problematic products (cigarettes, medicines, alcoholic beverages, etc.) and practices (e.g., advertising to children and the disguising of advertising as editorial text in publications), and (3) undefined "gray zones [*Grauzone*] at the limit of the law."[11]

The DWR tends to define "taste and opinion" in terms of "offending the public" since taste is a very subjective notion, but "offensiveness" is also difficult to pinpoint objectively. While codes of conduct for the tobacco and pharmaceutical sectors (among others) were left to their trade associations, the DWR issued its own Rules of Conduct (*Verhaltensregeln*) for advertising to children (1974) and for alcoholic-beverage advertisements, which can appear in all media.

These early exercises in standards development provided a lesson that still marks German advertising self-regulation. The federal government incorporated the cigarette rules into law in 1974, and unsuccessfully tried the same for advertising to children. This unanticipated turn of events sobered the mood of the ZAW and DWR, which have since become reluctant to "hold the stirrup for regulation." Thus, although the Werberat endorses the advertising code of the International Chamber of Commerce, it decided not to include new ICC guidelines on advertising to children as part of its own Rules of Conduct about this practice, for fear of encouraging rather than discouraging new regulations. Subsequently, the ZAW and DWR have only issued decision rules (*Entschliessungen*), position statements (*Verlautbarungen*) and guidelines (*Richtlinien*) about such issues as women in advertising, the presentation of unsafe situations in advertisements, tire advertising and the separation of ads from editorial materials in periodicals. Implicit standards have also emerged from the cases decided by the DWR since 1972 (for a compilation of rules and decisions, see the ZAW publications listed in the References section).

Several statements by the ZAW and DWR make general references to "gray zones," where "red cards" can be waived at offending advertisers (ZAW, *Deutscher Werberat* 1985, p. 21), but these "gray areas at the limit of the law" are not explicated. Instead, the Werberat is free to select well-founded complaints related to "the law, ZAW guidelines, and the International Code of Advertising of the International Chamber of Commerce, provided they fall within the domain of the German legal order (ZAW, *Deutscher Werberat* 1985, p. 21)." However, the examples given in ZAW-DWR publications only refer to "soft" cases of sexism, encouragement of violence, racism, etc., rather than to "hard" cases of false and misleading advertising. As such, one cannot conclude that the Werberat "applies the law" in the sense of readily and regularly accepting cases of deceptive and otherwise illegal advertising that fall under the 1909 unfair-competition law and consumer-protection regulations.

Preadvertising Advice and Clearance. Censorship is a touchy issue in postwar Germany in view of the abuses of the Nazi regime. In fact, the German Constitution (Basic Law) forbids it for all media (Article 5); and the DWR bylaws specificallly mention that it will not engage in the preclearance of advertisements (Article 1.5). General advice can be provided to advertising practitioners but the availability of legal advice within large firms and by associations such as the ZBUW (see above) makes such advisement rather rare. In any case, the Werberat refuses to comment about particular ads before their publication.

Case Generation. Anyone—competitor, consumer, association, government agency, etc.—can lodge complaints with the DWR, except that anonymous ones are ignored. The DWR does not usually assume complaints as its own, but serves primarily as an intermediary between the complainant and the incriminated party. Still, the Werberat occasionally initiates its own cases since the sponsoring ZAW is genuinely concerned with advertising abuses—whether complained about or not.

Caseload and Disposal. The Werberat engages in very little systematic monitoring of German advertisements for the purpose of spotting violations. This has been done, however, for brief periods when broad criticisms have been expressed about such matters as alcohol advertising and "women in advertising." Thus, an analysis of newspapers was made in 1983 to detect objectionable ads in terms of inappropriate nudity. Instead, the Werberat generally waits for the 200 to 300 complaints it has received in recent years about both local and national advertisements in all media, including radio and television. Most complaints come from consumers since competitors tend to rely on the 1909 UWG law to go after one another.

These complaints are handled by the Werberat's director (who spends about 15 percent of his time on DWR activities), a half-time lawyer and a secretary— the equivalent of one full-time employee. The DWR Secretariat settles most complaints directly—either dismissing them as unfounded or obtaining that the advertiser withdraw or modify the ad after requesting him to respond to the complaint. The relevant advertising agency and medium are usually alerted; and clear-cut infringements of the 1909 law may be referred to the ZBUW. Should the advertiser and/or agency refuse to comply with the DWR Secretariat's request for justification, or assert that the complaint is unfounded, the case is brought before the full DWR Council (ten industry members). This body meets three or four times a year to decide by a majority vote in the case of audio-visual commercials and of difficult or novel cases, but otherwise decides by mail. In all cases, the complainant is notified in writing about the outcomes, which were as follows in 1984–1986:

	1984	1985	1986
Advertiser agreed to discontinue the ad	44	49	88
Advertiser modified the ad	9	10	13
Unjustified complaints	61	111	143
Complaints beyond the DWR's jurisdiction	56	52	39
Competitor complainant was advised to enforce his rights independently	16	9	14
Complaints dismissed owing to pending lawsuit	6	7	2
Complaints referred to proper agency	5	19	16
Public censure	0	4	1
Total cases	*197*	*261*	*316*

As can be seen, the Werberat interceded directly with the advertiser and was successful in obtaining their cooperation in 28 percent of the cases—a fairly steady proportion since, from 1972 to 1986, the Werberat handled 4,621 complaints, which resulted in 1,331 withdrawals or modifications (29 percent). In the other cases, the complaints were unjustified, or required referral to other bodies.

Some of the "matter and opinion" cases decided by the Werberat have dealt with such issues as irreverent references to God and angels in Christmas advertising; showing Arab sheiks in a derogatory manner; stating in an ad for car seatbelts that it is worse to be crippled than dead (a slur on cripples); claiming that it is better to own a home for retirement purposes than to have to live in a nursing home (an aspersion on those who live there); showing children throwing stones at windows while remarking that their father does not have to worry since his insurance policy covers such occurrences (an incitation to reckless behavior on the part of the young); a motorcycle ad displaying a terrorist speeding away from the scene of the crime, shortly after the president of the Federation of German Industries was kidnapped and murdered; a beer ad inciting young people to drink; direct-mail ads putting undue pressure on consumers; a temporary-job illustration implying that many sick workers are in fact drunk; and several ads making improper use of the female body. The ZAW and the Werberat believe and repeatedly stress that ads of this sort are undesirable for the general image and effectiveness of advertising.

Sanctions. Basically, the Werberat works through: (1) persuasion if possible, (2) public censure if appropriate, and (3) general warnings or recommendations based on past complaints and decisions as well as on other relevant developments. From the beginning, the DWR stated that it would not act like a court dispensing justice. Instead, it relies on voluntary compliance with its requests for justification and its recommendations to withdraw or modify the ad. Practically all incriminated advertisers comply with DWR decisions, since in only seven cases, since 1972, has the name of a noncomplying firm been publicized in ZAW-DWR publications and the press. Moral pressure is also put on the agency and medium associated with the incriminated ad since they are informed of the complaint and of the case's disposal. While the media are not bound to follow DWR recommendations, most do. Publicity is also used, but its main role is to provide guidance to others rather than to "pillory" an advertiser.

Most advertising abuses now emanate from smaller firms or those at the margin of the industry (e.g., ads about hair loss, bust development and impotency), although large firms are not averse to hit-and-run tactics testing the limits of the law (see below). Since the general public, the consumer movement and government hold the entire industry responsible for such objectionable behavior in the "gray zones at the limit of the law," the Werberat handles such cases quite readily because they cannot be justified, but provide opportunities for stating and restating that the industry cares.

Publicity. As in most other advertising self-regulatory systems, the preferred approach is to address and convince the erring advertiser in private rather than censure him in public. Consequently, the Werberat provides general statistics about its cases and their disposition (see above), but few of its decisions are reported in detail (about 20 percent), and even fewer mention the advertiser's name. However, the offending company can sometimes be identified in the Werberat's anonymous vignettes if the slogan, claim or situation used in the ad is well known.

Advertisers can be named in DWR reports if the case has already drawn some public attention in the press or otherwise, so that it is desirable to present an official ZAW/DWR position on the matter. When the advertiser or his agency refuses to cooperate with the investigation, or to withdraw or modify an ad found to be objectionable by the DWR, the latter "can inform the public of its objections about the named company but the advertiser and/or the advertising agency must previously be clearly notified of this possibility (ZAW, Deutscher Werberat 1985, Article 12.2)."

Clearly, the Werberat is discreet about most of its specific negative decisions, which are usually reported with some delay. Still, uncooperative advertisers are immediately denounced in the ZAW-Service magazine; while important issues are frequently discussed through general commentaries in ZAW publications, and may even lead to new recommendations, so that "lessons" may be drawn even when a particular negative decision has not been reported in detail.

The Werberat and the ZAW issue various regular and occasional reports about their activities, and the media often refer to them. These publications are essentially aimed at advertising practitioners[12] but the advertising self-regulatory system has been publicized every few years through public-service campaigns by cooperating media members. A recent campaign, for example, points out that there are a few "black sheep" in every group but that the advertising industry is committed to their eradication.[13] No direct invitation to complain was included in those public-service ads but the reader/viewer's attention was directed toward the Werberat and one of its publications ("The Pros and Cons of Advertising"), which discreetly mentions that complaints can be addressed to it. Other campaigns have invited complaints in a more direct manner, but it does not appear that the ZAW and Werberat are keen on increasing the number of consumer complaints. No survey has been made of public awareness of, and satisfaction with, the Werberat.

Effectiveness. A somewhat controversial study by Udo Beier provides some insight about case selection and disposal by the Werberat. Among the "weaknesses" he reported, was that: "Complaint handling takes an extraordinary long time: an average of 32 days for complaints which were successfully filed. This means that a suspect advertisement can appear for quite some time before it is stopped by the opinion of the DWR (Udo Beier 1979, p. 313)."

In fact, the Werberat now takes only one to three weeks to dispose of most cases. Besides, compared to other national self-regulatory systems, thirty-two days is rather fast, since sixty to ninety days are not unusual elsewhere (see Chapter 15). Moreover, when complaints deal with "gray zones" not readily amenable to legal treatment, thirty-two days seems reasonable to handle rather subjective issues. However, when warnings and cease-and-desist orders can be issued within a matter of hours or days under German fair-competition law (see above), thirty-two days or even one to three weeks is slow if the Werberat's purpose is to get an ad rapidly withdrawn or modified.

Beier also concluded that: "There are, in the view of the author, many wrong decisions [by the Werberat], especially in the case of misleading advertising (ambiguous, hyperbolical, incomplete, untrue claims) (Udo Beier 1979, p.

313).'' This conclusion has been strongly challenged by the Werberat as well as some more dispassionate observers. Not only did Beier, at first, rely on his own subjective judgment to conclude that his complaints were valid, but many of them were cases of deceptive (false or misleading) advertising, which do not fall within the main purview of the Werberat, which deals mostly with matters of taste and opinion and with some undesirable advertising practices (cf. ZAW-Service, 44–45, 1976, p. 12). Beier conceded as much when he stated that: ''Fifty-two [out of 235] of the advertisements which had been judged acceptable by the DWR [''no reason to object''] could be stopped with the help of other institutions [such as the ZBUW] (Udo Beier 1979, p. 313)''—but the latter focuses on the types of cases clearly falling under the 1909 UWG law, rather than on the matters regularly handled by the Werberat.

Still, Beier's challenge throws some light on the types of cases that the Werberat is willing to consider. It has already been mentioned that the Werberat's scope is somewhat ambiguous outside of ''soft'' issues of taste, opinion, sexism, racism, etc. Still, some ZAW-DWR documents imply that the Werberat does apply the 1909 unfair-competition law and consumer-protection laws. Beier subsequently referred his complaints to a couple of consumer-protection associations, which succeeded through warnings and court injunctions in obtaining that a significant number of the challenged ads be withdrawn or modified.[14] This outcome reveals that: (1) there were problems with these ads although the Werberat ruled that there was ''no reason to object'' to them, and (2) the Werberat does not normally deal with clear-cut cases of deceptive and otherwise illegal advertising although it claims to ''apply the law.''[15]

Finally, Beier complained that: ''[In] cases of ambiguity, interpretations usually favor the advertiser. Of the complainants, DWR demands proof that an advertiser's claim is untrue, whereas the advertiser remains in the clear if he makes some vague statements to the effect that the claim is true or the complainant's arguments are incorrect (Udo Beier 1979, p. 313).'' This is a trickier issue to settle in view of the impossibility of exactly reconstructing the criteria and analytical processes used by the DWR Secretariat and full Council when handling complaints.

In the first place, all advertising self-regulatory bodies face the difficult task of sorting out complaints into ''frivolous'' and ''serious'' categories—especially when taste and opinion are at stake. Besides, any self-regulatory body that does not include ''outsiders'' is readily vulnerable to changes—valid or invalid—of lacking objectivity and of favoring its members. Moreover, the general legal principle of *non liquet* (it is not clear) tends to favor the defendant when he can provide sufficient counterarguments even when the complainant can substantiate his complaint. Furthermore, German advertisers are generally opposed to the ''reversal of the burden of proof,'' that is, to the requirement that it is for the defendant to justify his action, although this objection is voiced more in the context of complaints clearly falling under the 1909 unfair-competition law. In any case, the ''gray-zone'' complaints typically handled by the Werberat do not lend themselves well to rigorous proof and counterproof, since they are subjective by nature. Consequently, it is difficult to prove that "the Werberat usually favors the advertiser," but this statement must now be put in a broader context.

The True Role of the Werberat

As in other countries, a central and unified body—such as the ZAW (Advertising Federation) in Germany—involving advertisers, agencies, media and directly related professions is needed to start, finance (at least initially) and supervise an advertising self-regulatory system. The problematic question is whether the resulting ASR system then assumes significant autonomy from its sponsors.

It can never be fully autonomous because it depends on sponsoring organizations not only for money (in practically all cases) but also for moral and personnel support. Its norms have to be in fair correspondence with those of the industry—neither lagging nor leading too much. It needs prominent members of the industry to sit on its board of directors and on complaint-handling committees, and they cannot be antagonized. Most important, it ultimately depends on voluntary compliance with its recommendations and decisions, since coercion is foreign to the spirit of self-regulation and even vulnerable to antitrust charges. ASR leaders have to operate within these serious constraints—a subtle process of "institution-building," which requires understanding and responsible board members as well as politically astute ASR leaders and professionals. Crises in the form of serious attacks on an ASR system's effectiveness and credibility are usually necessary to give it greater autonomy (see Chapter 1). While this study was unable to investigate these factors in great depth, it appears that the Werberat is not sufficiently autonomous—at least in comparison to some other ASR systems—because it remains too much subordinated to the ZAW's objectives of promoting and defending German advertising.

For one, the industry strongly believes that ads offensive to the public are detrimental to its image and harm its effectiveness in a country where advertising is still somewhat suspect since good products are supposed to sell themselves on their own merits (Fullerton and Nevett 1986). Therefore, the industry is willing to support an ASR system designed to identify and handle "bad sheep"—particularly in those "soft" areas at the limit of the law, since other mechanisms are already effectively handling most clear-cut cases of deceptive and unfair advertising. As such, the Werberat was set up to process largely unsolicited complaints from consumers and competitors on the basis of a broad if loosely defined mandate to hand out "red cards to gray advertisers" on the basis of a variety of external standards (the law and the ICC Code of Advertising Practice) and of its own rules of conduct, decision rules, position statements and guidelines. However, its role is more "preventive" than "corrective," since the Werberat is more concerned with developing "self-discipline" on the basis of its guidelines, recommendations and reports than with providing "external discipline" through sanctions (ZAW, *Deutscher Werberat* 1987, p. 30).

Consequently, the Werberat is not expected to act too zealously. First, Germany is still considered to be a country where consumer protection is a relatively minor goal compared to the preservation of orderly and respectable competition, and the Werberat operates in that German tradition. More concretely, any aggressive solicitation and handling of consumer complaints would not only antagonize some important ASR supporters, but would also contradict the Advertising Federation (ZAW) claim that, by and large, German advertisers behave properly. This is, of course, one possible explanation of why the Werberat refused to handle the kinds of deceptive-advertising cases that Udo Beier threw at it in order to test its "seriousness." Focusing on the "gray areas at the limit of the law" also helps avoid having to brand advertisers as "liars" or "deceivers"—something alien to the industry's self-image that most of them are "honorable merchants" who may sometimes "slip" at the margin, but will readily correct their ways when approached by their peers.

One may counter that the Werberat refers deceptive cases to other institutions such as the ZBUW and the courts and is, therefore, interested in their resolution for the good of the advertising industry. However, the complaints handled by the ZBUW, other trade associations and the courts emanate mostly from competitors, so that they can then be labeled as disputes among merchants rather than as cases concerning consumer protection.

Is the Werberat then truly concerned about consumer protection, as it claims to be? Obviously, most self-regulatory efforts to eradicate undesirable advertising behavior ultimately serve the consumer's interest. Besides, the Werberat accepts and even solicits (to some extent) consumer complaints, and it gives them a fair hearing in the light of its own criteria of relevance and resolution. However, it turns down a sizable number of consumer complaints that appear to be actionable under the law (cf. Udo Beier) on the ground that self-regulation plays a lesser role in Germany because the application of the 1909 unfair-competition is so well developed there (ZAW, *Deutscher Werberat* 1987, p. 9). It is also apparent that dealing with cases of deceptive advertising would require a much larger complaint-handling apparatus in view of their complexity, while cases of "taste and opinion" and other offensive behavior can be handled in a lighter and cheaper manner.

Only 10 percent of the ZAW's budget is devoted to Werberat activities, and the latter functions with a very small staff (the equivalent of one full-time person) while the resources of ASR systems in comparable countries (e.g., France and the United Kingdom, but also Belgium, which is only one-fifth the size of Germany) are much larger. Consequently, the ZAW's refusal to increase the Werberat's resources to handle more complex cases directly related to consumer protection weakens its claim to be centrally concerned with the latter. Other ASR systems also refuse to serve as full-blown "consumer-redress" institutions—something that consumerists and even governments usually expect them to be. Still, they handle a much greater variety of cases than the Werberat, and do not exclude most complaints related to deceptive advertising.

Therefore, one can conclude that the consumer-protection role of the Werberat is a subordinate one, and that the main tasks of its complaint-handling activities are: (1) to serve as an antenna or radar for emerging "gray zones" so that new industry recommendations, guidelines, etc., may be developed and issued; (2) to develop "self-discipline" among advertising practitioners, and (3) to serve as a "public-relations" appendage to the Advertising Federation (ZAW) to prove that the advertising industry "cares" as a way of fending off propositions to further regulate advertising—"the State made dispensable" (Den Staat entbehrlich gemacht) argument (ZAW, *Deutscher Werberat* 1987, p. 25).

This is where one can rejoin Udo Beier's (1979) criticism that the DWR acts leniently toward advertisers. The Werberat is not expected by its sponsor, the ZAW, to "lean hard" on erring members, since it is not, and refuses to be, a court. Behind-the-scene persuasion is used to resolve cases among gentlemen or honorable merchants—"among the daughters of pastors," as Germans say. Even the publicity given to DWR decisions is more a matter of providing examples of acceptable and unacceptable advertisements—almost in the spirit of the vast jurisprudence developed in connection with the 1909 fair-competition law—than an exercise in singling out wrongdoers. This has led one consumerist critic to label the Werberat as a "figleaf" designed to show that the advertising industry cares while actually not going after single advertisers extensively and vigorously (Dimper 1979).

This guild-like philosophy is vulnerable, however, when advertisers are tempted to act less than "honorably." Several interviewees commented about how recent unfavorable economic conditions have intensified competition and resulted in more aggressive advertisements testing the legal and self-regulatory limits of fair competition. Consequently, there has been an increase in the number of warnings and cease-and-desist injunctions issued under the 1909 UWG law, which are now at an all-time high. Besides, there seems to have been more cases of "tasteless" advertisements falling under the purview of DWR rules and recommendations as some advertisers are tempted to run shocking or controversial ads, which are immediately spotted in a milieu of rather dull advertising (as several foreign observers have commented). Well advised by in-house or outside legal experts, large and small advertisers can then be tempted to use more provocative ads, reasoning that by the time a complaint is issued and the Werberat takes its "thirty-two days" or even one to three weeks to reach a decision, the advertising campaign will have run its course and can then be withdrawn or modified as a token of one's behavior as an "honorable merchant."

It is impossible to prove if this is the reasoning actually used by some German advertisers, but there is sufficient misbehavior in German advertising to upset consumerist critics who then expect the Werberat to act promptly and sternly. Since German consumer associations lack sufficient expertise and financial resources to engage in numerous class actions to obtain consumer protection and redress against deceptive advertisements, they may have anticipated to find the Werberat ready to handle expertly and freely all of their advertising complaints.

What consumerist critics may not understand, however, is that the tasks of identifying problem areas in advertising, of developing new appropriate standards to cope with them, and of making them broadly accepted by practitioners does not require a large number of complaints—quality is more important than quantity—nor harsh disciplining of every single offender (see chapters 1 and 16). Indeed, self-regulatory bodies everywhere—just like regulatory agencies everywhere—refuse to invite all cases of consumer dissatisfaction with advertising, not only on account of a perennial lack of sufficient resources, but because many complaints are repetitive so that an ASR body need not handle each one of them in order to make its points about what constitutes good advertising behavior.

However, the Werberat can be criticized for cultivating some ambiguity about its scope and activism by making unqualified and loose claims that "the State has been made dispensable," that "red cards will be given to [all] gray advertisers," and the like. Advertising self-regulation plays a very useful if limited role in Germany. While its limited contribution is often misunderstood, some of that misunderstanding must be blamed on the industry itself for claiming too much or for misstating its true functions. Part of this problem results from the relatively poor relations between the Werberat and consumerist bodies.

Outsiders and the Werberat

The Werberat represents a unique exercise in pure self-regulation, since non-industry members or employees do not serve on its board and in its Secretariat. Admitting outsiders as inside participants would amount to creating "another republic" foreign to the spirit of self-discipline (ZAW, *Deutscher Werberat* 1987, p. 11). However, the Werberat has engaged in various communication exercises that have amounted to short-lived or limited forms of outside participation. Particularly noteworthy is an early unproductive attempt at dialogue and even concertation with the German consumerist movement, but there have been more recent and successful attempts in connection with the women-and-advertising issue.

The German Consumerist Movement

While large, this movement is not considered to be very representative, powerful or effective (cf. Biervert et al. 1984; Reich and Micklitz 1981; Rock et al., 1980). The federal and state governments recognize and subsidize a number of consumerist organizations engaging in product-testing, information, education, legal advising and/or collective actions such as suing for cease-and-desist orders and obtaining the favorable settlement of consumer complaints. Also government-subsidized is the capstone Consumer Association (Arbeitsgemeinschaft der Verbraucher, AgV) which articulates consumer interests in the political arena and occasionally interacts with the business community. Compared to many smaller consumerist organizations—particularly, in the North of Germany—which lean toward the political Left and favor radical regulatory solutions, the AgV broadly supports the market system and is less extreme in its regulatory proposals, although it does not exert much control over its member organizations. However, there is no general organization with wide individual membership, that would represent consumers on a direct basis, although certain segments of the consuming public (car owners, tenants, etc.) are well organized on such a private basis.

Shortly after its creation, the Werberat involved the Consumer Association (AgV) in some of its activities on an informal basis. Meetings were held with AgV officials to generate support for the Werberat and to settle various issues. Some success was achieved about the advertising of cosmetics and vitamins, but these meetings no longer take place on a regular basis. Various interpretations were given for this situation.

Werberat respondents stressed incompatible philosophies, with consumerists more interested in the extension and reinforcement of legal remedies while business considers present regulations to be adequate and self-regulation sufficient to deal with what the law ignores. Consumerist respondents, however, justified their withdrawal from these early informal interactions on the grounds that: (1) there was no advantage in being associated with what they consider to be an ineffective self-regulatory system not primarily concerned with achieving consumer protection, and (2) the Werberat was trying to involve them in its functioning without really granting them any significant influence over the development and application of self-regulatory standards—that is, the Werberat wanted the AgV to help sort out frivolous from nonfrivolous complaints, but kept the development of its standards and the actual disposal of the retained cases for its own internal system, which does not involve outsiders. They concluded that they were being used to grant legitimacy to a self-regulatory system that they do not view as capable of fostering consumer interests as they see them, and which competes with their aim of strengthening consumer protection through regulatory and other means (e.g., negative publicity campaigns).

Both interpretations are compatible. It is normal for ASR systems to try to obtain outside support "for free," so to speak, and for the other side to resist such exploitation. Besides, the Werberat has remained determined to keep self-regulation "pure," particularly in view of the fact that the AgV is not directly representative of consumer interests and does not constitute a "middle-of-the road" association (as exists in Canada and the United Kingdom, for example), which can interact with business in a fairly nonideological manner. Moreover, if the Werberat is subordinated to the ZAW's mission of improving the industry's image (see above), there is no room for outsiders who would challenge such a limited role.

It is noteworthy that one consumerist respondent mentioned that the AgV would lack the resources to be a full participant in DWR case-adjudication for lack of sufficient personnel well versed in advertising as well as product laws and techniques. In the same vein, several other respondents commented that German consumer-protection organizations lack adequate resources to ferret out cases of deceptive advertising, and to use the warning and court-injunction systems to combat them. In a private communication, Udo Beier remarked that two sizable consumer-protection associations, which had been quite successful in pressing the numerous complaints he had prepared for them, stopped engaging in such massive actions after he discontinued his assistance: "There were no competent persons in both organizations to continue my work of discovering and complaining about untrue, etc., ads." Besides, as was mentioned before, the loser assumes most of the legal expenses of both sides in Germany, but the major consumer-protection associations lack sufficient government funds to assume such a risk unless it is a sure-fire case. This is why consumerists would like the Werberat to be much more active in soliciting and handling consumer complaints—including those dealing with deceptive advertising—although this is an activist role, which the Werberat has declined to assume for the reasons presented before.

Therefore, it would appear that any meaningful involvement on the part of the capstone Consumer Association (AgV)—or of any other consumerist organization—would require: (1) real expertise on its part regarding products, advertising and the law; (2) a significant decision-making role for the AgV about standards and their application (no more "fig-leaf" mission); (3) harder disciplining by the Werberat of erring advertisers, and (4) more monitoring on the part of a Werberat no longer content to wait for complaints and other criticisms, but systematically investigating various industries and techniques. Clearly, the last three requirements are unlikely to be accepted by the ZAW—and by most ASR systems around the world, for that matter. Meanwhile, the AgV considers that using the media to publicize consumerist gripes as well as complaining directly to advertisers or even associations[16] is currently more effective than working through or with the Werberat.

Other Organizations

In view of concerns expressed about sexism in advertising and proposals to restrict it legally, the Werberat has recently engaged in regular discussions with the German Women's Council (Deutscher Frauenrat) (Nickel 1982, pp. 217–218; ZAW, Werbung '85, pp. 22–23).[17] This organization lodged twenty-six complaints in 1984, fifteen of which were sustained by the Werberat (six out of fourteen in 1985; and three out of five in 1986). The Werberat has also been cooperating with the ministry of Youth, Family and Health Affairs regarding the stereotyping and exploitation of women in advertising. It is supporting this ministry's study of the issue, and will issue new recommendations, if necessary.

The Government

General Position toward ASR. As a trade association, the Werberat comes under the purview of the Act Prohibiting Restraints of Competition (GWB), which forbids trade restrictions (Reich and Micklitz 1981, pp. 119–20).[18] However, considering that the Werberat relies mostly on recommendations and very mild sanctions, it has not encountered antitrust problems.

The ZAW and Werberat are currently benefiting from Germany being in an antiregulatory phase: "There is enough government!" This has put a brake to the serious consideration of major regulatory proposals,[19] but has not brought forth any noticeable deregulation, since Germans are generally satisfied with their legal system.

The German advertising industry interacts regularly with the federal and state governments—particularly through the lobbying efforts of the ZAW. Conservative parties, politicians and ministers but also Social-Democrat ones have expressed support for advertising self-regulation and the Werberat on repeated occasions, although such expressions tend to be either very general or rather perfunctory (cf. Lambsdorff 1979; and ZAW, *Deutscher Werberat* 1987). The bureaucracy, however, has been generally silent on this subject, although it has lodged a few complaints with the Werberat.

Therefore, one can conclude that explicit public policy toward advertising self-regulation is largely nonexistent in Germany—a reflection of the broadly accepted view that the legal system can readily cope with most abuses and is flexible enough to handle new significant problems. Both the consumer movement and advertising self-regulation emerged after the legal system had developed some sort of a balance among competitor, consumer and public interests. In this context, the Werberat's activities are useful in handling marginal issues that could escalate into major ones, but it is believed that legal remedies will be found through existing or new regulations when such critical points are reached.

Still, the federal government has come to realize that in fluid matters such as "women and advertising," it is difficult to legislate and that advertising self-regulation should be given the opportunity to straighten out problems through voluntary methods (Nickel 1982, pp. 217–18; ZAW, *Werbung '85*, pp. 22–23). This issue brought the ZAW and Werberat into frequent contacts with a couple of ministries that suggested that representatives of women's organizations be made members of the Werberat, but this suggestion was rejected as foreign to the concept of pure self-regulation (ZAW, *Deutscher Werberat* 1985, pp. 11–12).

EEC Directives. In 1984, the European Communities issued a long-fought Council Directive on Misleading Advertising. The Germans—like the British—opposed many of its original provisions because they would have imposed new obligations and administrative procedures that they considered unnecessary and foreign to their advertising-control philosophies. In particular, the German advertising industry feared that new domestic regulations would be required by the EEC directive in a country where legal restrictions are already perceived as burdensome, and where new regulations automatically mean new obligations and more litigation since the law is taken seriously and used effectively in Germany.

After much prodding by the British, the EEC directive on misleading advertising finally referred to self-regulatory bodies as an alternative avenue of first redress for consumers and competitors.[20] However, the Werberat may not qualify under the EEC directive since it does not deal predominantly with matters of misleading advertising. German legislation seems adequate for that purpose—except, perhaps, regarding the burden of proof now to be put on the advertiser "if appropriate (Article 6.a)," while the current use of private litigation based on the 1909 unfair-competition law will continue to serve as a form of "self-regulation" à la Germany.

The New Media. In a country where radio and television have been a monopoly of the states for many years, the advent of private stations and the growing "footprints" of foreign broadcasters via cable, of-the-air and satellite technologies are definitely changing the governmental control of programs and commercials. There will be more ads on radio and television in contrast to the present situation of strict limits (twenty minutes a day on each state network, concentrated in three or four time blocks between 6:30 PM and 8:00 PM, with none on Sundays and holidays); and some of the new commercials will come from abroad (Luxembourg's RTL, the British Sky Channel, etc.). The new regulatory framework for old and new media is hard to predict in the midst of all these developments, although commercial broadcasters will certainly be allowed more time to advertise.

There have already been problems with ads inserted in foreign publications or coming through the mails. However, the German legal system of warnings and injunctions based on the 1909 UWG law has proven somewhat ineffective in stopping problematic advertisements originated by foreign-based advertisers; and the Werberat is equallly impotent, although for different reasons. National authorities, the EEC Commission, the European Parliament and the Council of Europe are debating appropriate controls for the new advertising "without frontiers." The difficulties involved in developing EEC-wide, European-wide and even worldwide legal controls are real; and there is a growing opposition to undue restrictions of advertising now considered to be somewhat protected by the principle of freedom of commercial expression. Consequently, self-regulation is increasingly mentioned as a desirable form of control for international advertising.

However, the ZAW and Werberat are worried that the net outcome may still be more restrictions, since foreign self-regulatory codes—typically more developed and stricter than German ASR rules and guidelines—may become the norm. For example, all alcoholic beverages (including liquor) can be advertised on all German media (including television), but pressure is building up to have "voluntary" international rules forbidding or limiting the satellite advertising of alcoholic beverages as well as of over-the-counter medicines and of advertisements directed to children. The ZAW is opposing such an extension of self-regulatory guidelines or rules, but the relatively underdeveloped standards of the Werberat do not put it in a strong bargaining position vis-à-vis other European self-regulatory bodies in terms of negotiating what voluntary standards should prevail. This is a case where the industries involved in the controversy—tobacco, pharmaceuticals, alcoholic beverages—will have to carry out most of the fight through their national and international associations.

Another bothersome area is that of commercials broadcast on the new videotext cable service. ASR systems everywhere are faced with the difficulty of monitoring and handling complaints about thousands of brief and evanescent advertising messages emanating from individuals and firms, and presenting problems similar to those encountered with personal classified ads and "back-of-the-book" small ads for all sorts of products and services—some of them disreputable or deceptively presented. The only workable solutions appear to be greater media discipline, competitor suits and government prosecution of fraudulent uses of the mails and other media.

One consumerist also complained about the misleading title "Consumer Information" (*Verbraucherinformation*) used by some manufacturers for programs of their own making, but which consumers may think to be of independent origin. This seems to be an area that the Werberat, other German trade associations and the new media could readily handle in a responsible manner.

Conclusions

In a country where it is widely perceived that the law is necessary to solve most problems among competitors as well as between firms and consumers, the Werberat was set up to demonstrate that legal remedies are not indispensable to cope with taste-and-opinion issues and other undesirable practices that can be responsibly handled by self-regulation in advertising. The German Werberat is unique among ASR systems in its predominant focus on such matters, which is designed to complement a unique legal system offering relatively simple and inexpensive remedies against deceptive advertisements—particularly to competitors and, to a lesser extent, to consumers via their associations. In view of this special German situation, one can conclude that it was correct to restrict the Werberat's scope to these "gray zones at the limit of the law" in a country that is basically conservative in outlook.

This uniqueness, however, has not granted the Werberat extensive reach and credibility. This is largely because it is subordinated to the grander scheme of the Advertising Federation (ZAW) to promote and defend the industry, and to develop "self-discipline." This subordination to higher ZAW purposes has made the Werberat largely reactive to external developments, that is, individual complaints and more general criticisms of advertising—an attitude readily understandable in a country where industry is vulnerable to numerous and easy legal challenges. As in other countries, advertising self-regulation has been developed to prove that more regulation is not necessary and that the industry cares about consumer interests.

While suiting a system of pure self-regulation, the exclusion of outsiders from the Werberat's functioning is questionable to the extent that it limits its expertise, objectivity and credibility about the very subjective matters of taste and opinion. Some outside participation, however, may prove inevitable in view of similar developments in other countries, the recommendations of various supranational bodies (e.g., the European Economic Community and the Council of Europe), and/or some crisis that may threaten the German ASR system's legitimacy (e.g., the "women-in-advertising" issue).

It may not be essential for an ASR system to include outsiders to be credible: the U.S. NAD also excludes them, yet is considered to be independent and effective. Much more important is the perception of autonomy. If it is viewed as a mere "public-relations" project designed to prove that industry "cares" and/or as a pure internal dialogue among "honorable merchants" eager to wash their linen in private, an ASR system loses or lacks sufficient credibility. This is the fundamental dilemma faced by the Werberat: it exists and functions well within self-imposed limits, but is it credible enough as an independent body? The evidence gathered during this study suggests that it has not reached this level yet.

Finally, one can question the credibility of an ASR system limited to what the law does not cover—mainly, "soft" matters of taste and opinion. Self-regulation must remain distinct from the law, and it often plays a fundamentally complementary role to it where the latter has not proven effective. The vast and easy reach of the German legal system makes such a division of labor logical and plausible, although difficult. Yet, an ASR system cannot readily distance itself completely from issues of false and misleading advertising, which loom equally large in criticisms of the industry. A commitment to eradicating all forms of bad advertising behavior—whether defined under the law or through voluntary codes and guidelines—is essential to its credibility. Otherwise, complainants who are told that their complaint cannot be accepted because it does not fall within the purview of German self-regulation may well feel that it is the system itself that is frivolous or capricious—not their complaint. Of course, all ASR systems exclude some types of complaints—about religious, political and controversy advertising, for example. Such exclusions, however, are more easily justified because they do not deal with "commercial" advertising, which is what private industry can only be concerned about. Simply referring a few cases to the authorities or the ZBUW because they are the proper vehicles for handling deceptive and otherwise unfair advertising matters is not credible either.

Consequently, German advertising self-regulation may well have to broaden its scope to deal with matters other than those of taste and opinion and other "gray zones at the limit of the law." Currently, the law copes adequately with most infringements of good advertising behavior, but the Werberat may be well advised to handle more of them too in a complementary or parallel manner in order to achieve greater credibility.

Altogether, this analysis largely corroborates Udo Beier's (1979, pp. 311ff) and Brandmair's (1977, pp. 256 and 276) recommendations to have the Werberat: (1) achieve greater automony vis-à-vis the advertising industry; (2) expand its publicity efforts to the general public and invite more complaints from it; (3) monitor German advertising more systematically; (4) increase outside partici-pation in at least some of its activities (e.g., in identifying problematic areas), and (5) reach beyond the "gray zones" of advertising to handle other types of complaints that consumers also consider to be valid. While it is doubtful that the ZAW and the Werberat will readily accept such fundamental changes in the latter's philosophy, structure and operations, some changes appear inevitable on account of various domestic, foreign and international pressures, precedents and other developments.

NOTES

1. A popular treatise on competition law devotes some 500 pages just to Article 1 of the 1909 UWG law: Wolfgang Hefermehl, and Adolf Baumbach, *Wettbewerbsrecht* [Advertising Law] Munich: G. H. Beck'sche Verlagsbuchhandlung, 1983.

2. In any case, only competitors—not individual consumers—can sue for damages. Corrective advertising may be ordered by the courts, but is rarely imposed by them.

3. For example, food and drug regulations, while of an administrative nature, can be enforced under the UWG law because violation of their provisions will be regarded as an act of unfair competition.

4. Government agencies cannot sue firms under the 1909 UWG law, which is civil in nature and designed to solve problems between private parties, but these agencies can prosecute violators under criminal laws (Reich and Micklitz 1981, pp. 118–119). German courts must handle complaints submitted to them under the purview of the 1909 UWG law, while governmental agencies—as in other countries—exercise much greater latitude in assuming complaints.

5. There have been proposals to allow individual consumers to sue for an injunction under the 1909 law, but they have not been enacted into law yet. A 1986 draft of government-proposed amendments grants consumers the right to cancel a contract in the case of misleading advertising, but no right to damages.

6. Germans often complain—like the British—that foreigners do not understand their legal system and, therefore, mistakenly ask for more administrative- and criminal-law remedies of the sorts available in other European countries (public prosecutors, consumer ombudsman, etc.) and in the United States (FTC).

7. This section focuses on what is relevant for understanding German advertising self-regulation. Yet, it is well to realize that there is an ongoing debate about the short-comings of German legislation dealing with unfair competition and consumer protection, as well as various proposals to extend or improve its coverage. Recent regulatory pro-posals, however, are not so much about advertising (except, perhaps, regarding medicines) as about premiums, competitions, special sales, liquidations, price comparisons, pyramid selling and door-to-door selling.

8. German law requires that an interest organization be set up either to promote business interests or consumer interests, but not both. Of course, pursuing one such goal may have beneficial effects for the other. The ZBUW's importance is reflected by the fact that about 25 percent of advertising complaints are handled by it, rather than by competing organizations of a similar nature, trade associations, and Chambers of Commerce and Industry. The German Highest Court (*Bundesgerichtshof*) has also sustained more of its cases than for other organizations. However, it is not necessary to go through the ZBUW or similar organizations; and warnings are not necessary, although they are used in most cases because legal costs are recoverable only if a warning was issued. Besides, most legal action is designed to stop a particular practice, and warnings have proven effective for that purpose.

9. There is a sizable German-language literature on advertising self-regulation— mainly, Brandmair (1977), but also the numerous publications of the ZAW (reports, newsletters, pamphlets, publications by its leaders, etc.). Practically nothing has been written about it in English, however, apart from the brief section on Germany in: J. P. Neelankavil and A. B. Stridsberg's *Advertising Self-Regulation: A Global Perspective* (New York: Hastings House, 1980), pp. 78–80. This section borrows mostly from Brandmair (1977) and Nickel (1982).

10. As elsewhere, there were criticisms of cigarette, alcoholic and drug advertising and of advertising to children. The concentration of commercials in a few blocks of time also generated public annoyance. As usual, advertising was criticized for making people buy what they do not need. These issues are still current, although less highly charged.

11. Political, religious and advocacy/controversy (about general issues such as taxation) advertising are not handled by the Werberat, as is true in other countries too.

12. The moral support given by member associations to the Werberat was not systematically studied. However, they do relay ZAW/DWR information to their members, endorse its activities, and occasionally lodge complaints with the Werberat.

13. One such DWR ad states that: "We will take the initiative if someone dishonestly violates the rules of fair play in advertising. In a free-market system it is logical that advertising also be free. However, this does not mean free from responsibility vis-à-vis customers. The advertising industry supports this principle and therefore established a control institution on a voluntary basis—the German Advertising Council. This Council watches advertising campaigns and it challenges cases where the advertisement does not follow the rules of honesty and decency. In the unlikely case that a 'slip' is observed, the Council will take action to clear up the matter. We are always at your service and will send you at your request a free copy of the interesting information brochure: 'Advertising Pros & Cons' [the DWR's address follows]."

14. Udo Beier recounts this episode in the *Berliner Anwaltsblatt* 12 (1983): pp. 287–292.

15. This answer was given by the Werberat in the 1986 International Advertising Association survey reported in Chapter 15.

16. The AgV has recently alerted medical associations about allegedly undue claims made by vitamin manufacturers.

17. There were pronouncements by Social-Democratic parliamentarians, the Minister of Youth, Family and Health Affairs, and the Christian-Democratic Party against sexist and denigrating advertisements, which the ZAW challenged on the basis of its own 1983 analysis of 2,614 newspaper ads.

18. However, the Federal Ministry of Economics allowed the Orderly Marketing Ar-

rangements of the tobacco industry in 1973 in order to enable it to self-control cigarette advertising in terms of quantity and quality. Other associations (insurance, pharmaceuticals, branded goods, etc.) have also registered various industry rules with the authorities.

19. From around 1977 to 1978, there were various proposals to strengthen the 1909 law against unfair competition, but little came of them, so far as advertising is concerned. The present conservative government is probusiness, but cannot appear to be too lenient so that it may well entertain further special regulations as in the matter of medicine advertising.

20. Article 5 states that: "The Directive does not exclude the voluntary control of misleading advertising by self-regulatory bodies . . . if proceedings before such bodies are in addition to the court or administrative proceedings referred to in [Article 4]."

REFERENCES

Beier, F. K. "The Law of Unfair Competition in the European Community—Its Development and Present Status." *IIC* [International Review of Industrial Property and Copyright Law] 16, no. 2 (1985): 139–64.

Beier, Udo. "Schwachstellen der Werbeselbstkontrolle: Aufgezeigt am Beispiel des Deutschen Werberats" [Weakness of Advertising Self-control: The Case of the German Advertising Council]. *Journal of Consumer Policy* 3, no. 3 (1979): 300–13.

Biervert, Bernd et al. "Alternatives for Consumer Policy: A Study of Consumer Organizations in the FRG." *Journal of Consumer Policy* 7, no. 3 (1984): 343–58.

Brandmair, Lothar. *Die Freiwillige Selbstkontrolle der Werbung* [The Voluntary Self-Control of Advertising]. Cologne: Carl Heymanns Verlag, 1977.

Dimper, M. F. "Werbeselbstkontrolle—ein Feigenblatt [Advertising Self-Control—a Figleaf]." *Jahrbuch der Werbung* [Advertising Annual] Volume XVI. Dusseldorf: Econ Verlag, (1979): 37–39.

Fullerton, R. A., and T. R. Nevett. "Advertising and Society: A Comparative Analysis of the Roots of Distrust in Germany and Great Britain." *International Journal of Advertising* 5, no. 3 (1986): 225–41.

Lambsdorff, Otto Graf. "Self-Regulation in Advertising: A View from West Germany." *Advertising* [U.K.] 62 (Winter 1979–1980): 13–15.

Nickel, Volker. "German Admen Think Legal before Thinking Creative." *Advertising Age* 50, no. 48 (November 12, 1979): S–32.

———. "Werbeselbstdisziplin in Deutschland [Advertising Self-Discipline in Germany]." *Marketing-ZFP* 3 (August 1982): 213–19.

Reich, Norbert, and H. M. Micklitz. *Consumer Legislation in the Federal Republic of Germany*. New York: Van Nostrand Reinhold, 1981.

Rock, Reinhard et al. "A Critique of Some Fundamental Theoretical and Practical Tenets of Present Consumer Policy." *Journal of Consumer Policy* 4, no. 2 (1980): 93–101.

Zentralausschuss der Werbewirtschaft [ZAW]. *Spruchpraxis des Deutscher Werberats* [Case Practice of the DWR]. Bonn: various dates.

———. *Deutscher Werberat: Ordnung, Leistungen und Ergebnisse* [Groundrules, Achievements and Results]. Bonn: 1985, 1987.

———. *Werbung '85*. [Advertising 1985]. Bonn: 1985. Other issues were also used.

———. *ZAW-Service* [a monthly publication of the ZAW]. Bonn: various dates.

ACKNOWLEDGMENTS

The assistance of the following people is gratefully acknowledged: Uwe Albrecht (Deutscher Werberat/ZAW), Dr. Udo Beier (University of Hamburg), Dr. Frauke Henning-Bodewig (Max Planck Institute, Munich), Dr. Lothar Brandmair (Bayerische Staatskanzlei), Manfred Dimper (AgV), Hans Fiuczynski (M&M/Mars), Dr. Norbert Reich (University of Bremen), Tassilo Schwaller (Gesellschaft Werbeagenturen), Dr. Gunther Silberer (University of Bremen), Hans C. Sieh (Bayer and DWR), Dr. Hans Tonner (Hamburg), and Lutz Wallraven (formerly of the ZBUW). Dr. Helmut Soldner (University of Koblenz) provided very valuable research and editorial assistance in this project.

7

France: Bureau de Vérification de la Publicité

Structurally speaking, nonmembers of the French advertising industry play a minimal role in its self-regulatory body, the Bureau de Vérification de la Publicité (BVP, Advertising Control Bureau), since its board of directors includes only a tiny minority of outsiders, while all decisions about consumer and competitor complaints are made by the BVP staff itself. Yet, the BVP's effectiveness and credibility have not suffered from this arrangement.

The major explanation for this situation is that the BVP has managed to develop cooperative side-relationships with part of the French consumerist movement and with the government in developing and administering its advertising standards. Thereby, its self-regulatory structure has been kept fairly intact while some elements of outside participation have in fact been woven into its functioning. These conclusions are based on a review of the literature as well as on field interviews and correspondence with BVP and other advertising-association executives, government officials, experts and consumerists from 1981 to 1987.

Structure

The Bureau de Vérification de la Publicité (BVP) was founded in 1935 (under a different name) at the initiative of the major French advertiser, agency and media associations to become their capstone self-regulatory body. (These associations, however, have retained their own self-disciplinary activities about the professional behavior of their members.) Its official mission is to promote fair, truthful and wholesome advertising in the public interest, through freely accepted self-regulation.

Its present name, Bureau de Vérification de la Publicité, was adopted in 1953. The BVP was reformed in 1970–1971, at the suggestion of government, when its board of directors (Conseil d'Administration) was broadened to include, among others, representatives from the National Consumer Institute (Institut National de la Consommation, INC)—a government-sponsored and subsidized research, information and education body designed to assist consumer associations. The BVP also acquired a president chosen from outside the advertising industry (*BVP Echos* March 1985, p. 1).

The president is the thirty-third member of the Board of Directors, and has to be an "independent high-status person" (haute personnalité indépendante). The last four have had a legal background and judiciary experience in high-level French courts and councils. Except for the three seats granted to the INC (only one of which is in fact used), one seat to the distribution sector, one independent lawyer and one media-sales representative, all other members come from the advertising industry (including the former government-controlled television commercials sales monopoly).

The actual administration of the BVP has in fact been delegated to the president, a managing director (until recently a man with an advertising background, and currently a former executive of the INC) and a fourteen-person staff including three lawyers and one monitoring expert. Its financing comes entirely from the industry, apart from minor donations and revenues.

Functioning

Since the BVP's control activities are fairly traditional (cf. BVP *Recueil des Recommandations* 1983; Conseil Economique et Social 1980; Haas 1983; and Scrivener et al. 1979), the following sections focus on what is novel or different.

Norm Development

The BVP applies a broad array of rules:

1. *Government laws and regulations pertaining to advertising*—mainly the 1973 Royer Law on Consumer Protection and Information (as amended in 1978), which forbids all forms of false and misleading advertisements, puts the burden of proof on the incriminated advertiser in such penal cases, and allows for rather strict penalties (jail, fine, corrective advertising). This is currently the major basis of action for the BVP since 80 percent of its recent interventions have been grounded in that law. This major reliance on the law totally differs from U.K. practice, although it is also found in Belgium.

2. *The International Code of Advertising Practice* of the International Chamber of Commerce (ICC), which provides broad guidelines and is frequently cited by the BVP, particularly in matters of taste and social responsibility, where the law is relatively silent.

3. The guidelines (*Avis*) of the now inactive National Advertising Council (Conseil National de la Publicité, CNP), which was the official spokesman, promoter and defender of the broad interests of the advertising "interprofession"

(advertisers-agencies-media). CNP *avis* were intended to improve the "quality and morality" of advertising, and dealt with "soft" topics not readily amenable to hard and fast government regulations or to the BVP's own Recommendations (see below): (a) the proper identification of advertisements, (b) the exploitation of human credulity, (c) the handling of race and religion in advertising, (d) violence, (e) sex stereotyping, and (f) film advertising (the indirect denigration of competitors was also discussed). These CNP guidelines are essentially elaborations of various provisions of the ICC Code and of the BVP's General Recommendations.[1] CNP *avis* have now become an intrinsic part of the BVP's own set of General Recommendations, and are directly applied by the BVP staff.

4. *The BVP's own "Recommendations,"* which are of two kinds. General Recommendations cut across all product and service categories and deal with the proper identification of ads and of the advertiser, testimonials, children, the representation of women, classified ads, safety, price advertising, look-alike models and the use of superlatives. They are developed by the BVP's staff and submitted for approval to the BVP president and to its eight-member Specialists' Committee (Comité de Spécialistes). The latter are appointed by the Board of Directors and include a representative from the National Consumer Institute (INC) and one from the government-appointed Television Commercials Sales Office (Régie Française de Télévision, RFP). These General Recommendations parallel those developed by the International Chamber of Commerce and the CNP's guidelines (see above).

Sectoral Recommendations are about the advertising of specific products and services—from model agencies to direct-mail advertisements. There are some forty-five of them by now, and they provide a fair amount of details about the applicable legislation, the meaning to be given to various terms used in advertising these goods and services, the use of research findings, and about references to performance specifications. These Sectoral Recommendations are developed by special BVP Technical Commissions made up of the relevant industry's representatives but also of outsiders as advisers, namely, representatives of the appropriate ministry (e.g., Health), the Television Commercials Sales Office (RFP), and the National Consumer Institute (INC), which delegates the appropriate product-testing expert. Ultimately, they are submitted for advice to the BVP's Specialists' Committee and to the BVP president, but they constitute mainly commitments of a particular industrial sector, which plays the key role in their drafting.[2]

This use of technical commissions is unique and represents the most significant use of outside participation in French advertising self-regulation. It is clever too since it precludes the BVP from being accused of having developed "internal" rules designed exclusively to serve the self-interest of advertisers. Besides, it helps prevent the multiplication of separate advertising codes and guidelines by industrial sectors, as is the case in the United States, since the BVP provides a focal point for their elaboration and application.

Still, the BVP does not have a monopoly on advertising standards since professional associations (e.g., of advertisers and of advertising agencies) as well as the Television Commercials Sales Office (RFP) have their own guidelines. However, there is a growing similarity among these standards on account of the interlocking structure of all these bodies, that is, their representatives sit on each other's standards committees (see below).

Advising the Industry

Some 28 percent of the cases handled by the BVP in 1986 (1,067/3,762) consisted of free prepublication advice given to advertisers, agencies and media by the BVP staff. This proportion fluctuates from year to year (it increased by 23 percent from 1985 to 1986) but is higher than in the mid–1970s, thereby revealing a significant use of the BVP by its members.

Ad Monitoring (Pige)

Monitoring represents a sizable function for the BVP, which examines a sample of publications and radio spots (television is not monitored) as well as ads in problematic sectors (e.g., health and financial schemes) on a constant and systematic basis, although to a lesser extent than in the United Kingdom.[3] Thus, 407 monitoring cases were followed up with advertisers in 1986 (there was an average of such 360 follow-ups during the period 1975 to 1981) out of thousands of ads examined by the BVP on its own initiative. Again, this activity is carried out by the BVP staff.

Handling Consumer and Competitor Complaints

This activity is performed by the BVP's three in-house jurists, who handle some 900 to 1,200 cases a year (some of them deal with the same ad). Over half of the 3,762 cases in 1986 came from consumers (1,990, an increase of 56 percent over 1984) and 8 percent (298 in 1986) from other outsiders—mainly competitors.

BVP jurists contact the advertiser or its agency, ask for proper substantiation of the claims made, and urge them to make the necessary changes (modification or withdrawal) if some law or BVP Recommendation appears to have been violated. In the case of recalcitrant violators (113 cases in 1986), the BVP's jurists submit to its managing director a proposal requesting the media to stop diffusing the incriminated ad. The managing director either accepts the proposal or asks the jurists to reexamine the case or to contact the advertiser anew. Ultimately, this proposal comes before the BVP president, who has to make the final decision. If he agrees, the relevant media who are members of the BVP are requested to comply with its request to stop publishing the advertisement, something achieved in some 95 percent of the requests.

To avoid legal problems, the BVP states in its request to the media that this is only advice open to the ultimate appreciation of the courts—actually, the BVP carries insurance to protect itself against advertiser suits, but has never been sued for wrongful denunciation. The Paris Court of Appeals has sanctioned the right of a medium to refuse or suspend the publication of an incriminated ad, following an unfavorable BVP opinion (*BVP Echos* May 1980, p. 6). Conversely, a favorable BVP prepublication written opinion would probably be accepted by the courts as a proof of good faith on the part of the advertiser (*BVP Echos* April 1981, p. 4).

On rare occasions, the BVP lodges a formal complaint with the French authorities charged with enforcing advertising regulations, particularly in the case of drug, medical device and treatment advertising; and it has applied for symbolic civil damages (*partie civile*) in connection with the public prosecution of violators (see below). It also collaborates with magistrates that solicit its advice; in return, the courts have referred to its standards in cases where the law remains silent.

Publicizing Sanctions

The name of the advertiser and a brief synopsis of the case are subsequently published regarding ads: (1) whose withdrawal was requested of the media, and (2) whose prohibition was ordered by the Ministries of Health and of Social Affairs (some of these government decisions were precipitated by BVP denunciations to the authorities). Such publicity is provided in *BVP Echos*, the organization's newsletter, which is widely distributed to BVP members, the press, consumer associations, various governmental bodies and magistrates, experts, etc. A limited number of cases that led to the voluntary modification or withdrawal of an ad are also briefly, although anonymously, described in this publication.

Outside Participation in BVP Activities

The BVP Board of Directors includes no representatives of consumer associations (the INC is not a consumer association) or of government ministries, nor does it have "independent" or "moral" representation (e.g., public figures, pastors, academics, experts) as in the United Kingdom. Yet, the above analysis reveals a steady pattern of participation by key outside public bodies.

The National Consumer Institute (INC)

This government-created and subsidized autonomous establishment is not a representative consumer association (there are about twenty of them in France) but is at the disposal of such associations, as their "technical arm," through its research and product-testing facilities. In fact, it acts at times as a militant consumer organization via its well-known publication *50 Millions de Consommateurs* and its regular television and radio programs, which discuss issues and advise consumers.

According to BVP statutes, three INC representatives can sit on its Board of Directors.[4] Other INC delegates serve as advisers on the BVP's Specialists' Committee and Technical Commissions, where BVP Sectoral Recommendations are developed (see above), thereby gaining valuable information about advertising issues and problems that the INC can use in its publications as well as other educational and informational activities.

This mutual relationship is not without its problems. While the competition between the INC and consumer associations is a topic in itself (Burson-Marsteller 1981), it is enough to point out that the ambivalence of its role makes the INC reluctant to be seen as too closely associated with the BVP. Hence, the INC has only designated one representative to sit on the BVP Board of Directors instead of the three it is entitled to (a recent INC representative became the new BVP managing director in January 1983). For one thing, its extreme minority position (out of thirty-two possible directors) is just as well served by one member. Besides, the INC feels that the BVP—and the former National Advertising Council (CNP) for that matter—does not represent the entire advertising industry, since it does not include numerous smaller advertisers, regional newspapers and private local radios (Conseil Economique et Social 1980, pp. 13–14), although the BVP had some 300 media members in 1985.[5]

Conversely, a few advertising-industry members, who sit with INC representatives on various BVP bodies, feel ill at ease airing and discussing their problems in front of such outsiders. They would in fact prefer to meet with INC and other consumerist representatives in other loci, such as the Concertation Commission (see below) where confrontation is more readily expected and accepted. Some purists would even want to exclude all outside representation in BVP activities on the principled ground that self-regulation should be handled exclusively by insiders. However, it does not appear that the BVP will choose to end INC participation on its various bodies, since there are compensating advantages in terms of implicit endorsement of BVP activities, and technical inputs from the INC.

Government Authorities

There is significant formal interaction between the BVP and various government authorities. Delegates from the relevant ministries sit as invited advisers on BVP Technical Commissions, while the BVP has been represented on the Prescreening (*visionnage*) Commission of the government-controlled Régie Française de Publicité (RFP), which has had a monopoly on the sale of commercials on French state television and radio channels. The government-appointed president of the RFP has been a member of the BVP Board of Directors and of its Specialists' Committee; and the RFP Prescreening Commission's set of rules and guidelines has paralleled those of the BVP (see below for new developments in this area). Besides, medical and pharmaceutical advertising is supervised and prescreened by special government committees of the Ministries of Health and

Social Affairs. On all of these bodies, the BVP interacts with INC and other consumer-association representatives.

Outside of these formal channels, there are constant informal contacts between the BVP and the authorities—particularly the former departments of Consumer Affairs (Consommation) and of Communications under the Mitterrand Socialist governments. While other advertising associations participate in such exchanges, the BVP focuses only on technical issues related to its domain. For example, it would leave it to professional associations to lobby against increased taxes on advertising, but it negotiated with the government a 1982 BVP Sectoral Recommendation about liquor advertising, which was saddled by various restrictive and protectionist regulations that had come under EEC criticism. Actually, several BVP Recommendations have been developed at the government's request (cf. *BVP Echos* October and December 1984).

The BVP recommended at one point that the Royer Law be amended to explicitly authorize interprofessional (tripartite) associations such as the BVP to sue for civil damages (*action civile*) because the courts have limited such recourse to professional (e.g., advertisers or agencies) and consumerist associations concerned with the protection of consumer interests. The BVP would have trouble proving damages resulting from misleading advertising, although lower courts have occasionally granted it one symbolic franc, but this was not tested in higher courts, which would probably have voided such a decision (*BVP Echos* March 1983, p. 3; and May 1984, p. 3). While the BVP can denounce violators to the government, like anybody else, being able to sue in order to defend the industry's interests would provide the BVP with another "dissuasion" tool.

Government Positions toward the BVP

Support

Much of the 1970 reform of the BVP (see above) was strongly suggested by the French government (BVP Cinquantième Anniversaire 1985). While this reform did not prevent the enactment of many new regulations during the 1970s, BVP initiatives and contacts have been welcome by the authorities under both the Giscard d'Estaing and Mitterrand governments, who repeatedly acknowledged the existence and usefulness of the advertising self-regulatory system. Thus, former Socialist Prime Minister Mauroy instructed government bodies to abide by BVP Recommendations when engaging in advertising (Circular of November 4, 1981). Besides, the Scrivener Report commissioned under the Centrist Giscard d'Estaing government strongly praised advertising self-regulation:

Self-regulation presents two essential advantages. First, it unequivocally confronts firms with their ethical and social responsibilities, and derives therefrom an educational capability which regulation lacks. Second, self-regulation is often more effective than the latter because advertising is a complex, multiform and rapidly evolving phenomenon which does not lend itself to the formulation and, even more so, the application of regulatory measures (Scrivener et al. 1979, p. 91).

It is also fast and cheap—a big plus in times of budgetary constrictions. While the Scrivener report stressed that French advertising self-regulation was still weak and deficient in some respects (see below), it urged its expansion and reinforcement rather than its replacement by further regulation. In 1985, the Economic and Social Council (a government advisory body) also singled out the positive contributions of the BVP to better advertising. Furthermore, the 1985 report of the Consumer Law Reform Commission concluded that advertising regulations should not be multiplied, except in the case of major abuses. Instead, the role of self-regulation must be acknowledged because, better accepted by professionals than government intervention, it helps minimize detailed rules (Calais-Auloy 1986).

In a sense, the BVP approach of developing sectoral recommendations elaborated by representative professional organizations in cooperation with the appropriate governmental authorities has been typical of the "French planning" approach (Shonfield 1965); that is, the government has involved the appropriate business bodies in developing their own norms, but under government supervision in order to avoid collusive behavior detrimental to the public interest. The relatively minor role played by consumer organizations in this process even parallels that of the labor unions under the French Plan.

Under the 1981–1985 Socialist governments, contacts between the advertising industry (including the BVP) and the relevant ministries[6] maintained the same pace, quality and openness as in the past, even though the latter considered new regulations in such specific areas as: the stereotyping and degrading of women in advertisements, advertising directed to children, and the advertising of easily abused products (tobacco, alcohol, over-the-counter drugs, fatty and sugary products, etc.). The BVP as well as other representative organizations were consulted by these governments on such matters, but only application decrees pertaining to consumer-credit advertising were enacted during this period.

Reservations

Yet, the 1981–1985 Socialist governments pointed out the limits and limitations of advertising self-regulation. Thus, a representative of the Consumer-Affairs Ministry, speaking for the minister, stressed that: "The BVP is a professional body whose purpose is to put the best face possible on advertising, but it is not a consumer-protection organization. It cannot substitute for public authority. It complements legislation but does not free the authorities of their own responsibilities (*BVP Echos* November 1981, p. 7)." Similarly, Mrs. Lalumière, when Minister of Consumer Affairs, concluded that: "Public authorities have no business substituting for consumer-protection associations, nor counting on the self-discipline of [advertising] professionals; but neither should the BVP consider itself as a consumer-protection nor as a regulatory body (*BVP Echos* April 1982, p. 1).''

Clearly, these views conflict with the BVP's self-proclaimed task of consumer protection (*vide* its attempts to qualify as a consumer-protection association under the Royer Law). Besides, beyond these statements of principles lurk problems about the proper boundaries of regulation and self-regulation. If the government presses the BVP to develop too many recommendations, the burden of self-regulation could be perceived as too heavy and no longer as the expression of the industry's own wishes and volition. Moreover, laws and regulations already provide the basis for a very large proportion of BVP interventions (see above). This makes the BVP a quasienforcer of the law—a role which the administration, the courts and advertisers themselves do not always appreciate nor accept since guarantees of due process are not equally developed under self-regulation.

However, the French government expressed the thought that some BVP Recommendations could be translated into official regulations once their usefulness and effectiveness had been established (*BVP Echos* April 1981, p. 8). In this perspective, self-regulation would serve as the proving ground and antechamber of regulation—if only to reach non-BVP members as well as recalcitrant BVP violators.

"Hard" vs. "Soft" Law

The French government makes an implicit distinction between "hard" (e.g., false and misleading advertising) and "soft" (e.g., bad taste in advertising) issues. The former would be the subject of laws and regulations that can readily handle objective violations, while industry guidelines and sanctions would focus on "fairness" (at least in relation to consumers since unfair competition is handled by the law) and "good taste." As Calais-Auloy (1986) points out, consumers have practically no legal recourse in the case of unfair advertising, but must turn to the BVP for such complaints. In fact, the BVP has handled sexist and indecent ads, those presenting products in dangerous circumstances, and even the improper use of the French and foreign languages; and it often comments about such issues in *BVP Echos*.[7]

This "soft law" role is one where outsiders are useful if not essential, but the Deontology Commission of the former National Advertising Council (CNP) and the BVP staff have not included outsiders. Thus, the appreciation of what is in good taste, decent, fair, etc., has not benefited from opinions that are more independent and broader than those found among advertising practitioners and officials, except for what has been achieved through "concertation" with consumer associations (see below). Consequently, the distinction between "hard" and "soft" topics and jurisdictions resurrects the issue of outside representation, which the BVP can ignore or minimize only so long as it focuses on hard Sectoral

Recommendations where industry perspectives can legitimately predominate, although, even there, outsiders are invited to act as advisers.

In any case, it is likely that the French government will sooner or later deal with such "soft" topics as advertising to children and sex-stereotyping, where self-regulatory experience around the world is helping to develop fairly specific rules. In the short term, however, the current antiregulatory climate in France bodes well for the development and greater use of advertising self-regulation in lieu of massive new consumer-protection regulations.

Industry-Consumer Concertation

If self-regulation excludes or minimizes the formal participation of nonindustry members, how else can advertisers and consumerists interact? Here, the European Economic Community has urged that consultation take place among these bodies; and the Scrivener Report pressed for "the reinforcement of professional self-discipline, enlightened by true concertation with consumers (Scrivener et al. 1979, p. 7; see also Conseil Economique et Social 1984)."

What does this concept stand for? It starts with the recognition that advertisers and consumers both have legitimate but at times conflicting interests, so that some new equilibrium is needed between them. This requires mutual understanding through dialogue without denying the specific objectives of each side: "Concertation does not deny militant action by consumer associations, nor commercial action by firms (Scrivener et al. 1979, p. 98)." If understanding can be achieved, both sides can negotiate agreements about what constitutes appropriate professional behavior. Ultimately, such agreements may be extended by government to an entire industry in order to reach those practitioners that are not members of the relevant associations. In other words, industry-consumer agreements can become "collective conventions" similar to the ones negotiated between employers and unions, and formally recognized by governments as applying to all firms (Calais-Auloy 1984). Concertation, however, is not meant to replace self-regulation. The two should interact but "this articulation must not generate role ambiguity or confusion: self-discipline is the business of professionals [and] will remain effective only if its management and financing are clearly left to their responsibility (Scrivener et al. 1979, p. 100)."

The Concertation Commission

The Scrivener Commission's wish that concertation be given a try for an experimental period was soon followed in June 1980 by the creation of the Commission de Concertation Consommateurs/CNP by the National Advertising Council (CNP). This Commission has had some thirty members equally divided between consumer-association and advertising-industry representatives (with two cochairmen), with the National Consumer Institute and the BVP sitting on the side as "expert witnesses." They have met regularly, mostly as a discussion forum but with some resulting action (CNP 1983). Both sides agreed to exclude government representatives from their meetings so that they may choose their topics and discuss them freely and secretly. Actually, this pledge of secrecy led the Union Fédérale des Consommateurs—one of the largest but Left-leaning consumer associations—to stop attending meetings after the initial one.

The negotiation of agreements between business and consumer associations has been postponed indefinitely. French industry has been scared by this novelty and afraid that it could be extended to other sectors. Besides, it considers that consumer associations are not fully representative and that they cannot commit the entire movement anyway—both sides use that argument, as was seen above. Advertisers also feel that negotiation would be one-sided anyway since consumerists refuse to accept a deontology of their own (see below). In any case, advertisers prefer agreements dealing with sectoral problems, rather than with general issues where ideology is more likely to predominate.

Hence, meetings of the Concertation Commission have been devoted to airing general issues and discussing a few specific topics. Essentially, the industry position is: "Tell us what is shocking or bothering you about advertising." This is supposed to be "therapeutic" for the consumerist representatives, while industry answers are expected to "demystify" or "demythologize" ideological objections, or to point out that such concerns have already been taken care of by the law, BVP Recommendations and CNP *Avis*. This dialogue appears to have been largely one-sided, with consumerist representatives doing most of the questioning, while industry responds and defends itself.

Some workgroups, however, have focused on more concrete problems such as the advertising of dangerous products, classified ads, games of chance, and mobile-truck advertising (Le CNP cinq ans après, 1982; CNP 1983), with both sides approaching the government together, regarding the latter. Consumerist representatives have also asked for information about the prescreening of commercials, the functioning of the BVP, and the size and use of advertising expenditures—among others. Some BVP Recommendations have been amended accordingly.

Consumerist Demands

Altogether, advertisers consider such informal and private discussions as useful and preferable to external confrontation. Yet, they recognize that consumerists are not going to shed their ideological biases—whether legitimate or not—and that they will not stop resorting to confrontation in the media nor stop pressing for further regulation and taxation of advertising.

While it is hard to generalize about consumerist demands, the 1981 Socialist Party's platform included a special tax on advertising expenditures to finance consumer associations, equal time on television to counteract advertising messages and stricter regulation of advertising to children (Burson-Marsteller 1981, p. 29). The Socialist-inclined Union Fédérale des Consommateurs, the National

Consumer Institute, the Leftist INDECOSA consumer association and the CGT union of advertising workers (SNETCP) have had similar demands designed to promote consumer interests and further advertising control (CGT 1981).

The Government's Positions

The Socialist government's positions toward advertising, consumerism and self-regulation never clearly emerged. While definitely in favor of a greater role and expanded means for consumer associations and the National Consumer Institute, it did not want to be perceived as totally associated with consumerist views. Thus, the former minister for consumer affairs stated that: "It is out of the question for the Ministry . . . to be a super consumer association. To each his own responsibilities and role. . . . This ministry is not directed against producers, and it does not intend to alter their freedom (Burson-Marsteller 1981, p. 30)." It would also not act as the spokesman for consumer associations in negotiating with the advertising industry, since it must also consider the more general "public interest."

Regarding concertation, the Socialist government's former Consumer-Affairs department favored it in principle but was realistic about its prospects: "Outside of the prescreening of television commercials [where both consumerist and advertising representatives participate], the government cannot mandate concertation (private communication from a government official)." Still, this department kept track of what happened in the Concertation Commission, and brought up some topics of discussion (e.g., about comparison advertising) before the Conseil National de la Consommation (CNC), where representatives of government, industry and the consumer movement sit together.

Concertation's Outcomes

With or without the government's backing, consumer associations and militants have refused to bind themselves to agreements with advertisers. To industry suggestions during Concertation-Commission meetings that consumerist publications and broadcasts be more objective, and that they prenotify advertising organizations of such campaigns, consumer representatives replied: "You don't tell us in advance what you're going to advertise, so why should we submit to your prescreening?" Short of outright libel, they prefer to keep their freedom of speech, which is less regulated than that of advertisers. As militants, they have to take the offensive and always ask for "more." Better to single out advertising offenses and offenders, hit them on the run, and argue with the advertising industry later. That way, both attack and concertation can be effectively used by consumerists.[8]

Altogether, the French attempt at concertation has not proven very fruitful to date, echoing the Belgian experience with the Belgian Conseil de la Consommation, where official industry and consumer representatives "talk" but seldom compromise or reach agreement (Conseil Economique et Social 1980). In any case, in March 1984, the CNP was "put to rest"—not dissolved—because of a lack of moral and financial support by its media members, particularly the periodical press. Other reasons included: (1) the feeling that the threat of excessive government regulation and taxation of advertising—key factors in the creation of the tripartite CNP—no longer existed, and thus no longer justified a formal effort on the part of the industry, and (2) the printed-press segment wanted to distance itself from the audiovisual media, which threaten it, and it was unwilling to increase its financial contributions to the CNP. Now, the professional associations of advertisers, agencies, media and other supports meet informally on an ad hoc basis without the financial burden of a CNP staff.

However, the Commission de la Concertation Associations de Consommateurs/Professionels de la Publicité (its new name) survived, with the BVP providing its permanent Secretariat. It meets every two months and has issued a few *communiqués*, for example, about advertising on the new local radios, which had begun to proliferate under the socialist governments. The BVP has referred to these regular concertation efforts as "self-regulation enlightened and assisted by consumer organizations (*BVP Echos* August-September 1985, p. 6)."

Related Issues

Underlying or accompanying these developments and problems, are other issues bearing on the structure and functioning of the BVP.

BVP Reach

It has been estimated that through its 1,200 associational and individual paying members, the BVP reaches some 80 percent of French advertisements, excluding television commercials, which have been prescreened and posthandled by the Régie Française de Publicité. It is mostly smaller advertisers as well as a significant segment of the regional and local press and radio that have not joined. Since a major BVP sanction is requesting the stopping of incriminated ads through BVP-member media, this is a major lacuna of the system, although not one proper to France. (The BVP also acts by approaching incriminated advertisers, of course.)

The BVP points to some progress in recruiting members among this group and in reaching them indirectly through such capstone organizations as the Press Syndicate and through "confraternal" warnings and exhortations. Only a corporatist system with compulsory membership could resolve this problem,[9] but the French government has not favored that solution at all.

The advertising industry defends itself against such corporatist charges, since it consults the INC and the relevant ministries before developing its Sectoral Recommendations. Besides, there are now countervailing forces in the consumerist movement and in government regulation, which preclude any return to the privileges enjoyed by the old corporations or guilds. In any case, the BVP does not have a monopoly on developing standards and penalizing excesses, since other advertising associations as well as the government have their other norms and controls (*BVP Echos* February 1982, pp. 5–6).

BVP Visibility

Some 26 percent of the respondents to an October 1985 national poll were aware of the BVP's existence and activities—a proportion similar to that of the British ASA (it is best known in the Paris area as well as among male, younger, better educated and better heeled people). This proportion has grown, compared to the 9 percent of notoriety achieved in 1975, and 16 percent in 1980 (notoriety dropped after a BVP publicity campaign was interrupted in 1978). New publicity campaigns have been launched since 1981, and they seem to have born fruit. Besides, the BVP is increasingly contacting advertising associations and professionals, schools, magistrates and opinion leaders to make itself better known; and it is participating in various consumer programs on radio and television. Most BVP members of the press also display the BVP symbol to indicate their adherence to BVP standards, although not to vouch for the conformity of each and every advertisement. However, a BVP 1978 campaign to encourage more consumer complaints was vetoed by press members who felt it might imply that the control exercised by newspapers over their ads was inadequate. Consequently, BVP publicity campaigns have stressed the positive (''The BVP contributes to fair, truthful and wholesome advertising'') rather than the negative (''The BVP fights false and misleading ads'').

The BVP has been criticized for the small number of consumer complaints it receives and for the declining number of its postpublication cases and sanctions (CGT 1981, p. 76). While recognizing that greater notoriety would help increase consumer recourse, the BVP points out in reply that consumers do use other channels, such as consumer associations and government control units (e.g., the ministries of Health, Social Affairs and Economic Affairs). Besides, the BVP has increased its advising activities, and this should lead to fewer problematic cases. More generally, a higher level of professional behavior, exhorted and assisted by advertising self-regulation, is expected to result in fewer violations— and nobody should complain about that (*BVP Echos* February 1982, p. 5). Finally, the number of BVP activities has definitely increased in recent years (see above).

BVP Financing

After receiving a 40 to 50 percent subsidy from the National Advertising Council (CNP) after the mid–1970s in order to expand its activities, the BVP has become entirely self-financed through dues and miscellaneous revenues since 1981. Its finances are in good shape, but would obviously benefit from the steadier and more independent flow of income obtained by the British ASA through an automatic levy on advertisement billings.

Such a solution was tried out from 1979 to 1980 by the National Advertising Council (CNP) in order to: (1) relieve the BVP of the burdensome task of soliciting and collecting membership fees, and (2) counteract the consumerist objection: "How can you be independent of Advertiser X who pays you large dues?" It failed on account of CNP members' reluctance to continue the financial support of that council. Only a crisis situation, internal or external, would precipitate such a desirable development, although the BVP is now financially sound at least as far as its present scope of activities is concerned.

BVP Speed

Results here are impressive. About half of the outside complaints and of the problematic cases detected through BVP monitoring are resolved within a two-week period (BVP Rapport d'Activité [Annual Report] 1982, p. 2). Similarly fast action is obtained through prohibitions requested from the ministries of Health and Social Affairs. This is a better record than in the United Kingdom on account of the BVP staff making all necessary decisions, compared to the slower ASA Council, which meets only once a month to deliberate on the more difficult cases. It is mostly smaller advertisers—whether members or not—who delay the resolution process in France, but only a larger membership as well as an additional improvement in professional ethics can resolve this problem.

The New Media

The French broadcasting industry is undergoing major privatization. Instead of a state monopoly, there are now several private television networks after a couple of state-owned companies were sold off and a couple of new private ones were created. More commercials have thus become possible, but the question of their preclearance and postbroadcasting control remains unresolved.

A new National Commission for Communication and Freedoms (CNCL) is now responsible for new general rules about the length and frequency of commercials, those products and industries that can be advertised on television and other matters. However, the "deontological" control of commercials in terms of truthfulness, fairness and wholesomeness—both before and after their broadcasting—is still up in the air.

The options are: (1) to have such preclearance and complaint-handling tasks assumed by the new CNCL body, or (2) to have each network perform these tasks. In either case, the role of the BVP remains uncertain, although it is hard to imagine that it will be left out in view of its productive association with the RFP monopoly, its broad acceptance and support by industry and government and the desire of the new private networks to avoid outcries about the quality of the expanded commercials. In any case, it appears that the BVP will be more involved with television commercials, an area that it did not have to handle under the RFP system.

Industry Spokesman

The demise of the National Advertising Council (CNP) has cast the BVP in the role of "interprofessional" representative of the advertising industry. It has not only assumed the CNP's tasks in the "soft" topics of taste and social responsibility, but has taken strong positions against comparison advertising. It is now striving to assume a major role in the pre- and post-control of commercials in the new media.

These may be considered to be legitimate tasks for an advertising self-regulatory body. Yet, they also cast the BVP into a political role, which, in other countries such as the United Kingdom, is assumed by a capstone advertising association now largely missing in France. Since the interests and positions of various advertising segments—large versus small advertisers, print versus broadcast media, etc.—often differ and clash, this is a potentially dangerous position to assume for a BVP totally dependent on the financial contributions of individual members. Instead of simply being an essential instrument of the advertising industry, the BVP is claiming to represent the latter before government and public opinion. The present "interprofessional" vacuum created by the demise of the CNP permits, invites and even demands such a new role on the part of the BVP, but one wonders if it is an appropriate and viable one.

Conclusions

French advertising self-regulation works well, industry backs it up adequately, and the government definitely values it. These real achievements have been accomplished without any significant structural departure from a pure type of self-regulation, from which outsiders are excluded. The French have done it essentially by integrating such outsiders—mainly from the INC and government—in the BVP *process* rather than in its *structure*.

Legitimacy and credibility have not suffered from such limited outside participation because: (1) the BVP is an interprofessional association formally recognized under French law; (2) it has been relentless in its furthering of French advertising standards, and is largely perceived as effective by government and some consumerists; (3) it has reached out for advice from the National Consumer Institute (INC) through its Specialists' Committee and Technical Commissions; and (4) it has associated itself with government endeavors in this field by internalizing various advertising laws and regulations, by tapping government expertise, and by cooperating with it in norm-setting and implementation. It is ahead of the rest of business in a country where "the notion of self-discipline is still often foreign to the ways of thinking of industry and commerce, [and where] the role of regulation and of control has traditionally been assumed by the State until recently (Scrivener et al. 1979, pp. 91–92)." In fact, the BVP has helped various industries and new media to get better organized and self-regulated.

In this context, the BVP has become some sort of a "moral judiciary" (BVP, Rôle et Devenir 1985, p. 4), besides being acknowledged by the courts as a reference point. Born and reformed to cope with the growth of advertising and new media as well as with the ascendancy of consumerism and the threat of greater regulation, it has progressively assumed greater responsibilities in close cooperation with the government and through selective contacts with the consumerist movement. The improved public image of advertising in France (unfavorable opinions declined by half between 1974 and 1984, and 72 percent of the French people liked advertising in 1985) is certainly indebted to the BVP's efforts.

It is not that all problems have been resolved, nor has the role of advertising self-regulation achieved a permanent scope and format. In particular, the problem of reaching marginal practitioners that refuse to embrace a voluntary code of professional behavior keeps plaguing self-regulation. In this context, the observation by a former minister of Consumer Affairs that the BVP represents "the best of its profession" is both an explicit compliment and an implicit criticism. False and misleading personal classified ads represent another problem that does not admit of any simple solution as yet in any country.

Furthermore, the advent of new media such as the new regional and national radio and television networks, cable-television channels, interactive two-way communication systems, the advent of true international broadcasting via satellites and the growth of direct-response advertising are generating new problems that French self-regulation will have to address and help resolve.

The BVP is aware of these inevitable problems and determined to cope with them, although additional resources (that is, new members and/or higher dues) will be necessary to handle such expanded responsibilities. Its present structure, which largely excludes nonindustry members, is unlikely to change in the foreseeable future, and outsiders will remain effectively involved in its functioning.

NOTES

1. The CNP's now defunct Deontology Commission handled cases dealing with the depiction of women; with eroticism, racism and humor in advertising; with alcohol and tobacco advertisements; with references to speed in automobile ads, and more generally with "good taste" and broad issues of values (*BVP Echos* May 1982, p. 5). If an intervention was deemed necessary, the CNP asked the BVP to approach the advertiser.

2. Some sectoral recommendations benefited from negotiations between the relevant industry and consumer associations, as with the recent one on driving-school advertising.

3. The BVP handles all media except television and flyers. In the case of classified ads, it has obtained a relatively high rate of withdrawal when pursuing false "personal ads" (e.g., when a real estate agency pretends to be an individual selling his own property).

4. Conversely, the advertising industry was officially represented on the INC Board of Directors, but the former state secretary for Consumer Affairs removed nonconsumer representatives from that board while admitting them in 1983 on the Conseil National de la Consommation (CNC), designated to be the official locus for dialogue between consumer and business representatives. The functioning of the CNC was not studied in this research, however.

5. There are some 15,000 publications in France, including free ones, of which 4,000 accept advertising. There are also some 1,400 private local radio stations (now combining into networks), of which 30 are members of the BVP. Private stations in France and peripheral countries are monitored to some extent by the BVP, which also accepts complaints about their commercials.

6. At first, there was a full-fledged Ministry of Consumer Affairs, but it was progressively demoted to a subministry level within Economic Affairs after December 1984.

7. See, for example, the February 1987 issue of *BVP Echos* for comments about erotic ads. However, the BVP has stayed away from the flouting of antitobacco-advertising laws because the government itself has vacillated about their implementation (see *BVP Echos*, September 1986, pp. 2–3).

8. It appears that the French consumerist movement is undergoing mutation and possibly weakening, but this topic was not studied here (cf. Weiss and Chirouze [1984]).

9. Thus, it has been suggested that BVP membership be required for accreditation by the Press Syndicate but this is unlikely to happen (Conseil Economique et Social 1980).

REFERENCES

Bon, Jérome, ed. *L'Etat et la Publicité; Réglementations et Campagnes Publicitaires* [The State and Advertising; Regulations and Campaigns]. Cergy, France: Centre d'Etudes et de Recherche du Groupe ESSEC, 1980.

Bureau de Vérification de la Publicité. *BVP Echos* (May 1980; April 1981; November 1981; February 1982; April 1982; May 1982; March 1983; May 1984; October 1984; December 1984; March 1985; August 1985; September 1985; September 1986; February 1987).

Bureau de Vérification de la Publicité. *Cinquantième Anniversaire du Bureau de Vérification de la Publicité, 1935–1985* [Fiftieth Anniversary of the BVP]. Paris: 1985.

———. *Rapport d'Activité* [Annual Report]. Paris: 1982.

———. *Recueil des Recommandations* [Handbook of Recommendations]. Paris: 1983.

———. *Rôle et Devenir de l'Autodiscipline dans la Société Francaise* [Role and Future of Advertising Self-Regulation]. Paris: 1985.

Burson-Marsteller. *Le "Pouvoir Consommateur" dans la France Socialiste* [Consumer Power in Socialist France]. Paris: July 15, 1981.

Calais-Auloy, Jean. "Collectively Negotiated Agreements: Proposed Reforms in France." *Journal of Consumer Policy* 7 (1984): 115–23.

———. "Le contrôle de la publicité déloyale en France" [The Control of Unfair Advertising in France]. Montpellier, France: 1986.

Calais-Auloy, Jean et al. *Consumer Legislation in France*. New York: Van Nostrand Reinhold, 1981.

"Le CNP cinq ans après . . . (Suite)" [The CNP: Five Years Later - Part II]. *Publi 10* 161 (September 13, 1982): 22–24.

Cohen, Alain-Gérard. "Réglementation et Autodiscipline [Regulation and Self-Regulation." In *L'Etat et la Publicité*, edited by Jérome Bon. Cergy, France: Centre d'Etudes et de Recherche du Groupe ESSEC, 1980, pp. 33–37.

"Comment le BVP Surveille la Publicité." *BVP Echos* 40 (February 1981): 4.

Confédération Générale du Travail (CGT), Centre Confédéral d'Etudes Economiques. *Besoins Sociaux, Idéologies et Institutions de la Publicité*. Paris: September 1981.

Conseil Economique et Social. *Avis sur la Place et le Rôle de la Publicité dans l'Information des Consommateurs*. Paris: March 12, 1980.

————. "Bilan et Perspectives de la Politique Francaise à l'Egard des Consommateurs" [Balance Sheet and Perspectives regarding French Consumer Policy]. *Journal Officiel* (July 20, 1984): 1–59.

Conseil National de la Publicité (CNP). *Bilan et Perspectives de la Concertation entre les Organisations de Consommateurs et la Profession Publicitaire*. Paris: April 7, 1983.

Haas, C. R. "Advertising Self-Regulation in France." Paris: Bureau de Vérification de la Publicité, 1983.

Scrivener, Christiane, Achach, D., and Y. Monier. *Rôle, Responsabilité et Avenir de la Publicité* [Role, Responsibility and Future of Advertising]. Paris: La Documentation Française, 1979.

Shonfield, Andrew. *Modern Capitalism: The Changing Balance of Public and Private Power*. New York: Oxford University Press, 1965.

Weiss, Dimitri, and Yves Chirouze. *Le Consommérisme* [Consumerism]. Paris: Sirey, 1984. Reviewed by D. Lassarre in *Journal of Consumer Policy* 8 (1985): 199–203.

ACKNOWLEDGMENTS

The assistance of the following people is gratefully acknowledged: R. Biguet (Institut National de la Consommation), Lucien Bouis (BVP Director), Jean Calais-Auloy (Montpellier University), A. G. Cohen (FR3 Publicité), Alain Decruck (formerly of the Conseil National de la Publicité), Jeanine Jacquot, (Ministère de la Consommation), C. R. Haas (former Director of the BVP), Martine Lenglet (BVP), Dominique Lassarre (Descartes University), Claude Marcus (Publicis International), Philippe Le Ménestrel (Régie Française de Publicité and Conseil d'Etat), Monique Vanbremeersch (Union des Annonceurs), and Jean Zurfluh (RSC & G advertising agency, and CGT Advertising Employees Union).

8

Italy: Istituto
dell'Autodisciplina Pubblicitaria

Italy represents an extreme case in outside participation in that outsiders entirely control the monitoring, complaint-handling and disciplining tasks of advertising self-regulation. Industry, however, still sets up the standards, publicizes them, advises advertisers and agencies, and appoints the outside members of the investigative and adjudicative bodies.

Early Outside Participation

In 1966, the Italian media, advertiser and agency associations adopted a Code of Advertising Fairness (Codice di Lealtà Pubblicitaria). Its purpose, inspired by the International Code of Advertising Practice of the International Chamber of Commerce, was to promote and defend advertising's role in social information and economic development. Many attempts to set up self-regulatory rules had been made in Italy in the 1950s by some media and by groups of advertisers—sometimes successfully as in the case of the state-owned radio-TV network whose subsidiary SACIS still runs a strict preclearance system based on a set of self-imposed rules. Yet, the 1966 Code was the first attempt to gather, under unified rules, those advertisers, media and agencies representing the vast majority of Italian advertising.

Ever since, the Code (now in its eleventh version) has consisted of a set of rules dealing with: (1) general topics such as deceptive and misleading advertising; the use of scientific terms, technical and statistical quotations; testimonials and endorsements; warranties; superstition, credulity and fear; violence, vulgarity and indecency; moral and religious beliefs; children; safety; imitation; disparagement and comparison; (2) advertising for particular types of sales (installment, direct-mail, promotions, etc.), and (3) particular products and services (alcoholic beverages, cosmetics, drugs, courses, financial and real estate investments, travel, etc.).

Initial Structure and Process

A Claim Investigation Committee (*Comitato d'Accertamento*) and a judicial board called the *Giuri dell'Autodisciplina Pubblicitaria* (Advertising Self-Regulation Jury) were established to apply the rules of the Code. The Committee's duty was to act as a monitoring office that would uncover unfair or deceptive advertisements, then bring up the cases before the Jury. The latter was to act as a body adjudicating complaints submitted to it by either the Committee or private plaintiffs (competitors and consumers).

The basic principles of due process of law have had to be observed by the Jury but without any excessive formality. If it upholds a complaint, a cease-and-desist order is issued and publicized with the name of the defendant. The publicizing of a summary of the decision to the press can also be ordered in the case of noncompliance with Jury decisions that cannot be appealed. All media adhering to the Code have to comply with Jury decisions.

Original Reactions

When the 1966 Code of Advertising Fairness was adopted, the initial public reaction was one of skepticism. A voluntary code, it was said, would not work in a country like Italy, where breaking the rules is a sort of national pastime and where everybody tries to be "clever." Private regulation, merely based on the self-discipline of advertising people, would be doomed to systematic transgression. More serious objections came from the radical wing of legal-doctrine scholars and consumerists. They pointed out that the self-regulatory structure was intrinsically frail since its rules were not backed by the law, and the Jury's judgments could not be legally enforced. They concluded that a code based only on voluntary compliance and not supported by hard sanctions could not be effective (Ghidini 1968, p. 223). Besides, they stressed that consumer protection against unfair and false advertising was a task that institutionally belongs to the State. It was unthinkable that the control of advertising could be entrusted to industry itself (Bessone et al. 1974b, p. 97; Bessone et al. 1974a, p. 190; Ghidini 1968). Some even insinuated that the Code of Advertising Fairness was a screen to protect the interests of the major print media and prevent interference by the government.

The Credibility Problem

Clearly, the main problem of the newborn system was credibility. Therefore, from the very beginning, the participation of independent persons of unobjectionable reputation was considered a basic condition for the survival of the Claim Investigation Committee and the Jury.

Originally, Italian self-regulation was governed by the Italian Advertising General Confederation grouping the most important Italian associations of advertisers, agencies and press media as well as the state-owned radio-TV company. The idea was to have the self-regulatory body partly made up of outsiders and partly of advertising representatives. Out of the nine members of the Jury, four were chosen from among independent and qualified experts (the presiding member was customarily a retired high-ranking magistrate from the Supreme Court, while the other three were university professors expert in juridical matters or consumer-protection problems); the remaining five members, all experienced in juridical matters, were appointed by the four major associations that supported the Code and by the state-owned radio-TV network. (Similar criteria were followed for the composition of the Claim Investigation Committee.) The result was a board with a slight majority appointed by the advertising industry, but this did not mean any indulgence toward advertisers, agencies and media. As a matter of fact, the members appointed by the advertising industry were usually legally trained people such as lawyers or law professors; and, in any case, the Code made it clear that all of them had to serve as individuals "according to their personal belief rather than on behalf of the appointing parties."

Early Performance

After it was put to the test, the Italian advertising self-regulatory system did not deserve either the skepticism or the objections that were raised. Advertising people did comply with the self-imposed rules from the very beginning; and a sense of self-responsibility developed among advertisers and agencies as if self-regulation was actually the expression of their professional ethics. The media also responded to their new task of "enforcing" the self-regulatory decisions by refusing to accept reproved advertisements. No single important case of disobedience to the decisions of the Giuri was reported. Only once did a losing party bring a lawsuit before a court on the ground that certain aspects of the self-disciplinary system were illegal, but the court rejected the claim and confirmed the decision of the Jury (Tribunal of Milan 1976, p. 91). Nor did the self-regulatory body display partiality or favoritism of any kind. On the contrary, it performed its duties fairly even when very important and influential advertisers or publishers were involved.

Day-by-day confidence began to replace skepticism. If in 1966 only one case had been handled by the Jury, six were in 1967, eighteen in 1970, twenty-nine in 1973, and thirty-eight in 1974. The "case law" developed by the Jury showed, thanks to the balance of opposing interests, a good deal of common sense and fairmindedness. In spite of its private nature, Italian self-regulation was proving to be effective. Still, the objections against a system administered by a private institution persisted. What is worse, they became commonplace and accepted internationally as there were some foreign reports that Italian self-regulation did not actually protect consumers (e.g., Reich and Micklitz 1981, p. 72) and was a screen meant to cover up the interests of the advertising industry (Ghidini 1980, p. 38). While such insinuations were never fully substantiated, rumors of the sort were difficult to silence. This accounts for the deep changes that were brought to the Code in the mid–1970s, especially regarding outside participation in the self-regulatory system.

Code, Structure and Process Revision

In 1975, the Code was broadly amended as several of the existing rules of behavior were strengthened and new ones were introduced. The general idea was to emphasize consumer protection and to present self-regulation as a complete system for the control of advertising in the public interest (Fusi 1975, p. 185; Fusi 1976, p. 222). Even the Code's name was changed from "Advertising Fairness" to "Advertising Self-Regulation" (*Codice di Autodisciplina Pubblicitaria*, CAP) in order to stress the disciplinary nature of its rules. With the same aim in mind, outside participation in the Jury was increased and new independent members were appointed—even the president of a consumer association and a Communist senator took part in the Jury in 1975–1976. As for the Claim Investigation Committee, its functions were broadened. Not only did it, as in the past, monitor advertisements in order to submit suspect ones to the Jury, but it was also appointed to act as the representative of consumer interests and, in this capacity, to handle complaints from individual consumers.

New Structure

In 1976, the advertising industry dissolved the Italian Advertising General Confederation and replaced it in 1977 with the Advertising Self-Regulation Institute (*Istituto dell'Autodisciplina Pubblicitaria*, IAP). This Institute is an independent society sponsored and financed by the associations of advertisers (UPA), agencies (ASSAP, OTEP), professionals (TP, ACPI, AIAP) and film-makers (ANIPA) as well as state and private media (RAI, SIPRA, FIEG). Many other advertising associations have since joined the Institute on a voluntary basis, including the Independent TV Association (UTEPA). However, consumer associations are not represented on it, nor does the government interfere in any manner with its functioning.

The Institute is run by an Executive Committee appointed by the private associations that support the CAP Code, and is made up of industry members. Its major role is that of revising the Code; and 1977 amendments strengthened its compulsory character for all advertising operators. The Institute also appoints the members of the Claim Investigation Committee and of the Jury.

The acceptance of the Code by individual advertisers, agencies and media comes, first of all, from their joining one of these associations whose bylaws provide for automatic adherence to the self-regulatory rules by all members. Furthermore, a new rule has been established according to which all media and agencies agree to put in their contracts a special clause of acceptance of the CAP Code by advertisers. As a result, advertising campaigns can hardly be carried out without being subject to the Code of Advertising Self-Regulation. In fact, even if the advertiser does not join any association that recognizes the Code, he will be forced by his agency or the media to accept its rules on a contractual basis, since almost all agencies and media have joined one of the associations supporting the Code.

New Processes

In 1977, the functioning of the self-regulatory system was more precisely defined. The Claim Investigation Committee's main tasks are to uncover false or misleading advertisements, to request that such ads be substantiated or modified, to negotiate and settle cases with advertisers by mutual consent and, if this fails, to bring them before the Jury. This Committee also provides preadvertising advisory opinions at the request of advertisers, agencies and media— for a fee.

It is worth noting that the task of uncovering false or misleading claims through monitoring is usually carried out by the members of the Claim Investigation Committee themselves, while the three or four employees of the Institute's Secretariat attend only to routine bureaucratic work. It is mainly from this fairly systematic monitoring that this Committee gets its "ideas" for complaints to be lodged with the Jury. Finally, it has to be pointed out that the jurisdiction of the Claim Investigation Committee is strictly limited to matters where the consumer interest is involved. If competitors want to bring an action, they have to file a complaint directly to the Jury on their own initiative. In late 1985, the Claim Investigation Committee was renamed Control Committee (*Comitato di Controllo*).

The Jury's task is to examine the advertisements that either the Claim Investigation Committee (now Control Committee) or a private plaintiff submits to it, and to decide whether they do infringe the Code of Advertising Self-Regulation. Such a decision is taken after having heard both parties at hearings that usually take place two to four times a month. After discussing the case, the Jury hands out its verdict, which is immediately self-executory, with no appeal possible. If the advertisement is deemed to infringe the Code, the sanctions available to the Jury are: (1) to order the campaign stopped, in which case all media members (practically all Italian media are members) have to comply with the Jury's decision, and (2) to have the Institute publicize a summary of the decision, including the name of the wrongdoer. Should the advertiser or media not comply with the verdict, a further sanction is available to the Jury, namely, to order that a "public notice" of such disobedience be published or broadcast. No fines can be imposed or indemnity be awarded by the Jury against the losing party, however.

Outside Dominance

The establishment of the Institute in 1977 also offered an opportunity to modify the composition of both the Jury and the Claim Investigation Committee (now Control Committee). Since then, none of their members can be directly nominated by the advertising associations that support the Institute. Instead, all members are appointed by the Executive Committee of the Institute and chosen from among independent experts in law, consumer problems and advertising—in other words, it is a self-regulatory adjudicative system wholly administered by outsiders.

Five of the members of the Jury are chosen from among jurists and four from among psychologists, sociologists, and economists, so that the former prevail on this body. Its present composition consists of two high-ranking prosecuting attorneys (both still in active service, with one of them serving as president of the Jury), a Court magistrate (now retired), two university professors expert in trademark and competition law, and four university professors of psychology, sociology, and economics. However, no experts in consumer problems or advertising have been appointed to date. As for the Investigation (now Control) Committee (nine independent members), its composition is more balanced since it includes experts in consumer problems, advertising techniques and communications, with a preponderance of consumer advocates. No problems have been encountered in recruiting outsiders since several high-ranking magistrates and university professors have applied for the rarely vacant positions.

Positive Impact of the Changes

First of all, the changes have generated greater credibility for the system. The objections raised by Left-leaning critics and consumerists have almost ceased, and the institution is now generally accepted by the public as an impartial and objective instrument, which works in the public interest (Ghidini 1984 and 1985).

Many features and programs have been devoted by the press and by broadcasting stations to self-regulation. Together with an informative advertising campaign carried out every year by the Institute with the support of the media in order to increase awareness of the self-regulatory system among consumers, they help improve its public image. As a result, Italian self-regulation appears to be enjoying a very favorable public reputation, although no systematic public-opinion survey has been conducted to date.

Besides, the Control Committee has broadened its field of action. Many important complaints have been lodged by the Committee since 1977 concerning advertising for alcoholic beverages, tobacco, children, financial investments and several other topics of great moment. Even if the preclearance carried out by the media (especially by the state TV network) acts as a filter that catches many infringing ads and commercials before they are published or broadcast, the Control Committee is not bound by such preclearance and often raises objections against ads previously approved by the media.

The number of cases handled by the self-disciplinary bodies has increased remarkably. During the 1982–1986 quinquennium, the Jury delivered 393 decisions—almost as many as during the first sixteen years of its life (Istituto 1986, p. 15). About 70 percent of the complaints handled by the Jury have come from the Claim Investigation (now Control) Committee, and the balance from private plaintiffs—mainly competitors.

Furthermore, the change of structure has improved the speed of the proceedings. Although this probably does not result from the full participation of outsiders on the Control Committee and the Jury, it is remarkable that the whole process before the Jury nowadays takes only fifteen to twenty days, so that many unfair or deceptive campaigns can be stopped before they run their full course.

As for the substance of the decisions, the case law developed in the past few years by the outsider-composed Jury has made a major contribution in certain areas where the law is lacking or inadequate. This may be said, first of all, for the advertising of financial and real estate investments, where it has expressed principles that are likely to become basic rules in this field. Similarly, the Jury has contributed many important rules as far as the advertising of cosmetics, alcoholic beverages and food products are concerned. Several important decisions have also broadened and better defined the concepts of imitation and disparagement in advertising. From a general point of view, it may be said that the jurisprudence developed by the new outsider-dominated Jury is more complete, effective and influential than the old one when the participation of industry members gave it the image of a friendly arbitrator rather than of an adjudicative body.

Finally, the full participation of outsiders has meant greater severity in the application of the self-regulatory rules. This may be noted first of all in the activity of the Control Committee. Consumer advocates play a leading role in this body, and this accounts for the strictness and even inflexibility that it displays in carrying out its functions. Negotiating and settling a case by mutual consent with this Committee is currently very difficult for advertisers. Consequently, it is often preferable for them to wait until the campaign is referred to the Jury and to face the latter's decision, hoping that it will not be too severe.

As for the Jury, no consumerist influences can be observed. The fact that this body is made up principally of experienced jurists of great reputation vouches for its impartiality, fairness and strictness. Figures show that complaints are upheld by the Jury in more than 80 percent of the cases, and only 20 percent are dismissed; and in more than 85 percent of the cases, the Articles of the Code aimed at protecting consumers are applied, with the remainder concerning competitor protection (Istituto 1986, p. 17). Orders for publication of its decisions have almost quadrupled. When, in 1984, the Jury upheld Kodak's complaint against Fuji's campaign "Only the best go to the Olympics," and ruled that such a claim was misleading because it induced one to think that Fuji films had obtained the Los Angeles Olympics' sponsorship thanks to their superior quality, there was no hesitation in ordering the publication of the decision in the press (Giuri, No. 21/84). This would have been unthinkable when advertising people sat on the Jury, but this decision does not represent an isolated example.

Industry Reactions

If all this pleases the public and silences the critics, the attitudes of the advertising industry are not so positive. There are no public statements to that effect, nor have surveys been conducted about it, but advertisers and agencies often express feelings of uneasiness about the development of Italian advertising self-regulation.

Concern about Overstrictness

Many advertisers and professionals are under the impression that the strictness displayed by the self-regulatory body is not always fully justified. They think that there is a deliberate intention to apply the Code at any cost, and to pick holes in every ad—a result often ascribed to the composition of the Jury and the Control Committee, which only have outside members and no advertising people. Here are some recent examples of what they perceive as overstrictness:

1. In a 1984 Volvo campaign, the advertisement quoted the results of a study carried out by the Swedish Motor Vehicle Inspection Authority about the "median life" of Volvo cars. Although the source was clearly mentioned in the ad, the Claim Investigation Committee filed a complaint and the Jury held that such results had "no meaning" in Italy, where car inspection takes place only every ten years instead of every two years as in Sweden, so that it ordered the campaign stopped (Giuri, No. 26/84).

2. The 1984 Peugeot-Talbot campaign claimed that the Peugeot 305 GT's fuel consumption was one liter per 15.9 km. at a speed of 90 km./hour. The source was not quoted, but the defendant produced documentary evidence proving that consumption tests had been carried out in strict accordance with EEC official standards. The Jury upheld the Claim Investigation Committee's complaint and ruled that the ad was deceptive because it did not mention the method used in the test (Giuri, No. 46/84).

3. In another case submitted by the Committee, the ads of a correspondence school had used the caption "Become a beautician." The Giuri held that the claim was misleading, since it might induce the public to think that anyone was able to open a beauty parlor when, instead, special licensing requirements are imposed under the law (Giuri, No. 2/84).

Concern about Social Activism

If all of this confirms a definite strictness in applying the self-regulatory code, many advertisers and other practitioners consider that other decisions display a sort of judicial activism, as if improving or modifying certain social patterns was one of the tasks of self-regulation:

1. In 1983, British Leyland commercials presented a sequence of very imaginary and grotesque situations involving its Metro car. The gimmick was evident to all those who knew anything about advertising. Yet, the Jury ruled that the campaign presented the product as an object of unscrupulous thoughtlessness and encouraged the uncautious use of cars. The Claim Investigation Committee's complaint was upheld (Giuri, No. 17/83).

2. A 1979 campaign for a branded custard showed a boy who refused a dish and told his mother: "If you don't give me Ciao Crem, I won't eat." The Jury held that the claim was "miseducational" as it induced children to blackmail their parents, whetted maternal anxiety and encouraged conflict within the family (Giuri, No. 29/79). A similar decision was made in 1981 regarding a brand of pudding. The ad showed a grumpy boy sitting at the table with his parents, under the following heading: "When your child is not hungry, forcing him won't do him any good. Feed him with something he likes." The Jury ruled that the campaign had to be stopped for the same reasons (Giuri, No. 12/81).

3. In 1984, the French yogurt company Gervais-Danone wanted to use a similar appeal in commercials for its new product Danito. Hence, the agency was very careful about presenting a quite different scene: a boy smiling and his parents not concerned at all. The Claim Investigation Committee lodged a complaint and the result was surprising: the Jury held that the commercial was "miseducational" since it induced parents not to take care of their children (Giuri, No. 29/84).

Concern about Overreach

According to some advertisers and agencies, such decisions represent alarming symptoms of interference in freedom of commercial expression. But what raises a greater concern among advertising people is the occasional tendency to go beyond the limits of advertising self-regulation and regulate the practice of trade itself, thereby restraining the freedom of private enterprise:

1. In 1983, Johnson Wax launched a new bathfoam under the registered trademark Tahiti. A competitor objected that the way Tahiti was presented was misleading about the origin of the product, which did not come from Polynesia. The Jury went far beyond the claim, held that the trademark itself was misleading, and ordered Johnson Wax to give it up (Giuri, No. 12/83).

2. In 1983, a group of toilet-soap manufacturers complained about a Beecham TV campaign for a liquid soap marketed under the trademark Supersoap. According to the plaintiffs, such a campaign was deceptive, since this liquid soap

does not come from a process of saponification and is not "soap" under the proper chemical meaning of the word. The Jury upheld the complaint, ruled that the product definition "liquid soap" was false, and ordered Beecham to stop using such a term in its advertising and packaging (Giuri, No. 23/83). As a result, the media requested all liquid-soap manufacturers to amend their campaigns accordingly, and the term "liquid soap," even though generally used and internationally accepted, has practically disappeared from the Italian market.

3. In 1984, Johnson & Johnson offered a temporary discount of 150 liras on its Baby Shampoo. Such rebates are very popular in Italy since, unlike other promotions, they are not subject to prior approval by the government. The Claim Investigation Committee lodged a complaint on the ground that Baby Shampoo was not sold at a fixed price so that the rebate had no meaning. The Jury held that rebate offers are unfair whenever retailers are allowed to fix the sale price at their own discretion so that the discount offered by the manufacturer may be totally or partially neutralized (Giuri, No. 30/84). In practice, this decision, recently confirmed in a subsequent case, will have the effect of eliminating most discount offers, since consumer goods are seldom sold at a fixed price on the Italian market. However, many advertisers and agencies think that ruling on trademarks, classification of goods and promotional systems does not belong to the domain of advertising self-regulation, and they wonder, therefore, where Italian self-regulation is heading.

Process and Structural Concerns

The way the self-regulation process works is another reason for concern because: (1) the burden of the proof is on the defendant; (2) very little time (from eight to fifteen days) is given for preparing and filing a defense; (3) no adjournments are granted, except under very special circumstances; (4) permission is given to both parties to produce new documentary evidence at the hearing so that the other side is cut off from any possibility of immediately countering such new evidence; (5) Jury decisions are immediately self-executory, and (6) there is no possibility of appealing or otherwise contesting these decisions since the system does not provide for a board of second instance.

Many practitioners think that, when the advertising industry was represented on the Jury, this summary way of proceeding was acceptable since it acted as a sort of friendly arbitrator. Now that this adjudicating board is entirely controlled by outsiders and enforces the Code in such a strict way, they believe that the system should provide better protection of the rights of defendants and grant the possibility of appealing judgments. "You cannot risk a million-dollar campaign in a one-hour trial" is the way some advertising practitioners express their concern.

Unwarranted Criticisms

Such overly pessimistic feelings are probably unwarranted; and the severity occasionally displayed by the Claim Investigation (Control) Committee and the Jury does not justify a generally negative judgment.

First of all, the case law developed by the Jury shows not only severity, but also a good deal of common sense based on a realistic knowledge of social sensitivity and human behavior so that, on several occasions, the Jury has displayed uncommon moderation and openmindedness. The cases CdA (Claim Investigation Committee) vs. Beretta (Giuri, No. 2/82) and CdA vs. Midy (Giuri, No. 23/84), concerning advertising campaigns for a shotgun and a contraceptive respectively, represent meaningful examples. The Jury ruled that advertisements dealing with hot social issues must not be judged as offending the beliefs of a certain part of the public when the message does not suggest any pattern of degeneration, depravity or gratuitous exploitation of the worst aspects of human nature. A similar equanimity was displayed in the cases CdA vs. Elah (Giuri, No. 75/84), CdA vs. Fiat (Giuri, No. 3/85) and CdA vs. Snaidero (Giuri, No. 30/85), regarding three TV campaigns in which children were involved since the Jury ruled that advertising cannot conceal what happens in everyday life. Again in the case CdA vs. Piaggio (Giuri, No. 26/85), concerning a commercial containing horrifying characters, the Jury held that self-regulation must not interfere with good or bad taste and has to accept the likings of a certain part of the public. An even more liberal 1986 decision concerned a television campaign that included a sexual double-entendre. The Jury ruled that the latter had to be accepted as a refined satire of Italian customs, since such an erotic joke was unlikely to cause a feeling of repulsion in the audience (Giuri, No. 100/85). These examples demonstrate that accusing outsiders of judicial activism or preconceived strictness is not quite justified.

Moreover, many of the criticisms from advertisers and professionals do not address the core of the problem, which often concerns the content of the rules themselves rather than the outsiders who apply them. If the Jury has sometimes gone beyond the traditional limits of advertising self-regulation and ruled about trademarks or promotions, this must not be ascribed to an abuse of power on the part of the outsiders involved in the system, but to the Italian Code of Advertising Practice, which gives the broadest possible definition to the term "advertising" as including every form of presenting products and services to the public, including trademarks, packages and sales promotions.

Similarly, the summary way the process works does not depend on outsiders since they did not establish the procedural rules. The Code was set up by the Institute, whose main concern has been to prove that self-regulation is fast and able to stop a campaign while it is still in progress, even if this may work against some basic rights of the defendant. On the contrary, outsiders (mainly jurists) have tried to temper some of the most controversial aspects of the self-regulatory process by applying many principles borrowed from the Italian Codes of Civil and Penal Procedures. Such principles now form some sort of informal guidelines usually followed in the hearings before the Jury, and they contribute some basic guarantees of due process of law.

Other Outside Influences

In the face of a complex and somewhat deficient legal situation (see Appendix), Italian advertising self-regulation was developed, at least in part, to avoid or mitigate further regulation. Its development, however, took place in a vacuum as far as the Italian government has been concerned. No governmental encouragement, support or demands for improvement have been evident; and no satisfaction or dissatisfaction has been overtly expressed despite the travails and metamorphoses of the Italian self-regulatory system and its increasing effectiveness and credibility. The ongoing revision of Italian advertising law also appears to be unrelated to the existence of active self-regulation.

The Italian consumerist movement is rather weak, is not explicitly involved in the advertising self-regulatory system, and has not taken any particular position vis-à-vis the latter. As was mentioned before, several individual consumer advocates have commented on that system and have sat on the Control Committee in a personal capacity. Still, Italian advertising self-regulation has had few ''silent partners.''

Conclusions

The Italian experience offers grounds for reflection about the pros and cons of a self-regulatory system dominated by outsiders. It is undeniable that the latter stand for the strictest impartiality, and grant legitimacy and credibility to self-regulation. When, as happened in Italy, such outsiders are people of great professional expertise and uprightness, this is of immense avail to its good public reputation. However, outsiders are not advertising people but bring different experiences and perspectives to the application of self-regulatory rules. As they have committed themselves to vouch for the earnestness and impartiality of rules self-imposed by a social group to which they do not belong, outsiders act as the most severe and inflexible guarantors of the legitimacy of the system by applying their own principles, even if the latter are not always shared by advertising people.

This situation is unavoidable and worth accepting as long as it contributes to improving the image of self-regulation. However, when the rules—as applied— enlarge the application of advertising self-regulation to some fields that do not properly belong to traditional advertising, or when the process works in such a summary way that would be hardly accepted in a modern legal system, this may undermine the spontaneous acceptance of self-regulation by advertising operators. In the long run, it risks putting the whole system in jeopardy since voluntary compliance is the basis on which self-regulation lies. Thus far, the Italian situation has not reached such a critical point, however.

The government does not interfere in the functioning of the system. Consumer associations, probably in view of the particular severity displayed by the self-regulatory body, appear to be satisfied and are not asking for further reforms. The public also seems pleased with the reformed system. As for the Istituto dell'Autodisciplina Pubblicitaria, which governs Italian self-regulation and is in charge of revising the Code and appointing the Control Committee and Jury members, it does not seem to be aware of any need to tone down the system or to change its composition by bringing advertising people back into it. For that matter, new restrictive procedures were approved in 1985, entitling the president of the Jury to issue preliminary cease-and-desist orders at the request of the Control Committee, without having to consult the advertiser beforehand.

It appears that the Institute and the advertising associations that support it are convinced that the post–1977 "new way" is the right one, and that occasionally extreme severity does not harm the institution but improves its image. That may well be the case. Still, a vague sense of uneasiness is spreading among advertisers and agencies as if self-discipline was something imposed from above—a sort of punishment to endure or to try to evade rather than a spontaneous expression of professional responsibility. "There is no more *self-regulation* in Italy," someone said recently: "*Self* has gone, only *regulation* is left."

Appendix: Basic Italian State Laws Applying to Advertising

Italian lawmakers, prior to World War II, did realize the power of advertising as an instrument of social persuasion. Hence, in accordance with the centralizing policy of the Fascist government, advertising was submitted to strong censorship aimed at protecting consumers, but also attuned to the political ends of the régime.

In this context, the 1931 Police Law (R.D. 18 June 1931, No. 773) required that all advertisements be approved in advance by the *Questore* (Chief of Police). At the same time, separate laws were enacted to deal with the advertising of particular types of products or services. The 1934 law on drugs and medicinal preparations (R.D. 27 July 1934, No. 1265) submitted all advertisements for health products to prior authorization by the Ministry of Health. Similar provisions were applied to the advertising of many other products and services such as mineral waters, disinfecting lotions, insecticides, medicated toothpastes, medical treatments and services, spas and physiotherapy treatments. A censorship system was established in 1936 for travel and tourism advertisements (R.D.L. 23 November 1936, No. 2523), and in 1939 for the advertising of clearance sales (R.D.L. 19 January 1939, No. 294). In 1938, the law on premiums, gifts and competitions (D.L. 19 October 1938, No. 1933) made such promotions conditional on prior authorization by the Ministry of Finance. Those who transgressed such laws by publishing or broadcasting unauthorized advertisements, were to be prosecuted on criminal grounds.

After the war, these laws were kept and are still in force (with the exception of the 1931 Police Law) so that, at the beginning of the 1950s, Italy could superficially boast to have one of the strongest legal systems in Europe for the control of advertising.

However, the system suffered from bureaucratic sclerosis and was unable to keep pace with the needs of the advertising industry and of consumer protection.

New postwar laws were enacted to regulate the advertising of many other products, but without recourse to the censorship formula. A 1953 decree (D.P.R. 30 May 1953, No. 578) regulated advertising for baby foods and dietetic products; a 1962 law (L. 30 April 1962, No. 283) prohibited false and misleading advertising for foodstuffs and beverages; another one (L. 10 April 1962, No. 165) banned the advertising of cigarettes and tobacco; a 1973 law (L. 26 November 1973, No. 883) controlled the marketing of textile products; a 1980 law (L. 19 March 1980, No. 80) dealt with the advertising of promotional sales, and a 1982 law (D.P.R. 18 May 1982, No. 322) on foodstuffs and beverages made their advertising regulations conform with EEC directives.

These new laws as well as many others regulating the advertising of particular products abandoned the prewar censorship system, and have limited themselves to prohibiting false and deceptive advertising as well as fixing certain rules with which advertisers have to comply. Thus, the coexistence of prewar and postwar laws and the lack of a grand design to regulate advertising as a whole, have created an odd legal mosaic where some pieces are missing and many others overlap. After publication of the EEC Directive on Misleading Advertising of 10 September 1984 (No. 84/450/EEC), an attempt has been made to unify and harmonize all these regulations; and a bill banning false and deceptive advertisements on a general basis has been prepared. It is too early to tell whether the Italian Parliament will pass it without substantial changes because many criticisms have been raised about this bill. Still, the general opinion is that a new law will soon come into force.

References

Bessone, Mario et al. *Dal Codice di Lealtà Pubblicitaria al controllo amministrativo dell'advertising* [From the Advertising Fairness Code to the Administrative Control of Advertising]. *Giurisprudenza Italiana* 4 (1974a): 184–9.

———. *Materiali per uno studio della disciplina giuridica della pubblicità commerciale* [Materials for the Study of the Legal Discipline of Advertising]. *Giurisprudenza Merito* 4 (1974b): 97–104.

Burleton, E. N. "Self-Regulation of Advertising in Europe." *International Forum on Advertising Self-Regulation*. Mimeographed. Venice, Italy: October 1984.

Fusi, Maurizio. "Autodisciplina e controllo della pubblicità nell'interesse dei consumatori" [Self-Regulation and Advertising Control in the Interest of Consumers.] *Diritto Radiodiffusione e Telecomunicazioni* (1975): 185–214.

———. "Sul Nuovo Codice d'Autodisciplina Pubblicitaria" [The New Code of Advertising Self-Regulation]. *Rivista Diritto Industriale* 1 (1976): 222–47.

Ghidini, Gustavo. *Consumer Legislation in Italy*. New York: Van Nostrand Reinhold, 1980.

———. *Introduzione allo studio della pubblicità commerciale* [An Introduction to the Study of Commercial Advertising]. Milano: Giuffrè, 1968.

———. *La Repubblica*, November 30, 1984 and February 3, 1985. (Ghidini used to be one of the foremost critics of Italian advertising self-regulation.)

Giuri's decision No. 21/84, Kodak vs. Fuji.

Giuri's decision No. 26/84, CdA vs. Volvo.

Giuri's decision No. 46/84, CdA vs. Peugeot.

Giuri's decision No. 2/84, CdA vs. Elettra.

Giuri's decision No. 17/83, CdA vs. British Leyland.

Giuri's decision No. 29/79, CdA vs. Star.

Giuri's decision No. 12/81, CdA vs. Standard Brands.

Giuri's decision No. 29/84, CdA vs. Gervais-Danone.

Giuri's decision No. 12/83, Tikichimic vs. Johnson Wax.

Giuri's decision No. 28/83, Mira Lanza & others vs. Beecham.

Giuri's decision No. 30/84, CdA vs. Johnson & Johnson.

Giuri's decision No. 2/82, CdA vs. Beretta.

Giuri's decision No. 23/84, CdA vs. Midy.

Giuri's decision No. 75/84, CdA vs. Elah.

Giuri's decision No. 3/85, CdA vs. Fiat.

Giuri's decision No. 30/85, CdA vs. Snaidero.

Giuri's decision No. 26/85, CdA vs. Piaggio.

Giuri's decision No. 100/85, CdC vs. Fassi.

Istituto Autodisciplina Pubblicitaria. *Autodisciplina Pubblicitaria—Annuario* [Yearbook]. Milan, Italy: 1986.

Reich, Norbert, and Micklitz, Hans. *Le droit de la consommation dans les pays membres de la CEE* [Consumer Law in EEC Countries]. New York: Van Nostrand Reinhold, 1981.

Tribunal of Milan (January 22, 1976). *Rivista Diritto Industriale* 2 (1977): 91–117.

ACKNOWLEDGMENTS

Dr. Maurizio Fusi, a jurist specializing in Italian advertising regulation and a foremost specialist on Italian advertising self-regulation, was the main coauthor of an earlier version of this chapter: "Advertising Self-Regulation by Outsiders: The Case of Italy," *International Journal of Advertising* 4, no. 3 (1986): 93–107. The updated and expanded version in this chapter is indebted to Dr. Fusi, who is the coauthor (with Paolina Testa) of *L'Autodisciplina Pubblicitaria in Italia* (Milano: Giuffré, 1983). Dr. Fusi is also the author of *La comunicazione pubblicitaria nei suoi aspetti giuridici* [The Legal Aspects of Advertising Communication]. Milan: Giuffré, 1970. On May 13, 1986, the Istituto dell'Autodisciplina Pubblicitaria held in Milan an International Symposium on "Advertising between Regulation and Self-Regulation: Twenty Years of Self-Regulation in Italy," but only brief Italian summaries of the presentations were circulated.

9

Japan: Japan Advertising Review Organization (JARO)

Since 1974, JARO has played a significant role within Japan's extensive advertising self-regulatory system. It was created at the initiative of major advertising-related associations, and it interacts with them regularly and fruitfully. Within the Japanese self-regulatory network, JARO stands apart as the national, all-media and all-products body devoted to disseminating principles and rules of good advertising behavior, and to inviting and handling inquiries and complaints from consumers, competitors and other societal elements affected by advertising. There are standards to apply; preadvertising advice is available to advertisers, agencies and media; inquiries and complaints are systematically handled; practically all erring advertisers comply with its decisions, and publicity is given to its availability and decisions. Yet, JARO is limitedly used by consumers and their organizations; government agencies do not significantly rely on it, and some industry supporters are uncertain about its proper role and direction. This paradoxical situation provides the focal point for the following analysis.

Data for this study were obtained during a one-week series of interviews in Tokyo with JARO officers, industry leaders, government officials, consumer-organization executives and qualified observers. These interviews were organized, in October-November 1984, by JARO leaders who set up four luncheon sessions attended by anywhere from three to ten representatives of these various sectors, and handled through interpreters. Secondary sources were also used, but the paucity of English-language studies on Japanese consumerism, advertising regulation and self-regulation make this analysis tentative. Additional interviews took place with individual experts; and correspondence from 1985 to 1987 was exchanged with several people in connection with the drafting of this chapter (see Acknowledgments).

Why JARO Was Founded

The Japan Advertising Review Organization (JARO)[1] was launched in August 1974 at the initiative of the Advertising Federation of Japan (AFJ) and of major advertiser, agency and media associations, many of which already had codes of ethics. The need was felt for a central body to coordinate and expand the self-regulatory efforts of these and industry-specific associations (e.g., for medicine and food) in order to enhance consumer satisfaction and improve industry behavior.[2] JARO was also to interface with industry, government agencies, consumer organizations and the public at large about advertising issues, and to engage in various informational and educational activities (JARO 1976 and 1978).

Impetus

Reaching back to the 1950s, there had been a series of business "scandals" involving defective and polluted products (e.g., the arsenic contamination of a powdered milk in 1955), fraudulent advertisements (often in connection with the offer of premiums) and other objectionable marketing practices (e.g., bait-and-switch schemes). From them resulted the modern Japanese consumer movement as well as the Consumer Protection Fundamental Act [Basic Law] of 1968 and related legislation (Kirkpatrick 1975; Cohen 1977; Economic Planning Agency 1983; Miracle 1985).

JARO was launched in reaction to these developments in the hopes that: (1) criticisms of business and advertising could be defused by displaying concern and by engaging in meaningful consumer-redress activities, and (2) regulatory restrictions could be kept to a minimum through self-regulation and better organized contacts with government agencies and consumerists. Its launching also represented a sincere exercise in social responsibility to achieve "reconciliation among industry, consumers and government" and to have business assume responsibility for its actions (JARO 1978, pp. 2–3).[3]

At first, the organization was to be named the Better Business Association—a reflection of the U.S. Council of Better Business Bureaus, which served as a model and handles all sorts of complaints about products, contract fulfillment, advertisements and the like. Ultimately, JARO's scope was limited to advertising and labeling, although the latter receives little attention nowadays.

The Japanese are known as ingenious borrowers and adapters of Western innovations. This practice, however, reaches beyond the "hard" technologies associated with products and production processes and applies also to the "soft" technology of movements and institutions. As one business interviewee put it: "First, we borrowed consumerism from the West, then self-regulation as a reaction to it." JARO studied and adapted various features of the U.S., British and French self-regulatory systems. The credit given, to this day, to such foreign models reveals that the Japanese want to keep learning from others.

How JARO Works

Standards

JARO does not have an advertising code nor detailed guidelines of its own but relies on five "basic principles" that advertising and labeling should: (1) be fair and truthful; (2) not be detrimental to the recipients' interests; (3) consider their influence on the young; (4) respect and conform to social customs, and (5) accord with the law and public order.

Originally, detailed standards had been contemplated by Article of Organization No. 5.3, but this turned out to be a very difficult task in view of the variety of situations in heterogeneous industries. Ultimately, it was not found necessary "to put a roof over the roofs" of the numerous codes already available (JARO 1979, p. 1). Consequently, JARO applies standards derived from the law ("'advertising must abide by the law" says the Japan Advertising Federation), the provisions of numerous advertising and industry codes,[4] and its own "case histories"—just like the U.S. NAD/NARB system.[5]

Complaints and Inquiries

JARO clearly distinguishes between an "inquiry" and a "complaint." "Inquiries" refer not only to demands for information and advice from JARO members, consumers and their associations, government agencies, etc., but also to "incomplete" complaints. To be handled as a "complete" complaint, a communication to JARO must: (1) provide the full name and address of the complainant; (2) deal with advertising truth, accuracy and fairness—not with broad issues of taste or opinion, and (3) allow the ready identification of the print ad or commercial so that a copy of it may be obtained. About 40 percent of communications to JARO fall into the "complete complaint" category.

Obviously, JARO can only handle traceable advertisements, and it is within its prerogatives to limit its investigations to "hard" issues of truth and accuracy rather than "soft" expressions of dissatisfaction with advertising in general or with the promotion of particular products (e.g., liquor)—most advertising self-regulatory systems abroad apply similar restrictions. However, JARO also declines to handle complaints whose source cannot be fully identified. The rationale for this policy is that JARO wants to be able to notify the complainant about the disposal of the case. Besides, it does not want "to assume responsibility for intermediating between an unidentifiable person and an advertiser (JARO letter to author, May 2, 1983)."

In this matter, JARO does not follow the U.S. NAD's practice of assuming a complaint as its own even if it appears that the incriminated advertisement raises questions about the proper substantiation of the claims made, and about their truth and accuracy. Thus, besides not systematically monitoring ads,[6] JARO does not pursue potential leads provided by outsiders. Instead, such incomplete complaints (if identifiable) are sent to the relevant advertiser, agency and/or medium for further processing at their own discretion. The net outcome of this policy is that JARO handled only 24 complete "complaints" in 1986 versus 1,317 "inquiries," although higher proportions of complaints have prevailed in the past (see Table 9.1). Thirteen of these twenty-four complaints led to formal recommendations for modification or discontinuance of the advertising.

JARO handles inquiries and complaints about both national and local ads as well as about all types of media, goods and services. In recent years, most cases have involved deception, misleadingness and exaggeration, but also violation of the law and unfairness. Cases have often involved real estate and supermarket ads, but there has been a recent increase in those pertaining to help-wanted, work-at-home, health and beauty ads. The "mini media" of inserts, flyers and direct-mail communications—which contrast with the "mass media" of television, radio, print and outdoor advertising—have also become more problematic.

Table 9.1 indicates that more than two-thirds of the inquiries now emanate from individual consumers, and that this proportion has increased over time. Consumer associations and activists as well as governmental agencies play a much smaller role; while advertisers, agencies, media and their associations are in an intermediate position, but have not increased their use of JARO, which is mainly oriented toward consumers anyway. The recent decline in complaints, recommendations and final decisions has prompted JARO to ask whether this indicated that "dubious advertisers are dramatically disappearing (JARO 1984b, p. 31)." While acknowledging that major advertisers, agencies and media have probably learned to behave better, and that problems rest mainly with smaller firms and particular industries (real estate, supermarkets, etc.), JARO answered this question in the negative on the ground that most consumers still do not know how to file a complete and acceptable complaint, so that the present level of complaining may not be representative.

Complaint Handling

In the case of an acceptable complaint, the JARO Secretariat gets a copy of the ad and queries the advertiser, asking for substantiation of the claims made, if any. When the advertiser's evidence satisfies JARO and the complainant, or when he modifies or withdraws his ad, the case is closed unless JARO is still not pleased with his response. In the latter case, the complainant's letter, the copy of the ad and the advertiser's reply, together with other relevant data, are forwarded to one of five Ad-Review Subcommittees made up of middle-level executives from JARO's member organizations. This subcommittee discusses the evidence and decides whether the complaint should be dismissed or referred to the full Primary Ad-Review Committee for further examination. In the case of a referral to this Primary Committee, the subcommittee drafts a recommen-

Table 9.1
Complaints, Inquiries, Recommendations and Final Decisions Handled by JARO

FISCAL YEAR	COMPLAINTS	INQUIRIES	RECOMMEND-ATIONS	FINAL-PANEL DECISIONS	SOURCES OF INQUIRIES (I) AND COMPLAINTS (C) (in percentages of the total)							
					INDIVIDUAL CONSUMERS		CONSUMERIST BODIES		GOVERNMENT BODIES		ADVERTISING UNITS	
					(I)	(C)	(I)	(C)	(I)	(C)	(I)	(C)
1986	24	1,371	13	0	73.8%	63%	0.4%	0%	2.0%	13%	21.9%	25%
1985	24	1,598	10	0	72.4	83	0.3	0	2.6	4	18.8	13
1984	31	1,359	10	0	67.4	74	0.1	0	2.7	3	26.0	23
1983	39	1,098	17	0	68.2	74	1.8	0	1.6	5	25.3	21
1982	37	1,102	27	0	65.5	73	0.0	3	3.7	8	30.4	16
1981	71	1,060	47	0	60.3	70	0.2	0	4.2	13	34.6	17
1980	73	1,034	42	2	60.9	77	0.3	0	5.1	7	33.3	16
1979	71	906	34	2	53.5	61	3.0	4	5.2	11	37.3	24
1978	77	829	30	5	56.2	55	3.7	29	4.0	5	35.8	12
1977	59	518	15	3	44.7	69	6.7	10	2.7	14	45.9	7
1976	143	270	2	0	53.1	83	1.7	2	3.9	10	41.3	6
1975	145	108	4	0	65.8	79	0.0	1	5.4	12	28.8	7
1974	37	15	5	0	77.0	92	0.0	5	0.0	3	23.0	0

Notes: 1. "Government Bodies" include local consumer centers, the National Center for Consumer Affairs and Information, Fair Trade Associations and various administrative departments.

2. "Advertising Units" refers to advertisers, advertising agencies, media and related associations.

dation that usually urges the advertiser to modify or discontinue the ad. Related self-regulatory organizations are consulted at this stage, if necessary.

The Primary Review Committee, made up of eighteen executive-level people from member companies, re-examines the case and prepares the Recommendation to be issued under its name to the complainant, the implicated advertiser, his agency, the involved media (to alert the latter to watch for similar violations and refuse such ads), all members of JARO and related advertising associations. Such a Recommendation is really an expression of wish, desire or expectation addressed to the advertiser but, in practically all cases, he complies by modifying or withdrawing his ad.[7]

When the advertiser or complainant disagrees with the Recommendation, but also when some major novel issue is involved that the Primary Ad-Review Committee cannot resolve, the matter is brought before the Final Review Panel made up exclusively of seven independent experts. This panel can either confirm the Primary Ad-Review Committee's Recommendation, modify it or simply advise JARO about improving its policies. A Final Review Panel's decision cannot be appealed and has always been heeded by the incriminated advertiser. Otherwise, JARO would publicize his name to its media members.

Thirteen Recommendations were issued by the Primary Review Committee in 1986 (more in prior years), but no Final Decisions have emerged from the Final Review Panel since 1980 (see Table 9.1).

Length of the Process

Ad-review Subcommittees and the Primary Ad-Review Committee meet every month, and the Final Review Panel every three months. Subcommittees take one to three months to draft a Recommendation, which is then handled within the next month or two by the Primary Ad-Review Committee. Altogether, at least two to four months elapse before a Recommendation is sent to the advertiser and complainant. Several more months are needed for a Final Review Panel decision so that the whole process can take up to four to six months and even a year, and publicity of the decision may be even further delayed.

JARO acknowledges the slowness of its complaint-handling process, but counters that one of its goals is to prevent the reoccurrence of similar problems by pursuing the matter even if an advertiser decides, when first approached, to modify or discontinue the ad. Thereby, a beneficial result (ad modification or discontinuance), a precedent, and wide publicity are generated, although some harm may result in the short run from the ad remaining in circulation for a while.

Case Histories

From 1979 on, 191 (as of December 1986) synopses or "case histories" of major JARO decisions have been prepared by the Primary Ad-Review Committee and approved by the Final Review Panel. They are made available to JARO members, government agencies and consumer offices, major consumer associations and various experts.[8] These case histories have been selected as typical of problems encountered in various product categories and as useful for guiding advertising practitioners and policymakers. In this respect, JARO mirrors the U.S. NAD/NARB, which also publicizes its decisions to serve as precedents and as an educational tool. However, neither the product nor the company are identified in the JARO case histories—as is done in the United Kingdom and the United States—for fear of member defection and as a way of "saving face" for all concerned.

A perusal of these case histories reveals that the issues are not trivial; advertisers are often asked to substantiate their claims; JARO invokes various laws, regulations and industry codes; related associations have been asked to improve their rules or guidelines, and JARO ad-review committees do consider the public interest seriously rather than gloss over business shortcomings or treat them as peccadilloes. In most cases, the offenders are smaller firms rather than large advertisers, as far as can be told from the anonymous case histories.

Limited Outside Participation

The members of the Primary Ad-Review Committee and its subcommittees are all from industry. Only the Final Review Panel is made up of outsiders, that is, of seven nonindustry members chosen for their "knowledge and experience." Current members include five university professors (law, economics, history), one former member of the Fair Trade Commission (FTC), and one former editor of a woman's magazine, chosen for her insight on consumer problems. However, there are no representatives from consumer organizations perceived to be "antibusiness, too much on the consumer side, not fair to business, and too demanding," as some JARO respondents put it.

However, JARO officers meet with government officials and consumer representatives two or three times a year in order to exchange information and seek advice.[9] A former FTC member is on the JARO staff at the request of the government, but not to provide any official input. JARO also relies on other industry organizations to provide information when inquiries and complaints are being handled, although their inputs are mostly technical (e.g., how should distance be fairly expressed in an ad claiming proximity to a particular locale?) Besides, the various industry codes on which JARO relies were often developed in consultation with consumer and government bodies. Therefore, some outside input is being indirectly provided as far as the standards used by JARO are concerned. However, outsiders remain largely absent when most inquiries and complaints are handled.

Membership, Staffing and Financing

The bulk of JARO's revenues of about $1 million in 1986 (149 million yen) comes from initiation and regular dues paid by individual advertisers, media, agencies and interested persons. In 1986, there were 779 member companies (363 advertisers, 124 agencies, 255 media, 36 production units, and one personal member) paying an average of 120,000 yen (about $400 to $700) a year per member. Since most large firms already belong to JARO, there has been a slowdown in the growth of memberships recently.

A rather large Board of Directors (up to 120 members)[10] determines and supervises JARO's general policies, although a smaller Board of Standing Directors (up to 40 members) oversees their administration through JARO's officers and Secretariat. The latter is made up of fourteen full-timers, including four executive officers and four inquiry and complaint reviewers; with the rest engaged in administrative tasks, public and government relations.

Most of the top executive positions in JARO are held by men seconded from business. This practice is common in Japan, where employees are frequently rotated from department to department and even lent to related business and organizations, while the government often places some of its older employees in business associations and firms. JARO's officers and staff tend to be experienced advertising and media practitioners with a university education, but they do not have specialized economic or legal training (Miracle 1985, p. 56). They learn on the job under the supervision of their seniors and through experience.

This structure provides for broad financial support, some autonomy from other advertising and business associations, and a large base through which to diffuse JARO's philosophies, policies and decisions. However, direct reliance on individual companies creates dependence on larger firms (which tend to pay multiple dues) and fear of offending them; and it hampers major policy changes, since a large constituency has to be consulted and satisfied. The fact that several of JARO's top officers come from major member firms further reinforces this dependence.

Sanctions

JARO can recommend to its media members to refuse ads from an advertiser who does not comply with its Final Review Panel's decisions. In fact, compliance has practically always been obtained at earlier stages, thanks to the Japanese sense of shame of having been caught doing something socially improper, with the risk of losing face should the matter become widely known. More important still is the fact that most advertisers agree that the kind of good advertising behavior promoted by JARO and other advertising associations should, in fact, be adhered to. The media's commitment to JARO also helps ensure that compliance takes place.

Publicity

JARO publicizes its existence and activities through various brochures, newsletters and reports (e.g., "Red Reports" and case histories), which are broadly circulated to members, business associations, government agencies, consumer organizations and other interested parties. Some media members also run public-service ads, prepared by JARO, in the press and on television in order to make JARO better known to the general public. By one estimate, this free publicity was recently worth some $13 million—many times JARO's budget.

A 1979 survey conducted for JARO revealed that 16.7 percent of the general public knew of JARO. The proportions were higher among JARO member firms (33 percent) and particularly among ad agencies (70 percent). However, these data pertained to the greater Tokyo area, where JARO concentrates its activities.[11] Another JARO survey of member companies, and addressed to the JARO liaison person in these firms, revealed general satisfaction (67 percent) with its activities, although they also requested greater local activities in order to involve more members—a request being satisfied through additional local JARO offices and "caravan" meetings in major cities to bring together business, government and consumer representatives. Some unfamiliarity with JARO's activities was apparent, however, since a sizable number of these supposedly informed respondents thought that JARO engaged in monitoring and preclearance activities when, in fact, it does not.[12] Still, the growing number of inquiries reveals that consumers are approaching JARO in greater number and proportion to voice their concerns and inquire about various matters (see Table 9.1).

A telephone survey of 600 people in the Tokyo area as well as in the city of Sendai was conducted for JARO in March 1987, and it provided much better scores. Thus, 39.7 percent of general consumers were familiar with JARO (half of them about its activities, besides its name), compared to 16.7 percent in 1979. A somewhat smaller increase (from 19 to 34 percent) had taken place among "special consumer groups," that is, people highly aware and active regarding consumer matters. JARO members' familiarity had also increased from 33 to 76 percent. Satisfaction with JARO activities had also generally improved. Public-service announcements on television had been particularly effective in making JARO better known.

Interaction with the Advertising Industry

It has been mentioned that JARO constitutes only part of the Japanese advertising self-regulatory system, that it was created at the initiative of various advertising-related bodies, and that it has borrowed most of its rules from them. While not dependent on them financially, JARO interacts with them in many fruitful ways.

For one thing, JARO does not engage in the prescreening (prevetting, prior approval) of print ads and commercials, even though it provides general advice to advertisers, agencies and media at the preadvertising stage. Instead, most of this preclearing is done by various media associations and the media themselves. Thus, the Newspaper Advertising Review Council (NARC) precleared and investigated 3,211 ads in 1984, including cases where an ad was turned down by a newspaper, and this decision was challenged by the advertiser. Similar roles are played by the Japan Magazine Advertising Association and the Japan National Association of Commercial Broadcasters. This situation explains why the issue of prior substantiation of claims is not a major one for JARO, which only requires that advertisers have sufficient evidence to back up their claims after a complaint has been lodged. It is really the media that have such a presubstantiation requirement when the advertisements are submitted to them or their associations for approval (Miracle 1985, p. 63).

Second, other advertising and industry associations relay some of the consumer complaints they receive to JARO, because they are not equipped to handle them, they do not invite such complaints, and they have sponsored JARO precisely for that purpose. However, JARO does not adjudicate quarrels among advertisers—a task largely left to industry organizations such as the NARC as well as some ninety-five Fair Trade Associations (see below). It is only when such a case impacts consumers on account of deception, misleadingness and the like that JARO steps in—whether such a complaint is brought forth by a consumer or a competitor.

Finally, JARO depends on the moral support of other advertising-related organizations to uphold principles and rules of good advertising behavior in general, as well as when specific JARO Recommendations are circulated to them in order to illustrate the application of these standards and alert others to the emergence of new problems. Such a cooperation between JARO and these organizations appears to be fully operational.

Government Preeminence and Preemption

Much has been written in recent years about the close relationships between business and government in Japan, although mostly in the context of industrial policy and foreign economic relations (cf. Beer 1984). What transpired from this study, however, is that: (1) Japanese consumers trust their government more than business; (2) an elaborate network of national, prefectural (county-level) and municipal regulations and centers provides extensive information and support to consumers and their associations, and (3) JARO plays a relatively minor role in this governmental scheme.

Trust in Government

Japanese politicians are occasionally involved in major scandals; social policy is still deficient in a number of respects, and consumer associations keep militating for stricter consumer-protection legislation and greater government intervention against various business practices (Kirkpatrick 1975; Cohen 1977, Chira 1986). Yet, the Japanese basically trust their governmental bureaucracy perceived as competent and concerned. Consequently, various ministries (MITI, Agriculture, Health and Welfare, etc.) and governmental agencies (Fair Trade Commission, Japan Consumer Information Center, prefectures, municipalities, local consumer centers, etc.) are readily approached and used by consumers and their organizations.

Recourse to the executive government is also enhanced by the Japanese reluctance to engage in direct confrontation with opponents, whether through complaining or suing (Birnbaum 1986, p. 29). In this context, public agencies do provide third-party intervention between consumers and firms, thus sparing both parties the danger of "losing face" or of causing such affront to the other side. JARO, while also a third party, is essentially a business organization staffed and operated by insiders—except for the Final Review Committee, but there are no real consumer or government representatives sitting on the latter whose interventions are rather rare in any case (see above). Consequently, JARO appears less suitable for third-party intercession than government agencies, even though it does play such a role to a significant degree by handling mostly consumer complaints (see Table 9.1).

Government Preemption

Since the 1960s, the government has developed a consumer-protection program that is quite elaborate and operational by now. From the prime minister's level down, coursing through major ministries and agencies, and found in all prefectures and most major municipalities are various consultative, policy-making, regulatory, enforcement, research, informational and complaint-handling structures and processes (Economic Planning Agency 1983; Miracle 1985). Besides the Consumer Protection Fundamental Act of 1968, which established the basic directions of consumer policy and clarified the roles of various governmental levels, business firms and consumers, there are numerous laws and regulations pertaining to specific industries (e.g., food and medicines), fair and free competition (including antitrust legislation and the Act against Unjustifiable Premiums and Misleading Representations, UPMR Act), and contracts. Ministries as well as the Fair Trade Commission (FTC) and the National Police Agency implement these laws, which often contain clauses pertaining to advertising.

Like JARO, the government obtains a high level of voluntary compliance, but advertisers may also be ordered to publicize a negative judgment, to issue corrective advertising, and to submit similar ads to the FTC for approval during the following year. Furthermore, the FTC and local governmental bodies disseminate information about individual firms found to have contravened the law— apparently faster than JARO. However, FTC handling of cases is not any speedier than JARO's.

The FTC often pressures problematic industries into creating Fair Trade Associations (FTAs), which then issue Fair Competition Rules under the UPMR Act, to be approved by the FTC after a public hearing, and dealing with various practices, including advertising.[13] By mid–1986, 95 FTAs in more than 60 industries had issued 125 rules: 74 for representations (including advertising matters) and 51 for premiums. Most FTAs can handle consumer complaints and can also refer them to JARO (there have been few referrals, however). Instead, they deal mostly with complaints from competitors who also approach media associations and government agencies with their problems.

JARO, however, is not a FTA but a private nonprofit and public-interest association (*Shadanhojin*) approved by the Ministry of International Trade and Industry (MITI) and the Fair Trade Commission (which is part of the prime minister's office). As such, JARO is free of detailed administrative controls, unlike the FTAs' whose codes and structures must be approved by the FTC, but neither does it readily fit into the government's regulatory system.[14]

Much of the implementation of consumer-protection regulation has been delegated since 1972 to local public entities, which actively carry them out so that thousands of additional orders, warnings, and advices are issued to business firms every year. There is at least one consumer center in each prefecture, and many more in major municipalities (a total of 270 by April 1985). These centers handle some 260,000 complaints of various kinds a year, besides carrying out various research, informational and educational activities. Additional consumer-protection ordinances have been promulgated and are enforced by lower-level governments. Those complaints that cannot be handled by a consumer center are referred to a local Complaint Handling Committee for conciliation or mediation, although financial assistance may also be provided for a consumer to sue.

At the national level, the Japan Consumer Information Center handles complaints (5,933 in fiscal 1984) and collects statistics about them so that problematic industries, firms and practices may be readily identified. Besides, the central and local governments use thousands of "monitors"—often housewives and members of consumer associations—to report on illegal or undesirable business practices; and they train consumer consultants to handle complaints and provide mediation.

JARO's Role in Public Policy

This review of governmental activities reveals that many regulations and FTA rules bear on advertising, and that Japanese consumers and their organizations receive plenty of attention and assistance when dissatisfied with business activities, including advertising. Consequently, the role of JARO is rather modest, and its 1,500-odd annual inquiries and complaints represent only a fraction of those handled by government units, which greatly benefit from their "third-party" position, ready accessibility and reputation for independence and effectiveness.[15]

However, this relatively small role on the part of JARO must be carefully put into context. The nature and image of Japanese advertising are such that relatively little dissatisfaction has been felt and expressed about it. Thus, one report of consumer complaints received by government agencies in 1981 classified only 3.2 percent of the 205,162 cases as pertaining to "labeling, advertising and packaging" (Economic Planning Agency 1983, p. 36)—a rather broad category; and this percentage dropped to 1.9 percent in 1985 (private communication from the Economic Planning Agency). Instead, most complaints registered with government bodies have dealt with sales methods, contracts, quality, performance and servicing. Therefore, JARO, which appeared rather late on the complaint-handling scene, can only tap a relatively small pool of consumer expressions of dissatisfaction with advertising.

Since it is public policy to have enterprises "properly handle consumer complaints,"[16] government officials do approve of JARO, whose constitution was encouraged by the government and which received the approbation of the prime minister and MITI (JARO, What Is JARO 1978, p. 3). Besides, the government-issued *Consumers Handbook* (EPA 1985) refers to JARO, Fair Trade Associations and the consumer-affairs departments created by major business firms, although these are relatively recent references.[17] However, only a small fraction of the inquiries and complaints received by JARO since 1974 have emanated from governmental organizations, public enterprises and consumer centers (see Table 9.1), but this is also true in other countries with an advertising self-regulatory system.

Altogether, it is difficult to position JARO as a major "agent of public policy" (see Chapter 1) in Japan.[18] On the one hand, the government called for the establishment of a central self-regulatory organization by the advertising industry when consumer legislation was enacted and amended in the late 1960s. Ever since, it has encouraged self-discipline by private firms and associations as well as a "business-government-consumer partnership." Besides, there are fairly regular contacts between JARO and relevant government agencies (FTC, EPA, Ministry of Health and Welfare, etc.); and one of JARO's officers is a former FTC member who provides liaison between the two organizations. JARO is also appreciated for providing "finer-grain" responses than government agencies, for dealing with "gray areas," which the law overlooks, and for enhancing and propagating advertising-industry standards. Furthermore, no negative comments were elicited from government interviewees about JARO's role and effectiveness. On the other hand, one gets the impression that JARO is considered by some government officials to be a late and relatively minor player, compared to other business self-regulatory bodies (NARC, FTAs, etc.); and that greater public-policy expectations are placed on government-supported consumer centers as well as on business consumer-affairs departments. Besides, the levels of consumer dissatisfaction and complaint-behavior about advertising being rather low, JARO can only make marginal contributions to Japanese consumer policy.

Consequently, one can conclude that JARO plays a useful if relatively small complementary role to government initiatives. As one government respondent put it: "JARO is not a large organization but, in my opinion, consumer policy is the accumulation of small contributions from each local government consumer center, self-regulatory body, and company consumer-affairs unit so that JARO matters.''

Consumerism and Advertising

The consumer movement is rather well developed in Japan. There are numerous associations with large (although overlapping) memberships; they have emerged as a significant political force, and they receive explicit moral and financial support from the government in the context of its social policy (Kirkpatrick 1975; Cohen 1977; Chira 1986).

Consumerist Concerns

Interviews as well as the scant English-language literature on the subject reveal that advertising is not a very salient or important problem so far as consumerists are concerned; and Japanese consumer associations have not developed any single or strong position about it. Consumerist associations have identified various issues, but they mostly concern certain kinds of small-scale operators rather than large advertisers. Recent problems, for example, have focused on real estate promoters who misrepresent the size of houses as well as their location or distance from well-known areas and means of transportation. Inserts or leaflets enclosed by distributors (not by publishers) in newspapers, and containing false or misleading information about price and product availability (''bait-and-switch'' tactics) in retail stores have also been singled out.[19] Besides, some consumer groups have expressed dissatisfaction with advertising addressed to children or to which children are exposed (e.g., liquor ads) as well as with food and vitamin claims. Major advertisers and media, however, are seldom criticized by consumerists, although Japan is a major advertising nation permeated with countless billboards, print ads (the country has one of the highest rates of print readership in the world) and commercials (some 2,000 to 3,000 on television each day, diffused through numerous stations) for branded products.

"Mood" Advertising

The paucity of ad-related complaints reflects the fact that most Japanese advertising (except in the problematic categories mentioned above) is not of the hard-sell, conflictual or unique-selling-proposition types. As one observer put it: ''In Japan, one tries not to upset people, and certainly not with outspoken opinions. The communications business reflects this concern for harmony. . . . Head-on conflicts in advertising with competitors are usually avoided. Advertising . . . is created to please the prospect as opposed to making a direct sale. The more it pleases, the more likely it is to move the product. The real battle is fought at the distribution level . . . [Wagenaar 1978, p. 79; see also Miller 1985]."

Consequently, most Japanese ads evoke emotions and moods of the "Oh, oh, oh, what a feeling: Toyota!" variety, rely on fantasy or use celebrities as subtle endorsers—mostly through fifteen-second spots, which do not offer much time for specific points anyway. Their purpose is to create a "good feeling" and to communicate that the company is a reliable one with which to deal. Therefore, comparison ads contrasting brand names and product features are practically taboo, although not illegal. (FTA rules often oppose comparisons—see Boddewyn and Marton 1978—but the FTC developed new guidelines in 1987 and is now pressuring FTAs to allow comparative advertising as a way of alleviating trade frictions between the United States and Japan.) This being the general practice, it is very difficult to fault an ad for being false, misleading or unfair— except perhaps to juveniles when unsafe situations or incomplete information is provided, as a few of JARO's case histories reveal. Consequently, there are relatively few occasions to complain to JARO or the government. The prevalence of "mood" advertising also helps explain why few claims need substantiation— before or after the ad is issued—since nothing verifiable has been stated nor any hard comparison made.

General Satisfaction with Advertising

Japanese consumers appear to enjoy advertising and be satisfied with what they see and hear. Japanese advertisements may not deliver much product information by Western standards, but they generate what consumers appear to want, namely, assurance and reassurance about a company's overall reputation and reliability. As such, advertising assumes a relatively low salience in Japan; and consumers as well as government agencies are more concerned about product delivery, safety and performance after goods and services have been bought. This helps explain why consumer-policy pronouncements stress the development of consumer-affairs departments within firms rather than JARO and other self-regulatory bodies that deal only with advertising.

Consumerists and JARO

Interviews with the leaders of three Japanese consumer organizations[20] revealed that they are concerned with a few advertising issues centering on particular industries and practices (see above). However, they prefer to approach the appropriate advertisers, media and associations directly with their inquiries, complaints and requests, or to use the consumer centers and other government agencies that they trust more than JARO. Besides, they feel that some of the standards used by JARO are lower than theirs so that complaining to it will not be productive, since the two sides will probably disagree about the existence of a problem. These consumerists also believe that JARO is too much of an "in-

sider'' organization, since consumer associations are not represented on ad-
review committees. Consequently, they do not tell their members to use JARO
but instead assume their complaints—handling them themselves or referring them
to a consumer center or a government agency. These organizations also conduct
various surveys and studies, which help pinpoint problems that are brought to
the attention of business firms, associations and/or the government, but few of
them have dealt with advertising.

Implications and Recommendations

Altogether, one observes that JARO constitutes a well-developed self-regulatory system handling a sizable number of requests from consumers, business
and other bodies; making and publicizing considered decisions; obtaining compliance from advertisers and related parties; and reaching out to government and
consumerist bodies for mutual information and education on an informal basis.
Yet, JARO's impact is limited and its leadership is uncertain about future courses
of action. The following sections summarize problematic areas and suggest
possible remedies. Four related problems stand out: (1) relative lack of uniqueness; (2) low outside participation; (3) constricted leadership and (4) limited
government recognition.

Relative Lack of Uniqueness

While both consumerism and advertising self-regulation were borrowed from
the West, consumerists have managed to find their own targets and to rally the
government as well as many consumers around them. JARO, however, appeared
rather late on the scene, after an extensive and effective scheme of regulations
and consumer centers had already been developed. Besides, JARO chose to
focus on advertising—a major business activity in Japan, for sure, but one with
relatively low salience because of the overall satisfaction with advertising and
the prevalence of ''mood'' and pleasant ads, which generate few complaints.
Consequently, there was little opportunity to crusade for ''truth and accuracy''
as with the U.S. NAD/NARB system, which found fertile investigative grounds
in aggressive, fact-laden and comparative advertisements, and has a powerful
tool in the presubstantiation requirement also used by U.S. courts and the Federal
Trade Commission.

Still, JARO has been able to provide a centralized locus for whatever complaints could still be directed at advertising through a self-regulatory system, in
view of the large number of associations with general or advertising codes of
their own but less disposed or equipped to handle consumer complaints. Thus,
it has offered a focal point for handling a relatively small number of complaints
and more numerous inquiries.

JARO itself has recently raised the question of whether it should extend the
scope of its activities by concerning itself with additional problems such as the

quality, performance and other attributes of products and services as well as with the reputation of business firms.[21] Actually, this had been contemplated when JARO was founded, but such matters are now referred to firms and relevant associations. JARO could also increase its reach by opening additional offices in key cities, as was originally contemplated and is being progressively implemented.

However, this approach would require a totally different structure (such as the one developed by the U.S. Council of Better Business Bureaus throughout the United States) as well as larger financing of another type through local business and advertising associations or chapters. Besides, it would simply duplicate the well-dispersed consumer centers sponsored by the government so that such a broader scheme would probably meet with the same relatively low level of consumer interest experienced by JARO now. In any case, member companies are opposed to expanding the scope of JARO's activities on account of a lack of financial resources to develop the necessary testing facilities (JARO 1984, p. 3).[22]

There may be a simpler solution that would not require JARO to set up its own testing facilities. Instead, it could adopt the presubstantiation requirement found in Canada, the United Kingdom and the United States that advertisers have adequate evidence in hand before any claims be made. This would force firms and/or associations to develop or help develop such testing facilities, while JARO itself would not need new resources. This requirement makes sense since the reputation and credibility of advertising depends on its truth and accuracy; and no responsible advertiser should wait to develop the necessary substantiation until he is challenged. It would also put JARO in an innovative position vis-à-vis government, which, until now, has been the leader in developing advertising controls. Still, it is well to remember that claim substantiation is a relatively minor matter in Japan.

JARO could also change its policy of handling only "complete" complaints. Instead, all identifiable complaints that turn out to be problematic on the basis of a preliminary investigation could be assumed by JARO as its own—as is done by the U.S. NAD. This would not alter JARO's mission, since Article of Organization No. 5.2 states that it "shall monitor advertising and labelling." Handling more "inquiries" as "complaints" would amount to a form of inexpensive monitoring, which has not been possible on account of limited resources; and it would not fundamentally alter JARO's role of a "go-between" complainant and advertiser. Of course, there would be more work to be done by JARO's Secretariat, but its credibility is at stake since the number of complaints handled as well as recommendations and decisions issued has been declining in recent years (see Table 9.1), raising questions about its very raison d'être. Actually, this could be initiated by focusing at first on problematic areas such as real estate ads and inserts in "mini media"—a road that JARO is beginning to follow in a quasimonitoring manner.

Besides, JARO could well increase its publicity efforts in order to invite more consumer contacts. Currently, only JARO's name, address and telephone number have been mentioned in its publicity campaigns, with little attempt to instruct people on how to register a "full" complaint or even to "inquire." More extensive and informative campaigns could also be developed, although it must be kept in mind that Japanese consumers are less prone to complain and have relatively little to complain about so far as advertising is concerned.

The above recommendations are based on the assumption that JARO's credibility vis-à-vis consumers and government bodies rests in part on the sheer volume of cases handled and decisions issued—particularly in view of the larger number of complaints tackled by government-related bodies. However, even if JARO were to remain a relatively small player as far as consumers are concerned, it could also become a consultant to its members. This is the case in Sweden, where traditional advertising self-regulation was eliminated once the government's Consumer Ombudsman's system had preempted the field (see Chapter 12). Swedish business, instead, set up a consulting bureau, which advises advertisers, agencies and media for a fee.

As of now, JARO does not engage in preclearance work (which is done by the media and their associations), although it provides advice to its members for free. Considering the voluntary character of such a preclearance mission, a new consultant role may not encounter too much opposition on the part of JARO members. However, it would require a different staff made up of lawyers and other experts more versed in the intricacies of Japanese advertising regulations (which JARO also applies), but separate consulting fees could be levied to finance the hiring of such people.

Finally, JARO could develop uniqueness by preempting fields not yet regulated. New media, such as teleshopping via interactive cable, are beginning to grow in Japan, and they are bound to generate more consumer complaints as well as requests for their control. (Inserts are another problem that JARO is already tackling.) As mentioned below, the government is urging business to organize itself to deal with such emerging problems, but whether JARO can and will seize such opportunities is a function of other factors discussed in subsequent sections.

Low Outside Participation

JARO is not alone in its limited use of "outsiders" in the handling of consumer complaints, since this is also the case in most other countries. Despite its rather objective treatment of complaints, JARO is perceived as relying on norms developed and applied by business since only the rarely used Final Review Panel is made up of "independents." There are, of course, regular discussions of issues with government and consumerist representatives; and JARO is not insensitive to the concerns they express. However, its fundamentally "insider" system raises questions of objectivity, and it clashes with the Japanese preference for relying on independent third parties to mediate disputes.

Three alternatives are relevant here. The first one is to include outsiders in the ad-review committees that handle complaints and make recommendations—as is done in Canada, Italy, the Netherlands and the United Kingdom. Information gathered in this study suggests that this would be very difficult to achieve because the Japanese consumer movement is highly fragmented so that it would not be easy to recruit outsiders acceptable to all parties concerned. Besides, consumer associations have a vested interest in their own complaint-handling systems and may not be interested in supporting a rival one set up by business. JARO itself views consumerists as "too demanding" and probably threatening to the consensus-building practiced in Japanese organizations. Finally, interorganizational relations are very difficult in Japan, where "vertical" hierarchical structures predominate and hamper the reaching of agreements with other "outside" groups (Nakane 1970, pp. 53 ff).

The second alternative is to accept that JARO is in fact an "insider" organization designed to serve its business members rather than to provide redress to dissatisfied consumers. Under this perspective, JARO would still accept consumer complaints, but would assume them as its own for the purpose of improving the behavior and raising the standards of its members—as is done by the U.S. NAD system. For such a mission, no "outsiders" need be incorporated into the JARO structure, although contacts would be maintained with governmental and consumerist bodies; and complaints—complete or incomplete—would be solicited from consumers and other nonbusiness units.

Finally, no outsiders are needed for JARO to devote more attention to the industries (real estate, supermarkets, etc.) and practices (inserts, etc.) that are currently problematic. Again, it is an "internal" task of getting certain sectors to create or strengthen a trade association, which, in turn, would develop a code of ethics whose implementation would be left to them or delegated to JARO. Such a task would require the assistance of other advertising bodies (e.g., the Japan Advertising Federation) and even of the government, since the FTC can pressure industries into creating a Fair Trade Association with appropriate fair-competition rules. This role would shift JARO's mission to one of having large and generally responsible advertising firms—which constitute the bulk of JARO's members—police the behavior of smaller companies. Being an internal policing task, this shift would not require outside participation either.

— Constricted Leadership —

Japanese decisionmaking is a complex affair rooted in many indigenous—old and modern—variables. Consequently, one expects a Japanese trade association such as JARO to be run along "Japanese" lines, since its support rests on many "traditional" companies; and the resulting consensus in decisionmaking is likely to be conservative and cautious, with few sudden or abrupt policy changes.

Besides, the Japanese practice of borrowing executives from member organizations and of appointing end-of-career business and government officers to head such associations (sometimes with their salaries still paid by the former employer or subsidized by the latter's dues paid to JARO) is not conducive to creating a permanent bureaucracy of fairly independent ''professionals'' keen on building their own personal record and on striking new paths. The top officers of JARO fit this pattern, which is good to the extent that they are close to prominent JARO members, and have a good sense of what such firms will accept. However, they lack distance and/or independence from the membership. Yet, it seems unlikely that these JARO staffing practices will be changed in the near future because of their serious personal, structural and financial implications. Therefore, the present leadership will be the one to chart new courses of action.

The fact that JARO does depend on hundreds of individual company fees rather than on the financial sponsorship of a few capstone organizations complicates and slows down the adoption of new orientations and policies—but this is true of most Japanese associations and not proper to JARO. One wonders whether a different structure—such as exists in the United States—where a few major associations directly finance and control the advertising self-regulatory system—would give JARO greater freedom of initiative and action. Of course, each association in turn would have to develop a consensus among its members so that the process could remain as complex and lengthy as is now the case, or even more so. An automatic levy on all advertising expenditures—as is practiced in Ireland and the United Kingdom—would also relieve JARO of having to solicit old and new members, and give JARO greater independence. However, this method of financing usually encounters strong opposition from members who would lose control of a then financially independent system. To succeed, such a scheme would require the full moral support of the key advertising associations, which would become the sole members of JARO's board of directors. Since JARO was in fact created at the initiative of such associations, such a move is not out of the question but its design and likelihood of success are beyond the scope of this study.

Limited Government Recognition

The Japanese bureaucracy is rather safe in its reputation and public acceptance. Having preempted the field through regulations and ubiquitous consumer centers, it has not significantly relied on JARO to substitute for its extensive consumer-protection activities. Only budgetary restrictions could really make it want to rely more on private initiatives to improve advertising behavior.[23] Actually, there are indications that Japanese budgetary allocations to consumer protection have peaked (OECD, various years). In that context, greater private assumption of advertising-control activities may prove attractive to the government. Thus, the Consumer Policy Planning Subcommittee, together with the Economic Planning Agency, has recently suggested that media and information suppliers develop self-regulatory devices to preempt possible government regulation regarding the amount, truthfulness and complaint-handling of advertisements in new electronic media—for example, in the case of teleshopping via interactive cable television (IAA 1985). This could provide an opening wedge for JARO to seize if it is true that it will not get any new resources from its members until "new ways and new targets are found"—as one business interviewee put it. However, it has not yet developed any initiative in this direction.

Conclusions

JARO is now faced with old and new challenges to its existence, but also with opportunities to refocus itself. It has developed into a relatively strong "private government," but remains a marginal "agent of public policy." According to its original purpose, it has served its member organizations well by centralizing, coordinating and servicing other self-regulatory initiatives. However, it is a relatively minor player in the handling of consumer complaints, which do not focus very much on advertising matters and are mainly handled by government-sponsored consumer centers. Having reached a plateau in terms of credibility, use and effectiveness, it needs to be repositioned, just like any other service, along new lines such as the ones mentioned above. JARO's Middle-Term Project has recently been set up to study and recommend changes of the sort, which are needed since advertising, consumerism and government intervention are themselves evolving in Japan.

NOTES

1. The English acronym JARO is widely used, even in Japan, but the official name is Shadan Hojin Nippon Kokoku Shinsa Kiko.

2. For further historical (1885–1976) details, see Miracle 1985 and Yamaki 1984. JARO has issued various reports about its creation and development.

3. See also *JARO's Articles of Organization* (JARO 1976) for expressions of civic responsibility through advertising integrity.

4. JARO relies on eight advertiser codes (e.g., by the Japan Advertisers Association and for pharmaceuticals, banking, department stores and outdoor advertising), five newspaper codes, one broadcasting code, two magazine codes, the Advertising Ethics Code of the Japan Advertising Agencies Association, and at least seven other codes—besides the relevant clauses of Fair Competition Rules developed by various industry associations. Yamaki (1984, p. 1) refers to 37 rules and codes used by JARO.

5. JARO case histories sometimes refer to foreign precedents as with Case History No. 44, which mentions a similar case handled by the U.S. NAD/NARB.

6. Yet, Article 5 of JARO's Articles of Organization provides for such monitoring of advertising and labeling. However, JARO offers free advice to its members when ads are being prepared.

7. Members of ad-review committees come from industry but do not serve on a panel when their own company is involved. Subcommittees include at least one member of the Primary Ad-Review Committee, and they refer the results of all their deliberations to the latter.

8. The "Red Reports" broadly circulated by JARO publicize its Recommendations well before the case histories are published at a more leisurely pace.

9. There is a division of labor between JARO and the Japan Advertising Federation: the former "works with" government agencies, while JAF does the adversary lobbying in such matters as the regulation and taxation of advertising.

10. Only the president and the executive director, among JARO's Board of Directors, are on JARO's payroll, while other directors serve without compensation.

11. There are JARO offices in Osaka, Sapporo and Shimane—the last two very recent additions, with a further one to open in Nagoya. The thirty-five local advertising clubs that make up the Japan Advertising Federation (which shares a common chairman with JARO) also provide some local representation for JARO.

12. JARO letter to author (2 May 1983). Only 33 percent of middle-level managers in JARO member organizations knew of its existence. Lack of comparable data about self-regulatory bodies in other countries make it impossible to conclude that this lack of information is unusual.

13. Under the Act against Unjustifiable Premiums and Misleading Representations, enterprises are forbidden to issue misleading, exaggerated and deceptive advertisements or other misrepresentations to consumers, concerning the contents of products and services as well as contract terms. The Fair Trade Commission may issue cease-and-desist orders and warnings to firms considered to be in violation of this Act. In fiscal 1985, 5 orders and 474 warnings were issued by the FTC. Some FTAs are headed by former FTC officials; and, as bodies approved by the FTC, they can impose sanctions that are beyond the legal scope of JARO, which is not a FTA.

14. Of course, MITI and the FTC, which approved JARO, supervise its activities and account in a general manner. Media associations such as the NARC and JMAA are also not FTAs, and are free of administrative controls—a reflection of the postwar policy of avoiding press and broadcast censorship by the government.

15. It is difficult to compare JARO and government statistics, but if JARO handles some 1,500 inquiries and complaints while both the FTC and local governments issue some 6,000 orders and warnings under the Act against Unjustifiable Premiums and Misleading Representations, one obtains a ratio of 1 to 4. However, many other laws and ordinances are also applied at the national and local levels so that the true ratio is probably lower and the government's role even larger.

16. Article 4 of the Consumer Protection Fundamental Act (Law No. 78, 30 May 1968), which is included in *Consumer Protection in Japan* (EPA 1983, pp. 4–5).

17. The EPA pamphlet *Consumer Protection in Japan* (1983, p. 35), which has been prepared for foreigners, does not mention JARO. Neither have Japan's sections in the *Consumer Policy in OECD Countries* annual reports.

18. It was impossible to accurately ascertain governmental attitudes toward JARO since hundreds of units and thousands of functionaries are involved. Interviews with a group of national government officials were conducted in the presence of JARO leaders, so that some of these officials' views were possibly not expressed.

19. The "inserts" problem is being tackled through the newspaper industry in cooperation with JARO, which is receiving more complaints about these inserts in so-called "mini media," which escape the self-regulatory controls effectively applied by the "mass media."

20. Chifuren (National Federation of Regional Women's Organization), Shokaren (Consumption Science Organization) and Shufuren (Japan Housewives' Association).

21. JARO letter to author (2 May 1983), and JARO 1984b.

22. The Japan Advertising Federation is also thinly financed. Some respondents com-

mented unfavorably on the unnecessary duplication of Japanese business and advertising associations with fairly similar objectives, which share "thin bread."

23. Of course, the government already uses Fair Trade Associations for self-regulatory purposes, but they are not very much involved in advertising matters that concern consumers (see above).

REFERENCES

Beer, L. W. *Freedom of Expression in Japan.* Tokyo and New York: Kodansha International, 1984.

Birnbaum, Phyllis. "Honorable Fussy Consumers." *Across the Board* (March 1986): 24–30.

Boddewyn, J. J., and K. Marton. *Comparison Advertising; A Worldwide Study.* New York: Hastings House, 1978.

Chira, Susan. "Diffuse Goals Set by Naders of Japan." *New York Times,* July 14, 1986, D10.

Cohen, S. E. "Consumerism Powers Basic Changes in Japan." *Advertising Age* 48, no. 14 (April 4, 1977): 12 ff.

Economic Planning Agency [EPA]. *Consumers Handbook '85* [in Japanese]. Tokyo: 1985.

———. *Consumer Protection in Japan.* Tokyo: 1983.

International Advertising Association [IAA]. *Intelligence Summary* 46 (June-July 1985): 4.

JARO. *JARO's Articles of Organization.* Tokyo: 1976.

———. *History of Ten Years of Progress, 1974–1984* [in Japanese]. Tokyo: 1984a.

———. "JARO Handled 1390 Complaints and Inquiries in 1984." Tokyo: 1984b.

———. "JARO Issued 'The Case History' as an Ad Review Standard." Tokyo: September 30, 1979.

———. *What Is JARO?* Tokyo: 1978.

Kirkpatrick, M. A. "Consumerism and Japan's New Citizen Politics." *Asian Survey* 40 no. 3 (March 1975): 234–46.

Miller, Richard. "The Cultural Nuances of Japan and Italy." *Back Stage* (June 21, 1985): 6B ff.

Miracle, G. E. "Advertising Regulation in Japan and the USA: An Introductory Comparison." *Waseda Business and Economic Studies* 21 (1985): 35–69.

Nakane, Chie. *Japanese Society.* Berkeley, Calif.: University of California Press, 1970.

Organization for Economic Cooperation and Development. *Annual Reports on Consumer Policy in OECD Member Countries.* Paris: 1981, 1983 and 1985.

Wagenaar, J. D. "Creativity in Ads: Hard on Mood, Soft on Conflict." *Advertising Age* 49, no. 3 (January 16, 1978): 79.

Yamaki, Toshio. "Advertising Regulation in Japan." Tokyo: Nikkei Advertising Research Institute, June 20, 1984.

ACKNOWLEDGMENTS

This research is greatly indebted to those JARO officers and staff members who arranged numerous interviews with a variety of industry, government, media and consumerist people with the assistance of generously provided interpreters; and who themselves answered numerous queries with great care and diligence: Mssrs. Shizuo Kawaguchi, President of JARO; Izumi Shimotani, Chairman of the Primary Ad-Review Committee; Yoshiyuki Adachi, Chairman of the General Affairs Committee; Shuji Yanagida, Consultant; Yoshio Kimura, Executive Director; and Chiaki Shimada, External Relations. Pertinent advice about this report was also received from Katsuhiko Amano (Dentsu), Dr. Kumi Itotagawa, Yasuyo Maruyama (Hakuhodo advertising agency), Gordon Miracle (Michigan State), Yoshiro Nakajo (Economic Planning Agency), Yoshi Tsurumi (Baruch College) and Toshio Yamaki (Nikkei Advertising Research Institute).

10

The Netherlands: Reclame Code Commissie

The Dutch advertising self-regulatory system is a relatively old and original one. Its creation predates the 1970s, which witnessed the establishment of most other systems; and from the start, it has involved significant support and participation by consumer associations, a rarity among such systems. While other forms of advertising control in the Netherlands also include nonindustry members (see Appendix), this analysis focuses on the Advertising Code system and the participation of outsiders in its functioning (cf. Hondius 1980 and 1984; Kabel 1983; Verkade 1981). Literature reviews, personal interviews and correspondence with self-regulatory administrators, consumer and industry representatives, government officials and experts from 1981 to 1987 have provided the data for this analysis. Relatively few Dutch-language sources were used but many of them are cited in Hondius (1984).

The Advertising Code System

Three interrelated bodies handle nonbroadcast advertising as well as "noncommercial" advertising (e.g., campaigns for the Red Cross and against South African policies).[1] They all involve nonindustry participation.

The Advertising Code Foundation

This capstone body (Stichting Reclame Code, SRC) was founded in 1964 to develop the Dutch Advertising Code and to maintain relations with the government, the consumer movement and other relevant external organizations. Nine organizations have sponsored and financed it: one represents advertisers, another the agencies, four the media, and one the advertising industry at large, but the two principal Dutch consumer associations are also involved, namely, the Consumentenbond (Consumer Alliance) and the Konsumenten Kontakt, which were founding members of the Foundation. The financial contribution of the latter two is proportionately smaller, however.[2]

The Dutch Advertising Code (Nederlandse Code voor het Reclamewezen) contains general rules (e.g., about good taste, comparisons and testimonials) as well as special provisions for certain products. The Dutch Code borrows from the International Chamber of Commerce's International Code of Advertising Practice, but new rules are developed by the Foundation after consultation with the relevant industry groups.

The Advertising Code Commission

The Reclame Code Commissie (RCC) is the implementing or "judiciary" arm of the system, which handles the complaints generated by consumers, consumer associations, competitors and trade associations as well as by its own minuscule monitoring. Its work is handled by two five-member committees,[3] each headed by a Foundation-appointed independent chairman with a legal background (preferably a judge), but not affiliated with advertising-related organizations. The other four members are nominated by: the advertiser (one), agency (one) and media (one) associations as well as by the two consumer associations (one)—with the Consumentenbond member sitting on the committee handling complaints emanating from the Konsumenten Kontakt association, and vice versa. Once appointed by their own organizations, these four members are not considered as representatives of these organizations but are expected to act independently. This structure amounts to a 40 percent rate of "outside participation" (the Chairman and the consumer representative)—less than in Italy (100 percent) and the United Kingdom (66 percent), but about as much as in Canada.

These two committees handled 298 complaints in 1986, out of which 183 resulted in either private recommendations to the advertiser (138) to have the advertisement modified, or in public ones (45) in the case of severe violations and of matters of general interest (Stichting Reclame Code [SRC] annual reports). The latter are communicated to: (1) the media who normally stop publishing or broadcasting the objectionable advertisement; (2) member organizations of the self-regulatory system, and (3) the relevant government departments. Outside advice is sought from research laboratories, universities, the National Food Council, etc., when complex technical claims are involved.

No preadvertising advice is provided to advertisers for fear of creating a conflict if an advertisement advised to be in compliance with the Code becomes the subject of a later complaint. Some other countries, however, separate these two functions, with the Secretariat providing advice while a separate board handles complaints.

The Appeals College

The College van Beroep, which handles all appeals to the decisions of the Advertising Code Commission, has five members: an independent Chairman; one member from consumer associations, and three from industry (advertisers, agencies, media). The rate of outside participation is 60 percent, to the extent that one of the three industry's representatives has to be an independent "outsider."

The above three bodies share a rather small staff made up of three part-time lawyers and two secretaries. Their current annual budget is in the vicinity of 350,000 guilders (about $140,000) provided by the member associations (including the two consumer organizations).

The Bases of Outside Representation

Consumer representatives have fruitfully participated in the Dutch advertising self-regulatory system since its inception in 1964. What has brought about such cooperation and conditioned its effectiveness?

The Consumer Movement

Most analysts of the Netherlands have observed the high degree of organization in Dutch society, where many groups are active in all spheres of social and political life, with high percentages of individual affiliation (Lijphart 1968, p. 206; Bekke 1983). In particular, there is a small number of moderately powerful, independent private consumer associations—particularly, the Consumentenbond, which reaches one-tenth of all Dutch households, and the Konsumenten Kontakt, linked with two major trade unions, the national family organization (NGR) and the Housewives' Association, but there are also a few other specialized consumer associations (e.g., for motorists and home-owners). As such, Dutch consumers are among the best organized ones in Western Europe (Hondius 1980, p. 7; Box, 1983).

These organizations are bent on creating "a framework of behavioral patterns, agreements, standards and laws for commerce and industry, consumers and the government, which enable each to play its appropriate, mutual economic role in a safe and effective way (Hondius 1980, p. 9)." This accommodating stance resembles that of the major consumer associations in Canada and the United Kingdom, and it contrasts with the highly fragmented and ideology-laden situations in Belgium and France. However, the political power of these consumer associations appears to be somewhat limited with the Dutch administration and Parliament (Hondius 1980, p. 12; Box 1983). Thus, there is no separate consumer-protection agency, although the Ministry of Economic Affairs has a Consumer Affairs section. Therefore, it seemed desirable for the two major consumer associations to be "inside" the self-regulatory system in order to be better able to influence it—what Hirschman (1970) calls the "loyalty" (versus "exit" or "voice") route.

Although in a minority position, the consumer representatives on the Advertising Code Commission carry weight because of: (1) the moral importance of their participation (e.g., they threatened to leave the Advertising Code Commission over the matter of cigarette advertising); (2) the preliminary work done by their sponsoring organizations, which have substantial resources, thereby allowing consumer representatives to be well informed about Code violations, and (3) the implicit threat of demands for more government regulation, should self-regulation prove inadequate. Consumer associations do not feel circumscribed by their participation in advertising self-regulation but continue to favor additional regulations (Kasper 1979). Thus, consumer representatives have pressed for and accepted stricter voluntary-code restrictions against cigarette advertising, but their associations keep lobbying for greater government regulation in this and other matters (e.g., the World Health Organization's code regarding breastmilk substitutes).

Still, most Commission decisions are based on a consensus among all represented parties; and the fact that consumer associations keep lobbying for further regulation has not poisoned the relationships between business and consumer representatives. As members of the Code Committees, consumer representatives investigate whether a complaint is justified in the light of the Code's provisions, but they do not challenge the wording and amending of the code itself, which are "political" tasks left to the Foundation (SRC). Since the Commission also applies government laws, any increase in the latter benefits the consumer movement both via regulation and self-regulation.

There is a specifically Dutch component present here—but one hard to pinpoint and define. As one consumerist respondent put it: "We talk to each other and invite the other side to our conferences. We tolerate each other even though we have conflicting interests. Success depends a lot on representatives being willing to compromise and not being angry or radical. We also respect what has been achieved to date."

The Government

Both industry and consumer associations interact regularly with government: (1) through institutionalized advisory councils (e.g., the capstone Social and Economic Council and its Commission on Consumer Affairs, CCA, where various economic and social sectors are represented; and the Interministerial Commission for Consumer Affairs (ICC), set up by the Ministry of Economic Affairs), and (2) on an informal ad hoc basis.

As far as Dutch consumer-protection legislation is concerned, most of the relevant rules are judge-made on the basis of the general-tort provisions of the Dutch Civil Code or are scattered over many acts, which were originally intended to protect competitors (Hondius 1980, p. 20). Still, a misleading-advertising section was enacted in 1980 as an amendment to the Civil Code. It provides for reversal of the burden of proof, that is, the advertiser must prove that he did not violate the law (similarly, under the Advertising Code, he must establish that the advertisement was accurate and complete) as well as for damages, corrective advertising and cease-and-desist injunctions.

The 1983 revision of the Dutch Constitution explicitly excluded equal freedom-of-speech protection for commercial advertising because, if the latter were covered, the laws applying to advertising could well turn out to be unconstitutional. Some members of the industry, however, argue that Article 7, Section 4 of the new Constitution will not unduly restrict advertising (ter Kuile et al. 1983). Besides, the European Convention on Human Rights holds that "commercial speech" is not outside the protection it grants.

The government does not participate directly in the functioning of the advertising self-regulatory system. Still, it has legitimized its existence since this system has been registered as a legal public-interest body for the self-regulation of advertising. Outside participation—particularly, the 60 percent rate at the appeal level—was devised in order to satisfy the procompetition and antitrust requirement of the law. The government also communicates various requests to the self-regulatory system. For example, following a parliamentary question, the Ministry of Economic Affairs inquired in 1981 about the possibility of the Advertising Code prohibiting appeals based on "greed and envy." The Advertising Code Foundation answered that it was opposed to including such subjective criteria in the Code, but that the Code Committees can make recommendations about "extreme" abuses of such appeals by advertisers. Government threats of introducing further regulations have also been effective—as in the case of cigarette advertising. For that matter, the Dutch advertising self-regulatory system was originally set up to forestall legislative intervention (Hondius 1984).

In recent decades, there has been a progressive shift in the Dutch political system from interest representation through which an important role in policy-making and policy-implementation has been played by semiprivate groups and institutions, to greater unilateral intervention on the part of the State (Bekke 1983; Hondius 1984). The consumer-affairs staff in the Ministry of Economic Affairs has been greatly expanded in recent years; and there was a government proposal to ban alcoholic-beverage advertising on radio and television. However, recent recessionary economic conditions and stressed budgets have led the government to become more cautious about expanding its role and more willing to rely again on intermediary bodies (Koopman 1986). Thus, the 1987 revision of the Broadcasting Act, by shifting the handling of complaints about broadcast commercials to the Advertising Code Foundation (see Appendix), offers renewed evidence of government willingness to rely on self-regulation.

The Industry

Dutch trade and industry have a long tradition of self-regulation. Major business associations have emphasized that it should be left to firms themselves to minimize or prevent the less attractive societal consequences of their behavior by means of self-regulation and voluntary codes (Kasper 1979). There is general agreement about its usefulness in view of the incompleteness of consumer-protection legislation:

From a consumer point of view, self-regulation plays an important role in the advertising area. Whereas civil law concerning advertising is usually invoked by competitors, the self-regulatory code is often applied at the request of consumers or consumers' organizations. . . . That no change of the law has been felt necessary in recent years, is no doubt a result of the rather effective self-regulation. The Netherlands Advertising Code, as interpreted by the Reclame Code Commissie, provides far stricter rules than the common law (Hondius 1980, pp. 74 and 85).

Conversely, the industry has supported self-regulation because of the expectation of stricter laws, should it fail. Although opposed to further regulation, the industry has come to accept the new 1980 law on misleading advertising as a last-resort instrument to be used against "diehards" with a record of sustained violations of the Advertising Code.

Self-Regulation's Acceptance and Effectiveness

From the outset, consumer organizations have participated in the application and implementation of the code, which is considered to cover approximately 90 percent of the advertising that falls within its scope of application (Hondius 1984, p. 145). Thus, over two-thirds and even four-fifths of the complaints handled by the Advertising Code Commission since 1980 have come from the consumer side:

	1980	1981	1982	1983	1984	1985	1986
Consumer associations	21	33	48	19	15	12	14
Consumers	308	275	270	201	281	219	228
Competitors	113	171	158	69	29	42	30
Business organizations	0	0	0	17	7	2	25
Monitoring	3	1	12	1	12	18	1
	445	480	488	307	344	293	298
Proportion of consumer-related complaints	74%	64%	65%	72%	86%	79%	81%

Industry stresses the expertise, flexibility, inexpensiveness and relative speed of self-regulation. However, an average of sixty-five days in 1985 elapsed between the receipt of a complaint and the issuing of a recommendation, while only one to two weeks are needed to obtain action in court under the new 1980 misleading-advertising legislation, although such action is more expensive, and the typical judge does not know much about advertising. In any case, only a handful of cases are brought up yearly under the legal system, compared to hundreds under self-regulation.

Criticisms of Dutch advertising self-regulation have centered on the fairly traditional grounds that: (1) there is a lack of full publicity of its decisions since not all RCC recommendations are made public;[4] (2) the Commission exercises too much discretion in accepting or rejecting complaints; (3) sanctions seldom involve fines, compensation or rectification (e.g., corrective advertising)[5] but rely instead on recommendations to the advertisers and the media; (4) monitoring of advertisements by the Commission is very limited for lack of sufficient resources so that it depends mostly on the complaints that reach it; (5) only advertisements appearing in member media can be impacted (of course, they represent most of Dutch advertising), although complaints about advertisements in all nonbroadcast media are accepted; (6) the extent of advertiser compliance with RCC recommendations is not well known; (7) little if any preadvertising advice is provided to advertisers, and (8) consumers (although not consumer associations) are not sufficiently aware of this redress avenue—again a reflection of the Commission's limited resources. Hondius (1980, pp. 181–182) also mentions that the Advertising Code Commission has seldom used its power to forbid a firm to advertise until approval of its subsequent advertisements has been granted, following evidence of renewed good behavior on the part of the incriminated advertiser. In partial response to these criticisms, RCC meetings were opened to the public in 1986 unless one of the parties has valid objections. Besides, copies of RCC decisions are now immediately made available to anyone for a small fee.

Conclusions

Dutch advertising self-regulation has performed rather well, except in the matters of preadvertising advice and of postadvertising monitoring. It displays strong outside-participation features on the part of consumer organizations, which use it and even share in its financing. Interaction with the government seems more limited than in Canada and the United Kingdom—probably a reflection of the Netherlands' stronger traditions of corporatism, private policy-making and negotiations (Bekke 1983; Koopman 1986). Besides, recent government retrenchment on account of recessionary and deregulatory pressures is granting the self-regulatory system another chance to prove its complementary role in controlling advertising behavior, particularly since the system appears to satisfy key consumer organizations.

Appendix

Besides the Advertising Code System, three other forms of advertising control involve nonindustry members in the Netherlands.

The (Broadcasting) Advertising Council (Reclameraad)

This body was created under the Broadcasting Act (1965, 1969) to develop and implement a mandated code bearing on programs and commercials in the interest of the public, the broadcasting system and the advertising industry. It has been financed through income derived from broadcast commercials. Its government-appointed board includes representatives of the broadcasting system, the advertising industry (press, advertisers and agencies), consumer organizations, major cultural bodies, small and medium business and the Advertising Society (Genootschap voor Reclame), as well as various independent experts.

The Reclameraad has handled complaints by consumers and competitors against commercials originally found acceptable by the radio-television authority (STER, Stichting Etherreclame), which reviews all commercial materials prior to broadcasting, and determines whether they are acceptable in the light of the Reclameraad Code.

A new 1987 law has replaced the Broadcasting Act and no longer provides for the Reclameraad, whose functions will probably be assumed by the Stichting Reclame Code.

Drug Advertising Boards

Two bodies (KOAG and KAMA) are sponsored and financed by the pharmaceutical industry, the advertising industry and the media. They preclear all proprietary (over-the-counter) drug and medical-treatment advertisements to the public, which are not accepted by the media without their approval (de Vroom 1985). Since KAMA deals with all health claims, including those associated with food, it is not restricted to the pharmaceutical industry.

Industry Complaint Boards

Eight retail industries (which include furniture, travel agencies, flooring, kitchen appliances, dry- and wet-cleaning and public utilities) have set up complaint boards (*Geschillencommissies*). A Code is typically developed through negotiation between the Consumentenbond and the industry, while complaints are handled by a three-member panel made up of an independent chair (typically, a lawyer) plus one representative each of the industry and the Consumentenbond. This system is financed by these two groups, but also by government subsidies predicated on the joint establishment of such boards. This is an example of "negotiated" codes or "concerted action" rather than of "pure" industry-initiated and run self-regulation. These boards, however, rarely deal with advertising complaints, nor do they issue rulings bearing on future advertisements.

NOTES

1. Noncommercial advertisements are mainly handled on the basis of truthfulness, although complaints about "bad taste" can also be considered, provided public opinion is carefully considered in such a matter. Only "advice" to the media, rather than "recommendations" (see below), can be issued about noncommercial advertising, however.

2. There are four major contributors (one each from the advertiser and agency sides, and two from the media side), and their contributions amount to about 230,000 guilders (around $100,000); others pay a total of 40,000 guilders (about $16,000). Industry associations, for which special provisions have been added to the general code, pay a minimum annual fee of 10,000 guilders (about $4,000) for a total of 80,000 guilders: alcoholic and tobacco products, sweets, consumer credit and investment, direct-marketing (which has its own self-regulatory body, BBH, now integrated into the Foundation) and

Viditel (viewdata). There are only eight financing organizations left since 1983 when the cinema-advertising association was expelled from the Foundation for not paying dues for three years. However, two cinema-advertising agencies have joined the Foundation. Since 1982, business complainants must pay 500 guilders (about $200) to have their case handled.

3. Since 1984, there is a third five-member Direct Mail Committee headed by an independent chairman (an academic jurist), one representative of the two consumer associations, and three members jointly appointed by the Direct Marketing Institute and the advertiser, agency and media associations—a 40 percent ratio of outside participation.

4. Once a year, the Advertising Code Commission (RCC) publishes a compendium of all its decisions. The Dutch publishing firm Kluwer has started publishing a journal on copyright and advertising law (IER), which reports some of the decisions of the Reclameraad, Code Commissie and College van Beroep, although their nonpublic recommendations do not name the parties involved, according to the current practice of the Code Commission. Besides, major newspapers and the monthly publication of the Consumentenbond often publicize the recommendations of the Code committees.

5. However, the Tobacco Code provides for a maximum penalty of 50,000 guilders (about $20,000); and the Direct-Marketing Code enables the Code Commission and Appeals College to have the advertiser: (1) diffuse the Commission's or College's public recommendation to those who received the original advertisement, and (2) pay damages to the complainant.

REFERENCES

Bekke, Hans. "Private Organizations and the State: Mutual Prisoners Blocking Debureaucratization." Mimeographed. Nijmegen: Institute for Political Science, University of Nijmegen, October 1983.

Box, J. M. F. "Consumerism in an Era of Decline: Does It Still Have a Future?" Mimeographed. Delft, Netherlands: Department of Industrial Design, Delft University of Technology, 1983.

"Bremen Workshop." *Consumer Affairs* [J. W. Thompson, London] 66 (November–December 1983): 19–20.

de Vroom, Bert. "Quality Regulation in the Dutch Pharmaceutical Industry." In *Private Interest Government*, edited by Wolfgang Streeck, and Ph. C. Schmitter. London, England, and Beverly Hills, Calif.: Sage, 1985, pp. 128–49.

Hirschman, A. O. *Exit, Voice and Loyalty*. Cambridge, Mass.: Harvard University Press, 1970.

Hondius, E. H. *Consumer Legislation in The Netherlands*. New York: Van Nostrand Reinhold, 1980.

———. "Non-legislative Means of Consumer Protection: The Dutch Perspective." *Journal of Consumer Policy* 7, no. 2 (1984): 137–56.

Kabel, J. J. C. "Zelfregulering en Recht; Basiscriteria voor Zelfregulering van Reclame in Nederland [Self-Regulation and Law: Basic Criteria for Advertising Self-Regulation]." *Sociale en Economische Wetenschappen* 31, no. 3 (March 1983): 151–65.

Kasper, Hans. "Consumer Policy and Consumption Policy in the Netherlands." Reprinted in *Consumerism, Public Policy and Consumer Protection; Proceedings of the 5th*

ESSEC Seminar on Marketing and Public Policy, edited by M. J. Baker, and
    Daniel Tixier, pp. 230–39. Cergy-Pontoise, France: ESSEC, December 1979.
Koopman, Joop, "New Developments in Government Consumer Policy: A Challenge
    for Consumer Organizations." *Journal of Consumer Policy* 9, no. 3 (1986): 269–
    86.
Lijphart, Arend. *The Politics of Accommodation; Pluralism and Democracy in the Neth-
    erlands*. Berkeley, Calif.: University of California Press, 1968.
Stichting Reclame Code [SRC]. *Jaarverslag* [Annual Report]. Amsterdam, various dates.
ter Kuile, B. H., Ribbink, G. J., and D. Schut. "Report re Article 7, Section 4 of the
    [Dutch] Constitution and the Freedom of Commercial Advertising." Mimeo-
    graphed. Amsterdam: Dutch Advertising Association [Genootschap voor Re-
    clame], October 1983.
Verkade, D. W. F., ed. *Praktijkboek Reclame- en Aanduidingenrecht* [Handbook of
    Advertising]. Deventer, Netherlands: Kluwer, 1978–1981.

ACKNOWLEDGMENTS

The assistance of the following people is gratefully acknowledged: Jo M. F. Box (Delft
University of Technology), A. E. de Gelder (Stichting Reclame Code), L. Donia (Kon-
sumenten Kontakt), H. F. Heijting (Stichting Reclame Code), P. A. E. Hollander (Re-
clame Code Commissie), E. H. Hondius (Utrecht State University), J. J. C. Kabel
(Amsterdam University), Ineke Kamphuisen-van der Schraaf (Stichting Reclame Code),
Hans Kasper (SWOKA), Joop Koopman (Ministry of Economic Affairs), R. E. Lunshof
(Reclameraad), G. J. Ribbink (Lawfirm Geerling, Amsterdam; Agencies' Association),
D. Schut (Stichting Reclame Code), Marion van Delft-Baas (Utrecht State University),
A. J.M. van den Biggelaar (Konsumenten Kontakt), J. A. van Haren (Keuringsraad),
D. W. F. Verkade (Catholic University, Nijmegen; Lawfirm Stibbe, Blaise & De Jong,
Amsterdam) and C. H. M. Wirtz (Advertisers' Association).

11

The Philippines: Philippine Board of Advertising

Advertising self-regulation in the Philippines originally derived its mandate from the government after former President Marcos imposed martial law in 1972. As such, it represents a form of ''corporative associationism'' (Streeck and Schmitter 1985), whereby industry is delegated some regulatory power. However, outsiders are relatively minor actors in Philippine advertising self-regulation—a situation that raises questions about the compatibility of corporative associationism with outside participation. A research trip to Manila in 1984 elicited most of the information contained in this chapter, the contents of which were checked by various practitioners and observers (see Acknowledgments).

Creation and Original Character of the PBA

The Philippine Board of Advertising (PBA) was created and is controlled as well as financed by all the associations of advertisers, agencies, media, supports and suppliers.[1] Only minor media, often regional and local, as well as some forms of direct-mail or leaflet advertising remain largely unreached or not influenced through the PBA system and even the law (see below). There had been earlier attempts by the Philippine Association of National Advertisers (PANA) to develop self-regulation after 1956, and by advertising agencies and various media thereafter. On their own, such efforts would probably have resulted in a capstone organization of the PBA type as well as a code of advertising ethics designed to upgrade, defend and promote advertising. However, political events gave an immediate impetus to the creation of the Philippine Board of Advertising.

Martial Law

In September 1972, former President Ferdinand E. Marcos declared martial law to cope with major political, social and economic problems that had resulted in impoverishment, violence, cynicism and other ills in the Philippines.[2] In order to quell criticism from the political factions opposing the government, to promote his "New Society" scheme, and to galvanize Filipinos toward overcoming their problems, President Marcos suspended the Parliament and started ruling by decrees, presidential orders and the like, some of which drastically affected the media.

In particular, the declaration of martial law brought strict curbs on press freedom. A number of media operations were closed, in some cases permanently. Subsequent resumption of operations was allowed only with operating permits and supervision by government representatives. All government media operations were merged under the Department of Public Information, which issued decrees detailing guidelines for journalists as well as procedures for censorship and control. Implementation and operation of these decrees was initially handled by a military office, but in November 1972 they were transferred to the newly created Mass Media Council (Vreeland et al. 1976, p. 169).

In January 1973, this Council met with the heads of all communication associations in the Philippines to develop new rules and regulations for the conduct of media and advertising agencies, which were at that time loosely classified as "mass media." One of the several councils formed at this meeting was the Council for Advertising, Public Relations, Research and Sales Promotion. A subcommittee was then formed, consisting of representatives from what were to become the PBA's founding associations, the Office of Civil Relations, the Institute of Mass Communications and the consumer sector in order to forge a Code of Ethics and Rules and Regulations for all firms engaged in advertising and sales promotion. After fifteen months of preparation, such a code was signed, approved and ratified by all participating organizations in March 1974. It was then presented to the Secretary of Public Information for minor editing and approval.

Following its formation in May 1974, the Philippine Board of Advertising agreed in principle with the above Code as appropriate for its purposes. The secretary of public information released the Code on 4 April 1975, and the PBA adopted it formally on 15 April 1975. Subsequently, on 19 June 1975, the Philippine Board of Advertising adopted a revised version of the Code, which clarified the position of the Board as the self-regulatory body referred to in the Code, and included certain other modifications. Additional amendments of the Code of Ethics were adopted by the Board in 1979, 1983 and January 1984 after a series of multisectoral consultations (PBA Code of Ethics 1984, Preface), with some additional fine tuning in 1986 and 1987 (see the list of PBA documents in the References section).

Meanwhile, Presidential Decree No. 756 of 9 November 1974 had created the Print Media Council and the Broadcast Media Council to replace the Media Advisory Council (successor to the Mass Media Council). This 1974 decree stated, among other things, that: "Since the abolition of the Mass Media Council and the creation in its stead of the Media Advisory Council, the various sectors of mass media have shown capability for self-regulation and internal discipline within their ranks, and have demonstrated responsibility for maintaining standards for professional conduct and excellence . . . The Print Media group and the Broadcast Media group are hereby authorized to organize and determine the composition of a body or council within each group, which shall be responsible for instituting and formulating systems of self-regulation and internal discipline within its own ranks."

Subsequently, the PBA was deputized on 20 February 1976 by these two councils to implement their task of "elevating the ethics and standards of excellence" of the mass media. Being more interested in censoring news, programs and editorials than advertisements, which were less dangerous and about which it knew little or nothing, the government was quite willing to leave the pre-screening of advertising to the industry. Since the Print and Broadcast councils had served a censorship function, the Code of Ethics inherited by the PBA provided for the screening of all advertisements—prescreening in the case of broadcast commercials[3] and postscreening for print ads. Such screening was justified by the fear of unbridled competition (there had been severe abuses in the past) and the desire to protect gullible consumers.

Explicit Government Endorsement

The PBA sought to have its powers formalized and backed by the government. A letter of 1 August 1977 from Secretary of Trade T. T. Quiazon, Jr., to the Philippine Board of Advertising, is very revealing in this regard:

This will serve to formalize our basic agreement . . . for a working arrangement wherein the Department of Trade will provide all the necessary assistance and support to the Philippine Board of Advertising in the screening of all advertising materials, as well as in the implementation and enforcement of the PBA's decisions relative to the advertisements screened. . . . Based on its experience so far, the Philippine Board of Advertising has informed the Department of Trade that it needs a more direct involvement of the Department in order to more effectively coordinate all decisions made with reference to cases involving violations of the industry-promulgated Code of Ethics and other existing laws on unfair trade practices involving the use of mass-media advertising. Pursuant, therefore, to the powers vested upon me by law, I am hereby directing that:

1. All cases and/or complaints of alleged violations of accepted fair-trade practices or laws involving the use of mass-media advertising brought before the Department of Trade or any of its instrumentalities be referred to the Philippine Board of Advertising for proper hearing and adjudication;

2. The PBA be authorized to screen all advertising as may fall within the jurisdiction of the Department of Trade. In this connection, at least two senior officials of the

Department of Trade shall be appointed by the Secretary of Trade who shall participate in the activities of the screening committees of the Philippine Board of Advertising;

3. The Philippine Board of Advertising shall submit its screening procedures to the Department of Trade for endorsement;

4. The sanctions provided for by law will be imposed by the Department of Trade upon recommendation of the Philippine Board of Advertising on parties found guilty of violating existing laws and/or governmental rules and regulations relative to fair-trade practices in the use of mass media for advertising.

The Department feels that the implementation of this basic agreement, which shall be covered by the necessary Department Administrative Orders and Circulars, will enhance the development of the concept of self-regulation of an industry vital to the development of our national culture, in the dissemination of information and in the conduct of trade. Finally, it is understood that this agreement is being formalized pursuant to the government's philosophy that self-regulation by an industry often serves to inculcate a greater sense of responsibility. We wish the Philippine Board of Advertising success in this endeavor.

The government's endorsement of the original PBA Code was important in order to stress that recalcitrant advertisers would not be left unpunished. However, the progressive extension of the *pre*screening requirement has reduced the importance of this threat, since all broadcast commercials must now be approved in advance, thereby minimizing the likelihood of *post*broadcasting complaints.

Recent Government Policy

When martial law was lifted in January 1981, the Print Media Council and the Broadcast Media Council were dissolved, but the PBA retained its screening function as well as other self-regulatory tasks, albeit under a vaguer governmental mandate.[4] In his letter, Secretary of Trade Quiazon probably used the correct term "philosophy" to characterize the government's position regarding advertising self-regulation. There are no constitutional provisions, laws, regulations, presidential orders and decrees and the like that currently state that the advertising industry has been delegated explicit mandates and powers to self-regulate this industry, although the Quiazon letter (see above) has never been formally repudiated by the government under subsequent secretaries of trade (and industry).

However, government officials—all the way down from former President Ferdinand Marcos and powerful First Lady Imelda Marcos to ministers and high-level bureaucrats—have kept referring favorably to advertising self-regulation and the Philippine Board of Advertising. Thus, former Prime Minister Virata stated in a speech of 15 October 1982 that: "I would like to assure you that we would like to make the advertising industry self-regulative as much as possible. It is true that there are a number of bills in [Parliament designed to restrict advertising]. To me this is a normal event [but] as much as possible, if there is capacity for self-regulation, it would be much better and I hope we can keep it that way."

The PBA has maintained excellent relations with the Ministry of Trade and Industry—particularly its Bureau of Domestic Trade—and the Ministry of Health, particularly, its Bureau of Food and Drugs. Informal consultations take place about complaints received by these bureaus[5] and are transmitted by them to the PBA as well as about PBA Code revision and regulatory proposals.[6] Government officials used to sit on PBA screening panels but have stopped doing it because they have other priorities. The Bureau of Food and Drugs is supposed to approve all relevant advertisements but in fact has delegated this task to the PBA. More significant is these bureaus' basic trust in the PBA's functioning. As Director De Lima of the Bureau of Domestic Trade put it: "The PBA does it well although we keep an eye on it. It has done a better job than other industry associations [e.g., repair shops] in policing its members. They hardly come to us, and we do not intervene. Government action is a last resort (personal interview)."

The net result is a government that, on the one hand, is prodded and advised by consumerists about a variety of issues including advertising, but, on the other hand, is fundamentally satisfied with the PBA's activities. The government remains in the wings, ready to threaten the industry with further restrictions and stronger enforcement but unlikely to do so, barring major crises. As in the United States, it is really the "silent partner" of advertising self-regulation, although in a semiformal context, since the arrangements engineered during and after the martial law episode.

Toward New Regulation

Various bills were introduced in previous Parliaments[7] to ban the advertising of tobacco and alcohol products and of outdoor advertising along national highways;[8] to require health warnings and government preclearance in the case of food, drug and cosmetics ads; to restrict television advertising, and even to create a Philippine Advertising Council or a Consumers Board of Advertising involving consumerist representatives. While practically no regulatory changes have been made, these legislative proposals help understand the legal environment of Philippine advertising self-regulation.

The Need for Regulatory Reform

These restrictive parliamentary bills supported by the Filipino consumer movement do not appear to reflect fundamental dissatisfaction with the Philippine Board of Advertising's performance. Instead, they mirror concerns about what might be called "soft" advertising issues—namely, cigarette and liquor advertisements (allowed in all media), outdoor advertising seen as marring the environment, and children-directed commercials—which the advertising industry tries to control through application of the acceptance rules of the media and the provisions of the PBA Code of Ethics.[9]

Regarding the "hard" matters of false (fraudulent), misleading and unfair (e.g., disparaging) advertising, the PBA and media codes are quite strict and rather well enforced. However, there is fairly general agreement that the laws bearing on these matters are rather antiquated (several date from the 1930s during the U.S.-control period), incomplete, ineffective and very poorly enforced—therefore justifying demands for a consumer-protection code (Reyes 1982).[10]

The advertising industry generally acknowledges the need for legal reform although worrying and lobbying about its exact content, since it has been drafted with the assistance of the University of the Philippines Law Center, some of whose members are active in the consumer movement and draw some of their inspiration from the rather radical International Organization of Consumers Unions (IOCU). This industry position, however, must be put into the broader context of growing business reaction against other initiatives of the former Marcos government (e.g., increased taxation, endless presidential decrees lacking precise guidelines for business behavior, and the unwarranted creation of state enterprises).

Negotiations with Government

To counter these inimical proposals, representatives of the advertising industry met with parliamentarians in 1983 and 1984. Agreement was reached that laws dating from the 1930s ought to be updated, and that the various parliamentary proposals and other proposed revisions ought to be examined in the context of an Omnibus Advertising Code, which would consider both the welfare of consumers and the legitimate interests of business enterprises, while also recognizing the desirability of self-regulation. A draft Advertising Code of the Philippines was submitted by the industry to the Parliament's Committee on Public Information in order to combine, update and expand existing legislation.[11] It was to be further negotiated by all interested parties, including consumer organizations, but this did not happen owing to the election of a new parliament in 1984 before the Marcos' fall.

During the preliminary negotiations, the industry recognized the government's preeminence in economic regulation but stressed the need to: (1) avoid overregulation as well as the Advertising Standards Authority advocated in the proposed Consumer Protection Code (see below), and (2) encourage self-regulation through the Philippine Board of Advertising or an equivalent organization to be backed up by a strong body of laws (de Joya 1984, pp. 3–4). Besides, the industry acknowledged that: "The principle of self-regulation that is being advocated does envision the participation of consumer organizations in the screening of advertising. As a matter of fact, this is already being done under the aegis of the Philippine Board of Advertising, and there is a modus vivendi that has already been established (de Joya 1984, p. 4)"—a statement that contradicts recent practice.

The advertising industry had no objection to the Bureau of Domestic Trade obtaining quasijudicial power in the case of fraudulent advertising[12] although "the present practice of close cooperation between the Ministry of Trade and Industry and the Philippine Board of Advertising [should] continue (de Joya 1984, p. 5)." Regarding the "fringe advertisers" who are not members of the PBA[13] and thus avoid its purview and control (e.g., massage parlors), the industry was "in favor of any legislative mechanism that will strengthen the Philippine Board of Advertising and therefore enhance its ability to bring under its fold all advertisers and advertising agencies (de Joya 1984, pp. 8–9)."

The overthrow of the Marcos regime in 1986, the drafting and adoption of a new Constitution in 1987, the absence of a Parliament until late 1987, and other more urgent problems have removed these proposals for new laws and regulations from active consideration in the past couple of years. Still, Article XVI.11(2) of the new Constitution provides that: "The advertising industry is impressed with public interest, and shall be regulated by law for the protection of consumers and the promotion of the general welfare."

Consumerist Views of Self-Regulation

Interviews with several leaders of the Filipino consumer movement[14] revealed a relatively low salience for advertising issues. There are really no burning issues in this area, apart from employment-agency and "switch-and-bait" advertisements, as well as advertising to children and other soft topics. While they promote the revision of laws applicable to advertising and the granting of more extensive enforcement powers to the Bureau of Domestic Trade and the Bureau of Food and Drugs in the case of false and misleading advertisements, there are more pressing consumer problems, such as abusive lending rates, low quality foods, hazardous products, improper labeling and the lack of low-priced basic commodities to absorb most of their energies and resources. Besides, the Filipino consumer movement is fragmented among at least six organizations lacking a strong unified voice.

The views of Attorney Zenaida S. Reyes, who is affiliated with the Law Center of the University of the Philippines and is very active in various national and international consumer organizations, are very revealing in this respect. She is an ardent advocate of various reforms, and has expressed the consumerist perspective on advertising self-regulation and regulation, which is more a plea for better laws and enforcement than a fundamental criticism of the PBA's role and performance within the limits of what self-regulation can achieve:

To the credit of the PBA, it has been instrumental in self-regulating the industry, which has resulted in withdrawal and modification of many commercial advertising claims. The Board has qualitatively improved the advertising industry, especially during the period when it was deputized by the Print Media Council and the Broadcast Media Council under P.D. No. 576 to uphold the excellence of mass media. Unfortunately, these Councils were abolished when martial law was lifted, and the PBA is left on its own capabilities.

Since false and misleading advertising serves no beneficial economic function and is illegal, private regulation will not be always desirable. The attempt by the industry to establish standards of truthfulness may not be within the standards required by law.[15] These standards, in fact, may conflict with government regulatory policy, considering that these [standards] will certainly be influenced, one way or another, by the industry's self-interested motive for commercial considerations. It would serve the general public better if the standards for beneficial advertising should be exclusively a governmental function. However, private agreements to refrain from airing certain proscribed advertising claims and methods will probably be justifiable because of the very limited enforcement resources of the government.

The Code of Ethics of the PBA establishes reasonable standards. The question that may now be raised is what and how are the sanctions enforced to secure substantial compliance with the Code's provisions? The KBP [broadcasters' association] is generally able to coerce advertisers to comply with PBA standards by refusing to air advertising materials. But the inherent tendency to limit the use of this power arises because, like the PBA, the media have more self-interest in generating more advertising revenue than in policing advertising claims to protect the public (Reyes 1982, pp. 21–22).

Still, Reyes argued (p. 22) for the maintenance of the PBA and its strengthening through stricter claim presubstantiation, corrective advertising, free counteradvertising and even an Advertising Standards Authority with a dominant consumer, academic and government representation. However, no criticism was expressed of the fact that consumer organizations are not consulted by, or involved in the activities of, the PBA. It appears that these organizations prefer to remain as outside critics rather than be PBA insiders in a minority position and with no voting power.

Outside Participation in the PBA's Functioning

The PBA's Code of Ethics for Advertising and Sales Promotion is fairly elaborate. Inspired in part by foreign examples (International Chamber of Commerce, Canada's Advertising Standards Council, and the International Advertising Association), it offers general principles and deals with twenty-nine topics (drugs, lotteries, gifts, comparisons, etc.).[16] Reflecting both its martial-law origin and developing-country environment, this code includes several references to advertising's role in economic and social development, its public responsibilities, its loyalty to the government with which "practitioners shall work hand in hand"; and "its pride in things Filipino (PBA, Code of Ethics 1986, Article I)." Self-regulation is presented as a necessary, speedy and inexpensive complement to legal controls—the classical justification of such a system. Voluntary adherence to the Code is stressed, although the required prescreening of advertisements makes the letter of the Code more compulsory than its spirit. A brief reference is also made to "the government policy that encourages self-regulation in the private sector (PBA, Code of Ethics 1984, p. 23; and PBA, ACRC Manual 1987, Article I).

Article V of the PBA Code used to deal with Trade Practices and Conduct—

a task now relegated to separate documents (PBA, ACRC Manual 1987, and PBA, TPCC Standards 1986), which include numerous provisions regulating the relations among advertisers, agencies, media and advertising supports—another clear expression of "corporative associationism," which would not be acceptable under U.S. antitrust laws.

Code Development

The original 1974 Code definitely involved some outside participation since the consumer sector (the Philippine Consumers Movement) and various government agencies participated in its drafting (PBA, Code of Ethics 1984, Preface). Besides, the first executive director of the PBA, Oscar P. Lagman, Jr., had been very active in the consumer movement. Since then, no formal outside consultation has taken place in subsequent code revisions even though the close informal links between the PBA and the Bureau of Domestic Trade (and its predecessor, the Fair Trade Board) as well as the Bureau of Food and Drugs have generated useful inputs. Besides, the already quoted letter of 1 August 1977 from the then secretary of trade to the PBA, designed to formalize their mutual involvement, stated that: "The Philippine Board of Advertising shall submit its screening procedures to the Department of Trade for endorsement." In principle, this requirement is still in force, although the repeal of martial law in 1981 has left many such agreements in limbo.

Publicizing the PBA

No formal direct campaigns have been conducted to make the consuming public aware of the PBA's existence and complaint-handling procedures so that consumer complaints reaching the PBA seldom exceed five or ten a year; while those forwarded by government bureaus amount to a bare two per annum. Still, the business press reports on the PBA's activities (e.g., Quiogue 1984), and consumer-organization newsletters and publications refer to it occasionally as a channel for complaints, although consumerist bodies prefer to direct their members' complaints to the Bureau of Domestic Trade in order to assert their independence from the PBA.

PBA Screening and Complaint Handling

Since martial-law times, PBA actions have centered on the screening of advertisements on the basis of its Code of Ethics for Advertising and Sales Promotions, the ACRC Manual and the TPCC Standards. Prescreening is required in the case of broadcast commercials (except for regional and local ones) and may be extended to print ads, which have been postscreened until now, that is, reviewed on the basis of complaints emanating from competitors, consumers, consumerist organizations and the government (mainly, the Bureau of Domestic Trade).

Prescreening could have been dropped by the PBA when martial law was repealed in 1981, but the industry felt that retaining it enhanced its credibility in the face of various parliamentary bills proposing restrictions on advertising as well as alternative "advertising boards" where consumerists would have had a stronger voice. Besides, it is still felt that most media do not screen well on the basis of their acceptance rules—particularly during the current severe economic recession when everybody is hungry for advertising revenue.

In principle, the approval of a PBA screening panel is required before member media will accept such advertisements, although an accelerated and simplified procedure was introduced in 1986 (see below). Since all major national media belong to the PBA through their associations, this requirement is very hard to avoid. Screening-panel members are all professionals and practitioners affiliated with member companies or associations although technical experts (e.g., medical and dental associations) and consumerist groups may be invited "to render additional opinions (PBA, ACRC Manual 1986, Article 6.6)." Actually, the latter have not been invited in recent years; and in any case, they do not have the vote. Besides, there is no reference in PBA documents to government officials who were supposed to be appointed to participate in the activities of the screening committees (cf. Quiazon letter of August 1, 1977).

Some 120 people used to be assigned to 8 screening panels meeting in rotation 3 or 4 nights a week to prescreen some 1,300 to 2,000 commercials a year. Panel members tended to develop fatigue after several months, to absent themselves more frequently and even to drop out. It was sometimes difficult to have an appropriate quorum present. Besides, decisions to accept or reject an advertisement varied from panel to panel, creating skepticism about their competence, the exact meaning of PBA standards and the impartiality of panel members. In view of these problems, prescreening procedures were simplified in 1986: (1) radio scripts and TV storyboards can be presented to the PBA every day for prescreening by the Executive Director of the PBA and his staff; (2) when the materials raise no questions of violating the Code of Ethics, the Executive Director gives his approval for production, and (3) only controversial materials are referred to a Screening Panel convened as soon as possible and drawn from a pool of seventy professionals. This new system works faster and appears to function satisfactorily, with not more than 5 percent of the submissions being referred to a Screening Panel.

Appeals of prescreening decisions are now handled by the new (1984) Advertising Content Regulation Committee, which also deals with complaints from competitors, consumers and government bureaus about commercials and print ads that have already been aired or published. Here again, "technical experts, trade professionals, or consumerist groups etc." may be invited "for added opinion" but without a vote.

Other Contacts

Recognizing the importance of the consumer sector and the need to reconcile consumer interests with those of the advertising industry, the PBA—in cooperation with the Philippine Consumers Movement (KMPI) and the Consumers Federated Groups of the Philippines (CFGP)—established the Consumer Protection Board, which functions as a two-way channel of communications between the advertising industry and the consumer sector.[17] This Board is a forum where consumers and advertisers may discuss subjects of mutual concern prior to determining a course of action to be recommended to the Philippine Board of Advertising. Such rapports have been episodic at best, and they have usually centered on matters of taste and opinion in advertising.

The PBA as a Form of Corporative Associationism

Definitional Problems

How can the PBA self-regulatory system be categorized in political theory? It is probably best located somewhere between "corporatism" and "pluralism" as defined by Schmitter:

Corporatism can be defined as a system of interest representation in which the constituent units are organized into a limited number of singular, compulsory, non-competitive, hierarchically-ordered and functionally pre-determined categories, certified or licensed (if not created) by the State and granted a deliberate representational monopoly within their respective categories in exchange for observing certain governmentally imposed controls on their selection of leaders and articulation of demands and supports (1979, pp. 93–94).

The 1974–1981 PBA definitely exhibited most of these characteristics, although they resulted more from the accidental imposition of martial-law-based censorship than from any attempt to restructure the Filipino economy along corporatist lines. Since the lifting of martial law in 1981, the PBA has lost its compulsory, state-mandated character and has assumed roles closer to Streeck and Schmitter's "corporative associations," which are voluntary, self-determined, not specially licensed, subsidized, created or otherwise controlled by the State, but which, as "private-interest governments," also become "agents of public policy" through explicit recognition (if not exact delegation) of their self-regulatory task as an essential complement to government regulation:

From the viewpoint of public policy, neo-corporatism amounts to an attempt to assign to interest associations a distinct role between the "state" and "civil society" (market and community) so as to put to public purposes the type of social order that associations can generate and embody. As an alternative to direct state intervention and regulation, the public use of private organized interests takes the form of the establishment, under state license and assistance, of "private interest governments" with devolved public responsibilities (Streeck and Schmitter 1985, p. 16).

Actually, the corporative associationism of the PBA has only been one of several similar initiatives of former President Marcos after his imposition of martial law in 1972. They reflected his effort to impose some order on a people who acknowledged a need for greater discipline in a period of major social and political unrest while also valuing their individual freedoms. To the extent that his "New Society" scheme came to terms with this felt need for fairly mild participatory self-discipline, he had reason to assume that it would be accepted with little opposition.

The Benefits and Limits of Self-Regulation

The present Philippine Board of Advertising constitutes a "private-interest government" to the extent that peers rather than outsiders formally control the establishment and enforcement of self-imposed and voluntarily accepted behavior rules—including mandatory prescreening. Its major enforcement power currently rests on the media refusing to accept advertisements that have not been precleared by the PBA. This is particularly true in the case of radio and television commercials, since the Broadcasters Association (KBP) includes all stations, and strictly enforces adherence to the PBA Code and prescreening requirement. Besides, the PBA's Advertising Content Regulation Committee can issue cease-and-desist orders against aired commercials "deemed to adversely affect public interest (PBA, ACRC Manual 1987, Article VII.A.1.c)."

The PBA has been diligent in its task of self-regulating the industry, although the effectiveness of the self-regulation it enforces is very difficult to ascertain—as is the effectiveness of regulation, for that matter. On the one hand, it is almost certain that, without it, more Filipino advertisements would have been false, misleading, unfair and unwholesome—particularly in the light of inadequate regulation and limited enforcement by government. Besides, its absence would most likely have precipitated some regulatory reaction and even overreaction—as has happened in other developing countries where self-regulation is absent or moribund. On the other hand, exactly how much healthier Filipino advertising is nowadays cannot be measured.

Probably unique among advertising self-regulatory systems is the PBA's comprehensive screening of all national broadcast advertisements. This allows it to control them *at the source*; and it can make its decisions stick since all major national broadcast media require the production of a PBA clearance sheet before accepting a commercial. Consequently, the classical self-regulatory problem of the "noncomplier" or "free-loader" who does not care about self-regulation is largely eliminated; and dubious broadcast campaigns are no longer stopped only *after* they have started running—as is the typical case in other countries. Of course, there are still *post*screening complaints, but they are bound to be less numerous and severe than in the absence of broadcast prescreening. However, the print media as well as some minor media (e.g., direct-mail advertising) remain free of prescreening requirements—as do personal ads and advertisements in regional and local media, which do still occasionally accept questionable materials. However, the government itself would be unlikely to actively prosecute violators in these problem areas, even if regulation were to be re-enforced.

The PBA's Code of Ethics is not perfect. Certain areas such as credit advertising rate only three lines when they fill pages in Canada, France and the United Kingdom. Moreover, self-regulation is unlikely to satisfy those critics who would like it to ban or severely restrict the advertising of certain goods (e.g., tobacco and liquor) while the PBA's objective is only to make their advertising truthful, not misleading or unfair. Still, within these constraints that keep evolving under social and political pressures, Filipino self-regulation has promised and helped deliver better advertising.

The Problems of Corporative Associationism

Reverting to Streeck and Schmitter's definition (1985), the PBA system certainly represents a partial "delegation of public-policy functions to private governments" as well as the utilization of "the collective self-interest of social groups to create and maintain a generally acceptable social order (p. 16)." The PBA born of martial-law conditions and operating in the context of a strong autocratic government has certainly suited the current social order as envisioned by the former Marcos regime. While there was significant opposition to the latter, the advertising self-regulatory system does not seem to have been perceived as a tool of that regime nor significantly out of step with general community expectations. Some consumerists may want stricter regulations but the latter's need has been acknowledged by the advertising industry; and the PBA and its supporting organizations have not been deaf nor blind to evolving social concerns, but have tightened their rules accordingly.

Being endowed with a quasipublic function has made the PBA serious about its objectives of upholding good advertising practice in the midst of a somewhat chaotic developing economy and polity—no small task and achievement indeed. As such, Filipino advertising "private government" has become a true "agent of public policy," however vague this delegation of power may have become after martial law was ended. Yet, certain features of the system can bother a "Western" observer. Five aspects of the PBA system will illustrate these concerns.

Prescreening. In the PBA system, a proposed ad is, in principle, scrutinized by a screening panel made up of advertiser, agency and media representatives. The applicant must bare details not only about his campaign, but also about what is new about his product or service on account of the perfectly reasonable requirement that the advertiser must be able to presubstantiate his claims. Such presubstantiation is also required in other developed self-regulatory systems (e.g.,

Canada, United Kingdom, United States) but only in the context of postadvertising cases, that is, after the advertisement has been published or broadcast.

In the Filipino system, however, other industry members may see it beforehand. Of course, only noncompetitors may sit on screening panels whose members, in any case, are sworn to secrecy. No evidence of leakages was unearthed or revealed, but still one wonders how "secret" trade secrets can remain within a relatively small advertising community. Certainly, Western antitrust aficionados would shudder at the mere thought of such a potential invasion of competitive privacy. Even when prescreening is required in Western countries, it is done by government officials or the permanent staff of the advertising self-regulatory body—not by practicing industry members—although the new accelerated procedure has recently introduced fast prescreening by the PBA staff in most cases.

Advertisement Proximity. The PBA Code of Ethics proscribes billboards for competing products or firms "side-by-side or on the same line of vision," ads for competing products or firms on the same page of a newspaper or magazine, and broadcast commercials "within the same commercial cluster (PBA, TPCC Standards 1986, Articles 4.2.6, 4.3.3 and 4.4.3)." No rationale is given for these restrictions although one PBA commentator explained it in terms of avoiding "consumer confusion." Still, one can guess that they are related to advertiser demands (see the discussion of comparison advertising below). A particular advertiser or his agency may rightly object to his advertisement being shown next to a competing one, but this could be handled through negotiation with the involved medium. However, when the self-regulatory system ordains such a proscription, can one readily argue that it has been enacted with the public interest—rather than self-interest—in mind?

Comparison Advertising. In 1976, the Philippine Advertising Board amended its code to forbid "direct" comparisons that name the competitor's brand (Boddewyn and Marton 1978, pp. 163–167). Obviously, this is a controversial practice that has adversaries in every country. What is questionable, however, is that this amendment was based on an investigation conducted by the *advertisers'* association (PANA), which could hardly be considered partial to the use of direct comparisons usually directed against leading brands. High "public-interest" rhetoric was used in the PANA report[18] that was accepted by the PBA at a time when it was chaired by an advertiser representative.

Even more serious in the context of evaluating "corporative associationism" is the fact that the government (the Fair Trade Board at the time) chose not to intervene and present a public-interest perspective vis-à-vis the rationale presented by the advertiser group regarding comparison advertising. It appears, instead, that the interests of leading firms (e.g., the San Miguel conglomerate) loosely connected with the Marcos family and its friends were allowed to prevail, despite the objections of other advertisers and agencies. This does not mean, however, that large advertisers have not had to abide by PBA rules and decisions on a regular basis.

Print-prescreening. While broadcast commercials have had to be prescreened since February 1976, the imposition of print prescreening has been repeatedly postponed, although it had been contemplated and even urged by the government from the beginning (see the 1977 Quiazon letter above).[19] The PBA itself has always considered it ideal for print ads to be prescreened, but the sheer magnitude of the task—compared to the smaller number of radio and television commercials—as well as the lack of financial and human resources has repeatedly postponed the implementation of this decision of principle. Besides, the head of the Print Media Organization (PRIMO) has been opposed to any measure that might smack of press censorship, since such charges were common under the Marcos regime.

Of course, what is good for the goose (broadcast media) should be good for the gander (print media), since there is no reason to assume that print ads are less prone to bad practices than commercials are.[20] Besides, faced with stagnant advertising expenditures, some broadcasting media claim to have witnessed cases of advertisers shifting to print advertisements in order to avoid the mandatory prescreening of commercials or to work around negative decisions of PBA screening panels. Consequently, the decision to extend prescreening to print advertisements has been rationalized in terms of the public interest, although the private interests of the powerful broadcast media have also influenced this decision, which is less popular with advertisers and advertising agencies.

Outside Participation. While falling short of pure corporatism, corporative associationism delegates power—explicitly or indirectly—to an industry in order to develop and implement rules of good behavior that complement or parallel government regulations. However, self-regulation works best when a strong government not only encourages it but also watches over it, and is ready to correct its shortcomings through regulation or its threat (cf. Chapter 1). At this time, however, the Filipino government, while highly supportive, is not yet in a position to monitor and intervene when self-regulation goes slack or verges on the collusive.

Besides, corporatism and even neocorporatism (in the form of corporative associationism) are not quite geared to explicit outside participation. They are more attuned to negotiation with equal external bodies (such as consumer organizations) for the formulation of government regulations as the resulting compromise of conflicting interests. However, the Filipino consumer movement is much less developed than industry—a situation endemic to developing countries—and it has not received an equivalent "delegated power" to speak up for consumers so that it is not quite "equal" to the PBA when it comes to negotiating.

Conclusions

The record of the Philippine Board of Advertising is hard to fault. Under the circumstances, it has assumed a mantle first dictated by martial law, but ultimately based on the aspirations of an industry anxious to avoid regulation and willing to assume responsibility for good advertising behavior—both in its own interest and for the public interest of a developing economy, polity and community.

Yet, the above analysis suggests that corporative associationism is fundamentally adverse to outside participation by nongovernmental bodies such as consumer associations, because it has enough "internal" battles to fight among conflicting industry interests, and because it is more attuned to negotiating with "external" interest groups than to incorporating them in its system. Besides, its integrity requires strong government prodding and threat. At least as far as Filipino advertising is concerned, there is probably too much laissez-faire on the part of a government preoccupied with other political, social and economic problems as well as unable to monitor, goad and threaten self-regulation when its reach and grasp fall short of what consumer protection and competition enhancement would truly require. Under the present circumstances, the PBA's reach and grasp have been adequate, but they are likely to be challenged and constrained in coming years as consumerism and governmental capability keep developing.

These conclusions could be challenged as being too "ethnocentric" because based on Western views and procompetitive ideologies.[21] The latter are probably more suitable for advanced economies while the Philippines is caught—like other developing countries—between a weak regulatory environment and somewhat wild competition. In this context, some self-regulatory excesses and cartel-like behavior may well be inevitable and even condoned on the ground that they are acceptable in the short run, but remediable in the long run as better business ethics become more routine and government regulations become more up-to-date and better enforced.

NOTES

1. Advertising Suppliers Association of the Philippines (ASAP); Association of Accredited Advertising Agencies—Philippines (4A's); Cinema Advertising Association of the Philippines (CAAP); Kapisanan ng mga Brodkaster sa Pilipinas (KBP—Broadcasters Association of the Philippines); Marketing and Opinion Research Society of the Philippines (MORES); Outdoor Advertising Association of the Philippines (OAAP); Philippine Association of National Advertisers (PANA), and Print Media Organization (PRIMO).

2. There have been many analyses of the martial-law episode in the Philippines but its exact antecedents, motivations, precipitating circumstances, features and demise need not be related here, except as they apply to the media and advertising. This study relied mostly on the account in Vreeland et al. (1976).

3. In fact, it was First Lady Imelda Marcos, in her capacity as governor of Metropolitan Manila, who engineered the maintenance of broadcast prescreening in order to facilitate the enforcement of PBA standards: "We appeal to all radio and television networks to assist in [the task of screening all advertisements presented to the media] by having all advertisers obtain a clearance from the Philippine Board of Advertising and the Broadcast Media Council before allowing the broadcast/telecast of advertisements (Marcos 1976)."

4. Presidential Decree No. 1784 of 15 January 1981, which abolished the two coun-

cils, stated that: "The print and broadcast media may, however, in accord with their demonstrated regard for excellence and a high sense of responsibility as constant objectives, establish other self-regulatory bodies of their own in such form and with such rules and regulations as they may respectively see fit (Section 3)."

5. Complaints from competitors are normally transferred by the Bureau of Domestic Trade to the PBA, which typically tries to obtain voluntary compliance from the advertiser. The results of such actions are then reported to the Bureau, which may be asked to issue a cease-and-desist injunction in the case of recalcitrant advertisers.

6. The PBA was consulted by the Bureau of Domestic Trade (BDT) when the latter revised its rules applying to sales promotions for which prior BDT approval must be obtained.

7. The last "pre-Revolution" Parliament was elected in May 1984. Several new bills were introduced such as one for a code for the marketing of breastmilk substitutes, which would have restricted their advertising.

8. There are already rather strict municipal restrictions on outdoor advertising, prompted by former First Lady Imelda Marcos' keen interest in beautifying the environment.

9. PBA screening panels really focus on the "hard" issues of adequate claim substantiation and other violations of clear-cut rules, such as the ban on the use of direct comparisons naming competitors. It is really the media—particularly television stations—and their associations that cope with such "soft" issues as decency (e.g., sexy ads), good taste and the scheduling of commercials for sensitive products (e.g., feminine-hygiene goods, liquor and cigarettes).

10. The basic laws (Act No. 3740 of 1930 and Commonwealth Law No. 46 of 1936) against misrepresentation are criminal statutes, which have resulted in very few convictions and other legal actions in the field of advertising. This has been owing to consumer apathy, the cost of litigation, official preference to prosecute more serious crimes, the need to prove fraud beyond a reasonable doubt and the burden of proof resting with the complainant. Even provisions of the new Civil Code against misrepresentation put a heavy burden of proof on the complainant and can result in only minimal recovery. Besides, misleading advertisements cannot really be prosecuted under current law. The Bureau of Domestic Trade can recommend immediate suspension of a fraudulent ad to the Ministry of Justice if informal negotiation with the advertiser fails, but it lacks formal enforcement and injunctive-relief power—hence, the recommendation to empower this Bureau to apply civil and administrative remedies. The Bureau of Food and Drugs focuses more on labeling than on advertising, although food and medicine ads must in principle be approved in advance—as is also the case with financial ads (Reyes 1982). The Movies and Television Review and Classification Board for Motion Pictures (a government entity) handles advertisements for films.

11. Certain matters such as the length and frequency of broadcast commercials were to be left to separate legislation to be developed by the media (KBP) in cooperation with the appropriate government agency (NTC). The advertising industry is really not too keen about such a mandated code, since it could not be changed without government approval. However, the draft Advertising Code of the Philippines was couched in very general terms about which there is general consensus within the industry. Actually, the advertising industry has been providing inputs for the Consumer Protection Code being drawn-up since 1974 by consumer organizations (mainly, the Consumers Federated Groups of the

Philippines) under the aegis of the University of the Philippines Law Center (de Joya 1984, p. 4).

12. Both the Bureau of Domestic Trade and the Bureau of Food and Drugs have received more explicit rule-making and adjudicatory powers since 1982–1983.

13. The PBA reaches advertisers that are not members of PANA to the extent that they use agencies that subscribe to the PBA Code or use the broadcast media, which all belong to the KBP, also a supporter of the PBA.

14. Mrs. Julita C. Benedicto (Chairman), Attorney Zenaida Reyes (First Vice-President), Mrs. Lourdes Casas de Quezon (Secretary) and Miss Mary Mendeza (Executive Director) of the Consumers Federated Groups of the Philippines. The CFGT represents the major Filipino consumer organizations before the government and the International Organization of Consumers Unions.

15. The industry, however, stresses that its Code and other rules mention that laws and regulations are taken into account by the PBA (cf. PBA, ACRC Manual [1987] Article III.A.1, which refers to "guidance by the Laws of the Land").

16. The Broadcasting Association of the Philippines (KBP) has its own television and radio codes, and so do various other industries (e.g., pharmaceuticals).

17. There had been a Consumers Bureau from 1974 to 1976, which brought together advertisers, agencies, media, production houses and consumerists in order to discuss advertisements found questionable by consumers. It was dissolved when the PBA was empowered to screen advertisements and limited the role of consumer representatives to being "resource persons" in the screening process. This was not acceptable to consumer associations, which stopped participating in this exercise.

18. Several interviewees commented that direct comparison advertising remains controversial in the Philippines because Filipinos abhor embarrassing other people. Besides, such comparisons may well complicate the task of already overloaded screening panels. However, superiority claims (e.g., "The Number One Beer in the Philippines") are acceptable, provided they can be substantiated.

19. Personal ads, restaurant ads, posters and direct-mail advertising would be exempt from this new requirement, which, in any case, would only apply to national print media affiliated with the PBA.

20. It is easier to run a false or misleading advertisement in print, and then remove it or apologize when complaints develop and the harm has been done—compared to broadcast commercials, which are more expensive to prepare and are usually intended for multiple uses. Many print ads are also prepared against hurried deadlines, which tempt the media to check them less carefully. Most competitor complaints have been about print rather than broadcast ads, for that matter.

21. This ethnocentric criticism can, of course, be addressed to various consumerist and supranational initiatives, such as those of the International Organization of Consumers Unions and the United Nations' Economic and Social Council, which are trying to impress "advanced" Western standards of consumer protection on developing countries, where nascent bureaucracies can hardly cope with even more elementary tasks. Besides, antitrust concerns are voiced to rail against multinational corporations when they dominate the local economy. Thus, there has been some grumblings in the Philippines against the branches of foreign (mostly U.S.) advertising agencies, which control more than half of agency billings. For that matter, the new 1987 Constitution severely restricts foreign participation in the advertising industry (Article XVI.11). A related concern is about

Western values being propagated through advertising—a frequent theme in former President and First Lady Marcos' speeches to advertising audiences.

REFERENCES

Boddewyn, J. J., and Katherin Marton. *Comparison Advertising: A Worldwide Study*. New York: Hastings House. 1978.

de Joya, A. R., and A. G. de Joya. "Year-End Report: Special Plans and Programs Committee of the Association of Accredited Advertising Agencies." Manila: AAAA, May 23, 1984.

Marcos, Imelda R. "Appointment Letter of PBA." In Code of Ethics, of Philippine Board of Advertising [PBA]. Manila: 1976.

Philippine Board of Advertising [PBA] *Code of Ethics, Rules and Regulations for Advertising and Sales Promotions; Rules of Procedure for Screening*. Manila: January 1984.

———. *Code of Ethics for Advertising and Sales Promotion*. Manila: January 1986 (plus subsequent amendments, no dates given).

———. Advertising Content Regulation Committee [ACRC]. *ACRC Manual of Procedure for Screening, Complaints and Appeals*. Manila: February 24, 1987.

———. Trade Practices and Conduct Committee [TPCC]. *Standards of Trade Practices and Conduct in the Advertising Industry*. Manila: 1986.

Quiazon, T. T., Jr. "Letter to the Philippine Board of Advertising." Manila: August 1, 1977.

Quiogue, M. P. "In Pursuit of Truth in Advertising." *Business Day* (November 6, 1984): 13.

Reyes, Z. S. "Advertising in the Philippines: Current Methods of Regulation and Some Proposals for Reforms." Mimeographed. Manila: Division of Research and Law Reform, Law Center, University of the Philippines. May 14, 1982.

Schmitter, P. C. "Still the Century of Corporatism?" *Review of Politics* 36 (January 1979): 85–131.

Streeck, Wolfgang, and P. C. Schmitter. "Community, Market, State—and Associations? The Prospective Contribution of Interest Governance to Social Order." In *Private Interest Government; Beyond Market and State*, edited by Wolfgang Streeck, and P. C. Schmitter. Beverly Hills, Calif.: Sage, 1985, pp. 1–29.

Vreeland, Nena et al. *Area Handbook for the Philippines*. Washington, D.C.: U.S. Government Printing Office, 1976.

ACKNOWLEDGMENTS

The assistance of the following people is gratefully acknowledged: Antonio R. de Joya, Alberto G. de Joya, Director Lilia De Lima, André S. Kahn, Oscar P. Lagman, Jr., Gregorio Macabenta, Chérie Mijares, Lulu C. de Quezon, Attorney Zenaida S. Reyes, Catalina C. Sanchez, Oscar T. Valenzuela, Stella Villegas and Virgilio Luzon.

12

Sweden: The Consumer-Ombudsman System and Advertising Self-Regulation

The Swedish consumer-protection system is often perceived as a strong body of laws and regulations that severely constrains business behavior. In fact, its development and implementation have involved significant business participation and influence; and it largely relies on government-issued guidelines based on business self-regulatory experience rather than on detailed mandatory rules. This experience reveals an unusual connection between advertising regulation and self-regulation.

Besides, the advent of Sweden's consumer-protection legislation and Consumer-Ombudsman apparatus led to the voluntary demise of its relatively sophisticated marketing/advertising self-regulatory system. Why did the latter happen when other countries with equally developed consumer-protection laws (e.g., France and the United Kingdom) have not witnessed a similar withdrawal on the part of business?

It may seem odd to investigate Sweden, since it no longer has an advertising self-regulatory body with a nationwide competence. However, it is important to analyze such an absence in a country usually considered to be a "pilot nation." Has Sweden really pioneered a way of controlling advertising behavior without self-regulation, or has self-regulation survived and simply assumed a new form? As this investigation progressed, the second explanation came to seem the more valid one, and a very ingenious one at that.

Relevant data and interpretations were obtained through published sources, on-the-spot interviews, and correspondence from 1981 to 1987. Unfortunately, only English-language sources could be used, although several Swedish experts were kind enough to review this paper (see Acknowledgments). While Swedish consumer policies cover many matters and include a sizable number of laws and institutions, this analysis focuses on those dealing directly with advertising.

Before addressing the central concerns of this chapter, it is necessary to review briefly the major components of Swedish consumer policy, with particular emphasis on business participation in its development and application.

The Consumer-Protection System

The 1970s were truly "the decade of the consumer" in Sweden as a number of statutes were enacted or amended, and a fairly elaborate legal and administrative system of consumer protection and information was set up (James 1972; Johansson 1978; Swedish Institute 1981 and 1983). The central purpose of the new system has been to protect consumers against misleading and improper advertising claims as well as some unfair marketing practices—for example, one-sided contract terms.[1] Not all of it was new or original since there were Swedish precedents as well as various borrowings from Germany, the United States and other Scandinavian countries (Thorelli 1981). Still, there have been novel ideas and emphases.

Our market economy will work satisfactorily only if the consumers are enabled to control the course of events through the exercise of well-balanced choices. However, the consumer is in a weak position vis-à-vis private enterprise. . . . To support the consumers and improve their position on the market, consumer policy is called upon to influence in various ways what the market has to offer and to help consumers make the best use of their resources (Swedish Institute 1981, p. 1; see also Johansson 1978; Bernitz 1976 and 1981; and Bernitz and Draper 1986).

Much of this purpose can be achieved through recommendations and negotiations, but compulsory legislation and other more direct interventions must also be used if the former approaches do not work (Freivalds 1986, p. 19)—for example, "when weaker citizens in their capacity as consumers . . . can be presumed to be less able to see through deceptive or suggestive advertising arguments (Bernitz 1976, p. 14)." Hence, there has been a marked tendency to regard consumer protection as being a permanent task for the State ("consumers will never be equal partners in the marketplace"), with particular emphasis on protecting the weak. However, Swedish policy does not state that consumers have fundamental rights, as has been done in the United States and by both the Council of Europe and the European Communities; and this policy is to be implemented within a market-economy system and in cooperation with business (Bernitz and Draper 1986, pp. 16–20; Thorelli 1977, p. 223).

The Marketing Practices Act

The heart of the Marketing Practices Act (1970, as revised and amended in 1975, 1980 and 1985) is found in a few general clauses: (1) Section 2 prohibits marketing practices (including advertising) that adversely affect consumers or businessmen; (2) Section 3 requires businessmen, as part of their marketing activities, to supply information important for consumers; and (3) Section 4 prohibits the sale to consumers of dangerous products and services as well as those manifestly unfit for their main purpose. These general clauses carry the sanction of an injunction, but consent orders can also be negotiated.[2]

The National Board for Consumer Policies

The key governmental consumer agency is the National Board for Consumer Policies (Konsumentverket, KOV, of 1972), which merged three previously separate agencies concerned with labeling, product-testing and consumer information. It is also related to the now distinct National Board for Consumer Complaints (Allmänna Reklamationnämnden, ARN), which processes consumer complaints about defective products, the quality of services rendered and delays in performance; and which can issue recommendations to producers and sellers to amend abuses that may have occurred.[3]

The KOV is headed by a Governing Council of twelve members, whose chairperson is also both the director general of the KOV and the consumer ombudsman (KO). The rest is made up of representatives of consumers and employees (three), business (two), political parties (two), the local authorities (one), the Director General of the National Food Administration and the staff of the KOV Board in an advisory capacity (two). Outside members are appointed by the Ministry of Finance (formerly of Commerce) on the basis of nominations offered by business and consumer organizations.

While the KOV Council has a broad policy-analysis and recommendation mandate, it does not issue specific regulations but limits itself to providing *guidelines* designed to define the meaning of the deliberately vague concepts embodied in consumer laws. It is worth noting that—unlike the U.S. Federal Trade Commission—the KOV Council is not obliged to hold hearings or ask for comments about its proposed guidelines. The latter—some forty of them by now—deal with such matters as special-sale advertising, price reductions and discounting, renewal of subscriptions, consumer-credit and car advertising, restaurant price advertising as well as travel and direct-mail advertising. Implementation of the law—as interpreted through these guidelines—is left to the KOV, the Consumer Ombudsman and the Market Court (Johansson 1978, pp. 472–473; Bernitz and Draper 1986).

The KOV guidelines, however, are not legally binding on business, although it is presumed that their violation will normally lead the Consumer Ombudsman to make a case of it before the Market Court.[4] *The latter is not bound by them either* since the guidelines represent only the position of one of parties—the Consumer Ombudsman—before that tribunal. Still, the Market Court views them as similar in relevance to the International Chamber of Commerce's codes of advertising and marketing practice (Bernitz and Draper 1981, pp. 76 and 117; Thorelli 1977, p. 231); and a recent government-sponsored committee report has recommended that the guidelines' legal character should be further stressed, although no changes ensued from that recommendation (Konsumentpolitiska 1983, p. 352). Altogether, these guidelines carry considerable weight as representing the position of the KOV/KO public agency in charge of consumer protection, and—in many cases—the position of the relevant trade association, or as otherwise expressing what is considered to be good commercial practice in that sector (Bernitz and Draper 1981, p. 76).

Since 1976, the National Board for Consumer Policies has been merged with the Consumer Ombudsman into one superagency, the Konsumentverket/KO—with the Ombudsman retaining a separate identity as the prosecuting authority under the Marketing Practices Act, the Improper Contract Terms Act and the Consumer Credit Act (Bernitz and Draper 1981, pp. 67 ff). It is worth noting that the KOV Governing Council is prohibited from exercising any review over the KO's selection of cases and over their handling before the Market Court in order to prevent business interests from affecting the choice of cases brought before that court, where these interests are represented (Bernitz and Draper 1981, p. 70). The KOV/KO system functions relatively independently of Parliament and of the sponsoring Ministry of Finance, which funds it and controls its key appointments. There have, of course, been numerous official studies of the functioning of Swedish consumer laws and institutions as well as bills aimed at strengthening the system, but nothing amounting to direct pressure on its administrators who are completely independent.

It must be added that the National Board for Consumer Policies (KOV) carries out many other functions such as research, testing, information and education (Freivalds 1986). A government-appointed Committee on the KOV Guidelines recently commented on the operations of the KOV/KO system and consumer policies at large, and suggested some relatively minor changes to the Minister of Finance and ultimately to Parliament (Konsumentpolitiska 1983). Business, government and consumers were represented on this committee headed by an independent expert. Subsequently, some of its recommendations were incorporated by Parliament in amendments to the Marketing Practices Act in 1985.

The Consumer Ombudsman (Konsumentombudsmannen, KO)

The KO is also director general of the National Board for Consumer Policies. Her main role is to deal with matters referred to her by the Marketing Practices, Improper Contract Terms and Consumer Credit Acts. In this context, the KOV monitors marketing practices, identifies violations of the above laws and negotiates with implicated firms, while the KO petitions the Market Court for injunctions and fines against uncooperative wrongdoers. In addition, the KO is empowered to bring precedent-setting cases to the Market Court to get a clearer ruling even if the incriminated firm is agreeable to the KO's demands, since such an agreement creates no legal precedent (Bernitz and Draper 1981, p. 66). The Ombudsman can also issue cease-and-desist orders in minor cases.

Complaints are received by the KOV from individual consumers (about three-fourths of the cases), business, regional and local authorities and associations, but problems are also detected through the monitoring of advertisements (about 13 percent of the cases in the early 1980s). The KOV then determines whether the advertising in question is in fact faulty, and whether the KO has jurisdiction (e.g., the Ombudsman deals mainly with the information received by consumers, not with product deficiencies, except in the case of unsafe and unfit products). If these criteria are satisfied, the KOV takes up the matter with the advertiser, pointing out where the problem lies, requesting justification or explanation, and asking that it be corrected. In over 95 percent of the actionable cases, the marketer or advertiser agrees and the matter stops there. Informal persuasion is thus the first technique used, while having the Consumer Ombudsman present a case before the Market Court is a last resort (only about twenty to thirty cases a year, with about half of them based on competitor complaints).

It is worth noting that the KO is not allowed to get involved in: (1) individual civil-law disputes, and (2) the resolution of specific cases, which are handled by the National Board for Consumers Complaints (ARN) and by the regular courts. Hence, the complaints received by the National Board for Consumer Policies (KOV) only serve to draw attention to apparent violations of the law, since the KOV/KO's role is to protect consumers as a *group* even though the KO cannot initiate class actions (Bernitz 1976, p. 34; Bernitz and Draper 1981, p. 30). In other words, it is not the purpose of the Marketing Practices Act to solve disputes between consumers and businessmen (and between businessmen), but rather to protect consumers in general from being subjected to unacceptable marketing practices (Bernitz and Draper 1986, p. 121).

There is strong evidence that Sven Heurgren who served as KO from 1971 to 1983 and was considered to be a Social Democrat remained fairly independent of political pressures, aided in this by his former record as a jurist and a judge. A former judge and KOV administrator, Mrs. Laila Freivalds, was appointed in July 1983 to replace him, but no major policy changes have surfaced since then.

The Market Court (Marknadsdomstolen)

When handling marketing cases, this tribunal has nine members representing business (three from manufacturing, wholesaling and retailing), labor and consumers (three), one independent expert on consumer affairs and an independent chairman and vice-chairman with judicial experience. The Market Court can force an advertiser to stop an incriminated practice through cease-and-desist injunctions and prohibitions, and to require more information in advertisements and labels. These decisions (based on majority votes) are enforceable with fines (up to $300,000) if its orders are violated, and they cannot be appealed.[5] Unlike traditional courts, the Market Court is not limited to prevailing standards but can refer to emerging ones. Its task, like that of the Ombudsman, is "to make the market better for the future'' since it can only enjoin businessmen from doing something from now on (consent orders are alsò used for that purpose).

Defining What the Law Means

The legislation enforced by the Consumer Ombudsman and Market Court is rather general and vague, and deliberately so. For example, the Marketing Practices Act's key Section 2 on "Improper Marketing" states that: "If a merchant, in the marketing of a product, service or anything else of value, advertises or takes other action which, *by conflicting with good commercial standards or otherwise*, adversely affects consumers or merchants . . . [emphasis added].'' Its Section 3 is aimed at merchants who omit to give "information of particular significance to consumers"; while the Act Prohibiting Improper Contract Terms lacks any precise definition of what constitutes unfairness in contract terms.

How then are terms such as "improper" (*otillbörlig*) interpreted by the Ombudsman and the Market Court? In the first place, there are the parliamentary documents expressing legislative intent. Second, there are Market Court decisions serving as precedents. Third, there are the KOV guidelines—but how have the latter been developed and applied?

Business Influence

From 1957 to 1970, there was a nationwide self-regulatory council on Business Practice (Näringslivets Opinionsnämnd) set up by Swedish industrial and commercial organizations (self-regulation had in fact started in 1929 to 1935). In later years, it included consumer representatives and was headed by a former member of the judiciary. This Council had developed guidelines based on its experience in applying the International Chamber of Commerce's (ICC) International Code of Advertising Practice to some 2,000 cases over the years. Thorelli (1977, p. 199) characterized it as "probably the most advanced self-policing advertising control machinery in the world," and other commentators gave it equal credit as well as to the underlying ICC codes.

The new KOV/KO organization and the Market Court have drawn on these guidelines and ICC codes ever since. In fact, the Swedish legislators intended as much. Their development in recent years has not been achieved in a vacuum but has been influenced by: (1) business representation on the KOV Governing Council and on the Market Court; (2) trade associations negotiating about guidelines and standard contract terms with the KOV and KO, and (3) firms litigating before the Market Court, which ultimately gives meaning to the law and the KOV guidelines.

For one thing, business has two out of the ten seats on the Governing Council of the KOV/KO (versus three for consumer and labor representatives), and it shares equal representation with the latter on the Market Court and on the National Board for Consumer Complaints (ARN). It must be stressed that these are decision-making bodies—not mere advisory or consultative ones as is the case with Belgium's Consumers Council. Besides, the guidelines about marketing practices and product design have always been worked out in cooperation with the relevant trade associations and key business firms, although the KOV Governing Council is free to issue them independently (Konsumentverket—KO, n.d.). In fact, it will probably not undertake negotiations with business representatives where the trade associations' positions on the issues are known or where no relevant trade association exists (Bernitz and Draper 1986, p. 77).

Crucial to business influence is the fact that Sweden has strong trade associations, which can ensure reasonable compliance by their members who represent a high proportion of their industry's business. Negotiations between the KOV/KO and these associations may even be based on drafts prepared by the latter. The KOV/KO then follows up the broad-based negotiations with non-member companies. Such agreements with trade associations are not legally binding on anyone, but neither will the KO challenge an agreement unless circumstances have changed or other special reasons have arisen, and—in any case—not before attempting to negotiate a new agreement, since obtaining the cooperation of business is a paramount consideration (Bernitz and Draper 1986, pp. 264–267).

Of course, the addition of ''or otherwise'' to Section 2 of the 1975 Marketing Practices Act (about advertising and other marketing actions ''conflicting with good commercial standards or otherwise'') reveals that business standards—old or new—do not limit the meaning of the law. Still, statements from trade associations and responsible firms about current business practices have been used by the Consumer Ombudsman before the Market Court—particularly in the case of the Improper Contract Terms Act (Bernitz and Draper 1981, pp. 74 and 225). Agreements between the KOV/KO and trade associations—although not legally binding on anyone—can be introduced in the Market Court by the Consumer Ombudsman as evidence of good commercial practice in that line of business; and this court has accorded official recognition to such evidence (Bernitz and Draper 1981, pp. 265–266).

Hence, business has had many opportunities to help shape the KOV/KO system's policies and actions ever since its beginning, even though this power is shared and circumscribed in some ways (e.g., it is the KO Secretariat that decides which cases will go before the Market Court, not the KOV Governing Council). Besides, business accommodation has taken place under the shadow of legal action—whether legal proceedings before the Market Court or the threat of further legislation. The fear of negative publicity has also been an important motivator of business cooperation in a country where the press strongly favors consumer protection (Bernitz and Draper 1981, p. 295).

Consumerist Influence

What about consumer associations, advocates and representatives who also sit on the same councils and boards as business? Have they not been equally influential or even more so in a country famous for its consumerism? A partial review of the literature (e.g., Bernitz and Draper 1981, pp. 22 and 290; Thorelli 1977, pp. 191–193; Thorelli 1981) as well as interviews revealed the following about the Swedish consumer movement:

1. There is no capstone or leading organization representing all or most of the Swedish consumer bodies—as is the case in Canada, The Federal Republic of Germany and the United Kingdom. The consumer movement is therefore as fragmented as in Belgium and France.

2. Consumer representatives on the KOV Governing Council and the Market Court are typically drawn from the cooperative union (Kooperativa Förbundet, KF), the Confederation of Trade Unions (LO) and the Central Organization of Salaried Employees (TCO). These organizations are economically and politically powerful—largely because of their size and their association with the Social Democratic Party (SD), which has ruled Sweden since 1936, with a 1976–1982 eclipse. This situation has allowed them to dominate the representation of consumer interests, although their multiple missions do not make them ideal consumer representatives and at times antagonize other more independent consumer organizations—KF is also a very large business organization involved in manufacturing, wholesaling and retailing; while LO represents workers and TCO salaried employees whose interests do not always coincide with those of consumers.

3. There are smaller consumer associations focusing on the specific concerns of handicapped people, tenants and home-owners, car- and boat-owners and so on. These are influential when their interests are at stake, but they do not work in unison, as is the case with business, which is much better organized.

4. Active, vocal and even radical individual consumerists are found everywhere in this well-organized society: in Parliament, in the Social-Democratic and Liberal parties, in the countless commissions established by government to study practically everything in Sweden, in the unions, among the intelligentsia, in the KOV departments and KO Secretariat, in district and municipal consumer-affairs bureaus as well as in the press and other media, including the state-monopoly broadcasting networks (for an analysis of more radical views, see Johansson 1978, p. 479).

Altogether, these fragments of the Swedish consumerist movement add up to a powerful constituency in terms of defining and supporting broad proconsumer goals, and in shaping up the concomitant legislative and institutional developments. However, they appear to have had less influence than business in: (1) the development of the KOV guidelines that interpret the law, and (2) the decisions of the Market Court, where the law is ultimately given meaning.[6] It is, after all, with business that the KOV negotiates—not with consumer associations. For that matter, very few complaints to the National Board for Consumer Policies (KOV) emanate from consumer organizations, but rather from individuals; and these organizations have not petitioned the Market Court directly when the KO has chosen not to use the latter, while business firms and associations have.

It would seem that the Consumer Ombudsman was a response to the weak condition of the consumer movement, and that—ironically enough—the broad success and public acceptance of the KOV/KO system have minimized the need for a unified consumer movement, since it is considered the State's task to protect consumers and even represent them in this consumerist society.

Why the Formal Self-Regulatory System Was Abandoned

This analysis so far has revealed considerable business influence in the implementation of the new consumer policy; this explains *a posteriori* why business could do without a self-regulatory system. It remains to examine the reasons why the very effective Council on Business Practice was dismantled in 1970, although this Council had been criticized for being dominated by business interests and for lacking strong sanctions (Hetzler 1984, p. 167).

The "Leftward Twist"

In the mid–1960s, the ruling Social Democratic Party took a radical turn and worked toward more regulation and greater government stewardship in economic affairs. It found in consumerism a new vehicle to revive good old-fashioned antibusiness agitation, which ultimately culminated in the creation of the Consumer Ombudsman as "St. George fighting the dragon advertisers (Thorelli 1977, pp. 196–199)." More conservative parties, on their part, were afraid of being labeled as reactionary or anticonsumer if they opposed the proposed new policy. In any case, even conservative legislators accepted the principle that the development of business norms and their application should be vested in government rather than left to the discretion—however well intentioned—of industry.

Business was intimidated by this "Leftward twist" and somewhat convinced by the "state responsibility" argument. In any case, there did not seem to be any way of preventing the passage of the proposed legislation. Hence, the new proconsumer policies found little opposition and even support among businesspeople since the new legislation was almost identical to the existing self-regulatory norms. There was really "nothing to fight against," as one business respondent put it.

Exit, Voice or Loyalty?

In view of these developments, the self-regulatory body faced what Hirschman (1970) calls the choice between exit (quit), voice (complain, lobby, etc., from the outside) and loyalty (work within the system). On the surface, Swedish business quit by disbanding its effective Council on Business Practice. In fact, it chose the voice and loyalty routes—particularly the latter. Many factors and actors have, of course, shaped that choice, but the following appear to be significant in interpreting its 1970 decision.

1. Self-regulation is a complex and costly proposition. Letting the government assume this financial and administrative burden was appealing. Of course, firms would still need advice to deal with the new bureaucracy, but this could be done through setting up a consulting firm that charges fees for such service in lieu of having to chase members for dues to support the self-regulatory body.

This was achieved by the creation of the Marketing Law Consultancy (Konsultbyran för Marknadsrätt) in 1969, shortly before the new marketing laws and institutions came into effect (1970–1972). Its team of expert lawyers have monitored the Market Court's and the KOV/KO activities as well as relevant developments in marketing law. They have advised firms (some 400 a year) at an early stage in the development of their marketing/advertising plans as well as when they get in trouble with the KOV or the Consumer Ombudsman. (The authorities do not, in principle, give preliminary advice, although there seems to be ways of obtaining it.) However, the Marketing Law Consultancy's lawyers have not represented clients before the Market Court and other tribunals.

The Consultancy's founder was the Trade and Industry Committee on Marketing Law Policy (Näringslivets Delegation för Marknadsrätt, NDM), which has been supported by twenty-six leading business organizations: chambers of commerce, associations of farmers, wholesalers, retailers, banks and insurance companies, advertisers, agencies and publishers as well as the capstone Federation of Swedish Industries (SI) and even the Cooperative Union (KF) by special agreement. The leadership of both the Consultancy and the NDM Committee has come from the former self-regulatory Council on Business Practice, with the NDM headed by a previous Competition Ombudsman—a classical way of achieving legitimacy and credibility. (The Marketing Law Consultancy was sold in 1985 to a private company because it became unprofitable after law firms started providing similar services.)

2. The wording of the key concepts of new marketing legislation was left deliberately vague, and the new Consumer Ombudsman and National Board for Consumer Policies (KOV) were going to need help to give them specific meaning. However, since business was going to be significantly represented on the decision-making KOV Governing Council and Market Court (see above), it would be in an internal position to influence the application of the new laws in a definite and positive manner. Why fight the new system—inevitable anyway—and keep an antagonistic distance on the outside when one could play a loyal and fruitful role on the inside? This stance fitted the Swedish model of trying to achieve consensus or compromise through discussion and negotiation rather than through open confrontation and conflict in what Swedes like to call a "small country" (8.3 million souls) that is quite homogeneous. There were precedents since policy elaboration and implementation are often left to special government agencies

involving interest groups and operating outside of the regular ministries (Jacobsson 1983).

3. In the same vein, the standards to be developed by the National Board for Consumer Policies and the Consumer Ombudsman were likely to parallel the much respected principles of good commercial behavior elaborated by the Council on Business Practice on the basis of the International Chamber of Commerce's codes and of its own precedents. In fact, there would now be greater predictability of what constituted "good business behavior"; while the influential small-business segment of Swedish industry saw in stronger regulation a way of taming down the competition from large firms.

4. The major criticism of the Council of Business Practice had been its problems with ensuring that the voluntary standards were observed by less reputable businessmen—the classical "noncomplier" problem (Bernitz and Draper 1981, p. 21; International Chamber of Commerce [ICC] 1978, p. 9). Now, however, the KOV guidelines and other agreements to be negotiated with business would amount to "codes of marketing ethics with teeth (Thorelli, 1977, p. 219)" and "You could hang the real crooks," as one business interviewee put it—the classical advantages of the coercive regulatory approach. Responsible businessmen and former leaders of the self-regulatory movement liked that prospect in view of their own frustration with noncompliers. In any case, business was not likely to be persecuted and vilified—except for irresponsible wrongdoers—under a system mainly based on negotiations and cease-and-desist injunctions rather than on penal sanctions meted out by the regular courts ("Entretien" 1982, p. 3).

5. Other criticisms of self-regulation had included the small number of cases handled, the lack of sufficient publicity about wrongdoers and the difficulty of tapping consumer inputs on a large scale (most complaints had come from competitors). The new Swedish consumer-protection institutions (KOV, KO, National Board for Consumer Complaints, Market Court, etc.) would remedy these defects, and—again—responsible businessmen could not disapprove of these new tools as long as they were handled fairly. Business representation on these bodies as well as eternal vigilance would see to that.

The New Blend of Regulation and Self-Regulation

How has the new system fared in terms of mixing government compulsion with loyal business cooperation?

The Pros and Cons of Regulation

First, the new Swedish laws of the 1970s have given the KOV/KO system a strong legal basis from which to negotiate with business associations and firms (Wikström 1984); and adherence to the KOV guidelines has been satisfactory

(Konsumentpolitiska 1983, p. 346). There seems to be general agreement that the KOV-KO system has proved superior to self-regulation in terms of discovering consumer concerns and dissatisfactions (Wikström 1983), since it can handle many more complaints and inquiries. Each year, some 60,000 letters reach the Konsumentverket, some 8,000 of them complaints that result in about 2,500 negotiations; and the National Board for Consumer Complaints (ARN) handles some 8,000 written complaints (plus 400,000 contacts at district and municipal consumer-affairs bureaus)—versus the 1,000 to 1,500 inquiries and complaints handled annually by the self-regulatory Council on Business Practice from 1957 to 1970.

The KOV/KO role and availability can also be more readily publicized than those of self-regulation. It is safe to assume that close to 100 percent of adult Swedes know about the Consumer Ombudsman (93 percent, in fact, according to a 1978 survey) while in France and the United Kingdom, where there have been aggressive efforts to make advertising self-regulation better known than anywhere else, only one-quarter of the population is aware of its existence. Still, a recent discussion had a member of the KOV outline some of the problems encountered with guidelines: "The production of guidelines takes a lot of time and work, and economic resources too; sometimes they provide more detailed regulation than is necessary; it is difficult to inform all traders of their contents so that there is a time lag before they take effect. . . . The ambitions of the Consumer Ombudsman and the National Board for Consumer Policies to produce guidelines are lower today than in the mid–1970s (Bremen Workshop 1983, p. 19; see also Thorelli 1981, and Wikström 1984)."

However, business has not always liked the new laws and guidelines. It has opposed the severe restrictions against premium offers; and the more coercive nature of the system has also generated some antagonism in contrast to voluntarily accepted rules of behavior ("Entretien" 1982, p. 3). Business has been rebuffed in such areas as the continuing ban of commercials on radio and television, which remain government monopolies. For that matter, Parliament discussed in 1982 a fairly general prohibition of advertising on videocassettes; and the government even considered the jamming of foreign-based satellite broadcasting (new mass-media parliamentary commissions have been studying this subject in recent years). However, we are dealing here with a different type of policy—"cultural" rather than of the consumer-protection and fair-competition varieties, where business carries greater weight and expertise (Gustafsson 1983).

The Realities of Regulation

Below the surface of the broad public and business acceptances of the new consumer-protection system, other realities must be acknowledged:

1. Its very existence has reassured the public, irrespective of its true content and effectiveness—something akin to Edelman's (1967) "symbolic uses of politics." The innovations have been presented as radical and the product of a new

political ideology when, in fact, they have been noncontroversial, since they involved standards already accepted or acceptable by most of Swedish business. The novel institutions of the National Board for Consumer Policies, the Consumer Ombudsman (there are other types of Ombudsman, going back to 1809), the Market Court and the National Board for Consumer Complaints have provided highly visible "symbols" for the new age of consumerism—as was unsuccessfully attempted with the aborted U.S. Consumer Protection Agency—but the rules of the game have not fundamentally changed (cf. Bernitz and Draper [1981, pp. 290–297] for a somewhat different interpretation). In this context, it is worth noting that there was no Swedish member on the fairly radical International Organization of Consumers Unions (IOCU) until 1985 when the KOV become a corresponding member.

2. As was seen before, the true meaning of the new regulations has in fact been shaped by their very target, namely, business. We are here on territory familiar to students of the regulatory process and of its "capture"—strong or mild—by private interests. When the Market Court includes three decision-making representatives each from the business and consumer sides—all appointed by the minister of finance on the basis of nominations from key representative associations—plus an independent expert as well as a chairman and a vice-chairman with a judicial background, how far have we really traveled from the self-regulatory Council on Business Practice, which had a very similar structure? Also, when: (1) KOV guidelines are largely based on the experience of the same Council on Business Practice in applying the International Code of Advertising Practice of the International Chamber of Commerce, and (2) business has a strong voice in shaping up new guidelines, which are nonbinding anyway on firms and on the Market Court, how radical a departure has really been achieved from the pre–1970 situation? In any case, the new policy has accepted the market economy, although claiming a commanding voice for the State in ascertaining, defining and defending consumer interests within that system.

Still, it would be erroneous to conclude from this analysis that business and government have somehow colluded at the expense of the Swedish consumer. Instead, business has assumed responsible attitudes, and KOV-KO administrators have applied laws and guidelines without prejudice. For that matter, a good number of Market Court decisions have been taken against the votes of business representatives.

3. In only a few cases has pressure been put on business to provide more informative advertisements on the basis of Section 3 of the Marketing Practices Act, although KOV guidelines have been somewhat useful in this respect (Wikström 1984); and it is noteworthy that Sweden has rejected the suggestion that the Market Court be empowered to require corrective advertising.

4. There has been a pause in the development of consumer-protection legislation since the late 1970s. This was not caused by the temporary eclipse of the Social-Democrats from power in 1976–1982, since there is broad agreement about consumer policy among all parties and in public opinion. Still, the pace

of reform has slowed down in the face of: (1) deficits that have resulted in reduced budgets for the KOV/KO system, (2) disaffection with bureaucracy, and (3) greater attention paid to comparing the costs and benefits of further regulations. Clearly, Sweden has been touched by the reality of recession and the ambient spirit of deregulation—and U.S. experience on this score has not gone unnoticed. In fact, a recent government-sponsored commission report (Konsumentpolitiska 1983) favored the resumption of a complementary role for self-regulation by business, under KOV supervision, as a way of alleviating the high costs associated with the full assumption by government of the control of business behavior.[7]

In late 1985, the Swedish Parliament approved a move toward a higher degree of "auto-activities" (*egen-atgärder*) by various business sectors. The government justified this development toward business assuming "more direct-responsibility for the maintenance of high standards of ethics in marketing" on the basis of the classical arguments favoring self-regulation: better adaptation to business circumstances, greater acceptance by firms, smoother and swifter enforcement (Flory and Tengelin 1986). Besides, the KOV is expected to consume fewer resources in supervising such a system than in developing guidelines from the outside (Bernitz and Draper 1986, p. 305).

Already, an "auto-action" program has been activated by the Swedish Direct Sales Association, with an extensive set of rules that have been approved by the KOV—somewhat along the lines of the British Office of Fair Trading system for the approval of industry codes of practices. This association will monitor its members while the KOV will oversee the practices of nonmembers. Two other systems applying to subscription offers and home-electronics advertising are being developed, but the results are not in yet.

Actually, both self-regulatory and self-disciplinary systems are already in place in a few industries. For example, an Information Practices Committee regulates information relating to prescription medicines. Likewise, in the advertising industry, each advertising agency has its own system of internal self-discipline. An executive, who is trained and experienced in Sweden's marketing law and known as the "responsible editor," reviews for acceptability all the advertisements and materials produced by an agency. Without his approval, no advertisement can appear.

The governmental system does not—in principle—provide for advance external review of advertisements, one of the tasks of advertising control. These functions are performed by the responsible editor and by the private law firms (e.g., the former Marketing Law Consultancy) to which agencies, advertisers and the media can turn for legal advice.

Therefore, self-regulation is alive and well in Sweden and may even face a better future, although it is not clear at this point if industry—outside of retailing—will broadly accept an expanded role for self-regulation, which it would have to finance.

Conclusions

Sweden is well worth watching because it is considered a "pilot nation" in the field of consumer policy, and it influences what happens in other parts of the world—particularly other Scandinavian countries, the Federal Republic of Germany (with which Sweden entertains strong legal ties) and the Netherlands. This reputation may be a bit inflated since Sweden has often followed German patterns and has been influenced by U.S. developments (Thorelli 1981). Still, it remains that its innovations and experience carry weight in such bodies as the Organization for European Cooperation and Development, the Council of Europe, the European Economic Community (via Danish membership) and the United Nations. Therefore, the above analysis brings up a series of implications well worth pondering.

1. The control of advertising behavior cannot be conceived or achieved without a blend of: (1) self-discipline on the part of individuals and firms, (2) self-regulation by peers at the industry level, and (3) regulation by the State. Sten Tengelin, one of the leaders and architects of Swedish business' cooperation with the new system, stressed this perspective in a private communication: "I cannot see any *real* difference, for example, between the present Swedish system formally based on law but where the 'law' consists of general clauses, the substance of which is created by voluntary codes and business-inspired guidelines, and the British [advertising] self-regulatory system where the norms applied are 'non-legal' but ultimately founded on basic legal principles (common law and equity)."

2. The real challenge then is to develop the proper blend of: (1) the law with its advantages of universal reach and compulsion, and (2) self-regulation, which can provide the necessary voluntary adhesion to the spirit and not just the letter of what constitutes good business behavior in the face of constantly changing consumer expectations and evolving commercial technologies (e.g., comparison advertising, videocassette advertising, and satellite advertising).

This is obviously a complex task, depending on what side can best handle any one of six basic tasks connected with the control of business behavior (see Chapter 1). The now defunct Swedish Council on Business Practice had performed rather well on these tasks, except that it encountered problems with: (1) tapping emerging consumer concerns; (2) making the system known to most consumers; (3) handling large numbers of complaints, had they materialized, and (4) changing the behavior of the unrepentant crooks. The post–1970 Swedish consumer-protection innovations have been able to remedy most of these deficiencies, *but only because business was coopted by the new system and chose to cooperate* for the reasons examined above. Both sides have emerged better informed from this institutionalized dialogue and cooperation.

A few advantages may have been sacrificed in the process, however: (1) self-regulatory systems are usually faster than the Market Court system (including the KO's preparatory work) in handling complaints (two months versus three to four months); (2) they often require advertisers to have prior substantiation for any claims they make, while the law only demands that they be able to substantiate them ex post facto; (3) member media usually cooperate with the self-regulatory system by refusing to publish (or broadcast) advertisements found to be in violation of voluntary codes; and (4) wrongdoers and questionable practices are more readily publicized under self-regulation than under the law, unless a diligent press cares to ferret out the necessary information—but the latter seems to be the case in Sweden, where Market Court decisions are readily publicized by the press. Most important, moral adhesion slackens as the burden of the law becomes more obvious—as evidenced by Swedish advertisers turning to more subjective advertising after the Consumer Ombudsman focused on violations of the more objective types of false, misleading and unfair advertising ("Entretien" 1982, p. 2).

3. It is not a matter of finding a permanent blend of the two approaches, but one of constant dynamic remixing since a "more perfect union" has to be regularly worked out between them. Self-regulation can go stale in terms of identifying and coping with new consumer issues, encountering financial difficulties, and the like. Similarly, the law can become burdensome and overwhelming, or come up short of workable solutions, Hence, both business and government have to remain open to new working arrangements without remaining wed to rigid ideological positions. Recent Swedish proposals provide evidence of such an openminded attitude in the context of the "auto-activities" previously mentioned.

4. Self-regulation needs nurturing by the State. Businessmen may favor it in principle but be unable to gather enough support for it, or direct it into anticompetitive and anticonsumer directions. The British experience with the Office of Fair Trading (OFT) is rather positive in this area in view of its mandate to encourage industry to develop codes of conduct that are then monitored by the OFT, which stands ready to propose new regulations, should the self-regulatory approach fail. The Swedes seem to be moving in the same direction although from the opposite side, since a recent commission report (Konsumentpolitiska 1983) and parliamentary action have suggested more self-regulation under KOV supervision in the light of the difficulties encountered by the present legal system. This might create for the KOV a role similar to that of the British Office of Fair Trading. The multiplication of new media will also create opportunities for self-regulation, both at the national and international levels.[8]

5. Finally, it is appropriate to stress the unique national dimensions involved in the blending of self-regulation with regulation. The Swedish and British situations show government coopting business to achieve its goals, albeit in different ways. In France, it is more a case of the industry involving government in the development of its standards. In Belgium and the United States, one finds government sitting pretty much on the side, although for different reasons—traditional U.S. fear of the anticompetitive aspects of self-regulation, and current

Belgian governmental indecision in the face of warring consumerist and advertising groups. Therefore, the Consumer Ombudsman system may work best in a small and highly homogeneous country with interacting elites and a gift for consensus (Thorelli 1977, p. 231), but may not be exportable to other countries. Its study, nevertheless, confirms that regulation and self-regulation are natural partners in improving standards of business behavior.

NOTES

1. There are also laws and a Competition Ombudsman that deal with restrictive trade practices (Freivalds 1986, p. 21).

2. The Act also includes criminal provisions outlawing intentionally misleading advertising (sections 6, 7 and 8). Upon the request or with the consent of the Consumer Ombudsman, violations of these criminal provisions are handled in the ordinary courts by public prosecutors. Unlike businessmen, however, consumers cannot claim damages on the basis of the Marketing Practices Act (Bernitz 1981, p. 242).

3. The ARN Board is made up of an equal number of consumer and business representatives, with a judge presiding as chair. Compliance with its recommendations is close to 90 percent.

4. What happens if the guidelines are not followed? A KOV document comments as follows:

If the wording in the guidelines is "shall" or "must not," this signifies that the National Board for Consumer Policies (KOV) considers it necessary or particularly urgent that marketing is adapted to the guidelines. If a "shall" rule is not adhered to, the Board will take action. In the normal case, this will mean that the Board contacts the firm which does not follow the guidelines. The Board believes that correction will be achieved in most cases through such contacts. If the contacts do not lead to an acceptable result, the Consumer Ombudsman may take action in the Market Court under the Marketing Act or issue a prohibition injunction or an information injunction. If there is the wording "should not" in the guidelines, this means that the Board considers it advisable that marketing be practiced according to the guidelines. If a "should" rule is not adhered to, the Board will consider in each individual case, whether or not to take action. Such an action will always be in the form of negotiating contacts in one form or another (no source given); see also Bernitz and Draper 1986, p. 77.

5. For discussions of Market Court decisions, see: Bernitz and Draper 1981 and 1986; Konsumentpolitiska 1983; and Freivalds 1986.

6. Specialized consumer organizations seem to be more influential in the development of standard contract terms in various trades, however.

7. A government labeling agency, which had assumed the tasks of a private volunteer organization, was subsequently eliminated so that informative labeling was ultimately abandoned in a country that had pioneered it.

8. Foreign broadcasts are already received in Sweden through cable and satellite systems. Commercials coming through satellite channels are tolerated, provided no specific direct commercial appeal is made to Swedish viewers.

REFERENCES

Bernitz, Ulf. "Consumer Protection: Aims, Methods and Trends in Swedish Consumer Law." *Scandinavian Studies in Law* 20 (1976): 13–36.

————. "Guidelines Issued by the Consumer Board: The Swedish Experience." *Journal of Consumer Policy* 7, no. 2 (1984): 161–65.

————. "Market and Consumer Law." In *Introduction to Swedish Law*, edited by Stig Strömholm. Stockholm: Norstedts, 1981, pp. 231–56.

Bernitz, Ulf, and John Draper. *Consumer Protection in Sweden: Legislation, Institutions and Practice.* Stockholm: Institute of Intellectual Property and Market Law at Stockholm University, No. 12, 1981 and 1986.

"Bremen Workshop." *Consumer Affairs* [J. W. Thompson, London] 66 (November– December 1983): 19–20. See the full report of this workshop in the special issue of *Journal of Consumer Policy* 7, no. 2 (1984).

Business International. *Europe's Consumer Movement.* NY: 1980.

Edelman, Murray. *The Symbolic Uses of Politics.* Urbana, IL: University of Illinois Press, 1967.

"Entretien avec Monsieur Sten Tengelin [interview with Mr. Sten Tengelin]." *BVP Echos* [French Advertising Control Bureau newsletter] 52 (December 1982): 1–3.

Flory, Ingrid, and Sten Tengelin. "The Role of Business in Swedish Consumer Policy Re-assessed; A Summary Presentation of the Declarations on Business Self-Regulation Made in the Government Bill 1984/85: 213, as Adopted by the Swedish Riksdag [Parliament] in December 1985." Mimeographed. Stockholm: February 1986.

Freivalds, Laila. "Swedish Consumer Policy." *Consumer Affairs* [J. W. Thompson, London] 80 (March–April 1986): 19–23.

Gustafsson, K. E. "Mass Media Structure and Policy in Sweden in the Early 1980s." *Current Sweden* 301 (June 1983).

Hetzler, Antoinette. "Sweden's Regulation of Consumer Affairs." *Journal of Public Policy* 7, no. 2 (1984): 167–69.

Hirschman, A. O. *Exit, Voice and Loyalty.* Cambridge, Mass.: Harvard University Press, 1970.

International Chamber of Commerce [ICC]. *Marketing: Discipline for Freedom.* Paris, 1978.

Jacobsson, Bengt. "Organized Interests and Political Control." Mimeographed. Stockholm: Economic Research Institute, Stockholm School of Economics, 1983.

James, Donald. "KO—The Consumer Ombudsman." *Sweden Now* 4 (1972): 48–52.

Johansson, J. K. "The Theory and Practice of Swedish Consumer Policy." In *Consumerism: Search for the Consumer Interest*, edited by D. A. Aaker, and G. S. Day. 3rd ed. New York: Free Press, 1978, 470–83. Reprinted from *Journal of Consumer Affairs* 10 (Summer 1976): 19–32.

Konsumentpolitiska Styrmedel: Utvärdering och Förslag; Betänkande av Riktlinjekommitten [Consumer Policy Instruments; Evaluation and Suggestions; Thoughts of the Guidelines Committee]. Stockholm: Statens Offentliga Utredning [Government-Commissioned Report], no. 40, 1983.

Konsumentverket-KO, *The National Swedish Board for Consumer Policies—The Consumer Ombudsman: Functions, Organization, Activities.* Vällingby, no date.

"Sweden: The Consumer Ombudsman." *EFTA Bulletin* 16 (March 1975): 16–18.

Swedish Institute, "Swedish Consumer Policy." *Fact Sheets on Sweden* (September 1981).

————. "The Swedish Ombudsmen." *Fact Sheets on Sweden* (January 1983).

Thorelli, H. B. "Swedish Consumer Policy, Its Transferability and Related Research Implications." *Advances in Consumer Research* [Association for Consumer Research] 8 (1981): 467–73.

Thorelli, H. B., and S. V. Thorelli. *Dynamic Analysis*: "The Case of Sweden Since 1940." In *Consumer Information Systems and Consumer Policy*. Cambridge, Mass.: Ballinger, 1977, Chapter 7: pp. 189–231.

Wikström, Solveig. "Bringing Consumer Information Systems Down to Earth; Experiences from a Swedish Experiment." *Journal of Consumer Policy* 7, no. 1 (1984): 13–26.

————. "Marketing and Business Consumer Policy, Contribution to Problem Solving." Discussion Paper No. 18. Lund: University of Lund, Department of Business Administration, January 1983.

ACKNOWLEDGMENTS

The assistance of the following administrators, academics, businessmen and experts is gratefully acknowledged: Johan Arndt (Norwegian School of Economics and Business Administration); Mikael Ankers (Ministry of Finance); Mathias André (University of Stockholm); Ulf Bernitz (University of Stockholm); Axel Edling (Deputy Consumer Ombudsman); Ingrid Flory (consultant; former KOV member); Johny K. Johansson (University of Washington); Lars Jonson (President, Market Court); Folke Olander (Aarhus School of Economics and Business Administration); Staffan Sandström (Ministry of Finance); Anders Stenlund (Sverges Industriförbund); Berit Ström-Thun (Public Complaints Board); Ake Sundquist (Chairman, Trade and Industry Committee for Marketing Law, NDM); Carl Anders Svensson (Marketing Law Consultancy); Sten Tengelin (Trade and Industry Committee for Marketing Law, NDM); H. B. Thorelli (Indiana University); Thomas Utterström (KOV); Ursula Wallberg (Konsumentverket); Göran Westlund (Kooperativa Förbundet); Bo Wickström (Göteborg University) and Solveig Wikström (University of Lund).

13

The United Kingdom: Advertising Standards Authority

The British advertising self-regulatory (ASR) system is the largest, most active and best financed one in the world; and its Advertising Standards Authority (ASA) has received many plaudits and been used as a model by other countries (e.g., India, Ireland and Singapore). The ASA has also been the subject of more academic, parliamentary and professional scrutiny than any other ASR system, so that many of its features need not be described or analyzed here (e.g., Advertising Association 1987; British Code of Advertising Practice [BCAP] 1985; Buell 1977; Jones and Pickering 1985; Miracle and Nevett 1987; Thomson 1983). Previous studies, however, have paid relatively less attention to: (1) the participation of outsiders (that is, nonindustry members) in the ASA system, and (2) this system's relationships with the British government.

Regarding outside participation, nonindustry members represent some two-thirds of the ASA's governing Council, but the impact of these outsiders on the ASA's functioning and effectiveness has not been systematically examined. In other words, does advertising self-regulation work even better when its code-development and complaint-handling arms include nonindustry members? While it is impossible to single out fully the impact of such outside participation—a structural factor—on the ASA's functioning and effectiveness, enough evidence suggests that the latter have improved on account of the former.

Regarding the relationships between advertising self-regulation and the British government, it will be argued that the latter has played a strong role of "outside partner" in terms of encouraging, threatening, defending and supervising it. As such, effective outside participation is not limited to the formal incorporation of nonindustry members in the structure and functioning of advertising self-regulation.[1] It is also appropriate to investigate why such close relationships do exist between the ASA and the British government.

To address these issues, interviews were conducted, starting in the Fall of 1981, with ASA Council members, consumer associations and government officials. Extensive correspondence and other contacts have since been maintained with these people as well as with other experts.

The British Advertising Self-Regulatory Structure

U.K. advertising practice had come under strong consumerist criticism as well as government investigation and "ultimatums" in the late 1950s and early 1960s. Also, a statutory code had been imposed in 1955 on broadcast advertising—a development that could have been extended to print advertising (BCAP 1985, p. 7). Consequently, it was thought necessary by the Advertising Association— a body of advertisers, agencies and media designed to promote and defend the industry as well as to upgrade its performance—to unify and improve existing codes of advertising behavior, and to enhance their application.[2]

From these efforts resulted the first edition (in 1961) of the British Code of Advertising Practice (BCAP; its seventh edition came out in 1985), and the constitution of a couple of code-development and application bodies, including the Advertising Standards Authority (ASA), created in 1962. The resulting advertising self-regulatory system is now responsible for: (1) updating the Code; (2) investigating complaints from consumers and competitors, (3) monitoring print, cinema, outdoor, videotext, viewdata and direct-mail advertisements;[3] (4) mandatory prescreening of ads for cigarettes; (5) providing prepublication advice to agencies and advertisers before ads are released, and (6) publicizing the British self-regulatory system and encouraging its use (some 30 percent of its budget is spent on this task).

In this scheme, the Advertising Standards Authority itself is only one of three major bodies that provide some check and balance vis-à-vis one another:

1. The Advertising Standards Board of Finance (ASBOF) funds both the ASA and the Code of Advertising Practice Committee's activities, and it appoints the ASA chairman. Only industry members sit on this board, whose income comes from a 0.1 percent surcharge levied on gross advertising billings outside of radio and television, since the ASA does not investigate complaints about TV and radio commercials, which are handled by the Independent Broadcasting Authority.

2. The Code of Advertising Practice (CAP) Committee is made up of some twenty trade association representatives from advertisers, agencies and media (cf. ASA Case Report 138). Its missions are: (1) to draw up and revise the Code in consultation with the ASA Council (see below); (2) to give advice on the interpretation of the Code to the industry, and (3) to handle complaints emanating from competitors (the ASA deals only with consumer complaints). The ASA and the CAP Committee share a common Secretariat headed by a director general.

3. The *Advertising Standards Authority* itself includes three classes of members. First, a chairman who is "not engaged in the business of advertising,"

and who should also be a person of public substance. He is appointed by the Advertising Standards Board of Finance after formal consultation with the members of the ASA Council, and informal consultation with the Advertising Association and the appropriate government units (currently, the Department of Trade and Industry and the Director General of Fair Trading). Subsequently, the chairman appoints: (1) independent members also not engaged in the business of advertising, and (2) advertising members drawn from advertisers, media owners and advertising agencies.

Together with the chairman, these two types of members constitute the Council, or governing body, of the ASA. Since 1975, typically two-thirds (currently seven out of eleven, plus the chairman, but the normal complement is twelve members) of this Council are "independents," although ASA Bylaws only require a majority of them. The functions of the ASA Council are: (1) to oversee the work of the CAP Committee in drafting and amending the Code; (2) to act exceptionally as an appeal tribunal on competitor complaints first handled by the CAP Committee; (3) to maintain and apply procedures for investigating complaints from members of the public; (4) to monitor advertising; (5) to publicize the existence of the self-regulatory system,[4] and (6) to supervise the ASA's research activities.

Outside Participation and Independence

The British self-regulatory system emphasizes the independence of the complaint-handling process as far as consumer complaints are concerned. Not only are the ASA chairman and seven out of eleven members of the ASA Council "independent" persons, but even industry members serve as individuals, rather than as representatives of any firm or association.

Yet, the ASA's independence is limited to the extent that the Code itself is not drawn up by the ASA but by the CAP Committee, which is exclusively made up of industry representatives, because it was considered appropriate to separate the functions of code-development and code-enforcement. Still, the ASA Council checks if the Code meets public expectations, and it puts pressure on the CAP Committee to make the necessary revisions. If these are not forthcoming, the ASA Council can always apply stricter or new standards of its own—at least, in matters of taste—and urge the industry to comply with them through its publications and pronouncements. Consequently, the ASA Council is really the senior partner of the CAP Committee, whose decisions it can ultimately overrule, although every effort is made to resolve differences consensually.

Second, ASA activities are financed by the advertising industry. However, this funding comes from an automatic levy on advertising expenditures, rather than from direct dues or contributions collected from sponsoring industry organizations or from advertising firms.

Third, the independent members are not appointed by outside bodies such as consumer organizations or the government, but by the ASA Chairman, who is an "independent" himself. This is, of course, at the heart of the issue of outside participation; and the government's Office of Fair Trading remarked in its 1978 review of the British self-regulatory system that:

It is an obvious point that the Advertising Standards Board of Finance's choice (after consultation with the relevant Minister) of the Council's Chairman, and his choice of its members are key determinants of the effectiveness of the whole control system. To date, these choices have been well made. We would suggest, however, that the Chairman's power to appoint all the members considerably increases the crucial nature of the industry's initial choice, and that circumstances could arise in which this could provoke criticism. We suggest that it would heighten the appearance of the ASA's independence if a consultative stage were applied also in the choice of members. Such consultation could extend not only to the relevant Minister but also to the Advertising Association and the National Consumer Council (Director General of Fair Trading [DGFT] 1978, p. 30).[5]

Informal soundings with such bodies now occur; and efforts are made to ensure that at least one member of the ASA Council occupies a senior position in either the National Consumer Council or the Consumers' Association. Still, it is felt that the ASA chairman's independence would be undermined if a more formal "advise and consent" procedure were to be introduced. Besides, the Advertising Association considers that any such consultation over the chairman's choice of members might be seen to reduce the ASA's independence from the advertising industry, on which the Association sets great store.

Selection Criteria for Independent Members

First, independent members are not chosen as representatives of the public at large—they are not "ordinary people"—but rather of "the great and the good," that is, better educated and better known people, with significant past or current public responsibilities, whether or not members of the so-called British "Establishment." Thus, the current ASA chairman is a Lord (so were his predecessors) and a professor; while recent independent members have been a director of the Immigrants Advisory Service and former Labour Member of Parliament; a chairman of the Consumers' Association (a private organization); a long-serving member of the National Consumer Council (a public body); a former president of the British Medical Association; the chairman of the Inner London Juvenile Court; a theologian and Canon of Exeter Cathedral, also professor emeritus at London University; the art correspondent for Scottish Television; and the former chairman of the Equal Opportunities Commission, previously a national officer of the Labour Party.[6]

Second, the independent members are balanced, as much as possible, in terms of age, sex, political affiliation, religion, regional origin and voluntary experience, although some of these criteria may apply to the same person. Outside members are selected to reflect "the diversity of national life (BCAP 1985,

p. 14)." However, these criteria are not designed to ensure representation or representativeness of any particular group, since the independent members serve (like the industry members) as individuals rather than as representatives. Systematic representation would be impossible in such a small body, in any case.

Third, professional expertise is not a criterion—for example, the physician member is not there to provide informed opinions about medical advertisements, nor the accountant about financial ones. For that matter, the ASA Secretariat retains expert advisers on technical, scientific and professional matters, whenever necessary for investigating consumer complaints. If anywhere, their expertise lies in their "independent thinking" when interpreting broad cultural patterns and trends. Indeed, most of their deliberations do not revolve around clear-cut violations of the Code, but deal with gray areas where ill-defined and evolving matters of taste and decency predominate, and where there are no obvious right or wrong answers.

The basic principle of the British Code of Advertising Practice is that "All advertisements should be legal, decent, honest and truthful." However, compared to the handling of "hard" violations of the Code, the ASA Secretariat does not prepare briefs on "soft" matters of taste and decency, but leaves them for discussion at the monthly meetings of the ASA Council. It is interesting to observe that the government's Office of Fair Trading is not anxious to tackle matters of "taste and decency, which we consider is best dealt with through individual publishers' house rules and through decision by the ASA Council [DGFT 1978, p. 46]." A typical dilemma involves considering whether the advertisement seriously offends a minority of the audience or taps a widespread concern: "If the Authority believes that a high proportion of viewers of an advertisement are likely to find it offensive, then we shall probably say to the advertiser that it therefore contravenes the Code (ASA officer's oral comment)." Independent thinking and judgment are clearly crucial for such a task.

Fourth, a major selection criterion is "workability." The ASA Council has to make a sizable number of decisions, and the credibility of the system rests in part on its speed in resolving complaints. For that matter, one of the major government criticisms of the self-regulatory system has been that complaint-handling takes too long (DGFT 1978, pp. 33ff), although complaint handling has recently been accelerated. ASA Council members receive through the mail some twenty brief summaries of cases to comment on every week (about 1,000 a year). Most of them represent fairly obvious open-and-shut cases, easily handled by mail voting, and likely to receive fairly unanimous approval on the basis of the Secretariat's recommendations. Others, however, require more extensive discussion in committee meetings held every month, where a dozen difficult cases are typically decided. The ASA Council also deals with policy matters such as code revision and the supervision of monitoring and research, which take time at the monthly meetings. Hence, the Council has to be a "working committee" and a "decision-taking body." This requires members who can listen, give and take, compromise, work together and reach consensus[7] fairly quickly without major personality or ideological wrangles—not people who take stands, go on record or make fusses.

Fifth, while the members must be independent thinkers, they can only be people who are not opposed in principle to advertising. The danger here, in the words of one respondent, is that the criterion of workability may result in "very deferential Establishment types who never get worked up." Both the Director General of Fair Trading and the National Consumer Council have commented somewhat unfavorably that the ASA Council "seeks to reflect public attitudes rather than influence them in matters of taste," and that they take "insufficient account of the consumer interest" by not assuming strong enough positions against the advertising of certain products such as tobacco and alcohol, of proprietary medicines, and of the portrayal of women in advertising (DGFT 1978, p. 30; Whincup 1980, pp. 150–55). Thus, the National Consumer Council, quoting the Code of Advertising Practice, has stated that:

It is arguable whether advertising for cigarettes can ever (even in the light of the new provisions in the Code of Practice) honestly "be prepared with a sense of responsibility to the consumer" and not "bring advertising into disrepute or reduce confidence in advertising as a service to industry and the public." And is it possible to effectively promote the sale of proprietary medicines, for which cheap, satisfactory British Pharmacopoeia equivalents exist, "without exploiting a consumer's lack of experience or knowledge?" (National Consumer Council 1977, pp. 11–12).

The ASA responds to these criticisms and related ones (e.g., about sexism and racism) by pointing out that this approach is mandated by the Code, which requires the Authority to use as its test of offensiveness the likely views of the audience for the advertisement concerned: "Any other approach would entail the Authority becoming a censor, a role which it has no wish to assume." That the banning of the advertising of controversial products (e.g., cigarettes) should be left to Parliament, is another view commonly held by industry and shared by the ASA (cf. Lawson [1985], p. 284). Besides, the ASA conducts surveys of controversial topics such as advertising to children and the depiction of women in advertising, and of the ways in which advertisements are likely to be taken by the average consumer, so that sufficient knowledge about these issues can be made available to the ASA Council.

Altogether, the key selection criteria for Council members are both external (credibility and fairness in judgment) and internal (compatibility/workability and speed). Formal expertise and representativeness are not significant considerations in this respect.

Why Outside Participation Has Been Possible

One can speculate about why the British have found it relatively easy to tap the services of independent outsiders—including consumerist representatives—

when most self-regulatory systems find it much more difficult if not impossible. The tradition of social responsibilities on the part of "the great and the good," the nonradical nature of major U.K. consumer organizations (mostly through the Consumers' Association), the prodding and public endorsement of government officials, and some corporatist tendencies in the British economy (see below) provide ready interpretations in need of further examination, however.

Hirschman's (1970) analysis of the "loyalty" (versus "exit" and "voice") route also helps explain why outsiders have preferred to operate "within" rather than "without" the British self-regulatory system. A written comment from a representative of the National Consumer Council is revealing in this respect:

Clearly, one of the reasons why consumer bodies do choose to co-operate is because we believe that by doing so we can strengthen the operation of the system and improve it, working, as it were, from the inside. The adoption of such a posture necessarily involves consumer organizations in a less confrontational position with the self-regulatory system, and this in itself is likely to lead to greater public credibility. One could therefore postulate the existence of a "virtuous cycle" in which, when a self-regulatory system becomes effective enough to command support from consumer organizations, its effectiveness is likely to increase through a continuing improvement in its public image and credibility (private communication, 1982).

This does not mean that consumerist groups have refrained from criticizing and prodding the ASA, but their interventions have probably been more informed and subdued than if they had chosen to use only "exit" (nonparticipation) and "voice" (external rather than internal criticism). Conversely, the participation of outsiders has required that they be satisfied with what is, after all, a burdensome, although remunerated, task. Their leaving the ASA Council, for lack of significant influence on code development and case disposition, would greatly harm the credibility of the British self-regulatory system, which has had to ensure that their participation be real and meaningful—again a demonstration of the "virtuous circle" mentioned above.

The Independence of the ASA Secretariat

Another test of the independence of the British self-regulatory system revolves around the role of the ASA Secretariat in the process of consumer-complaint handling, which is not minor at all. For one thing, it weeds out frivolous complaints, since it is estimated that some 25 percent of those received by the ASA are not about advertising but about something else (e.g., product performance). Another quarter are carpings about advertising in general or about matters of taste and opinion (e.g., animal furs should not be advertised) that do not typically fall under the purview of the Code (although they are notified to the ASA Council, which may instruct the ASA staff to investigate them). Other complaints deal with radio and television commercials, and are forwarded to the Independent Broadcasting Authority for action. Hence, the ASA Secretariat's work focuses on about one-third of the consumer complaints received by the ASA (there were 7,308 consumer complaints in 1985, and 12,433 from January 1986 through June 1987).[8] Some cases are resolved through initial inquiries that reveal no infringement of the Code. The rest may be submitted to experts or to a CAP Copy Panel,[9] but they ultimately reach the ASA Council in the form of briefs outlining the problem and any apparent violation of the Code, and requesting a vote.

In these sorting-out, analytical and recommendation processes, the composition of the Secretariat staff plays a very important role. Were this staff to be made up of "activist" or "militant" people, it is possible that more cases would come up for decisions, and that staff recommendations would be more stringent. Here again, one needs people tolerant to advertising, since their job is to enforce a code that presupposes that advertisements can be legal, honest and truthful. As one ASA officer put it: "What are wanted are people with perception and judgment who will not let their personal antipathies interfere with their work, or see the enforcement of the Code as an opportunity for an ego trip."[10]

In any case, all recommendations for the nonpursuit of cases by the ASA Secretariat can be challenged by the ASA Council. If even one Council member requests pursuit, the matter is reopened. Thus, nonpursuit is an ASA Council decision—not a Secretariat decision. Moreover, all complaints that are pursued, including those that the Secretariat proposes should not be upheld, go to the ASA Council. Since all cases within the Authority's remit go to the ASA Council, it is impossible that more could go, even if one had a different Secretariat staff. What might change is the nature of the suggested resolution (i.e., more complaints might be recommended to be upheld), but there is no evidence that this would change the outcome when ASA Council members are ready to challenge what is put before them by the ASA Secretariat.

Appraising Outside Participation

The ASA system is not one of "pure" self-regulation, since it includes close to two-thirds of outside independent members on the ASA Council, even though these members are not appointed with the advice and consent of the public at large, of representative consumer associations or of the government, but by the ASA's independent chairman. As such, this hybrid system represents a "middle way"—a typically pragmatic, nonideological British approach, which tends to avoid purist solutions while willing to improvise and compromise. As the legal adviser to the Institute of Practitioners in Advertising put it: "Our approach— which is much more in keeping with our instinct and general approach to life— is not whether a particular system equates with some theoretical principle, but whether it works; whether it makes sense and is demonstrative of the public interest (quoted in Schiffman 1985, p. 6)."

Regarding the participation of outsiders in ASA activities, the major effectiveness tests of the Advertising Standards Authority, as currently structured, are: (1) does it work in the public interest better than pure self-regulation or an even more representative system of self-regulation, in terms of the effectiveness and fairness of its legislative and adjudicative processes; and (2) is it perceived as effective and fair by its stakeholders? (Whether it works better than regulation is a separate issue.)

These are complex questions since gauging the effectiveness of self-regulation—whether pure or hybrid—is a very imprecise endeavor (see Chapter 1). An Office of Fair Trading study (DGFT 1978, p. 12) measured it in terms of how many print ads could be considered to conform to the British Code of Advertising Practice in a sample of such ads. It found 7 percent to be in apparent violation, although the ASA challenged some of the Code interpretations made in that study (Thomson 1983, p. 339). A 1981 survey published by the National Consumer Council found that 4 percent of a sample of respondents considered themselves to have been misled by advertisements in the previous year (NCC 1982).[11] However, the ASA's extensive and sophisticated monitoring system has recently detected very few additional breaches besides those reported through complaints—only 183 ads out of 2,388 publications scanned, and 4 percent of the valid cases pursued from 1984 to 1985.

A 1982 survey conducted for the ASA revealed that among those aware (23 percent) of the existence of the Advertising Standards Authority, some 69 percent agreed strongly or slightly that the ASA is able to ensure that any advertising seen in the press or on posters be truthful. They generally thought (48 percent) that the ASA acts independently of the advertising industry; that the ASA is the most sensible way of dealing with complaints from the public (72 percent) and that a government department would not handle the job better (only 13 percent thought that the latter would be the case) (ASA Case Report 101, 1983; Davidson Pearce Ltd. 1983). The 1984 and 1985 annual reports of the Advertising Association reported similar improvements in public, consumerist and parliamentary attitudes toward advertising and its self-regulation.

Such measures could be multiplied (cf. Jones and Pickering [1985], Lawson [1985], and Miracle and Nevett [1987]) but one cannot conceive that advertising control in the United Kingdom would be better off in the absence of the ASA system. For that matter, governmental and consumerist bodies have expressed overall satisfaction with that system. Thus, the Consumers' Association concluded in 1981 that:

Self-regulatory codes are seldom effective. . . . The one obvious success has been the British Code of Advertising Practice but it operates under conditions favouring success. For many years there had been the threat of legislation if the industry failed to regulate itself effectively. The publishers as well as the advertisers participate in the system of control; and because of this, the system includes an effective sanction—the media members will refuse to accept offending advertisements or, in extreme cases, all advertisements from advertisers who persistently ignore the code. (The loophole in the system is the difficulty of controlling direct-mail advertising.) Potentially the control could be so tight that questions would then be raised about the justice of a self-regulatory body having

Table 13.1

Direct Impact of Outside Participation on ASA Structure, Functioning and Effectiveness (*)

1.	KEY SECRETARIAT APPOINTMENTS	NONE, except through the ASA Chairman
2.	CODE DEVELOPMENT	SOME in that the ASA Council (dominated by independent members) oversees the CAP Committee's amending of the Code
3.	MONITORING OF ADS	SOME to the extent that all monitoring cases are reported to the ASA Council who can supervise this activity
4.	FINANCIAL INDEPENDENCE	SIGNIFICANT to the extent that the financing of the ASA is independent of direct contributions by the industry
5.	CONSUMER-COMPLAINT HANDLING	
	a. Credibility	SIGNIFICANT contributory factor
	b. Expertise	YES in the matter of applying specific provisions of the Code with the assistance of the Secretariat, and in resolving issues of taste and decency
	c. Objectivity	YES within the constraint of a body holding essentially positive views toward advertising
	d. Speed	YES compared to a more dissensual body but slower than if done exclusively by the Secretariat
	e. Consensus	YES but at the expense of not challenging broad standards of taste, decency and fairness
	f. Satisfaction of Complainants and Industry	YES as far as can be told
6.	ADJUDICATION OF VIOLATIONS	YES as far as can be told

(*) Only the direct impact is considered here. It is obvious that consumer complaints feed *indirectly* into Code revision and enhanced monitoring activities.

such power over traders' rights to promote their goods. As it is, the system works well (Consumers' Association 1981, pp. 3–4).[12]

Did the significant participation of outsiders in ASA activities contribute to this positive assessment? Table 13.1 summarizes their contributions and suggests that, indeed, they were positive although various qualifications are necessary.

1. Credibility: It is really the total independence of the system—an independent chairman, an automatically financed system, and a two-third majority of independents on the ASA Council—rather than the latter alone that have made

the ASA's control of advertising behavior credible. The government's close watching, soon to be analyzed, definitely contributed to this perception. An ASA Council totally made up of outsiders (as in Italy) could well have further enhanced credibility but not necessarily effectiveness and fairness (as will be argued next). In any case, informed observers and analysts of the British system have expressed satisfaction with the present system's independence. Thus, an Office of Fair Trading study concluded that: "By creating and financing the Advertising Standards Authority, the advertising industry has recognized the need to open up its system of self-control to independent scrutiny and guidance, so that the discipline applied reflects not only what the industry itself feels to be necessary for its own good but also what an independent body (the ASA Council) considers to be current public opinion and the public interest (DGFT 1978, pp. 27–28)."[13]

Similarly, a working party appointed in 1978 by the Labour government's Secretary of State for Prices and Consumer Protection,[14] concluded that:

It is present [ASA] policy to ensure that the proportion of independent to industry members remains at the maximum permissible level of 2:1. The preponderance of independent members on the Council as a whole, the mode of appointment of both ordinary Council Members and Chairman, the separation of the funding body (ASBOF) from both the Advertising Association and ASA (which therefore is not involved in soliciting contributions or chasing up reluctant contributors), together with the nature of the levy itself are, in total, designed to ensure that the supervisory element in the control arrangements is isolated from any possibility of pressure from the advertising business to support its interests against those of the general public (Department of Trade 1980, p. 4).

Still, criticism has been expressed that the lack of consultation by the CAP Committee with outside consumer interests, when formulating draft revisions of the Code, can impede it "from being fully in tune with society's requirements (Driver and Foxall 1984, pp. 8–9)." The ASA answers that the present approach is needed to ensure that the Code be perceived as "user-friendly" by the industry whose moral and practical support is essential for the working of self-regulation.

Besides, some criticism has been expressed about the recent appointment of new independent members by the chairman of the ASA Council—a situation precipitated by the departure of several of them. As was mentioned before, he does not have to consult with outside constituencies when making such appointments, although "some strengthening of the ASA Council" was recommended by the government in 1978 and 1980 (Department of Trade 1980, pp. 6 and 18). At worst, critics stress that several recent appointees are "distinguished elitist eccentrics lacking obvious qualifications and out of touch with advertising issues." They fear that such appointments will strengthen the hand of the chairman and of the ASA Secretariat for lack of members likely to argue strongly against their recommendations—a situation that could ultimately hurt the ASA's credibility but could not be corroborated in this study.

2. Expertise: The mixture of industry and independent members on the ASA Council has provided a broader perspective in the adjudication of difficult "hard"

and "soft" cases in the light of prevailing economic and social standards. The choice of middle-of-the-road outsiders interacting in a consensual manner with industry representatives has probably imparted a rather conservative and prudent tone to the interpretation of such standards. The Italian experience with a complaint-handling Jury composed entirely of outsiders suggests that more radical decisions are made when such a structure is used. However, the British seem content with their more temperate approach; and it remains to be proven that the Italian decisions have achieved an even better balance of the private and public interests—probably an insuperable research task. Still, the question raised about the quality of new independent members is troublesome in this respect.

3. *Speed*: The mixture of insiders and outsiders expected to decide in a consensual manner tends to slow down the adjudication process. Clearly, the French system, where all decisions are made by the Secretariat, is faster than the British one, where benevolent outsiders have to be gathered at their convenience. However, the ASA staff has accelerated its preliminary contacting of incriminated advertisers and its analysis of the substantiation the latter must provide (see below). In fact, many complaints refer to advertisements that have already ceased to appear so that "speed" is not essential in their case. Where an ongoing campaign is involved, however, a "fast-stream" procedure is used. Fewer cases could be referred to the ASA Council, as is done in countries where the staff makes most decisions, but only at the cost of reducing independent control of the system—something the British do not appear willing to abandon. In other words, there is a tradeoff between credibility and speed, which the British have resolved to their own satisfaction, although the average two months spent on handling valid complaints remains uncomfortably high for some critics.

4. *Stakeholder Satisfaction*: Various references have already been made to the votes of confidence cast by government, the general public and consumerists. The capstone Advertising Association, which launched the ASA and has kept a watchful eye on its performance, is also satisfied (see its annual reports).[15] Various public-opinion surveys have been conducted by the ASA, but they have focused on public awareness and overall evaluation rather than on direct satisfaction (ASA Case Report 101, 1983). Short of new studies bearing on this issue (for example, complainants could be surveyed in terms of their satisfaction with the disposition of their complaints), it is impossible to reach any definite conclusion about this matter. One could add that the presence of outsiders minimizes the risk of the ASA acting as a self-serving "cartel"—a criticism often addressed to industry self-regulatory systems. Since the ASA serves all industries in a "vertical" manner, there is much less danger that it would not take a broader view of the general interest.

The issue of taste and decency remains a difficult one for the CAP Committee and ASA Council. Some of the most troublesome complaints concern matters in which the capacity of an advertisement to offend is central. The ASA refuses to act as a censor in matters of taste and opinion, or to judge whether what is advertised is worth buying and consuming, nor does it offer itself as a basis for arbitration between conflicting ideologies, as in political advertising (BCAP 1985, p. 9). Lawson has commented about ASA-Council decisions bearing on such matters:

Complaints arising from sexism are not upheld by the ASA in general although equally few are condoned by complete acquittal. The majority of cases in this category are in the "no-decision" group, in which the ASA judges that there has been no breach of the code technically but warns advertisers that the copy may be regarded as being in poor taste or as irrelevant, and may ask them to refrain from further use of such techniques (Lawson 1985, p. 287; similar comments are made by Lawson about safety complaints).

The presence of independent outsiders on the ASA Council has provided some guarantee that the public interest will be seriously considered in such matters. However, the lack of representativeness of these "independents," the absence of major direct inputs from outside constituencies when the Code is revised and the principled refusal to distinguish between "good" and "bad" products suggest that outside participation in the British manner will not be sufficient to cope with such issues, and that regulatory solutions will predominate in the resolution of some of them (e.g., cigarette advertising).

The Government as Outside Partner

Outside participation on the ASA Council was not developed in a vacuum. Indeed, this and other improvements of the ASA system were often prompted by the British government, and have been closely monitored by it.

Government Pressures

It has already been mentioned that the British Advertising Code of Practice and the ASA system were set up in 1961–1962 in response to strong government and consumerist criticisms and pressures—essentially, the threat of further regulation even though the industry's genuine interest in "good advertising behavior" cannot be gainsaid. Their improvement ever since has largely been in response to further government initiatives—particularly from the Department of Trade and Industry and the Office of Fair Trading.

Between 1962 and 1974, the ASA and the Code of Advertising Practice Committee (which handles competitor complaints) had been relatively inactive, responding only to unsolicited complaints. At that point, the Secretary of State for Prices and Consumer Protection and the Director General of Fair Trading threatened statutory controls on the industry if the system were not made more effective (Cranston 1984, p. 148; Jones and Pickering 1985, pp. 26ff). In response, the Code was revised and expanded in 1974 at the high point of consumer-protection legislation; the independence of the system was progressively enhanced through separate financing[16] and the appointment of a majority of independent members on the ASA Council; and greater publicity of the Code, of the ASA's complaint mechanism and of its decisions (with names of the offending advertisers being given) was progressively introduced. Furthermore, the 1978 OFT investigation of the self-regulatory system resulted in: (1) the adoption of a better sampling method for ASA monitoring, and (2) the ASA reducing to ten days the time allowed advertisers to provide evidence of presubstantiation of claims made. (The OFT also considered further sanctions[17] in the forms of corrective advertising and fines, but they were deemed to be relatively ineffective.) In a related vein, publicizing the decisions of the Code of Advertising Practice Committee (which handles competitor complaints) was also initiated in 1980 at the instigation of the Office of Fair Trading.[18]

All of these initiatives resulted from government pressures, although they have been endorsed and adopted by the industry itself. *Clearly, major transformation of the British ASR system has resulted from strong and repeated government criticisms and pressures for reform.*

British Political Culture

Why did the government intervene so forcefully and successfully? Beer (1965), in his study of the role of parties and pressure groups in British politics, stressed "the widespread acceptance of functional representation in British political culture (p. 329)." That is, there is general agreement that: (1) the British government will be advised, helped and criticized by the specialist knowledge of interested parties, instead of acting alone, and (2) it must create and maintain confidence in the relevant industry's good faith (pp. 322 and 324). In this context, Beer quotes Harry Eckstein about "the persistent corporatism of British political culture (p. 330)." Similarly, Shonfield (1965) referred to the instinctive British objection to State overinvolvement ("positive government") in industry's affairs, notwithstanding its vast accretion of power to influence private business decisions (pp. 110 and 162).

In other words, the British government prefers, whenever possible, to rely on representative associations and "private governments" to express and enforce appropriate behavior rather than to regulate directly. This preference translates itself in "leaning" procedures designed to foster the development of codes of practice. For that matter, the Fair Trading Act 1973 (Section 124.3) imposes a duty on the Director General of Fair Trading to encourage trade associations to prepare codes of practice for guidance in safeguarding and promoting the interests of consumers. When an industry, such as advertising, is willing to "bend" in response, the British government is quite happy to rely on it for standards development and enforcement without, however, relinquishing its control of such "voluntary" action or its mandate to recommend new regulations whenever statutory standards are more appropriate. (There are already some eighty laws applying in one way or another to advertising, and more are forthcoming).

Vogel (1983, p. 94; and 1986), in his comparative study of UK and US environmental controls, commented on "the preference of [UK] regulatory officials for securing compliance through persuasion and negotiation." He went on to say:

Crucial to the effectiveness of the British regulatory system is the mutual respect that exists between industrialists and regulatory officials (p. 95). . . . If one compares the British and American approaches to insurance regulation, equal employment, banking regulation, consumer protection, occupational health and safety, or securities regulation, a clear pattern emerges: In each case Americans rely heavily on formal rules, often enforced in the face of strong opposition from the institutions affected by them, while the British continue to rely on flexible standards and voluntary compliance—including, in many cases, self-regulation (Vogel 1983, p. 101).

Vogel ascribes this difference in control styles to three elements, "none of which exists in the United States to the extent each does in Britain: a highly respected civil service, a business community that places a high value on acting 'responsibly,' and a public that is not unduly suspicious of business-government cooperation (Vogel 1983, pp. 101–102)." Similarly, Miracle and Nevett have commented, in the context of advertising self-regulation, that:

In the United Kingdom, there was little feeling that advertising was not fit to control itself, only that it was not doing the job as well as it might. In a sense there is something typically British about such a compromise which lets each side claim what it will. Politicians can claim either to have acted to curb advertising, or to have preserved the freedom of business from government interference, depending on their political allegiance, while the advertising industry can claim that it has taken voluntary action to curb its own excesses, conveniently overlooking the fact that it did so under threat. Honor is thus satisfied on all sides (Miracle and Nevett 1987, pp. 52–53).

Governmental Defense of the ASA

The parliamentary debates in London as well as the 1974–1984 negotiations in Brussels regarding the proposed European Community (EEC) directive on misleading (and unfair) advertising, have cast the British government as a firm defender of the advertising self-regulatory system (Jones and Pickering 1985, pp. 59–64).

Earlier drafts of this directive had required comprehensive legal controls to be readily enforced through administrative authorities and/or the courts. The UK government was particularly concerned that automatic access to the courts by complainants would undermine the ASA's work, while the House of Lords concluded in 1978 that the self-regulatory system should be supported as being in the best interest of the country. The Office of Fair Trading concurred that a rigid code of laws was not appropriate:

Government, the advertising industry and consumer groups are united in the view that the self-regulatory system could not survive a blanket imposition of legal control over the content of advertisements. The result would be to lose the benefit of a system which can reflect the spirit rather than the letter, which can be readily updated, and which commands a high degree of commitment from the advertising industry (OFT 1983, p. 356).

Earlier, the House of Lords Select Committee had observed that: "[If] advertisers could not be guaranteed that an adjudication from the ASA offered certainty that their advertisement was in conformity with accepted standards . . . the advertising business might have little incentive to continue to fund the self-regulatory system (House of Lords 1978, Paragraph 24)." Actually, the terms of reference ultimately adopted by the working party appointed by the government to discuss the EEC draft Directive in 1979 were clearly biased in favor of the ASA system: "To consider whether, and if so to what extent, the existing self-regulatory system of advertising control in the United Kingdom requires reinforcement (Driver and Foxall 1984, pp. 12–13)."

Following intense British and German pressure, the final 1984 EEC Directive on Misleading Advertising came to allow individuals, firms and certain associations with a legitimate interest to bring complaints before a court or an "administrative authority." When a complaint is upheld, this administrative authority must be able to: (1) order the cessation of, or institute legal proceedings for the cessation of, the misleading advertisement, and (2) order or institute legal proceedings for the prohibition of misleading advertisements not yet published but whose publication is imminent (Article 4.2). Clearly, the ASA would not be able to act in such a law-enforcement manner unless it were to be transformed into a corporatist organization—something that neither the advertising industry nor the government wanted at all (Thomas 1984, p. 201). Fortunately, the 1984 EEC directive allows the courts or administrative authorities to require prior recourse to "other established means of dealing with complaints" (Article 4.1); and Article 5 makes it clear that such "established means" may include self-regulatory bodies—something the British government insisted on.

Since the EEC Directive had to be implemented by early 1987, the British government made various studies and proposals that concluded that: (1) the ASA should provide the first line of redress for most nonbroadcast advertising,[19] and (2) the Director General of Fair Trading only needed "long-stop" and "back-up" power to "strengthen rather than diminish the authority of the self-regulatory system." This review gave the government another opportunity to defend and promote advertising self-regulation:

As a complement to statutory controls, self-regulation offers advantages in terms of efficacy, flexibility and economy on which an entirely officially regulated system would be most unlikely to improve. It is sometimes suggested that self-regulation tends to give the benefit of the doubt to those whose activities are being scrutinized. The record of the ASA suggests that this is not the case in the field of advertising control. The Authority's constitution and system of financing means that it is remoter from industry influence than, for example, a trade association enforcing a Code of Practice upon its members.[20] And indeed, operating on a non-statutory basis, it has the ability to maintain more exacting standards than those which might in practice often be possible for an official body mindful of statutory limitations (Department of Trade and Industry 1985, p. 2).

Consequently, there was no need for major statutory innovations—only that the Director General of Fair Trading be empowered to obtain court orders to prevent the publication of ads likely to deceive or mislead, as a reinforcement to the self-regulatory system of control rather than as a substitute for it, or an undermining factor of it (Department of Trade and Industry 1985, p. 1):

In the short term, additional procedures, provided they are sensibly integrated with the present ones, will discourage those who might otherwise be inclined to disregard ASA rulings. This could be particularly valuable in areas where the ASA currently find it more difficult to enforce their rulings, e.g., in relation to some forms of direct advertising. In the longer run, a back-up system can be seen as an incentive to the self-regulatory system to maintain its current high standards (Department of Trade and Industry 1985, p. 2).

Consequently, the Control of Misleading Advertisements Regulations 1987 gives the Director General of Fair Trading discretion to refer complaints to such "established means" as the ASA and local authorities, and to prevent plaintiffs from disregarding such referrals:

Before he considers a complaint, the Director of Fair Trading may require the person making the complaint to satisfy him that appropriate means of dealing with the complaint have been tried. (Such means might include complaining to a local authority trading standards department or to a self-regulatory body, such as the Advertising Standards Authority. It is, however, for the Director to determine what means he considers appropriate in any particular case.) In dealing with the complaints, the Director is required to bear in mind all the interests involved, including, in particular, the public interest, and the desirability of encouraging the control, by self-regulatory bodies, of advertisements (Explanatory Note to The Control of Misleading Advertisements Regulations 1987, draft version, 27 February 1987).

These developments reveal a strong governmental endorsement of the ASA but also gray zones of competence and discretion, which will need to be defined on the bases of negotiation and experience. The Advertising Association and the ASA have maintained extensive contacts with the Office of Fair Trading to argue that the prominence of the ASA be maintained and explicitly acknowledged, and that the discretionary powers of the OFT be spelled out as much as possible. However, a less sympathetic government could readily assume a greater first-line-of-enforcement role, provided greater resources were given to the Office of Fair Trading and to local authorities.

Meanwhile, the ASA is faced with more work since: (1) advertisers and agencies may come to seek greater prepublication advice,[21] and (2) the EEC Directive requires that adequate explanation be given to complainants about decisions (Article 4.3)—something the ASA already does, but greater care will probably have to be exercised in this matter. Its future responsibilities regarding financial advertising will change when the Financial Services Act 1986 becomes fully operative. The Securities and Investment Board (SIB) will make rules "as to the form and content of advertisements in respect of investment business." While these rules only apply to investment-business advertising (securities, market investment, futures, unit trusts and long-term life assurance), the ASA and the CAP Committee will continue to regulate all other financial advertisements, and they expect to work closely with the SIB along lines that are still under discussion.

A Duty to Trade Fairly?

In the background of this discussion of the EEC Directive lurk new proposals for consumer-protection legislation. On the one hand, there is concern about the cost-effectiveness of such legislation and the availability of resources to enforce it; on the other, codes of practice formally approved by the Office of Fair Trading are now more difficult to negotiate, since trade associations no longer perceive legislation as a realistic threat under the Conservative government if no code of practice is concluded.[22]

Consequently, it has been proposed that a requirement of "a general statutory duty to trade fairly" be imposed, where codes of practice (presumably including the BCAP) would provide the details for how the courts should interpret this general duty, which would be binding on all traders, irrespective of membership in a trade association (Borrie 1984; Office of Fair Trading 1986). In the case of advertising, it would mean a new statutory duty not to publish an advertisement likely to deceive or mislead[23] with regard to any material fact, with the Director General of Fair Trading having power to seek from the courts an order to prevent publication of an advertisement that appeared to breach that duty (this power is similar to that involved in the implementation of the 1984 EEC Directive).

Such a requirement would assist the ASA, which has a presubstantiation requirement, but has frequently found that advertisers cannot substantiate their factual claims, or do not do it promptly enough.[24] Since a general duty is more likely to be enforced by civil rather than criminal means, compliance with a code such as the BCAP could therefore be taken as evidence that a company is trading fairly (Jones and Pickering 1985, p. 59).

However, the Advertising Association has pointed out the dangers "which inevitably arise when codes of conduct become too closely linked with legislation (Advertising Association, *Annual Report and Accounts* 1984, p. 10)." That is, business finds it difficult to revise its voluntary codes when government depends on their specific contents for implementing its competition and consumer-protection policies. Besides, the Code of Advertising Practice could probably not be amended without consulting the Office of Fair Trading and even consumer organizations—something currently unacceptable to the industry (Advertising

Association, *Director General's Newsletter* January 1985, p. 3), which had previously declined to make the British Code of Advertising Practice one of those supervised by the Office of Fair Trading.

Business-Government Relations

These recent developments have been marked by intensive contacts between the advertising industry (mainly the capstone Advertising Association) and the government (mainly, the Department of Trade and Industry and the Office of Fair Trading, but also Members of Parliament, both in power and in the Opposition). For example, each new minister of trade and industry is briefed about advertising self-regulation, and invited to tour ASA facilities. These frequent communications, held in a spirit of good-faith cooperation, reflect the "British political culture" mentioned above. Besides, regulatory initiatives likely to minimize the ASA's role are immediately challenged, as with the recent City [London] Takeover Panel's ban on the contentious advertising of acquisitions, and with the Securities and Investments Board, which will constitute a separate administrative authority responsible (among others) for the control of investment advertising.

The advertising industry not only responds to such developments but also anticipates them, as with the mid–1986 appointment of a former permanent secretary of the department of trade to chair an Advertising Association's inquiry into the operation of the British advertising-control system—both regulatory and self-regulatory. This appointment reveals not only the esteem placed by business on the Civil Service, but also the ready availability of people considered to be independent of business, yet willing to assist it in a nonideological manner. It also illustrates the use of "Establishment" types to confirm the status quo, as one critic put it.

Such business-government relations were, of course, less cordial when the Labour Party was in power—for example, in the 1970s when strong pressures and regulatory threats were exerted on the self-regulatory system. More recently, the Labour Party's platform at the time of the 1983 national elections stated that: "We are not satisfied that voluntary codes of practice are sufficiently strong or sufficiently widely observed. We, therefore, intend to reform the law to give statutory backing to codes of practice which have been agreed with the Director General of Fair Trading. There will need to be powers to order advertisements to be substantiated, withdrawn or corrected with equal prominence (Consumers and the General Election 1983, p. 13)." Similarly, the Labour Party's *Charter for Consumers* concluded that: "The existing Code of Practice, which is run by a body set up by industry itself, has proved inadequate. Advertisements that break the law still appear. We believe we cannot rely on self-regulation, and propose a number of new measures [e.g., a statutory code of advertising practice, powers to make advertisers substantiate their claims, and powers to order corrective advertising] (Labour Party, Labour's Charter for Consumers 1986, p. 23).''

The Advertising Association (AA) keeps discussing such antagonistic programs with the Labour Party's shadow minister for consumer affairs as well as with that party's leadership in the hope that they will come to see the merits of the present self-regulatory system. The AA appears to be currently more concerned about the Opposition parties than with the consumer lobby, which ''is important but they do not hold strong reservations about advertising and so have a lower priority with us (Advertising Association, *Director General's Newsletter*, January 1985, p. 1).'' It remains that any return to power by the Opposition parties is likely to witness stronger consumer-protection initiatives.

Advertising Self-Regulation as Corporatism?

Allusion has already been made to ''the persistent corporatism in British political culture.'' Unfortunately, corporatism is an elusive concept that assumes various ideological and concrete guises in different countries and industries so that a definitive conclusion cannot be reached.

That British advertising self-regulation represents a ''private government'' that complements ''Market'' and ''State'' control mechanisms (Streeck and Schmitter 1985) is not in doubt. However, it goes well beyond ''parallel'' action by the ASA and the authorities, where each system would operate autonomously and free of mutual interaction and even interference. Much closer interaction and intermingling are revealed by the following elements.

1. The British government pressured the ASA to strengthen itself through the inclusion of more ''independents,'' the imposition of an automatic levy on most nonbroadcast advertising expenditures, and other measures.
2. The government is consulted, among others, when the chairman of the ASA Council is appointed.
3. The authorities have tried to keep the ASA as the central advertising self-regulatory system (outside of broadcasting) when complementary systems have been urged for such sectors as mail-order and securities/investments.
4. The government defended and promoted the ASA as an intrinsic part of the British advertising-control system when the EEC proposed a purely regulatory approach for the handling of misleading advertisements.
5. The ''British solution'' for implementing the EEC Directive on Misleading Advertising recognizes the ASA as an ''established means of dealing with complaints,'' with the Office of Fair Trading backing up the ASA.
6. By accepting the imposition of an automatic levy by the ASA on nonbroadcast advertising expenditures, which was not challenged as a restraint of trade, the government implicitly granted it taxing authority—surely a delegation of the ''monopoly of coercion'' associated with the State. This has made practically all display advertisers subject to the ASA's reach.
7. The ongoing discussion of ''a statutory duty to trade fairly,'' which would give codes of practice the status of norms enforceable in the courts, reveals a tendency on the

part of the British authorities to transform such "voluntary" norms into "statutory" ones. (The ASA has resisted such a development for that very reason.)

Do these arrangements add up to a "corporatist scheme?" According to van Waarden (1985, p. 197), they do: "Whenever such forms of self-regulation involve the State to a greater or lesser extent, one can speak of corporatist arrangements where the private and public spheres are interwoven. This may be the result either of private assistance in formulating and implementing public policy, or of state assistance in the formulation and implementation of private regulation."

However, what kind of "corporatist arrangement" is present in the case of the ASA? van Waarden acknowledges that such a mix of private and public responsibility is rather "opaque" in Western democracies, and stops far short of a representational monopoly (van Waarden 1985, p. 213) as in true corporatism (see Chapter 1 for a discussion of that concept). The pure corporatist label may be appropriate for the statutorily based Independent Broadcasting Authority, which controls television and radio commercials, and for the forthcoming Securities and Investments Board, but not for the ASA, which represents a voluntary industry initiative. While the associations that back up the British Code of Advertising Practice require adherence to this Code as a condition for membership, they cannot require membership, so that adhesion to the British advertising self-regulatory system remains voluntary—except that the automatic levy has to be paid by practically all advertisers in the nonbroadcast media.[25] This coercive levy allows one to label the ASA systems as corporatist in the light of Streeck and Schmitter's observation that: "Where the state strictly upholds the right of individuals not to be organized and not to be subject to any coercion other than that exercised by the state itself, a corporative-associative order cannot exist (Streeck and Schmitter 1985, p. 25)." Besides, the links between the ASA and the government are strong and constant, and the advertising self-regulatory system is definitely an instrument of British public policy in the matter of advertising control.

This conclusion, however, can be challenged on the ground that various authorities apply some eighty statutes, orders and regulations so that the ASA is far from having any monopoly in the development and application of advertising controls, and ASA sanctions are not legally binding. For that matter, the British government has never conceived of the ASA as exercising a monopoly over advertising control. Its official view is that it is a matter of complementation— what the Director General of Fair Trading has labeled as "horses for courses":

Studies by ourselves and others over the years have suggested that, in the field of advertising, some sort of mixture is needed. We have statutory legal controis through, for example, the Trade Descriptions Act and the work of the Independent Broadcasting Authority. But *complementary to these controls*, the self-regulatory system operated by the Advertising Standards Authority (ASA) is generally accepted to be both efficient and effective (Borrie 1982, p. 11; emphasis added).[26]

One could argue that the automatic levy on practically all display advertising expenditures is not a "tax" but a charge assented to on behalf of their members by those organizations that have agreed to uphold and enforce the British Code of Advertising Practice. For that matter, a small advertiser who does not use an agency and places his ads in publications not in membership of one of the publishers' associations would avoid paying it. More important, the advertising industry does not view the surcharge as a form of government coercion but rather as a means of escaping from it, since the levy finances an alternative to statutory control.

Consequently, the British system of advertising control partakes more of the "quasicorporatist" and "consensual-corporatist" types than of the "pure" mode (cf. Wilson and Butler 1985). One could add, in the light of this book's central focus on outside participation, that the inclusion of a majority of nonindustry members on the ASA Council reveals that this body is not purely "corporatist" since corporatism normally involves only "insiders."

Conclusions

Altogether, outside "independent" representation on the ASA Council has contributed to the effectiveness and acceptance of the ASA system. Of course, it is impossible to disentangle the contribution of outside participation from other factors that have also assisted such a favorable perception: greater publicity given to the ASA complaint system, and enhanced invitation of people to complain;[27] relative speed and "costlessness" of the system as far as complainants are concerned; increased strictness of the Code and of ASA monitoring activities, and studies of sensitive topics such as advertising to children—all well-publicized endeavors. Still, one can reasonably conclude that the participation of outsiders in advertising self-regulation can be made to work and contribute to the system "being fair and seen to be fair"—at least in the British context.

The British self-regulatory system has become highly effective even though it would be unreasonable to expect that full compliance with the Code could ever be obtained. For that matter, statutory control cannot achieve perfection either, as the Working Party concluded: "We do not think that it is realistic to aim for perfection and indeed, given the absence of universal prevetting [preclearance], which we accept as being impracticable, no system of control can achieve it" (Department of Trade 1980; see also Cranston 1984, p. 47; and Jones and Pickering 1985, pp. 68–70). Besides, a system based solely on regulation could reduce commitment on the part of practitioners, since only the "letter" rather than the "spirit" of the law would be respected. In all probability, a pure statutory system would also be much more costly to enforce (see the chapter on Canada for support of this point). The Clucas Committee report (Advertising Association 1987) has recently corroborated these positive evaluations of the ASA-CAP system.

The active involvement of the British government as prodder, supervisor, defender and "back-up and long-stop" complement to the ASA system reveals that outside participation is not limited to the formal inclusion of independents in its structure. Instead, a concerned and imaginative government, acting as a "silent partner," can effectively integrate advertising self-regulation into the overall advertising-control system, that modern societies need and want.

The British system works very well but its privileged position is being threatened by the proliferation of new media (teletext, videotape advertising, cable television, cross-border satellite broadcasting, etc.),[28] the fast growth of direct-mail advertising and of the international editions of newspapers and magazines that bring in advertisements from abroad, the recent initiation of advertising by various professions (lawyers, accountants, opticians, etc.), the increase in foreign-language ads in UK publications aimed at sizable foreign minorities in the country, the intractable problem of deceptive personal ads and the multiplication of new codes and/or statutory bodies related to advertising control (e.g., for direct-mail and securities/investments).

Also, consumers may soon be confused as to where to complain about different types of advertisements: broadcast vs. cable vs. display advertising, investment vs. other financial advertisements, certain forms of direct-mail and pharmaceutical advertising, etc. Consequently, there is the fear that: "Any fragmentation of the system is bound to lead to some loss of overall effectiveness and thus to invite intervention by a new government which might be less supportive of self-regulation (Advertising Association, *Director General's Newsletter*, June 1986, p. 1)."[29]

Whether the ultimate outcome will be further incorporation of the ASA system within the quasicorporatist British scheme of advertising control, or greater "positive government"—particularly if the Opposition parties return to power— will partly depend on whether the ASA system can resolve these problems in the near future. Its constant improvement over the past twenty-five years suggests that it will, although it may become increasingly difficult to retain its "user-friendly" character as its responsibilities expand.

NOTES

1. One could also argue that the large and increasing number of complaints lodged with the ASA amounts to a form of outside participation, but this line of reasoning will not be pursued here (see Jones and Pickering [1985] and the ASA Annual Reports for discussions of this issue).

2. Separate advertising codes are still maintained and administered for over-the-counter medicines and the mail-order publishing business, but they expressly make conformity with the BCAP one of their own rules; and their respective associations are members of the Code of Advertising Practice (CAP) Committee (BCAP 1985, pp. 9–10). The broadcast media have their own codes (see below), which are not applied by the ASA. Nor does the ASA deal with media operating from the United Kingdom but aimed at foreign audiences, with pharmaceutical advertising, with the contents of mail catalogs (handled by the Mail Order Traders' Association of Great Britain), and with

religious and political advertising. However, the ASA has a separate British Code of Sales Promotion Practice, which it also administers; while the Cigarette Code is administered through the CAP Committee, who carry out the mandatory preclearance of all cigarette ads. (See Thomson [1983] as well as BCAP [1985] for further details.)

3. For details about ASA monitoring activities, see ASA Case Reports 54, 69, 129 and 144 as well as the ASA annual reports. The prescreening (prevetting) of advertisements for cigarettes as well as the general prepublication advising of advertisers, agencies and media is not an ASA function, but is handled by the CAP Committee for nonbroadcast advertisements and by the Copy Clearance Secretariat for radio and television commercials. However, one independent member of the ASA Council sits on each CAP Copy (Advisory) Panel.

4. Consumer complaints came in unsolicited until 1974. Since then, the ASA has conducted regular campaigns designed to publicize the British self-regulatory system and to invite the public (including consumer associations) to address their complaints to the ASA. Decisions about competitor complaints are now publicized, as has been the case with consumer complaints since 1972, after remaining unpublicized until 1980. The dual approach—CAP Committee and ASA Council—about complaint handling is justified by the experienced feeling that competitors are better able to spot abuses and to resolve them under the judgment of their peers than in the case of consumer complaints—but also by the desire "not to wash dirty linen in public."

5. The National Consumer Council is financed by the secretary of state for consumer affairs who appoints its twenty-five members. Its role is to "speak up" for consumer interests, although it need not be consulted by the government.

6. Outside members have also included people associated with the British Standards Institution, the National Federation of Women's Institutes, the Boy Scouts movement, the Electricity Consumers' Council, the Methodist Church, secondary education and the trade unions as well as retired civil servants, among others.

7. Questions arising at any meeting of the Council are decided by a majority of the votes, with the chairman casting the deciding vote in the case of a tie-up. In practice, issues are scarcely ever decided by vote, the Council's aim being to attain consensus.

8. There are usually another 1,000 competitor complaints, but they are handled by the CAP Committee. Some 2,500 consumer complaints require investigation, with over half of them being upheld.

9. Copy Panels are used to advise the Secretariat. Sometimes, they are asked to give a view on material submitted for prepublication advice, sometimes to adjudicate on a finely balanced trade (CAP) complaint. However, the decision to involve them rests with the Secretariat or the parties involved in certain instances, so that the Copy panels are not a necessary part of the chain, but an optional extra link. Besides, the ASA Secretariat—which serves both the ASA and the CAP Committee under a common director general—frequently queries outside experts in complex cases and always where the matter is beyond its technical competence.

10. A related problem concerns the professional qualifications of ASA Secretariat personnel. There have been recent programs to second them to advertisers, agencies and media so that they may better understand the functioning of advertising and avoid unnecessary challenges to advertisers.

11. For further discussions of the matter of advertising misleadingness, see NCC 1977, pp. 12 ff and the ASA 1974–1975 Annual Report (pp. 16–25). As Jones and Pickering (1985, p. 37) point out, the number and proportion of complaints upheld by the ASA

have increased in recent years, but these increases may simply indicate an improvement in the quality of complaints, following greater publicity of the Code's contents by the ASA.

12. Reservations still expressed by the Consumers' Association and the National Consumer Council can be found in House of Lords (1978). While the British system of advertising self-regulation works better than in other industries, various criticisms are still expressed (cf. Cranston [1984, pp. 50–52]; Jones and Pickering [1985, pp. 67–70]; Murdock and Janus [1985, pp. 52–53]; and UNESCO [1985, pp. 52–53]). For a recent and rather positive assessment, see: "Legal, Decent, Honest and Truthful?" *Which?* (July 1986, pp. 309–312), a publication of the Consumers' Association.

13. This independent study was designed and supervised by a Working Party including representatives of the Advertising Association, the Consumers' Association (a private organization) and the Office of Fair Trading. Also involved were the National Federation of Consumer Groups, the National Consumer Council and various local-government bodies.

14. The office of the Secretary of State for Prices and Consumer Protection was eliminated when the Conservatives came back to power in 1979, and its tasks shifted to the Department of Trade and Industry's Secretary of State for Consumer Affairs.

15. However, on 1 August 1986, the Advertising Association announced the appointment of Sir Kenneth Clucas, a former Permanent Secretary of the Department of Trade, to chair its "inquiry into the operation of the advertising control system in the UK." This project was prompted by the recent proliferation of voluntary and statutory controls (see below) so that its scope is not limited to the ASA.

16. It has been suggested that the 1974 automatic levy system was also a response by the industry to proposals from the Labour government to set up a regulatory body to be financed by disallowing as a business expense 50 percent of advertising expenditures—the equivalent of a 16 percent tax on advertising. Clearly, one-tenth of one percent was a much better deal.

17. Present sanctions applied by the ASA include: (1) the negative publicity provided by the publishing of ASA decisions, (2) recommended denial of space in member media to recalcitrant advertisers; (3) the occasional expelling from membership in sponsoring organizations, and (4) rare denunciations to the authorities.

18. Additionally, the Post Office established in 1983 the Direct Mail Services Standards Board to raise the overall quality and image of direct mail as a form of advertising. To qualify, a direct-mail agency must satisfy this Board that it complies with the codes of advertising and sales promotion administered by the ASA, and that it provides services only to clients who subscribe to these codes—in return, a rebate is given to "good" direct-mail advertisers (ASA Case Report 118; Jones and Pickering 1985, p. 29). The Proprietary Association of Great Britain (for over-the-counter medicines), the Videotext Industry Association and the twenty industry codes of practice supervised by the Office of Fair Trading have similar requirements.

19. In the cases of television, radio and cable, the existing statutory bodies (e.g., the IBA and the Cable Authority) will constitute the "administrative authorities" envisaged by the EEC Directive. The investment and securities industry will have its own statutory body, possibly operating in conjunction with the ASA.

20. The stress on the ASA's independence reflects the Directive's requirement that administrative authorities and established means "be composed so as not to cast doubt on their impartiality (Article 4.3 of 1984 EEC Directive):"

21. However, the CAP Committee cannot give legal advice or interpret the law either to advertisers or lawyers because it is up to solicitors and the courts to do so. For references to the relations of the British Code of Advertising Practice to the law, see BCAP 1985, p. 11 and ASA Case Reports 66, 105 and 136.

22. The existing twenty codes of practice (not including the BCAP) were negotiated in the 1973–1979 period (cf. Jones and Pickering [1985]; Pickering and Cousins [1982]; OFT [1986]; and Thomas [1984]).

23. There is no single British statute that imposes a general obligation on advertisers to compete fairly and not to mislead (Lawson 1986; Thomson 1983, p. 327).

24. The Code requires that: "Before offering an advertisement for publication, the advertiser should have in his hands all documentary and other evidence necessary to demonstrate the advertisement's conformity with the Code. This material, together, when necessary, with a statement outlining its relevance, should be made available without delay if requested by either the Advertising Standards Authority or the Code of Advertising Practice Committee (BCAP, 1985, Article 1.2)." However, ASA Case Report 133 (14 May 1986) states that: "In a recent Case Report, no fewer than 39 complaints were about claim substantiation and of these, no less than 29 were upheld." Besides, over 30 percent of advertisers failed to reply immediately to ASA requests for claim substantiation. The 1985–1986 ASA Annual Report lists lack of substantiation as the second largest offense after misleading advertising (ASA, Annual Report 1985–1986, p. 24).

25. It is well to point out again that the BCAP Code is not one of the twenty codes of practice approved by the Office of Fair Trading whose approval is conditional on member firms of an association undertaking to abide by the provisions of its code. As Mitchell observes: "It is not open to a member firm to accept some provisions and not others. This . . . distinguishes a code of practice as such from the many recommendations or guidelines which trade associations produce (Mitchell 1978, p. 147)."

26. The Director General of the ASA has also referred to such complementariness (Thomson 1983, pp. 335 and 337).

27. The major theme of the 1980 ASA campaign was: "If an advertisement is wrong, we're here to put it right." Consequently, the number of consumer complaints doubled from 1979 to 1980, and their quality improved in terms of pertinence.

28. The ASA already covers the press, magazines, posters, aerial advertising, cinema and videocassette commercials, direct mail, viewdata services and advertising at exhibitions. Some 50 percent of all direct-mail advertisements was not yet monitored by the Direct Mail Services Standards Board as of 1985 (ASA Case Report 118, p. 2). Small advertisers spending fewer than 125,000 pounds a year on advertising accounted for some 60 percent of all complaints upheld (ASA Case Report 113, 1984).

29. The terms of reference given to the Clucas Committee of Inquiry into the Systems of Control of Advertising Standards, appointed by the Advertising Association in 1986, refer to problems associated with the proliferation of codes and raise questions about a possibly greater involvement of the ASA in their harmonization and coordination. See Advertising Association (1987) for its report.

REFERENCES

Advertising Association. *Advertising and Consumer Protection; The AA's Response to the Labour Party's "Charter for Consumers."* London: September 1986.

———. *Annual Report and Accounts.* London: various dates.

———. *Director General's Newsletter.* London: January 1985; June 1986.

————. *The Systems of Control of Advertising Standards; Report to the Advertising Association by the [Clucas] Committee of Inquiry*. London: May 1987. (The Advertising Association issued "Preliminary Comments" about this report on 10 September 1987.)

Advertising Standards Authority. *Annual Report*. London: various dates.

————. *ASA Case Report*. London: various dates.

Beer, S. H. *Modern British Politics*. London: Faber & Faber, 1965.

Borrie, Gordon. "A Duty to Trade Fairly?" *Journal of Consumer Policy* 7, no. 2 (1984): 197.

————. "Horses for Courses, Efficient Enforcement and Self-Regulation." *Annual Report of the Director General of Fair Trading*. London: HMSO, 1982, pp. 9–12.

The British Code of Advertising Practice [BCAP]. London: Code of Advertising Practice Committee, 1985.

Buell, V. P. *The British Approach to Improving Advertising Standards and Practice; A Comparison with the United States Experience*. Amherst, Mass.: Business Publication Services, School of Business Administration, University of Massachusetts, 1977.

"Consumers and the General Election." *Consumer Affairs*. J. W. Thompson, London 63 (May–June 1983): 12–14.

Consumers' Association. "Code of Practice (internal discussion paper)." London: 1981.

Cranston, Ross. *Consumers and the Law*. London: Weidenfeld and Nicolson, 1984.

Davidson Pearce Ltd. *Results of Omnibus Study into the Public's Awareness of the Advertising Standards Authority*. London: 1983.

Department of Trade. *The Self-Regulatory System of Advertising Control: Report of the Working Party*. London: 1980.

Department of Trade and Industry, Consumer Affairs Division. "Implementation of EC Directive on Misleading Advertising: Consultation Proposals." Mimeographed. London: July 10, 1985.

Director General of Fair Trading [DGFT]. *Review of the U.K. Self-Regulatory System of Advertising Control*. London: Office of Fair Trading, 1978.

Driver, J. C., and G. R. Foxall. *Advertising Policy and Practice*. New York: St. Martin's Press, 1984.

Hirschman, A. O. *Exit, Voice and Loyalty*. Cambridge, Mass.: Harvard University Press, 1970.

House of Lords, Select Committee on the European Communities. *Misleading Advertising; House of Lords Paper 230, Session 1977–1978*. London: HMSO, 1978.

Jones, T. T., and J. F. Pickering. *Self-Regulation in Advertising: A Review*. London: Advertising Association, 1985.

Labour Party. *Labour's Charter for Consumers*. London: Union Communications, 1986.

Lawson, R. W. "An Analysis of Complaints about Advertising." *International Journal of Advertising* 4 (1985): 279–95.

Lawson, Richard G. "The Legal Control of Unfair Advertising in the United Kingdom." Mimeographed. Paper presented at the Fifth European Workshop on Consumer Law. Louvain-la-Neuve, Belgium: September 1986.

Miracle, G. E., and T. R. Nevett. *Voluntary Regulation of Advertising: A Comparative Analysis of the United Kingdom and the United States*. Lexington, Mass.: Heath/Lexington, 1987.

Mitchell, Jeremy. "Government-Approved Codes of Practice." *Journal of Consumer Policy* 1, no. 2, (1978): 144–58.

Murdock, Graham, and Noreene Janus. *Mass Communications and the Advertising Industry*. Paris: UNESCO, 1985.

National Consumer Council [NCC]. *Advertising: Legislate or Persuade?* London: 1977.

———. *Shopping Attitudes Survey*. London: 1982.

Neelankavil, J. P., and A. B. Stridsberg. *Advertising Self-Regulation: A Global Perspective*. New York: Hastings House, 1979.

Office of Fair Trading. "Advertising and the Office of Fair Trading." In: *Advertising Association Handbook*, edited by J. J. Bullmore, and M. J. Waterson. London: Holt, Rinehart & Winston, 1983, 352–57.

———. *A General Duty to Trade Fairly: A Discussion Paper*. London, August 1986.

Pickering, J. F., and D. C. Cousins. "The Benefits and Costs of Voluntary Codes of Practice." *European Journal of Marketing* 16, no. 6 (1982): 31–45.

Schiffman, S. M. "Advertising Policy in the United Kingdom: An Interview with Phil Circus." *Advertising Compliance Service* 5, no. 4 (February 18, 1985): 4–6.

Shonfield, Andrew. *Modern Capitalism: The Changing Balance of Public and Private Power*. New York: Oxford University Press, 1965.

Streeck, Wolfgang, and P. C. Schmitter, eds. *Private Interest Government: Beyond Market and State*. Beverly Hills, Calif., and London: Sage, 1985.

Thomas, Richard. "Codes of Practice in the United Kingdom and the Consumer Interest." *Journal of Consumer Policy* 7, no. 2 (1984): 198–202.

Thomson, Peter. "Advertising Control: Advertisements in Media Other than Television and Radio." In *Advertising Association Handbook*, edited by J. J. Bullmore, and M. J. Waterson. London: Holt, Rinehart & Winston, 1983, 327–51.

van Waarden, Frans. "Varieties of Collective Self-Regulation of Business: The Example of the Dutch Dairy Industry." In *Private Interest Government*, edited by Wolfgang Streeck and P. C. Schmitter. 1985, pp. 197–220.

Vogel, David. "Cooperative Regulation: Environmental Protection in Great Britain." *Public Interest* 72 (Summer 1983): 88–106.

———. *National Styles of Regulation*. Ithaca, New York: Cornell University Press, 1986.

Whincup, M. H. *Consumer Legislation in the United Kingdom and the Republic of Ireland*. New York: Van Nostrand Reinhold, 1980.

Wilson, D. C., and R. J. Butler. "Corporatism in the British Voluntary Sector." In *Private Interest Government*, edited by Wolfgang Streeck, and P. C. Schmitter. 1985, pp. 72–86.

ACKNOWLEDGMENTS

The assistance of the Advertising Standards Association, and particularly of its Director General, Peter Thomson, is gratefully acknowledged, together with that of: Michael Barnes, Eric Burleton, Philip J. Circus, J. C. Driver, Trefor Jones, Patricia Mann, Rosemary McRobert, Charles Medawar, Gordon Miracle, Jeremy Mitchell, Terence Nevett, Brian Nixon, J. F. Pickering, A. E. Pitcher, Roger Underhill (Director General of the Advertising Association) and David Williamson.

14

The United States: The NAD/NARB System

U.S. advertising self-regulation at the national level involves very little formal participation by nonindustry members. Yet, the NAD/NARB interacts in many informal but effective ways with the Federal Trade Commission (FTC) and, to a lesser extent, with a few consumerist organizations. This symbiosis has been noted, but not explicity studied on account of a tendency to view regulation and self-regulation either as opposite approaches to advertising control or as leading parallel lives with little or no interaction.

Therefore, an explicit study of the interaction between the U.S. national advertising self-regulatory body (the NAD/NARB) and such outside bodies as the FTC is essential to understand that self-regulation does not operate in a vacuum, even when formal outside participation is absent. This chapter specifically argues that: (1) there is strong complementariness between the NAD/NARB and the FTC, even though both systems retain specific objectives, processes and sanctions; (2) the lack of major formal outside participation by nonindustry members in the NAD/NARB's functioning has not prevented it from tapping external outputs in the execution of its mission so that the FTC and some consumerist organizations are effective if silent "outside partners" of the U.S. advertising self-regulatory system, and (3) this mode of interacting with the nonadvertising world fits U.S. political culture.

The U.S. Advertising Self-Regulatory System

The present analysis focuses on the National Advertising Division (NAD) of the Council of Better Business Bureaus (CBBB) and its appeal-level National Advertising Review Board (NARB).[1] Both have been financed by the Council of Better Business Bureaus although national-level advertising associations

(American Association of Advertising Agencies, Association of National Advertisers and American Advertising Federation) helped create the system and strongly support it. Since it has been aptly analyzed by others (for example, Armstrong and Ozanne 1983; Meloan 1983; Miller 1981; Miracle and Nevett 1987; Zanot 1977 and 1979), only a few relevant features of the U.S. national advertising self-regulatory system, created in 1971, need be highlighted here.

1. U.S. advertising self-regulation has numerous components: both local (e.g., Better Business Bureaus) and national (the NAD/NARB studied here); both industry-specific (e.g., about pharmaceutical and alcohol advertising) and all-industry-wide (again, the NAD/NARB); and both media-type-specific (e.g., just for newspapers or direct-mail) and all-media-wide (again, the NAD/NARB).

2. The NAD/NARB system focuses on "truth and accuracy in advertising," that is, it deals almost exclusively with cases of false and misleading advertisements (print) and commercials (broadcast). Complaints related to unfairness, social responsibility, taste and morality are not handled by the NAD, although the NARB has issued a few papers about such issues as safety and women in advertising; and the NAD's Children's Advertising Review Unit (CARU) considers "the special nature" of this target group.

3. Except for advertisements directed to children, the NAD/NARB does not have codes or guidelines of its own but relies on those of the Council of Better Business Bureaus and of other associations, on standards developed by federal agencies and the courts, and on its own precedent-setting decisions.

4. Very few nonindustry members participate in the internal functioning of the national NAD/NARB system, since only the NARB uses "public members" (that is, nonindustry members) in its review panels (one out of five panelists is an outsider).[2] However, the NAD occasionally uses outside experts, and its Children's Advertising Review Unit (CARU) has an Academic Advisory Panel to help develop its standards.

5. The NAD's own monitoring of advertisements, together with competitor challenges, have provided some 70 to 75 percent of the 98 to 150 annual cases published in recent years, while consumer complaints represent only some 10 percent of them.[3]

Comparing U.S. Self-Regulation and Regulation

This section focuses on the differences, similarities and complementarities between U.S. advertising self-regulation and regulation, with particular emphasis on the relationships between the NAD/NARB and the Federal Trade Commission (FTC). This focus on the FTC, however, is not meant to imply that other outsiders do not affect the NAD/NARB's behavior. Thus, consumers and a few consumerist organizations feed complaints to the NAD, which also uses outside experts. Besides, public opinion bears on the NAD/NARB to the extent that legislators, regulators and consumerist leaders have commented on its functioning and effectiveness. These additional actors will be considered in later sections.

Regulatory and Self-Regulatory Differences

The National Advertising Review Board (NARB) was established in 1971 to sustain high standards of truth and accuracy in national advertising, with full regard for the public interest. The National Advertising Division (NAD) is responsible for receiving or initiating, evaluating, investigating, analyzing and holding initial negotiations with advertisers on complaints or questions from any source, involving truth or accuracy in national advertising. Each month, the NAD releases a public report of closed cases, which details the advertiser, advertising agency and product involved, the basis for questioning the advertisement, the advertiser's response and the NAD's decision, which can be appealed to the NARB (NARB 1985). On the regulatory side, government control over advertising is vested primarily in the Federal Trade Commission, which can use various means to stop or prevent the use of "any unfair method of competition or unfair or deceptive act or practice in commerce," according to Section 5(b) of the FTC Act.

These general missions of advertising regulation and self-regulation conceal several major differences. In the first place, regulation relies on laws, rules and court decisions that are binding on everyone and are backed by sanctions such as cease-and-desist orders, injunctions, corrective advertising, fines and imprisonment. However, the NAD/NARB system has no code of its own and no sanctions such as exclusion from membership, denial of access to the media or fines, although moral and peer pressure as well as publicity have been used to good effect.[4] Besides, the NAD—unlike the FTC—does not have to prove culpability or—unlike litigation—that competitors have been injured. Instead, it focuses on whether evidence supports the advertiser's claims (Smithies 1986).

In this context, a major difference between the operational mandates of the NAD and the FTC involves the concept of "public interest." Pursuant to Section 5(b) of the FTC Act, the Commission may not issue a complaint against an advertisement unless "it shall appear to the Commission that a proceeding by it in respect thereof would be to the interest of the public." The Supreme Court has interpreted this phrase as prohibiting the Commission from proceeding in matters that are essentially private controversies between competitors. Thus, it is unlikely that the Commission would proceed in a case involving competing "taste tests." The NAD, however, will participate in such controversies and try to resolve them (see note 10).

A second difference is less clear-cut. The FTC has an explicit consumer-protection ("consumer advocacy") mandate that complements its regulatory role in maintaining competition, while Armstrong and Ozanne (1983, p. 16) have argued that the NAD/NARB puts greater emphasis on "advertiser advocacy." By this, they mean that consumer protection is a byproduct of what the NAD/NARB does to maintain the general integrity of all advertising, to resolve disputes among competitors, to defuse consumerist concerns and to dampen the threat of government regulation. Their view is supported by the often mentioned facts that: (1) consumer and consumer-organization complaints represent only some 10 percent of the NAD caseload; (2) outsiders hardly participate in the system's functioning; (3) relatively little publicity is given to the NAD/NARB system outside of the specialized press;[5] (4) there are no campaigns to solicit more consumer complaints, and (5) the NAD/NARB does not deal with matters of taste, decency, morality and the like (tobacco and alcohol advertising, for example), which concern the public much more than "truth and accuracy in advertising."[6]

NAD officials, however, counter that such a distinction between consumer and advertiser advocacy is exaggerated if not misplaced. While it is true that NAD relies mainly on competitor complaints, only those that raise an issue of public interest are pursued. It does not act as the advocate for the complaining competitor or as an intervenor or tort-redressor between advertisers, but assumes complaints as its own (with possible additional charges, following NAD investigation) if it appears that the challenged advertisement raises questions about the proper substantiation of its claims.

A third difference is that the Federal Trade Commission is concerned not only with "deceptive"[7] but also with "unfair" advertising, while the NAD/NARB does not deal with the latter. However, the concept of "unfairness" is somewhat nebulous and its application rather controversial in law (Cohen 1982; Ford and Calfee 1986; Rice 1984); and the FTC was ordered by Congress in 1980 not to issue new industry-wide trade regulation rules on the basis of unfairness, which can still be used on a case-by-case basis, however.[8] Therefore, this difference from the NAD/NARB's avoidance of unfair-advertising cases has receded in importance, although still latently potent.

Altogether, the above contrasts between advertising regulation and self-regulation in terms of missions, processes and sanctions are significant, but they have not prevented the FTC and NAD/NARB systems from developing a complementary working relationship.

Regulatory and Self-Regulatory Similarities

The two systems display great resemblance in terms of: (1) limited outside participation; (2) emphasis on "hard" issues and criteria; (3) choice of cases to pursue; (4) shared standards, and (5) antitrust-law consensus.

Limited Outside Participation. Government bodies such as the FTC include only civil servants, although they rely to varying extents on public complaints, expert advisers and witnesses, advisory bodies and public hearings where the "vox populi" (or at least the voice of interest groups) can be invited and heard. Former FTC Chairman Michael Pertschuk had tried to make the Commission into the "greatest public-interest law firm in the country" responsive to consumerists, but this attempt got him and the FTC into trouble. Although still besieged by consumerist and other concerned pressure groups about such issues as advertising to children and tobacco and alcohol advertising, the FTC has tended since 1981 to deny their requests for amounting to "social engineering" and, therefore, lying outside of its concerns and best left to Congress to consider ("The New FTC" 1987; Molotsky 1985).

On its part, the NAD does not use outsiders, except as expert advisers, while forty-three NARB panels have included one "public" member out of five. This single public member has been there to vouch for the NARB's independence and credibility rather than to provide any special expertise—a task left to the permanent NAD staff and to occasional outside experts who focus on "hard" technical matters rather than on "soft" issues. Therefore, both the NAD and the FTC have formal structures, which exclude giving an explicit "voice" to outsiders in their respective deliberations.

Emphasis on "Hard" Criteria and Issues. Both the FTC and NAD/NARB focus on "hard" cases and refuse to handle "soft" issues by policy choice.[9] "Hard cases" revolve around such matters as deception and substantiation in interpreting an advertisement, while "soft issues" center on taste, social responsibility and the like, where there is a range of opinions about the proper norms to apply and about how to apply them. While the standards applied to deception and substantiation have varied over time,[10] there is some consensus about their applicability—something that is generally missing in the case of soft issues, even after Congress or the courts have spoken.

The FTC's "unfairness" mandate has, at times, included considering whether an ad is "immoral, unethical, oppressive, or unscrupulous [or] offends public policy (Rice 1984, p. 113)." However, since 1980, the FTC has proposed a definition of unfair acts or practices that excludes "offenses to taste or social belief (FTC Policy Statement 1980)." An analysis of what is currently discussed in FTC and legal circles reveals such an emphasis on "hard" issues and criteria;[11] and the NAD/NARB is equally interested in them rather than in "soft" ones (cf. Edelstein [1983] and Preston [1983]). In this regard, it is significant that the advertising industry opposed former FTC Chairman Miller's proposal to reconsider the presubstantiation requirement, which is one of the strongest tenets of U.S. advertising self-regulation. Any weakening of this FTC requirement would have made it more difficult for the NAD to obtain the necessary evidence from advertisers and agencies.[12]

The NARB has a second mission beyond that of hearing appeals to NAD decisions, namely, "to consider the content of advertising messages in controversy for reasons other than truth and accuracy . . . or a matter of social responsibility (NARB, Statement of Organization, 1985)." The NAD/NARB has generally declined to handle such cases on the ground that "there is no government agency to which such cases could be referred"—besides involving subjective judgments and evaluations.[13] Again, this stand reflects the complementary nature of the NAD/NARB and FTC.

Original procedures were amended to provide for specially appointed NARB consultative panels to consider questions of taste and social responsibility, determine problem areas and sponsor position papers to alert the industry to practices that should be avoided (Bell 1974, p. 60). A handful of such NARB papers has been published on comparative advertisements, safety, women in advertising and what people dislike about advertisements (NARB 1979). However, this general airing of larger and softer issues has received very low priority and has represented a very minor task with little or no impact on the NAD's casework; and no NARB report has been issued since 1979.

The original mandate of the Children's Advertising Review Unit mentioned that, beyond truth and accuracy, CARU would try to assure that children's advertising "is fair to children's still developing perceptions (CARU 1979, p. 1)." However, references to fairness have been removed from later versions of CARU's publication "An Eye on Children's Advertising," and expressions like "sensitive to the special nature of children" are now used.

Case Similarity. There has also been convergence between the NAD/NARB and the FTC regarding the choice of cases to pursue. Both bodies handle relatively few of them (a little over 100 a year for the NAD; fewer than 100 for the FTC) because of limited budget and staff resources.[14] Therefore, each tries to select cases that set precedents and send strong signals to business;[15] both emphasize cases of poorly substantiated and misleading advertisements, with the FTC also handling outright fraud cases, which the NAD leaves to government; and they both use a case-by-case approach now that the FTC has largely abandoned the pursuit of broad trade regulation rules and industry-wide rounds. This situation allowed the industry to conclude that: "The kinds of claims which will be pursued by the Federal Trade Commission, the broadcasters and the NAD are quite similar [although] the broadcasters and the NAD cast a much broader net and review many more claims than does the FTC (The American Association of Advertising Agencies [AAAA] 1983, p. 86)."

Shared Standards. Case similarity is facilitated by the fact that there are ample court and FTC jurisprudence, FTC trade regulation rules and guidelines, industry codes and NAB/NARB precedents that have progressively delimited the boundaries of good advertising practice. The relatively strong preclearance systems set up by large advertisers, advertising agencies and media (particularly, the networks) also reduce the likelihood of blatantly unacceptable national advertisements—at least in terms of "hard" standards. As Zanot (1985) put it, each "screen" may be crude, but superimposed they eliminate most of the chaff.

In any case, the NAD/NARB has repeatedly acknowledged that FTC and FDA rules and rulings constitute some of its main standards. Thus, Ronald Smithies, Executive Director of the NAD, mentioned as sources: "inputs from complaining advertisers, the guidelines of the Advertising Research Foundation, the rules and regulations of the Federal Trade Commission, pertinent decisions of the federal courts, and actions of the various consumer-affairs departments and state attorney generals. The most dramatic impact on NAD, however, is made by the Food and Drug Administration. FDA is most influential to NAD [because] food, nutrition and OTC drugs are our main categories."[16]

Similarly, FTC Commissioner Patricia Bailey (1984, p. 12) singled out the relevance of FTC standards for self-regulation:

Another point raised in support of the Commission's policy [to require prior substantiation of advertising claims] was its importance as a foundation for industry self-regulatory procedures, including the National Advertising Division of the Better Business Bureaus and the National Advertising Review Board. The Commission has, for example, developed an extensive body of case law, rules and formal guidelines that mark out areas of legality and illegality in relatively concrete terms. These are useful points of reference for all participants in a voluntary self-regulatory system—those who operate it as well as those who adhere to it.

She also referred to the NAB/NARB self-regulatory program "now grounded in FTC precedent and policy (Bailey 1984, p. 14)." Zanot (1979, p. 26) also concluded that "NARB decisions and guidelines are generally consistent with those of both the FTC and the courts." The NAD/NARB assumption of legal principles borrowed from the FTC reduces the latter's load, and allows the Commission to focus on unresolved cases and on those involving new legal questions.

Antitrust-Law Consensus. Finally, there has been basic agreement between the FTC, the Justice Department and the NAD/NARB about U.S. antitrust strictures against self-regulation. The consistently suspicious attitude of the U.S. government toward industry self-regulation and its attendant codes and sanctions (LaBarbera 1981, Smithies 1986)[17] is explained by fears that membership requirements to adhere to a code as well as sanctions such as exclusion, denial of access to the media (as is practiced by many other advertising self-regulatory bodies abroad) and fines would restrict freedom of entry and/or result in collusion to restrict certain practices, such as comparison advertising.[17] The 1982 federal-court decision, at the request of the Department of Justice, against some aspects of the National Association of Broadcasters' Code (mainly its restrictions of the number, duration and joint-sponsorship of commercials) represents a recent example of this attitude.

Since its inception in 1971, the NAD/NARB system has espoused this antitrust view by avoiding membership requirements, codes and sanctions. Instead, it uses only publicity through its monthly NAD Case Reports, peer pressure and the threat of referral of recalcitrant advertisers to the Federal Trade Commission. Therefore, there has been no antitrust-based conflict between U.S. advertising regulation and self-regulation, since private agreements to refrain from illegal advertising practices are safe under U.S. law. The only negative signal came in 1979 when the FTC warned all advertising self-regulatory bodies and the networks against restraining comparative advertisements and against requiring higher substantiation for such ads. However, no problems of the sort have surfaced since then.

Altogether, these five factors reveal far greater similarity between U.S. regulation and self-regulation than has been disclosed in previous analyses. But the symbiosis between the two systems does not stop here.

Mutual Support and Complementariness

The interdependence between the NAD/NARB and the FTC has not functioned in a vacuum. For one thing, the Reagan administration's support of deregulation—really started under President Carter—has been predicated on business assuming greater responsibility for its conduct. Virginia Knauer, Special Assistant to the President for Consumer Affairs, has stated this point rather clearly, besides alluding to budget cuts prompting government agencies to serve more as "facilitators" for the endeavors of private organizations: "Reducing the intrusion of government in our lives implies a greater responsibility for those who are governed. To every act there is an equal and opposite reaction. Therefore, to cut programs and taxes, and to reduce government regulation require not an abandonment of many of the objectives regulation was supposed to address, but a need for self-regulation and private-sector responsiveness to consumers and society (Knauer 1981, p. 4)."

Actually, well before James C. Miller III became FTC chairman in 1981, its leaders have generally lauded and encouraged the NAD/NARB, urging it to keep up the good work and not relent. Even former FTC chairman Michael Pertschuk had kind words for the NAD/NARB, observing that: "In one marketplace [the FTC has been] taking a beating: the competition to clean up shoddy and deceptive advertising. You've skimmed the cream of deceptive ads, outrageous frauds and misrepresentations. . . . It is entirely appropriate as a private body that you police cases in which the law and public policy are clear. And leave us, however painful, the close ones (Pertschuk 1978, p. 1)." In a policy statement, former Chairman Miller praised the advertising industry's self-regulatory efforts:

Advertising self-regulation is one area in which the private sector often outperforms the government. The informal methods of self-regulation often solve problems more quickly and at lower cost than the FTC could ever hope to achieve. But, of course, the Commission will continue to exercise its independent judgment in cases that come before it . . . [FTC's relations with self-regulatory groups] have been fruitful in the past, and I expect that to continue ("FTC Chairman Miller," 1984, p. 2).

Speaking before the Council of Better Business Bureaus, Daniel Oliver, the current FTC chairman, praised local BBBs as well as the national NAD/NARB's complementary role in one of his first public pronouncements: "There is no question that you have been able to resolve cases that normally would have come to us. Indeed, just last year, the Commission was able to defer action on a number of issues which had been quickly and effectively resolved by the NAD. Some may criticize this, but I applaud it. There is no reason why we cannot and should not play complementary roles (Oliver 1986, p. 3)."

Similarly, the advertising industry has emphasized its need of the Federal Trade Commission. As Len Matthews, president of the AAAA, put it: "We in our industry want and need the FTC to help industry fight the truly bad operators who will not respond to self-regulation (Matthews 1984, p. 10)." The AAAA also observed that "the very existence of the FTC's ad substantiation program enhances the effectiveness of all self-regulatory groups, since they can use the FTC or the appropriate regulatory body for referral of unresolved cases ("AAAA Response" 1983, p. 100)." (The NAD does not pursue cases already under formal investigation by a state or federal body.)

On occasions, the NAD refers matters to the Federal Trade Commission (FTC July 23, 1984, p. 67). Officially, no such referral to the FTC by the NAD/NARB has taken place to date, although it appears that open-and-shut cases of false or fraudulent advertising are immediately reported to the appropriate federal and state authorities rather than handled by the NAD. Similarly, the FTC at times recommends to complainants to bring up the matter to the NAD and other self-regulatory bodies. However, the FTC is more likely to do so in the case of competitors' complaints, since the latter are more amenable to the argument of "washing their own linen in private."[18]

Still, the FTC has steadfastly refused to relinquish its role to the NAD/NARB, mainly out of fear that self-regulation could result in "private restraints" in advertising.[19] For that matter, the FTC has recently reasserted its independence vis-à-vis self-regulatory bodies:

The Commission traditionally has enjoyed a close working relationship with self-regulation groups. . . . The Commission will not necessarily defer, however, to a finding by a self-regulation group. An imprimatur from a self-regulation group will not automatically shield a firm from Commission prosecution, and an unfavorable determination will not mean the Commission will automatically take issue, or find liability if it does (FTC Policy Statement 1984, pp. 12–13; see also FTC Advertising Substantiation Program 1984, pp. 63–68).

NAD Pioneering

More modest had been the NAD/NARB's role of "test pilot." It has steadily avoided the "soft" issues related to decency, taste and social responsibility (see above) so that it has not had to innovate and test ways of coping with them. The only exception lies in the matter of advertising to children, where it set up CARU, which has developed guidelines and a complaint-handling system—an initiative most welcome by an FTC less than eager to handle this kind of "social engineering" issue. Even here, however, the focus remains on "truthful and accurate advertising sensitive to the special nature of children."

Regarding "hard" matters, the NAD/NARB's requirement of prior substantiation of advertising claims coincided with the 1972 Pfizer FTC decision, which established the additional requirement that the advertiser and his agency have a "reasonable basis" in hand for their claims before an advertisement can be published or broadcast. However, the networks and other self-regulatory bodies already required prior substantiation before 1972 so that the NAD/NARB did not really innovate in this matter. The special NAD Case Report of October 1984 focused on "Food Cases Involving 'Natural' Claims," but this exercise did not represent an attempt to present consistent NAD standards, but rather to draw the attention of the food industry in an area where the FTC had been giving mixed signals or no signals at all. However, the NAD/NARB has pioneered in accepting the postsubstantiation of advertising (provided presubstantiation is also available); and the Federal Trade Commission (which also requires presubstantiation) has formalized its acceptance of this practice under certain conditions (FTC Policy Statement 1984).

In this context, Stanley Cohen (1980, p. 163) has deplored the NAD/NARB's reluctance "to play a conscience-raising role for the industry . . . by setting performance standards which are more demanding than law" although he concedes that this may have been the worthwhile price to pay for industry support of the U.S. national self-regulatory system.

Evaluation

Altogether, the FTC and the NAD/NARB have succeeded in sharing the task and cost of advertising control. In times of federal-budget cutting or containment, and in view of the limited resources granted to the NAD/NARB system by its sponsors (themselves strapped for resources),[20] such a complementary role saves money, time and people all around. This sharing reduces frictions between business and government—something that these partners appear quite happy to have, at least under the present administration. Besides, the fruitful interaction between the NAD/NARB and the FTC, while largely hidden from public view, reveals that advertising self-regulation can effectively function with little or no formal integration of nonindustry members in its structure and functioning. Instead, the Federal Trade Commission has played the role of "silent outside partner" of the NAD/NARB by: (1) providing it with significant norms, and (2) serving as a potential backup for it in the case of recalcitrant advertisers not amenable to self-regulatory ministrations. As will soon be discussed, a few consumerist organizations have also provided some inputs to the NAD/NARB, thereby adding another "outside" dimension to its operations.

Has this state of happy symbiosis between U.S. advertising regulation and self-regulation been in the public interest? Answering this question is complex and largely depends on one's view of the proper state of relations between business and government. Some people will always fear any cozy relationships between the two, and urge that government agencies be independent and not entangle themselves with private bodies. Even businesspeople feel ambivalent about cozy relationships, because they fear that self-regulation can be made to assume too many responsibilities and become just another "cop on the beat" for the government (see Chapter 1).

There is, however, another body of thought—mainly European and Latin American in origin and experience—that takes a more lenient view of what may loosely be called "neocorporatism" (see Chapter 1). For its proponents, the interdependence between the FTC and the NAD/NARB would not look sinister at all. The U.S. government has retained and repeatedly expressed its opposition to associational abuses; and its regulatory system remains strong, since Congress and the courts can always overrule the FTC, should the latter become too complacent toward the advertising industry. Besides, as was mentioned before, there are other venues for legal action against advertisers, such as private litigation, which have proven effective.

Whatever the imperfections still attached to the NAD/NARB and FTC, the comments of Carol Crawford, former Director of the FTC Bureau of Consumer Protection, sum up appropriately the benefits of the silent partnership between the two systems:

Ultimately, the complementary roles of the government and industry in the regulation of advertising amount to much more, of course, than a simple "dividing up" of cases. The end result is an environment of responsible cooperation between industry and government. In that environment, truthful and accurate advertising is encouraged and expected. Consequently, the marketplace is a source of better and more useful information, a result that benefits consumers and businesses alike (Crawford 1985, p. 10).

Interpretation

Why have the NAD/NARB and FTC systems managed to coexist and cooperate despite their overlap and possible rivalry? Answering this question requires analyzing the state of business-government relations in the United States.

U.S. Political Culture

The U.S. regulatory system has generally been viewed to be highly adversarial between business and government as the counterpart of a highly competitive economic system. Thus, Vogel (1986, pp. 249–50) has argued that U.S. business executives tend to regard government officials much as they view their competitors, that is, as challengers to be met as aggressively as possible; and they view any restraint on management's prerogatives as threatening. Vogel maintains that the individualistic ethos of U.S. business culture has often limited the role of trade associations as a vehicle for industry self-regulation, or relegated their role to opposing government regulatory initiatives. In this context, he views the heavy U.S. reliance on extensive formal laws and regulations as reflecting the frequent inadequacy of informal mechanisms of social control within a highly individualistic culture less susceptible to social pressure from government officials and business peers.

Yet, the NAD/NARB has managed to be broadly accepted as necessary and effective by the U.S. government and by the advertising industry. Even consumer activists have not voiced major criticisms of its operations after the first years of its establishment and shakedown.[21] To what can this acceptance and favorable appraisal be ascribed?

An Apolitical Instrument. In the first place, the NAD/NARB has been largely shielded from the occasional bruising battles between industry, Congress and regulatory agencies. The task of urging or opposing regulatory proposals (including the funding and redefinition of the FTC's purposes) has been left to such advertising associations as the AAF, AAAA and ANA. Fighting "unfair" and "moral" battles has also been remitted to these bodies as well as to associations in threatened industries (pharmaceuticals, liquor, tobacco, confectionery, cereals, etc.)

Instead, the NAD/NARB has been positioned as an apolitical technical instrument designed to foster truth and accuracy in advertising. This limited positioning reflects the fact that the advertising industry controls the NAD/NARB by financing it, by appointing its directors and executives, and by defining its functions—as exemplified by the NAD/NARB's progressive withdrawal from considering matters of unfairness, social responsibility, taste and morality. The fact that the post–1980 FTC has also avoided handling "offenses to taste and social beliefs," left for Congress to handle under the Reagan administration, has supported this division of labor between the NAD/NARB and other business bodies.

Still, this limited instrumental role has not totally shielded the NAD/NARB from political involvement. It is regularly paraded before congressional committees and new FTC commissioners to prove that self-regulation can do a better, cheaper and faster job than regulation. The NAD/NARB's structure and functioning were expanded to cope with advertisements directed to children in order to ward off further regulation in this area. As such, the NAD/NARB remains a political tool of the industry in its endless jousting with the U.S. government over the control of advertising, even though it has no political goals of its own.

A Nonrival to the FTC. The Federal Trade Commission and its staff could have viewed the NAD/NARB as a rival, but this has not happened. First, the FTC's activism of the 1970s was challenged and its resources curtailed by Congress—even its very raison d'être has been questioned in recent years under the deregulation principle and in the face of federal budget-cutting. FTC leaders, under the Reagan administration, have accepted such a reduced and allegedly more passive role, and have essentially limited their role to protecting consumers against certain cases of deception and unfairness ("New Directions FTC?" 1986). Squabbles between competitors have been gladly relegated to the courts and the ministrations of the NAD/NARB (if the public interest is involved); while moral and social-engineering issues about tobacco, liquor and children's advertising have been avoided as much as possible ("New Directions FTC?" 1986), as is also done by the NAD/NARB.

Even in the matter of consumer protection, there is not that much rivalry with the NAD/NARB because the FTC tends to focus on cases of fraud where the product itself cannot deliver what its advertising promises, or various services (delivery, maintenance, reimbursements, etc.) have not been provided as promised—something that the NAD/NARB largely ignores since it focuses on the substantiation of claims made in advertisements. The FTC has also continued to propose or issue new trade rule regulations covering an entire industry (e.g., funerals) or profession (e.g., opticians, lawyers and physicians)—an approach totally foreign to the NAD/NARB case-focused tack.

Consequently, instead of being rivals trying to dominate or eliminate one another, they have accepted and even fostered their overlap as an adaptive response to their respective limited resources, that contributes to the overall reliability and performance of each system as well as of the entire network.

An Ally of Consumerists. There is no great love lost between U.S. consumer activists and advertisers. Still, the former have not unduly criticized the NAD/NARB. For organizations such as the Center for Science in the Public Interest, it represents another venue for lodging complaints; and the NAD/NARB has successfully assumed some of them as in the Campbell Soup and Del Monte cases (Silverglade 1985, p. 20). Bodies such as Action for Children's Television are not so satisfied, but they probably realize and accept that the NAD's Children's Advertising Review Unit is not going to get embroiled in evaluating the "fairness" of such advertising—an issue better brought before Congress or even such regulatory agencies as the FTC and the Federal Communications Commission. The same applies to organizations concerned about cigarette and alcohol advertising. Again, this realistic appraisal of what the NAD/NARB can and cannot do helps keep it depoliticized.

An Accepted Controller of Advertising. Vogel's (1986) skepticism about the acceptance and effectiveness of industry self-regulation as a form of social control in the United States must be qualified, if not challenged, in the case of advertising. The obvious counterarguments are that self-regulation offers an alternative to regulation, and that business prefers the former to the latter because it ultimately controls the self-regulatory system. This is almost a truism, and the creation of the NAD/NARB in 1971 was clearly related to serious threats of further regulation of the advertising industry in the early 1970s. However, there is a major difference between creating a self-regulatory system for countervailing political purposes and accepting it as a necessary tool for "good advertising behavior."

There have been no systematic surveys of the acceptance and rating by business of the NAD/NARB, but the business literature (e.g., *Advertising Age*) has not been critical at all in recent years, compared to academic carpings about that system's limited reach, weak outside representation, etc. Why is this the case? In the first place, the NAD/NARB has not looked "heavy" in comparison to the FTC, since it does not have a code of its own, and its sanctions are largely limited to publicizing its reasoned decisions. While advertisers have practically always complied with NAD/NARB decisions, they remain free to ignore them, and do not incur penalties of the types governmental agencies and the courts can impose.

Second, the NAD/NARB has not acted like a court that adjudicates between a complainant and a defendant. Instead, it has initiated or assumed complaints as its own and examined them in the light of their substantiated truth and accuracy. Clearly, no advertiser likes to be asked to justify his claims, but the onus is lighter than if he were accused of having broken some law. Besides, large advertisers are now accustomed to having to provide similar evidence to the major media's acceptance (preclearance) units.

Third, the cooperation between the NAD/NARB and the FTC (and State Attorneys General) has been informal and largely hidden from view, so that the two have not been perceived as acting together to "get" infractors. Finally, any competitor dissatisfied with the NAD/NARB has alternative places such as the FTC and the courts in which to lodge complaints so that the former is not viewed as largely indispensable or unavoidable.

Still, private criticisms have been expressed by some advertisers and their legal advisers. They complain about having to "shadow-box" the NAD/NARB, which they accuse of using confidential experts that cannot be subpoenaed (cf. Kent 1985). Defendants can also play delaying tactics, which drag out NAD investigations for months while market shares may be lost so that going to court for fast legal relief is sometimes preferable. A few critics even view the NAD as a "one-man show" run by an "iron-handed" executive director who imposes his own views and acts almost as an independent "outsider."[22]

Whether the NAD/NARB system is losing its "user-friendly" touch is hard to determine without further investigation. Still, it has generally revealed itself as a light and alternative form of advertising control that fits the more open and loosely structured "pluralist" mode of interest-group organization and representation, compared to the "corporatist" granting of semiofficial status to an interest group expected to assist the government in its tasks (Vogel 1986, pp. 273 and 279). As such, it leaves room for the individualist ethos of U.S. business culture without, however, losing effectiveness, since the NAD/NARB has been able to obtain that unsubstantiated claims be modified or withdrawn. Also, the importance of the NAD as an advertising control body was emphasized in a 1985 court decision compelling an advertiser to comply with a settlement agreement to obtain a nonbinding advisory opinion from the NAD in a dispute over the propriety of advertising claims (Kent 1985, p. 1).

The Threat of Regulation

As is true of other countries, the development of U.S. self-regulation has taken place against a background of criticisms of advertising and of proposals to further regulate it (see, for example Miracle and Nevett [1987] and Zanot [1977]. As a former Vice-President put it at the onset of the NAD/NARB system: "We think it would be far better to wear a self-regulatory hairshirt now than a tight-fitting legislative straitjacket later on (Purdon 1972, p. 21)." Twelve years later, Charles F. Adams, former AAAA Washington representative, commented that: "I used to tell the regulators, when I was in Washington, that we didn't so much need the FTC as we needed the FFTC, that is, 'Fear of the Federal Trade Commission' (private communication)."

In this context, it is interesting to contrast the negative atmosphere surrounding the 1972 hearings held by the U.S. Senate's Committee on Commerce regarding a bill requiring the furnishing of documentation about advertising claims, with the positive results achieved today through FTC and NAD/NARB partnership. At that time, the Federal Trade Commission had just ruled that "It is an unfair practice in violation of the Federal Trade Commission Act to make an affirmative product claim without a reasonable basis for making that claim (81 F.T.C. 23)." The NAD/NARB immediately adopted that requirement. Since then, both the FTC and NAD/NARB have consistently required that prior substantiation be available, and this rule has had a salutary effect on most advertisers.

For sure, there are still serious complaints that various advertising campaigns are deceiving the public—as with the Center for Science in the Public Interest's charges against the beef and milk industries as well as against coffee and soft-drinks ads. However, there is much greater consensus than in 1972 that a combination of regulatory, self-regulatory and private-litigation remedies are now available to combat such deceptions. As such, no new demands have been put on the national advertising self-regulatory system to assume new tasks. The fact that the Center for Science in the Public Interest, which initiated or joined several "unfair-based" petitions to the FTC, has refrained from filing similar complaints to the NAD, reveals that the latter's focus on truth and accuracy is understood and accepted by this very militant consumerist organization.[23]

Yet, Armstrong (1984, pp. 51–52) observed that the NAD/NARB's caseload had declined in recent years, a parallel of the FTC's "lower activism," and that the level of case activity of the Children's Advertising Review Unit appears to fluctuate substantially with external pressures on children's advertising. For example, efforts peaked from 1978 to 1979 when the industry was threatened by the proposed FTC trade regulation rule on children's advertising, but they declined after this threat had passed, even though children-advertising cases still represent some 20 percent of the NAD cases in recent years.

One observes here the deplorable fact that business interest in self-regulation waxes and wanes in direct relation to regulatory threats—in the United States as well as abroad. The NAD/NARB's assigned missions and selection of cases to pursue are bound to reflect this reality. This is not to argue that it has become quiescent under the Reagan administration, but simply to acknowledge that self-regulation does not operate in a political vacuum. One may regret that the NAD/NARB has not taken advantage of the post-1975 deregulatory pause to further publicize its availability for consumer complaints, to accept taste-and-opinion complaints, to formalize its own standards and to increase the formal participation of outsiders in its structure and functioning—to quote some of the repeated criticisms of Armstrong and Ozanne (1983); Cohen (1980); LaBarbera (1980 a and b); Miracle and Nevett (1987); and Zanot (1979). However, this relative quiescence can simply be interpreted as another proof of the frequently parallel behavior of the FTC, also relatively quiescent, and of the NAD/NARB.

The relative decline in the number of cases handled by the NAD reflects the facts that: (1) competitor complaints have become more important, and (2) the latter tend to be more complex—as when comparative claims are challenged. These fewer decisions still set important additional precedents to guide business behavior. Therefore, it is not advisable to rely on raw statistics to conclude that the NAD/NARB system has become more quiescent or less influential.

The Threat of a Weak FTC

Around the time of the creation of the NAD/NARB, when major congressional hearings were debating possible new advertising regulations, Howard and Hulbert stressed that an effective self-regulatory system requires a strong regulatory counterpart: "We wish to make two points on the role of self-regulation: first, the National Advertising Review Board is likely to have a major impact only insofar as there is a strong [FTC] Commission policy operating. Second, as the procedures now provide, the extreme cases will have to come to the attention of the Commission (Howard and Hulbert 1973, pp. 93–94)." In other words, the real power of a self-regulatory body such as the NAD/NARB does not really derive from its membership—for that matter, the NAD/NARB has none—but from government prodding and the threat of further regulation and/or stronger enforcement of existing laws (see Chapter 1 for further discussion of this view).

This is not the place to discuss the validity of the criticisms that the Federal Trade Commission is not doing enough or not focusing on the right problems and wrongdoers.[24] Yet, a variety of consumerist organizations (e.g., the Center for Science in the Public Interest) have expressed concern about an FTC focusing mainly on clear cases of fraudulent (e.g., the product does not work) and deceptive advertisements involving in most cases relatively small firms, while purportedly neglecting large advertisers and misleading advertisements: "Practices which are simply half-truths or which are often described as manipulation of the consumer, those kinds of practices may simply have been ruled out as something that the FTC is concerned about (Zuckerman, May 1984, p. 6)."

In this context, acting FTC chairman Terry Calvani stated in early 1986 that the Federal Trade Commission is not very interested in cases of "search" and "experience" goods, where consumers can readily decide for themselves whether a product is worth buying or rebuying. Instead, it is more concerned about "credence goods" where consumers are really dependent upon information provided by the manufacturer or vendor because they cannot readily tell whether the claim is true or not, so that the claim substantiation doctrine is vitally important for such goods. Besides, Calvani related the relatively small number of FTC cases involving national advertisers to "the success of such ad-industry self-regulatory mechanisms as the NAD," and to large advertisers being "quick to police themselves" ("New Directions FTC?" 1986, pp. 4–5; also Crawford 1985, p. 8; and "The New FTC" 1987).

Indeed, Calvani's statement illustrates the complementary natures of the FTC and NAD, with he latter picking up such "search and experience goods" cases more readily. However, the major objection to this implicit "division of labor" is that it may give advertisers and agencies a wrong signal, namely, that the FTC itself is no longer interested in the kind of cases pursued by the NAD. Since the latter, like any other advertising self-regulatory system, depends on strong and diligent government agencies to threaten those not amenable to negotiation and voluntary compliance with its decisions, a lax or indifferent FTC would weaken the NAD's clout. Similarly, *Advertising Age's* Stanley Cohen, who has often commented on U.S. advertising self-regulation, has expressed concern about a weaker or less active FTC: "[We] should not forget that the ability of NARB to make its judgments stand may well diminish if there is no vigilant FTC hovering in the background (1980, p. 164)."

Moreover, one could interpret the laudatory comments that have emanated from the FTC about the NAD/NARB's "success" (cf. Calvani) not as an objective appraisal of the latter's effectiveness, but rather as a rationalization for the Reagan administration's policy in favor of deregulation (although some of them predate Chairman Miller's tenure). In other words, the FTC is happy about advertising self-regulation simply because it is opposed to more regulation—not because the NAD/NARB has truly assumed a greater and more effective role in advertising control.

Thus, the NAD has been criticized for terminating inquiries if the advertiser states that the incriminated ad has been discontinued or agrees that it will not be run again in that form without referring the unresolved questions to the NAD, prior to any future use of the claims—even though harm may have been done to some consumers and competitors. The FTC, however, can pursue such matters if the law has been broken, irrespective of any subsequent withdrawal of the advertisement, but some doubt that it does enough in this matter. Moreover, when the NAD keeps using the old FTC standard of "tendency or capacity to deceive," which has been replaced by "likely to mislead" at the FTC, will advertisers counter to an inquiring NAD that the legal standards have been lowered, and that they can no longer be threatened by a possible referral of the case by the NARB to the FTC?

Of course, the FTC does not provide the only venue for legal action; and Bergerson (1986) has argued that private litigation and industry self-discipline and self-regulation, relying heavily on many of the principles previously established by the FTC, have become the preferred means by which disputes over advertising claims are now regularly resolved. Besides, there is no evidence that advertisers have been less willing to accept NAD/NARB decisions even if they argue more strenuously. Still, a weaker or less active FTC—or one perceived as such by the industry—potentially undermines the NAD/NARB because of the standards they borrow from the FTC and the latter's role as backup for them.

Anticipation

What will the role of the NAD/NARB be in coming years? No institution stands still, so that U.S. national advertising self-regulation will continue to evolve because the regulatory environment itself changes.

New Battle Issues

Some people are anticipating and gearing up for another regulatory round after the present deregulatory pause terminates (cf. Molitor [1984], and Pertschuk [1982]). For that matter, tobacco and liquor advertising have re-emerged as major battlegrounds, with pharmaceutical advertising and advertising to children remaining latent powder kegs.[25] These are essentially "soft" matters of taste, opinion and social responsibility but even "hard" topics such as permissible wording in the advertising of foods and drugs are being fought (e.g., when can such words as "natural" and "light" be used). Moveover, the recent U.S. Supreme Court decision in the Posadas case (Docket No. 84–1903, 1 July 1986) has cast some doubts about First Amendment protection of "commercial speech" against undue regulation.

New Battle Arenas

Most of these battles, however, are likely to bypass both the NAD/NARB and the FTC, and to be fought in other arenas. Thus, the State Attorneys General of New York, Texas and California have accepted complaints filed by the Center for Science in the Public Interest, and used them to obtain compliance with state advertising laws as in the recent Campbell Soup and Coca-Cola Company (Nutrasweet) cases ignored by the FTC (Silverglade 1985, p. 20). The U.S. Congress itself is also acting more vigorously, banning the broadcast advertising of smokeless tobacco products in 1986, and proposing very restrictive limitations on tobacco advertising, all the way to a complete ban. Various legislative proposals to increase warning requirements in the labeling of such products as alcoholic beverages could spill over to their advertisements as well.

Both the NAD/NARB and the FTC are likely to be largely unaffected by these developments until an activist FTC chairman is appointed again, as has happened even under Republican presidents. Attacked industries—liquor, pharmaceuticals and even tobacco—are likely to have to strengthen their industry codes and enforcement, but this will not affect a NAD/NARB that remains focused on "truth and accuracy" and the proper substantiation of advertising claims.

Therefore, the symbiosis between the NAD/NARB and the FTC is likely to remain operational and effective in the foreseeable future even though their partnership has not been as formal and explicit as those prevailing in Canada, France and the United Kingdom.

NOTES

1. There are related dimensions of self-regulation that will not be analyzed here, such as the self-discipline exercised by advertisers, agencies and media, with the latter also performing a preclearance function about the advertisements submitted to them prior to publication or broadcasting. For a recent discussion of such complementary forms, see Janice Handler, "The Self-Regulatory System—An Advertiser's Viewpoint." *Food Drug Cosmetics Law Journal* 37 (January 1982): 257–263; Maddox and Zanot (1984) and Zanot (1985). See also the Practising Law Institute's annual handbooks on the *Legal and Business Aspects of the Advertising Industry*.

2. The local Advertising Review Committees (ARCs), jointly set up after 1981 by the Council of Better Business Bureaus and the American Advertising Federation, include representatives from the public at large, with the chairman selected from among the latter. However, ARCs are only advisory to local Better Business Bureaus.

3. Changes in recording methods preclude fully reliable computations of these percentages, but the relative orders of magnitude are essentially correct. These statistics are about published cases, but the NAD and CARU handle a much larger number of contacts or requests, of which only a fraction results in published decisions, because the others were dismissed for a variety of reasons (see: *NAD Case Report*, XIII, 6 of 15 July 1983, for a description of NAD/NARB case selection and handling). Therefore, consumer complaints are really more numerous than those emanating from competitors when contacts and requests are considered.

4. "While NAD decisions are not subject to enforcement by any government body, its 'teeth' are really the moral force of its position in the marketplace and the fact that the networks and other media may follow the NAD's views in any particular situation (Kent 1985, p. 1)."

5. The 167 local Better Business Bureaus (whose Council cosponsors and cofinances the NAD/NARB system) are much more publicized and better known, and they receive quite a few complaints—some of them about advertisements. The BBBs handle local advertising complaints (e.g., about retail ads) but pass on complaints about national advertisers to the NAD. Consumerist publications and the general press refer occasionally to NAD decisions, but the NAD has engaged in little publicity to make its existence and availability known to the general public, and to solicit consumer complaints. The NAD ran a couple of publicity campaigns in the late 1970s, but they resulted mostly in the kinds of complaints it does not handle (violence on television, boring or offending ads, etc.). Still, 5,600 copies of the *NAD Case Reports* are regularly circulated to some 800 newspapers, magazines, stations and interested parties.

6. There have been several public-opinion surveys about advertising by such organizations as Roper & Yankelovich, but a NARB-sponsored Gallup study reached similar conclusions about what bothers people regarding advertising (NARB 1979). This study found out that about 80 percent of consumer complaints involved issues of taste and morality.

7. The Federal Trade Commission Act does not mention "false" or "misleading"

advertising, but refers only to "unfair or deceptive acts or practices." However, the FTC in fact handles "truth and accuracy" as much as the NAD/NARB does.

8. This reaction followed the outcry and effective opposition on the part of both business and Congress against the "national-nanny" role assumed by the FTC in the context of the advertising-to-children issue, following a FTC-Staff proposal to limit it in the case of this "vulnerable group." The Commission, since Chairman James C. Miller III, has soft-pedalled the use of unfairness, claiming that, in most cases, deceptiveness can be used to handle advertisements that may also be considered as unfair. Still, the FTC requirement that advertising claims be adequately presubstantiated rests on the notion that unsubstantiated claims constitute an unfair act or practice (but see Ford and Calfee 1986, pp. 84–85).

9. The Federal Communications Commission (FCC) used to be more involved in soft issues as when it dealt with cigarette advertising and did invoke the Fairness Doctrine to press broadcasting stations to air antismoking viewpoints. The use of this doctrine has recently been eliminated on the ground that the multiplication of media—both old and new—provides enough avenues for dissent. The FCC had also praised and promoted the National Association of Broadcasters' Radio and Television Codes, which dealt with various taste and social-responsibility issues, until their demise, owing to an antitrust suit by the Department of Justice from 1979 to 1982 (see below).

10. The FTC now defines deception in terms of "unsubstantiated objective claims likely to mislead consumers acting reasonably under the circumstances to their [material] detriment [Crawford, December 5, 1984, p. 6]." The NAD is also interested in deception but mainly in whether the advertiser's claims had adequate prior substantiation. Thus, it will investigate taste-preference claims of the Pepsi Challenge variety on grounds of proper substantiation, while the FTC now ignores such subjective claims because of a lack of standards with which to evaluate them in terms of deception.

11. The FTC has had to implement various laws such as those mandating different types of warnings on tobacco products, but this has been a purely technical function. The FTC Staff has also had to comment on various petitions bearing—among others—on the advertising of alcohol and tobacco products, but it has regularly recommended against further regulation in these matters (e.g., FTC, "Omnibus Petition" 1985). In the case of alcohol advertising, various groups had charged that it was deceptive or unfair because of portraying alcoholic-beverage consumption in a positive or appealing manner, thereby causing increased consumption and abuse.

12. There have been rumblings to the effect that advertising associations—which are typically predominantly backed up by their larger members—do support presubstantiation because its burden is more onerous on smaller advertisers who are tempted to go after their larger rivals through comparison advertising (Cohen 1983, p. 39). Such a contention is hard to prove, however.

13. The Foreword to this 1979 report stresses that some of the grounds for dissatisfaction "are beyond the ability of the NAD/NARB to handle, or involve matters which neither government nor an industry self-regulatory group should interfere with." Still, it is worth noting that Ronald Smithies, NAD Executive Director, referred to an increasing number of NAD cases in 1986, that involved health claims in food and drug advertisements, where health claims not only are based on allegedly unsubstantiated fears, but also may unnecessarily exasperate these fears (cited in *AAF Washington Report* [January 1987]: 13). Such "exasperation of fears" may be construed to indicate some concern with "soft" issues.

14. The NAD published 98 decisions in 1987, and there were some 2,400 NAD/NARB/CARU cases over 17 years of operations—or an annual average of 140 NAD cases in 1971–1987 (there were also 43 NARB appeal cases). CARU resolved 182 advertising-to-children cases during its first eleven years of existence. In fiscal year 1983, the FTC acted on 98 consumer-protection matters, that is, complaints, consents, district-court actions, order modifications and rule-makings, although not all of them dealt with advertising. Former Chairman Miller claimed at one point that the FTC had issued more advertising complaints in the past one and one-half years than in the fiscal 1977–1980 period under his predecessor (*Advertising Compliance Service* 4, no. 8 (April 16, 1984): p. 8). For statistics on NAD/NARB and FTC activity, see *NAD Case Reports* (various dates) and the FTC's *Annual Reports* and *News Notes*.

15. NAD/NARB officials claim that they will handle any case where "truth and accuracy" is at stake ("Is there an objective statement or implied claim whose substantiation is subject to verification?"). However, it would seem that any organization with limited resources (as is also the case with the FTC) has to exercise judgment and will only select those cases where a large payoff (precedent-setting, publicity, etc.) is more likely.

16. "Effectively Using the NAD/NARB Process: PLI Conference Highlights." *Advertising Compliance Service* 4, no. 13 (July 2, 1984): 5–6. For a similar reference to the use of "FTC Guides and Trade Practice Rules and of the record of FTC consent orders and litigation," see: "Self-Regulation of National Advertising: Twelfth Year-End Report." *NAD Case Report* (July 15, 1983): 2–3. The Food and Drug Administration (FDA) does not handle food and drug consumer advertising—a task left to the FTC— but it supervises health claims used in food and drug labeling and in drug advertising to health professionals, thereby setting the underlying standards for what will ultimately be said in consumer advertising.

17. Even the sending of a letter by a self-regulatory body to recommend that an advertising medium require erring advertisers to amend their copy is not permitted under U.S. antitrust laws (LaBarbera 1981, p. 66). This practice of enlisting the cooperation of member media is common abroad, however; and overseas advertising self-regulatory bodies typically include media as members—unlike the NAD/NARB. It is worth noting that, as a matter of policy, the FTC itself does not cite the media used when issuing complaints, although the incriminated advertiser and agency are mentioned.

18. The FTC appears to assume that large advertisers can take care of themselves, and that its scarce resources should not be devoted to purely competitive squabbles better left to the NAD (if the "public interest" is involved), the courts and other forums. While these efforts are not linked to the NAD/NARB, it is worth noting that the Food and Drug Administration has teamed up with the Council of Better Business Bureaus to contact the advertising managers of some 9,500 publications with an offer of help in spotting advertisements for quack cures and other frauds (Irvin Molotsky, "Ads for Bogus Cures Under Attack," *New York Times*, May 31, 1984, B9). Similarly, the Direct Marketing Association has teamed up with the FTC to coauthor a consumer booklet on shopping by mail ("The FTC Is Striving to Achieve Cooperation Rather than Confrontation with America's Marketers: Miller." *AMA Marketing News* [September 2, 1983]: 10). However, doubts about the effectiveness of these approaches have been voiced by Virginia Knauer, Director of the U.S. Office of Consumer Affairs; and P. A. LaBarbera has revealed problems connected with "back-of-the-book" fraudulent advertisements rarely reached

by self-regulation ("The Shame of Magazine Advertising." *Journal of Advertising* 10, no. 1, [1981]: 31–37).

19. "Shouldn't Turn Ad Regulation over to NARB, FTC Argues." *Advertising Age* (November 15, 1976): 2, 80. Under the Pertschuk regime, A. H. Kramer, Director of the FTC's Bureau of Consumer Protection, had acknowledged that "self-regulation by the advertising industry is a critical component to the FTC's efforts," and he had even ventured to predict that: "If the industry takes anticipatory action through appropriate examination and self-regulation of new media advertising, future problems could well be averted, and the Commission's role might be reduced to overseeing compliance with a strong, self-imposed system of regulation" ("Industry and Government Can Work Together to Prevent Deceptive Advertising, Says Official of FTC." *FTC News Summary* (October 31, 1980): 2).

20. The NAD/NARB's recent annual budget of about $800,000 has been doubled since its inception in 1971. It appears to be adequate, since the goal is not to grow per se (private communication).

21. The Missouri Public Interest Research Group, which had been highly critical in the beginning and had monitored every NAD/NARB decision, later on petitioned the FTC to file complaints with the NAD first, before spending thousands of dollars of public funds. Quoted in: "The Process of Self-Regulation in Advertising; A Presentation by the National Advertising Review Council [sponsor of the NARB] to the U.S. Senate Commerce Committee, 17 September 1981," p. 8 (second part). This presentation was also made to the FTC. For additional favorable consumerist comments about the NAD, see Zuckerman (May 1984).

22. It is worth noting that one-fifth of appealed 1971–1986 NAD decisions have been reversed or modified by NARB panels where advertisers predominate (Miracle and Nevett 1987).

23. The advertising industry is also facing problems in connection with the multiplication of "new media" (cable television, cassettes, international satellite broadcasting, etc.). Their self-regulation is far from being understood or resolved. In particular, the matter of who would handle complaints emanating from overseas has hardly been discussed (cf. Boddewyn [1985]).

24. For a spirited set of charges and countercharges between former FTC Chairman Pertschuk and then current Chairman Miller, see: U.S. House of Representatives 1984. See also the two-part article "Assessment of the Miller Legacy at FTC." *Advertising Compliance Service* 5, no. 17 and 18 (September 2 and 16, 1985). For allegations of FTC inactivity see: "Deceptive Ads: The FTC's Laissez-Faire Approach Is Backfiring." *Business Week* (December 2, 1985): 136–40, and FTC Acting Chairman Terry Calvani's answer in the December 30, 1985 issue (p. 9). See also, his letter to the *New York Times* (April 29, 1986: A26). For recent consumerist concerns and plans, see the December 1986 issue of *Nutrition Action Newsletter*.

25. For recent advertising industry views about the emerging regulatory climate, see the papers presented at the November 1986 AAF National Advertising Law and Business Conference. For a brief summary, see: "Government Relations Reports; AAF Conference Highlights." *Advertising Compliance Service* 6, no. 24 (December 15, 1986): 5–7. The *AAF Washington Report* of January 1987 outlines many of the forthcoming advertising-related battles in Congress.

REFERENCES

AAAA. "The American Association of Advertising Agencies' Response to the Federal Trade Commission's Inquiry on the Advertising Substantiation Program." New York: July 13, 1983.

Armstrong, G. M. "An Evaluation of the Children's Advertising Review Unit." *Journal of Public Policy and Marketing* 3 (1984): 38–55.

Armstrong, G. M., and J. L. Ozanne. "An Evaluation of NAD/NARB Purpose and Performance." *Journal of Advertising* 12, no. 3 (1983): 15–26.

Bailey, Patricia F. "When Is an Ad Deceptive? The Regulation of Advertising at the FTC." In *New Trends in Advertising; Presentations at the American Advertising Federation's 1983–1984 Law and Public Policy Conferences.* Washington, DC: American Advertising Federation, 1984.

Bell, H. H. "Self-Regulation by the Advertising Industry." *California Management Review* 16, no. 3 (Spring 1974): 58–63.

Bergerson, S. R. "Ad Regulation: The Rules Are Changing and the Game Is Being Played in Some New Courts; Speech before the AAF National Advertising Law and Business Conference." Chicago, Ill.: November 5, 1986.

Boddewyn, J. J. "Advertising Regulation: Fiddling with the FTC While the World Burns." *Business Horizons* 28, no. 3 (May–June 1985): 32–40.

Children's Advertising Review Unit [CARU]. "An Eye on Children's Advertising." New York: CARU/NAD, 1979 and later versions.

Cohen, Dorothy. "Unfairness in Advertising Revisited." *Journal of Marketing* 46, (Winter 1982): 73–80.

Cohen, Stanley E. "Comments." *Advertising 1980; Proceedings of the Annual Conference of the American Academy of Advertising/1980.* Urbana, Ill.: Department of Advertising, University of Illinois, 1980, pp. 162–164.

———. "FTC Memo Hits Advertising Self-Regulation." *Advertising Age* (February 7, 1983): 39.

Crawford, Carol T. "Informal Dispute Settlement Programs and the Federal Trade Commission." Washington, DC: Federal Trade Commission, 1985.

———. "Remarks before the American Advertising Federation." Washington, DC: December 4, 1984.

———. "Remarks before the National Advertising Review Board." Washington, DC: December 5, 1984.

Edelstein, J. S. "Current Developments in Advertising Regulation." *Advertising Compliance Service* 3, no. 23, December 5, 1983: 3–8.

Federal Trade Commission [FTC]. *Annual Reports.* Washington, DC: various dates.

———. Bureau of Consumer Protection. "Advertising-Substantiation Program; Analysis of Public Comments and Recommended Changes." Washington, DC: July 23, 1984.

———. "FTC Policy Statement Regarding the Advertising Substantiation Program." Washington, DC: 1984.

———. "Omnibus Petition for Regulation of Unfair and Deceptive Alcoholic Beverage Advertising and Marketing Practices; Recommendations of the Staff of the Federal Trade Commission." Washington, DC: Docket No. 209–46, March 1985.

————. "Policy Statement on Unfairness." Washington, DC: December 17, 1980.

"FTC Chairman Miller Proposes Policy on Advertising Substantiation Program." *FTC News Notes* (March 30, 1984): 2.

Ford, G. T., and J. E. Calfee. "Recent Developments in FTC Policy on Deception." *Journal of Marketing* 50 (July 1986): 82–103.

Howard, J. A., and James Hulbert. *Advertising and the Public Interest; A Staff Report to the Federal Trade Commission*. Chicago, Ill.: Crain Communications, 1973.

Jacobson, Michael et al. *The Booze Merchants*. Washington, DC: Center for Science in the Public Interest, 1983.

Kent, F. H. "Control of Ads by Private Sector." *New York Law Journal* 27 (December 1985): 1ff.

Knauer, V. H. "Remarks before the SOCAP National Conference." Washington, DC: White House, June 22, 1981.

LaBarbera, P. A. "Advertising Self-Regulation: An Evaluation." *MSU Business Topics* (Summer 1980): 55–63.

————. "The Antitrust Shadow over Advertising Self-Regulation." In Leigh, J. H. and C. R. Martin, eds. *Current Issues and Research in Advertising 1981*. Ann Arbor, Mich.: Division of Research, Graduate School of Business Administration, University of Michigan, 1981, 57–70.

Maddox, L. M., and E. J. Zanot. "Suspension of the NAB Code and Its Effect on the Regulation of Advertising." *Journalism Quarterly* 61, no. 1 (Spring 1984): 125 ff.

Matthews, L. S. "Government Regulation and Self-Regulation in Advertising." A paper presented at the Fourteenth Asian Advertising Congress, Seoul, Korea, June 1984." New York: American Association of Advertising Agencies, June 20, 1984.

Meloan, T. W. "Advertising Self-Regulation: A Comparative Study [U.K. and U.S.]. Mimeographed. Los Angeles, Calif.: School of Business Administration, University of Southern California, 1983.

Miller, Mark. "Can Advertising Regulate Itself?" *Marketing and Media Decisions* (July 1981): 37 ff.

Miracle, G. E., and T. R. Nevett. *Voluntary Regulation of Advertising: A Comparative Analysis of the United Kingdom and the United States*. Lexington, Mass.: Lexington Books, 1987.

Molitor, G. T. T. "Plotting the Patterns of Change." *Enterprise* (March 1984): 4–9.

Molotsky, Irvin. "Ban on Beer Ads Is Called Unlikely." *New York Times*, February 8, 1985, C32.

National Advertising Division [NAD]. *NAD Case Reports*. New York: various dates.

National Advertising Review Board [NARB]. *Advertising Self-Regulation and Its Interaction with Consumers*. New York: 1979.

————. "Statement of Organization and Procedures of the National Advertising Review Board as Amended to June 19, 1980." New York: 1985.

"New Directions FTC?" *Advertising Compliance Service* 4, no. 2 (January 20, 1986): 4–5.

"The New FTC: Steady as She Goes; An Interview with Chairman Dan Oliver." *American Advertising* 3, no. 3 (January 1987): 9–11.

Oliver, Daniel. "The Coming of Age in Advertising Regulation; Speech at the Annual Meeting of the Council of Better Business Bureau; San Diego, Calif." Washington, DC: Federal Trade Commission, September 22, 1986.

Pertschuk, Michael. "Advertising and Inflation; A Speech before the Annual Meeting of the National Advertising Review Board." New York: November 8, 1978.

———. *Revolt against Regulation: The Rise and Pause of the Consumer Movement.* Berkeley, Calif.: University of California Press, 1982.

Preston, I. L., "A Review of the Literature on Advertising Regulation," in *Current Issues and Research in Advertising 1983* (Ann Arbor, Mich.: Division of Research, Graduate School of Business Administration, University of Michigan, 1983), pp. 1–37.

Purdon, R. A. "Advertising Self-Regulation: A New Reality." New York: American Association of Advertising Agencies, March 1972.

Rice, D. A. "Toward a Theory and Legal Standard of Consumer Unfairness." *Journal of Law and Commerce* 5, no. 1 (1984): 111–54.

Silverglade, B. A. "FTC Oversight Still Needed." *Advertising Age* (June 3, 1985): 20 ff.

Smithies, R. H. "Presentation before the American Advertising Federation's 1986 National Advertising Law and Business Conference." Chicago, Ill.: November 5, 1986.

U.S. House of Representatives, Committee on Energy and Commerce. *FTC Review, 1977–1984.* Washington, DC: U.S. Government Printing Office, Document 98-CC, September 1984.

Vogel, David. *National Styles of Regulation; Environmental Policy in Great Britain and the United States.* Ithaca, New York: Cornell University Press, 1986.

Zanot, E. J. "The National Advertising Review Board, 1971–76." *Journalism Monographs* 59 (February 1979): 1–46.

———. "The National Advertising Review Board: Premises, Precedents, and Performance." Unpublished Ph.D. dissertation, Ann Arbor, Mich.: University Microfilms International, 1977.

———. "A Review of Eight Years of NARB Casework: Guidelines and Parameters of Deceptive Advertising." *Journal of Advertising* 9, no. 4 (1980): 27–34.

———. "Unseen but Effective Advertising Regulation: The Clearance Process." *Journal of Advertising* 14, no. 4 (1985): 44 ff.

Zuckerman, Sam. "Booze on the Rocks." *Nutrition Action* [CSPI] 11 (December 1984): 6–10.

———. "FTC Abandons Food Ad Regulation." *Nutrition Action* [CSPI] 11 (May 1984): 5–9.

ACKNOWLEDGMENTS

The assistance of the following people is gratefully acknowledged: Ch. F. Adams (formerly of the AAAA), P. W. Allport (ANA), R. H. Alexander (NARB), P. P. Bailey (FTC), Howard H. Bell (AAF), Robert Chatov (SUNY-Buffalo), Stanley Cohen (*Advertising Age*), J. D. Forbes (British Columbia), Collot Guérard (FTC), Janice Handler (Lever Brothers), P. M. Hyman, Felix H. Kent, Priscilla LaBarbera (NYU), G. E. Miracle (Michigan State), I. L. Preston (Wisconsin-Madison), Lorraine Reid (formerly of the CBBB/NAD), W. W. Rogal, Bruce Silverglade (CSPI), R. H. Smithies (NAD), W. S. Snyder (formerly of the FTC, now with the AAF), W. H. Tankersley (Council of Better Business Bureaus), R. J. Watkins (Procter & Gamble), E. J. Zanot (Maryland), and Mitchell Zeller (CSPI).

___ III ___
Comparative Analyses

15

Data from a Sixteen-Country Survey

While this study was in progress, the International Advertising Association (IAA) conducted a 1986 survey of countries with an advanced ASR system at the national level. Sixteen organizations responded to this author's questionnaire; and the present chapter highlights the key findings of the IAA report (Boddewyn 1986)—particularly those questions focusing on outside participation in advertising self-regulation. This IAA survey added Australia, Ireland, Singapore, South Africa and Spain to the twelve countries covered in this volume, but did not include Sweden, which does not have an ASR system.

Highlights of the 1986 IAA Survey

1. Most advertising self-regulatory systems date from the 1960s and 1970s as a reflection of the rise of consumerism as a major issue and force during that period, and of the concurrent development of consumer-protection regulations.

2. The level of government regulation of advertising is considered to be high in seven countries and medium in another seven, while the Philippines and South Africa rank it as low. Eight expect no change, four more regulation, and four less. Eight countries perceive the consumer movement as moderately active, seven see it as very active and one (Spain) as not active at all. Altogether, the environment of self-regulation seems to have favorably stabilized.

3. Seven ASR systems have officially adopted the International Chamber of Commerce's (ICC) International Code of Advertising Practice. In the others, ICC principles and guidelines are usually incorporated in ASR rules. However, the sixteen countries reported that the courts make only rare references to the ICC Code, while in five countries they occasionally or regularly refer to local ASR principles, guidelines and/or codes.

4. Nine ASR systems have their own full-fledged code. Others rely on general principles, guidelines about some specific products (e.g., alcoholic beverages), targets (e.g., children), and practices (e.g., testimonials) and/or their own previous decisions. Nine ASR systems also apply national laws in addition to their own rules.

5. Eleven ASR systems require that advertisers have adequate substantiation prior to the release of an advertisement. (The ICC Code only states that "advertisers should be ready to produce evidence without delay to the self-disciplinary bodies.")

6. While all sixteen ASR systems accept complaints from customers, competitors, government agencies, etc., only six of them regularly monitor ads and commercials: Brazil, France, Italy, Spain, the United Kingdom and the United States. In other words, most systems define their role as an intermediary between advertiser and complainant rather than as a watchdog for the industry or the public. However, eleven ASR systems accept anonymous complaints and assume them as their own, if valid.

7. Complaints are typically settled within one to two months—faster in Germany and Ireland; much more slowly in Japan and the United States. An appeal system is available in ten of the sixteen countries, and it often includes nonindustry members.

8. All systems, except Germany's for the most part, handle complaints about false and misleading ads. However, about half of them, unlike the German system, shy away from cases of "unfairness" and "poor taste."

9. ASR systems vary in terms of whether they accept complaints about personal, help-wanted, opinion/controversy/advocacy and nonprofit ads. Nine of them handle ads in all media, while the others exclude such media as television, which are often handled by separate bodies.

10. The caseloads of ASR systems differ considerably. Some handle thousands of "inquiries" from consumers and competitors (e.g., France, Japan, South Africa and the United Kingdom). Regarding actionable complaints, the number of cases settled ranges from over 3,000 in the United Kingdom to 24 in Japan. These huge differences reflect varying policies: some single out important cases while others handle all valid complaints: some handle national ads but not local ones; some deal with all media while others handle only some of them, etc.

11. More inquiries and complaints come from consumers and their associations than from competing firms (except in Spain and the United States). However, complaints between competitors are more often resolved within their professional associations when the public interest is not at stake.

12. More than half of the sixteen ASR systems expect a higher caseload within the next two years, but no new types of complaints. Ads coming from abroad are seldom handled, but most ASR systems expect to scrutinize more of them in the future.

13. When an ad is found to be in violation of the rules, the advertiser is

always asked to withdraw or modify it. If he does not comply, fourteen ASR systems ask the media to stop printing or showing the ad—a practice restricted by antitrust law in Germany and United States. Various amounts of publicity are given to the ASR body's decisions and to the advertiser's compliance, but the names of noncompliant offenders are seldom publicized. Strong penalties such as expulsion, finjng and denunciation to the authorities are rarely used.

14. Most ASR systems provide free advice to advertisers and agencies. However, outside of Canada (for TV commercials addressed to children and about feminine-hygiene products), the Philippines (for all commercials) and the United Kingdom (for cigarette ads), practically no mandatory prescreening is provided.

15. Only five ASR systems have recently surveyed the public in terms of familiarity with self-regulation and satisfaction with its performance. From one-fifth to one-third of the surveyed public in these five countries were aware of the existence of an ASR system.

16. Press releases and publicity campaigns are the most common means used to publicize ASR systems. Also widely used are industry and public conferences as well as interaction with government bodies.

17. Outsiders are often informally consulted when self-regulatory guidelines and rules are developed and amended. In Australia, Canada, Italy, the Netherlands, Singapore and the United Kingdom, consumer representatives and independent members of the public play significant roles in deciding about complaints. Germany, the Philippines and Spain mentioned increasing outside representation at least informally, but no major changes appear likely (see below for further details).

18. Permanent ASR staffs are generally small, ranging from one person in Germany to fourteen in France and Japan, fifteen in the United States, and fifty-four in the United Kingdom. Secretariats tend to make routine decisions and prepare difficult ones for higher-level panels. Only in France and the United States does the staff make all the decisions.

19. In addition to the sixteen countries discussed above, fifteen survey responses came from countries with no central self-regulatory body, but with one or more professional advertising associations. In these countries, advertising-agency associations most frequently deal with self-regulation, and many of them have their own codes.

Outside Participation in ASR Activities

Two questions in the 1986 IAA survey dealt with the participation of outsiders:

1. "All advertising self-regulatory bodies interact to some extent with 'outsiders,' that is, people and organizations who do not belong to the advertising industry. Your organization may also interact with government agencies, consumerist organizations, legal experts and academicians on an *informal* basis. This question, however, is about the *formal or official* inclusion or participation of 'outsiders' (e.g., consumer and government representatives, independent members of the public, experts, etc.) in your

activities on a regular basis. To what extent do such outsiders participate in: (a) standards development, (b) choice of cases to handle, (c) deciding cases, (d) handling appeals, and (e) the general evaluation of ASR programs?''
2. ''Do you anticipate increasing the participation of outsiders in your activities?''

Outsiders of various types are used in most countries and in a variety of capacities. Three modes of outside participation stand out: (1) there is usually an ''independent'' person (often a former judge or jurist) serving as chairman of the ASR body; (2) various experts are frequently consulted on an ad hoc basis when ASR standards are developed and applied, and (3) more rarely, nonindustry members are involved in case adjudication. This third pattern was found in fewer than half of the sixteen countries.

AUSTRALIA	Eight out of thirteen adjudicating-panel members are ''independents.''
BRAZIL	Two out of eleven panel members come from outside the industry (physicians, journalists, lawyers, etc.).
CANADA	One-third of the case-handling panel (for difficult cases and appeals) is made up of consumer representatives, academics, Status of Women groups, YMCA, YWCA and the like.
ITALY	All members of the case-handling Jury are magistrates or legal experts (five) and academics (two).
NETHERLANDS	From 40 to 60 percent of the panels are consumerists and legal experts.
SINGAPORE	At least half of the adjudicating-panel members are consumer, government and trade-association representatives.
UNITED KINGDOM	Two-thirds of the panel are ''independent'' members of the public.

In Spain and the United States (at the appeal level), much smaller proportions of outsiders are used. In Germany, the Philippines and Spain, there are plans to increase outside participation. It is apparent that outsiders are used to a greater extent on appeal panels that at the first adjudicating level.

Outside participation is related to the role of ASR secretariats. Such permanent staffs either make most decisions (two countries), refer only difficult ones to adjudicating panels where outsiders may sit (six countries) or prepare the cases for such panels (seven countries). Only in Italy is the permanent staff not involved in adjudication. Still, the chairman and/or executive director of ASR bodies are often ''independents'' or, at least, professional administrators usually able to ensure that complaint-handling is managed competently and objectively.

Table 15.1
The Limits of Advertising Self-Regulation

	INDUSTRY IS WILLING TO SPEND SOME MONEY AND OTHER RESOURCES BUT NOT TOO MUCH (1)	PAST A CERTAIN POINT, ASR IS FELT TO BE AS BURDENSOME AS REGULATION (2)	SELF-REGULATION NEEDS TO BE BACKED UP BY REGULATION (3)	SELF-REGULATION CAN ONLY ASSIST PERSONAL SELF-DISCIPLINE (4)
AUSTRALIA	X	X		X
BELGIUM				X
BRAZIL			X	
CANADA	X		X	
FRANCE	X	X		
GERMANY			X	X
IRELAND	X		X	
ITALY	X		X	X
JAPAN	X			
NETHERLANDS				X
PHILIPPINES			X	X
SINGAPORE	X			
SOUTH AFRICA	X			X
SPAIN	X		X	
UK			X	
USA	X		X	X

The Limits of Self-Regulation

Four options were outlined in the IAA questionnaire about the limits of advertising self-regulation:

1. Industry is willing to spend some money and other resources on advertising self-regulation, but not too much.
2. Past a certain point, self-regulation is felt by industry members to be as burdensome as regulation so that its voluntary character decreases in intensity. Such a situation limits the moral, physical and financial support that the industry is willing to give to its self-regulatory body.
3. Self-regulation cannot perform the entire task of ensuring good advertising behavior but needs regulation to back it up and take care of those who refuse to act responsibly.
4. Self-regulation ultimately depends on personal discipline on the part of advertising people, and organized self-regulation can only assist such personal commitments.

Multiple answers were allowed, and they are presented in Table 15.1. The choices of options 1 (ten countries) and 2 (two countries) reveal what may be considered as self-imposed limitations, that is, the advertising industry is committed to self-regulation but wants to limit its scope and burden. They may also reflect the frustrations encountered by practically all ASR bodies outside of the United Kingdom in maintaining or increasing their relatively meager budgets. The selection of options 3 and 4 (nine and eight countries respectively) is more indicative of a recognition of the natural limits of self-regulation, which represents only one form of advertising control, since government regulation and the self-discipline of practitioners and media are also needed and used to achieve good and better advertising behavior.

Still, national answers varied considerably, suggesting that: (1) many factors affect the role, impact and effectiveness of advertising self-regulation around the world, and (2) no standardization of ASR systems is in sight.

16

Advertising Self-Regulation and Outside Participation: Comparative Conclusions

General Approach

Previous chapters have established that self-regulation, as a form of control of business conduct and performance by business itself, is a well-established function of the advertising industry in a score of countries, and that outside participation is present in practically all of these advertising self-regulatory systems, although in varying amounts and forms. They have also analyzed the potential contributions, constraints and shortcomings of advertising self-regulation and of outside participation by nonindustry members in its structure and operation. It remains for this chapter to (1) test through the country-study findings and in a comparative manner the hypotheses developed in Chapters 1 and 2, and (2) use these findings to critically examine the neocorporatist claim that self-regulation constitutes an alternative form of social control.

The hypotheses bearing on advertising self-regulation and outside participation were built around: (1) necessary conditions or prerequisites; (2) motivations and (3) precipitating circumstances that hasten what may already be possible and desired. These hypotheses are not testable in a rigorously quantitative manner for lack of suitable measures and data. In particular, the hypotheses centering on the development of advertising self-regulation (Chapter 1) can only be loosely tested, since the country studies did not provide a full historical analysis of the twelve ASR systems (and their predecessors), but focused on their more recent past. The effectiveness of advertising self-regulation and of outside participation is also very difficult to measure and compare for lack of adequate criteria, as was previously argued. Still, several comparative indices data will now be developed to indicate the intensity of various national factors uncovered by this research.

For each condition, motivation and precipitating circumstance, a rating of 1, 2 or 3 was given to each of the twelve countries: "1" means that this element is a minor one or rather weak; "2" stands for some significant influence; and "3" indicates that it is a very important and favorable factor.[1] Higher national scores are therefore related to: (1) a more developed self-regulatory system, that is, one buttressed by more conducive conditions, motivations and precipitating circumstances, and (2) high conduciveness to outside participation. While such ratings are perforce subjective, quantitative supportive evidence was used whenever possible. However, there is the danger of circular reasoning in this kind of analysis, since the overall states of advertising self-regulation and of outside participation in a particular country color the ratings given to that country's conditions, motivations and precipitating circumstances. Only independent evaluation of the latter factors through experts and/or the use of various socioeconomic indicators could remedy this problem.

Comparing the twelve countries is also complicated by the fact that each one of them warranted a somewhat different research approach. It would not have been productive to impose a methodological strait jacket on each national analysis because the ASR systems, outside participation in them and environmental circumstances varied so much. For example, the U.S. chapter could have been reduced to just a few pages if it had been limited to counting and explaining the very low number and influence of formal outsiders in the NAD/NARB system when, in fact, the Federal Trade Commission and a few consumerist organizations play an important if more informal role in that system. Similarly, the relatively high level of outside participation in Dutch advertising self-regulation is based on environmental factors other than in Canada, where there is also much outside participation, so that these two countries required somewhat different analyses.

A Comparison of ASR Systems

The nine hypotheses presented in Chapter 1 (in the form of ASR Conditions, Motivations and Precipitating Circumstances) were tested by assigning low ($=1$), average ($=2$) and high ($=3$) scores to those conditions, motivations and precipitators that the survey of the literature suggested were relevant to explain the existence, development and/or effectiveness of a national ASR system in eleven of the countries analyzed for this study (Sweden was left out because it does not have such a system). Tables 16.1 and 16.2 present the national and average scores for the nine hypotheses.

ASR Conditions

Hypotheses C1 and C2 achieved the highest score of 2.9 (out of 3) in this study, thereby revealing what might be called the interrelated necessary conditions for the existence and effectiveness of advertising self-regulation: (1) there must be some overarching advertising organization with the moral (and often

Table 16.1
A Comparison of ASR Systems' Existence and Effectiveness

ASR CONDITIONS	BELGIUM	BRAZIL	CANADA	FRANCE	GERMANY	ITALY	JAPAN	NETHERLANDS	PHILIP.	UK	USA	MEAN
C1. The existence of an industry-wide decision-making system (such as a capstone association) increases the probability of industry self-regulation.	3	3	3	2	3	3	3	3	3	3	3	2.9
C2. Industry self-regulation is more effective when it involves all inter-related levels.	3	3	3	3	3	3	3	3	3	3	2	2.9
C3. The development and effectiveness of an industry self-regulatory system are enhanced by government threat and oversight.	2	3	3	3	1	1	2	2	2	3	2	2.2
C4. The strength and effectiveness of an industry self-regulatory system are enhanced by its essentiality and non-substitutability.	2	2	3	2	2	3	1	2	3	3	2	2.3
C5. The existence and effectiveness of industry self-regulation are affected by cultural factors.	1	2	3	2	2	2	2	3	3	3	2	2.3

Average for ASR
Conditions   2.5

Table 16.1 (continued)

ASR MOTIVATIONS	BELGIUM	BRAZIL	CANADA	FRANCE	GERMANY	ITALY	JAPAN	NETHERLANDS	PHILIP.	UK	USA	MEAN
M1. Industry self-regulation is more likely in those situations where it can increase the overall demand for the industry's product.	2	2	3	3	2	2	2	3	1	3	3	2.4
M2. Industry self-regulation is more likely in those situations where the externally imposed cost from not undertaking such self-regulation would be greater than the cost of undertaking such self-regulation.	2	3	3	3	1	3	3	3	3	3	3	2.7

Average for ASR Motivations   2.5

ASR PRECIPITATORS	BELGIUM	BRAZIL	CANADA	FRANCE	GERMANY	ITALY	JAPAN	NETHERLANDS	PHILIP.	UK	USA	AVERAGE
PC1. The creation and improvement of an industry self-regulatory system are precipitated by the threat of government regulation.	3	3	3	3	1	1	2	3	2	3	3	2.5
PC2. Encouragement and support of industry self-regulation as an instrument of public policy is more likely when the limits of government intervention have become apparent.	1	2	3	2	2	1	2	3	3	3	2	2.2

Average for ASR Precipitators   2.3

financial) support of major advertiser, agency and media associations to launch, nurture and supervise an ASR system, and (2) the various levels in the advertising chain—from advertiser to agency to media—must actively participate in the ASR exercise. In particular, the participation of the media is crucial, because most advertisements need them to reach the public.

Separate codes of ethics and complaint-handling mechanisms on the part of advertiser, agency, media and/or product- or service-based industry associations have always paved the way for the development of a national, all-industry and all-media ASR system; and they still play an important role in resolving intra-professional disputes. However, such fragmented and uncoordinated efforts are generally insufficient to achieve the necessary scope, visibility and reach necessary to firmly position self-regulation as a credible alternative or complement to other forms of advertising control.[2]

If the media play such a crucial control role, could they not suffice to achieve advertising control? Their preclearance and acceptance roles are certainly crucial, but they need the "upstream" backup of advertisers and agencies committed to "good advertising behavior" as expressed in common principles, guidelines and codes. Otherwise, the media become overwhelmed with the total control task, and end up competing against each other on the basis of inconsistent standards.

The scores for France (on C1) and the United States (on C2) were lower because there is no true French capstone advertising association; while U.S. antitrust laws largely preclude the media from being involved in the administration of advertising self-regulation. However, there are effective informal arrangements in these two countries, that amount to an integrated approach. For that matter, their ASR systems reach some 80 percent of all national advertisements—a figure comparable to that found in the other nine nations.

Hypothesis C3 refers to the necessity of government threat and oversight for the development of effective self-regulation ("government threat" is also a precipitating circumstance analyzed below). The average score drops here to 2.2, reflecting a variety of national circumstances analyzed in the country chapters. The central argument in favor of this hypothesis is that advertising self-regulation works best when the government favors its existence, promotes and defends it, and keeps a watchful eye over its functioning. The United Kingdom represents the epitome of such a situation and of an extremely well-developed and well-rated ASR system; while Germany and Italy stand for the opposite case of government indifference. The other national scores corroborate this broad relationship between government involvement and ASR development and effectiveness, although the qualifications necessary to fully understand and support this general statement must be left to the country chapters.

Hypothesis C4 states that the strength and effectiveness of advertising self-regulation are enhanced by its essentiality and non-substitutability; in other words, it works best where it substitutes for the law or explicitly complements it. The average score of 2.3 reflects a variety of national circumstances, including historical ones, which cannot be fully considered here.

Ultimately, one can argue that industry self-regulation is always essential as a "private-interest government" necessary to complement other forms of social control, all of which exhibit certain limitations. Even if the law is reasonably developed and implemented, society benefits from overlapping controls emanating from the Community, the Market and Associations (see Chapter 1). Beyond this conceptual point, however, òne enters into the realm of implementation and acceptance. Self-regulation has the potential of manifesting its "essentiality and non-substitutability," but it may either: (1) not achieve it by failing to exploit its opportunities; (2) be overlooked or downplayed, notwithstanding its contributions; or (3) be overwhelmed by other forms of social control.

In both Germany and Japan, advertising self-regulation appeared after elaborate regulatory and redress systems were already in place, and it is still struggling to position itself there. In Belgium, the ASR system plays an important role in view of various regulatory shortcomings, but the very existence of the latter has militated against the honest recognition of its contributions by consumerists and government officials keen on strengthening regulatory and redress mechanisms. In many countries, advertising self-regulation lacks some of the resources (financial, moral, personal, etc.) truly necessary to become a major player in social control. These situations illustrate the overall validity of the C4 hypothesis, which, however, requires important subconditions to be present.

That the existence and effectiveness of self-regulation are affected by cultural factors (Hypothesis C5) is self-evident to the extent that all societal institutions, including ASR systems, are affected by a country's "culture" (see Chapter 1 for a discussion of this variable). Various country studies stressed such cultural factors as the general nature of business-government relations (e.g., the different "political cultures" of the United Kingdom and the United States), inclinations toward associationism and trust (e.g., in the Netherlands and Sweden) and public attitudes toward business and government (e.g., in Japan). Unfortunately, it is very difficult to generalize about the exact impact of cultural factors, because even unfavorable ones may be circumvented by resourceful ASR leaders (e.g., in France) or overridden by political threats (e.g., in the United States)—among other noncultural compensating elements. The average score of 2.3 for Hypothesis C5 reveals the difficulty of isolating the role of cultural conditions in explaining ASR systems.

ASR Motivations

Hypotheses M1 and M2 basically argue that ASR systems are developed for offensive and defensive reasons. On the one hand, the advertising industry realizes that the impact of its sizable expenditures can be crippled if people do not trust advertisements and advertisers. Therefore, self-regulation is positively motivated by the primary goal of enhancing the honesty and credibility of advertising through self-control, which can increase "the overall demand for the industry's product," that is, for commercial communications through the media.

On the other hand, advertising self-regulation demands resources (money, people, moral support, etc.) so that a cost-benefit calculus enters into the picture, and the ASR effort will roughly match the cost of not undertaking self-regulation. How many more costly regulations, suits, expressions of public dissatisfaction and disaffection with advertising, etc., will follow if self-regulation is not properly developed and implemented? Clearly one cannot exactly gauge such a tradeoff, but the negative alternatives of more regulation (from the State), unfavorable public reactions (from the Community) and unfair competition (in the Market) are always present to some degree, and provide significant motivations for advertising self-regulation. After all, the cost of ASR systems outside the United Kingdom pales in comparison to that of producing and broadcasting a major TV commercial in prime time.

These reasons are so obvious that one would expect a perfect 3.0 score for these two hypotheses, but M1 achieved only 2.4, while M2 reached a higher 2.7 average. For that matter, the national scores were sometimes difficult to determine, because of a lack of data about public satisfaction with advertising, the cost of regulation and the like. Higher national scores for Hypothesis M1 correspond roughly to countries where advertising expenditures are relatively high (e.g., Canada, the United Kingdom and the United States) or where advertising had been held in low repute (e.g., France). Under such conditions, positive motivation was particularly high in order to improve the acceptability of advertising. Regarding the cost benefit tradeoff (Hypothesis M2), the lower scores of Belgium and Germany reflect the limits of advertising self-regulation encountered in these two countries where the ASR system faces either high consumerist and bureaucratic resistance (in Belgium), or well-developed alternatives (in Germany), so that the payoff of additional efforts can only be marginal under the present circumstances.

ASR Precipitating Circumstances

Hypothesis PC1 states that "the creation and improvement of an industry self-regulatory system are precipitated by the threat of governmental regulation." In all countries, this factor appears to some degree. Yet, the average score was 2.5 instead of a maximum of 3.0 points. The lower scores simply reflect that the regulatory threat is less important in some countries. In Germany and Japan, the legal system is extremely well developed and used, so that further regulations are unlikely outside of particular sectors (e.g., drugs, tobacco and liquor), where ad hoc solutions are being developed through business-government negotiations. In the Philippines, a governmental vacuum and a quasicorporatist delegation of control to the ASR system have limited external threats, at least for the time being. Consequently, this hypothesis stands generally validated, although the threat of government regulation does not provide the sole explanation for the creation and improvement of ASR systems. Instead, the genuine desire of many advertising practitioners to raise standards—sometimes, in order to reduce unfair competition—must be acknowledged because, by doing so, they enhance their own reputation and effectiveness and those of the industry at large.

An even lower score (2.2) was ascribed to Hypothesis PC2: "Encouragement and support of industry self-regulation as an instrument of public policy is more likely when the limits of government intervention have become apparent." Still, this hypothesis is validated to the extent that the lower national scores simply reflect the fact that, in some countries, there is the reality (or the perception) that more regulation is needed (e.g., in Belgium) or, at least, wanted by some people (e.g., in the United States).

Of course, more advertising control is always needed to the extent that new problems emerge (as with the new media) or old solutions decline in effectiveness. The crux of the problem lies in what kinds of new controls will be preferred and ultimately prevail. The nature of the dominant problems (e.g., "soft" issues of taste and opinion versus "hard" issues of truth and accuracy), the political culture and the regulatory climate (e.g., the deregulatory pause in various countries), governmental budgetary problems, the perceived effectiveness of ASR solutions, the militancy of consumerists and the vested interests of bureaucrats are some of the factors that will affect the choice of particular social controls. Sometimes, parts of the same country exhibit different demands and solutions simultaneously, as in the case of English vs. French Canada; and particular industries may be under regulatory threat (e.g., tobacco, liquor and drugs) while "all is calm on the general front."

A Comparison of Outside Participation

Table 16.2 presents scores related to the conditions, motivations and precipitating circumstances related to outside participation (OP) in ASR systems, as was outlined in the form of hypotheses at the end of Chapter 2.

OP Conditions

The scores for all four hypotheses about OP conditions are the lowest for the entire series, reflecting an array of relatively unfavorable national elements regarding the participation of outsiders in advertising self-regulation.

Hypothesis C1 states that: "Outside participation is a function of the relative unavailability and ineffectiveness of other ways of obtaining consumer protection and of participating in public policymaking, as far as outsiders are concerned." The low score of 1.5 simply reflects the fact that organized outsiders (e.g., consumerists) either have alternative ways of expressing "voice" effectively or prefer to keep fighting for such influence, instead of settling for the "loyalty" route via participation in ASR systems (see Chapter 2 for an elaboration of these concepts). Actually, smart outsiders play it both ways, working both within and without the ASR systems, as in Canada, the Netherlands and the United Kingdom, or using it peripherally when appropriate, as in the United States. In other

Table 16.2
A Comparison of Outside Participation in ASR Systems

OP CONDITIONS	BELGIUM	BRAZIL	CANADA	FRANCE	GERMANY	ITALY	JAPAN	NETHERLANDS	PHILIP.	UK	USA	MEAN
C1. Outside practication is function of the relative unavailability and ineffectiveness of other ways of obtaining consumer protection and of participating in public policy, as far as outsiders are concerned.	1	1	2	2	1	1	1	2	2	2	1	1.5
C2. Outside participation is associated with cultures emphasizing cooperation and trust rather than conflict and distrust.	1	2	3	1	1	1	1	3	1	3	1	1.6
C3. Outside participation depends on the existence of a cohesive, middle-of-the-road and well-resourced consumer movement, or of a truly independent elite.	1	1	3	2	1	1	1	3	1	3	1	1.6
C4. Self-regulatory bodies accept outsiders only of they can control or neutralize them.	1	3	2	3	1	1	2	2	2	2	1	1.8
Average of OP Conditions												1.6

Table 16.2 (continued)

OP MOTIVATIONS	BELGIUM	BRAZIL	CANADA	FRANCE	GERMANY	ITALY	JAPAN	NETHERLANDS	PHILIP.	UK	USA	MEAN
M1. Outsiders - individually or collectively - accept to participate only when outside participation provides an effective way of achieving "voice."	1			2	2	3		3	1	2	1	1.7
M2. Self-regulatory bodies accept outsiders only when they provide legitimacy and/or expertise.	2	2	3	3	1	3	1	3	1	3	1	2.1
Average of OP Motivations												1.9

OP PRECIPITATORS	BELGIUM	BRAZIL	CANADA	FRANCE	GERMANY	ITALY	JAPAN	NETHERLANDS	PHILIP.	UK	USA	AVERAGE
PC1. Outside participation is linked to the emergence and salience of "soft" issues of taste and opinion, and the related need for new expertise about them.	1	2	3	1	1	2	1	1	1	3	2	1.6
PC2. Outside participation is precipitated by legitimacy crises.	1	2	3	2	1	3	1	2	1	3	2	1.9
PC3. Outside participation is more likely when public policy encourages and facilitates it.	1	1	3	2	1	1	1	3	1	3	1	1.6
Average of OP Precipitators												1.7

words, participating in self-regulation is never a necessity or, at least, is not perceived or accepted as one.

That "outside participation is associated with cultures emphasizing cooperation and trust rather than conflict and distrust" (Hypothesis C2) scored only an average of 1.6 points. Only Canada, the Netherlands and the United Kingdom scored 3.0 points, with most other nations standing at 1.0 point. This "cultural" factor is undeniably a major one, although, as was argued under ASR Condition No. 5, there are compensating factors in some countries.

Hypothesis C3, linking outside participation to the existence of a cohesive, middle-of-the-road and well-resourced consumer movement, or of a truly independent elite, got mostly national ratings of 1.0 (with four exceptions) and achieved an average score of 1.6 points. In a sense, Hypotheses C2 and C3 go together, since the lack of an unified and confident consumer movement is not only inconducive to outside participation, but is also a product of missing cultural cohesiveness in the country.

Finally, "Self-regulatory bodies accept outsiders only if they can control or neutralize them" (Hypothesis C4) scored an average of 1.8 points. Chapter 2 has already discussed outside participation as a departure from "pure" self-regulation, where only industry members participate in its functioning. In particular, the ASR system always retains direct control of its standards, because their acceptability by industry depends on their being "user-friendly" in order to generate voluntary adhesion. Even the application of these standards exhibits strong industry influence—outside of Italy—because of the difficulty of truly "encoding" and "diffusing" some of them in a simple and unequivocal way (see Chapter 2 for a discussion of these concepts). When independent outsiders are willing to participate, their number and selection as well as the preparation of the cases submitted to them remain largely under industry control.

Still, the relatively low score of 1.8 reveals the impossibility or difficulty of achieving such control over outsiders. Either they simply refuse to participate (e.g., Japan) or they occasionally precipitate crises (e.g., in Canada), while the industry is aware that mere "stooges" or "tokens" serve no real purpose in terms of achieving credibility or enhancing expertise. In any case, outsiders cannot be controlled outside the ASR system, where they can militate for more regulation (e.g., in the Netherlands). This delicate balancing problem is likely to persist because industry refuses to have nonindustry bodies choose their own representatives on ASR bodies.

OP Motivations

Here too the scores are on the low side. Outsiders accept to participate only when they can achieve "voice" (Hypothesis M1); and self-regulatory bodies accept outsiders only when the latter provide legitimacy and/or expertise (Hypothesis M2). Actually, this is a fair bargain between the two sides. The lower score of 1.7 points for M1 simply reveals that half of the ASR systems refuse to grant a significant decision-making role to outsiders or even to include them, so that "voice" becomes unattractive or impossible. However, the higher 2.1 score for M2 indicates that ASR systems need some outside participation for credibility and/or expertise purposes, and usually manage to get it even though they usually limit it when they can get it.

OP Precipitating Circumstances

Hypothesis PC1 links outside participation to the emergence and salience of "soft" issues of taste and opinion, and the related need for new expertise about them. A rather low score of 1.6 obtained here. There is no doubt that such soft issues are looming larger, if only because blatant cases of fraudulent and deceptive advertising have become relatively rare in more developed countries or are limited to hard-to-reach advertisers and media. However, there are soft issues and soft issues. Once some consensus has developed—after some initial industry resistance against racist or racy advertising or against showing some advertisements to particular audiences (e.g., in the cases of feminine-hygiene and contraceptive products) or against treating children like adults, etc.—the industry often acknowledges the need to include outsiders as some sort of a mini "opinion panel" at the preclearance and/or complaint-handling stages. Obviously, such outside participation remains impossible if the conditions previously examined are not present; and, in any case, the industry remains in control of its standards, as was previously discussed. Still, a few systems totally refuse to handle matters of decency, taste, opinion and even fairness—particularly, in the United States. When the soft issues shift to "social responsibility"—as with cigarette advertising—the advertising industry draws the line and simple declines to handle them so that outside participation is a moot issue in this respect.

Hypothesis PC2 states that "outside participation is precipitated by legitimacy crises." The Canadian, Italian and British cases are particularly supportive in this regard. Elsewhere, it is either a matter of outside participation being largely impossible (e.g., Belgium) or unnecessary, because the ASR system derives its legitimacy from other sources, such as an original government mandate as in the Philippines. This variety of circumstances helps explain the middling score of 1.9 points.

Finally, "outside participation is more likely when public policy encourages and facilitates it (Hypothesis PC3)." This factor has already been discussed under ASR Precipitating Condition No. 2 (which had a score of 2.2), but public policy is less effective when it comes to supporting outside participation, because the latter may not be readily feasible and obtainable in some countries on account of various cultural obstacles. Hence, PC3 obtained a relatively low score of 1.6 points.

Altogether, it is obvious from Table 16.3 that conditions, motivations and precipitating circumstances in eleven countries (Sweden being excluded) are

Table 16.3
The Impact of Factors Bearing on Advertising Self-Regulation and Outside Participation

	ADVERTISING SELF-REGULATION	OUTSIDE PARTICIPATION
CONDITIONS	2.5	1.6
MOTIVATIONS	2.5	1.9
PRECIPITATING CIRCUMSTANCES	2.3	1.7

Note: Scores on a minimum of 1 and a maximum of 3.

more conducive to the development and effectiveness of advertising self-regulation than of outside participation in it.

Of course, these scores represent only a snapshot in time after a relatively short experience with eleven national advertising self-regulatory systems, which date mostly from the early 1970s. Still, the significant differences between the two columns in Table 16.3 make it reasonable to conclude that outside participation, while desirable and even wanted, is much more difficult to achieve than a viable and effective ASR system, although time and experience will probably facilitate it. After all, it took decades to develop advertising self-regulation, whose birth and youth were often stormy and precarious.

Conclusions

Many observations about advertising self-regulation and outside participation have already been presented in chapters 1 and 2. Still, the country studies and their comparison in this chapter make it possible to reinterpret them in a neo-corporatist perspective.

ASR's Counterintuitiveness

Streeck and Schmitter (1985) have argued that private-interest government constitutes a natural form of social control, that complements the checks imposed on a socioeconomic institution such as advertising by the Community, the Market and the State. This view, however, is not a prevalent one, even though there are many historical precedents as in the medieval guilds and the professional orders in law and medicine as well as in current instances of effective self-regulatory bodies. Yet, the legitimacy and effectiveness of private-interest government remain questioned by its critics on account of the ''counterintuitiveness of the idea that organized special interests could be turned into promoters of the public interest (Streeck and Schmitter 1985,

p. 16).'' Why is this the case, and what does the experience of well-developed ASR systems in a score of countries contribute to the validity of the
Streeck and Schmitter claim?

Alternative Responses to Market Failures. For critics of self-regulation, it is
unreasonable to expect self-interested businessmen to seriously consider cur-
tailing their activities in the public interest. As Maitland (1985, p. 133) put it:
''Managers are largely unable to consider their firms' impact on society or to
subordinate profit-maximization to social objectives, no matter how well-intentioned they are.'' This happens, says Maitland, because it is not in the interest
of a group member to contribute to the costs of providing such ''public goods''
as truthful, fair and decent advertising, since ''no individual firm can be sure
that it is not placing itself at a competitive disadvantage by unwittingly interpreting its own obligations more strictly than its competitors do theirs (p. 134).''
Consequently, an economic system based on competition is bound to generate
''market failures'' such as the lack of perfect information about products, as
provided by advertising (Harris and Carman 1983, p. 51). The logical reaction
then is to develop ''regulatory responses'' designed to remedy such market
failures.

However, this line of reasoning overlooks the fact that the substitution of
acts of authority by the State for acts of market exchange in turn generates
''regulatory failures.'' As Carman and Harris (1986, p. 64) put it, after an
exhaustive review of regulatory responses: ''Despite the world's long history
of trying to improve on free-market performance, our knowledge of how to
design and implement an effective [regulatory] remedy is not very impressive.'' Of course, the critics of business and of its self-regulation will counter
that what this conclusion suggests is simply further refinement of regulatory
responses.

While there may be room for regulatory improvement in the light of new
problems and experiences, this absolute faith in regulation is misplaced.
There are readily observable limits to what regulation, as a form of social
control, can achieve (Carman and Harris 1986; Gupta and Lad 1983). This is
precisely the central position of Streeck and Schmitter, who argue that the
''social order'' rests on a combination of ''spontaneous solidarity'' (the Community), ''dispersed competition'' (the Market), ''hierarchical control'' (the
State) and ''organizational concertation'' (the Association or Private-Interest
Government). Each of these four institutions is imperfect and, therefore, requires the complementary contributions of the others: ''What is important is
that [these four institutions] at the same time require one another for their respective functioning; and that there are specific problems of order that each
of them is better equipped to resolve than the others (Streeck and Schmitter
1985, p. 4).'' In other words, ''market failures'' invite not only ''regulatory
responses'' but also other forms of social control, including self-regulation by

private-interest governments. Therefore, the appropriate model is not the simplistic one of "Market Failure → Regulatory Response" but the more elaborate one portrayed below:

```
                                  ( COMMUNITARIAN
MARKET      ⟶ COMPLEMENTARY   | MARKET
FAILURES    ⟋   RESPONSES      { REGULATORY
                                  | SELF-DISCIPLINARY
                                  ( SELF-REGULATORY
```

Communitarian responses generally assume the form of public revulsion against advertising on account of its perceived materialism, invasiveness, boringness, untrustworthiness, uselessness, etc., which reduce its overall acceptance and, therefore, effectiveness—even of "good" advertisements. Boycotts organized by various groups (consumerists, ecologists, human-righters, etc.) also represent a type of communitarian response, although generally focused on a particular industry or company (e.g., Nestlé's in the infant-formula case). *Market* responses include consumer rejection or discounting of particular advertisements, and competitor countering of improper ads with their own advertising. *Self-disciplinary* responses refer to auto-correcting measures by particular advertisers, agencies and media who realize that their behavior has proven unproductive. *Regulatory* responses assume many forms, such as prohibition, restriction, obligation, public provision and taxation (cf. Carman and Harris [1986], p. 52). *Self-regulatory* responses complement the above through peer pressure, moral suasion, denial of access to the media, etc. Another way of interpreting these responses is along Hirschman's (1970) "exit, voice and loyalty," whereby citizens, consumers, competitors and other concerned parties react by withdrawing, by complaining from the "outside," and/or by reforming from the "inside."

The State, in principle, reaches everybody, thereby eliminating the "free rider" problem of those who ignore their social responsibilities. However, it does it with a broad stroke through legal standards that lack the necessary nuances based on an intimate knowledge of business problems and concerns. Besides, the State can only provide a formalistic application of its rules, that does not readily take the specific conditions of individual cases into adequate consideration. As such, the regulatory approach is strong on the "letter" of the law but weak in obtaining adherence to its "spirit," because regulations are often "alien" to business in their design and implementation. Self-regulation, however, offers more realistic standards and better accepted decisions that can result in lower implementation costs and higher implementation effectiveness—an obvious set of "public goods" (Streeck and Schmitter 1985, p. 20 and passim). (These authors develop related arguments on the interrelationships between self-regulation, the Market and the Community from pages 22 to 27.) The country studies in this volume amply validate these social-the-

ory views. Most governments have come to realize the limits of their effective reach and to accept the contributions of self-regulation, even though this
beneficial situation will not preclude further State interventions nor further
Market and Community pressures on advertising practitioners.

The Special Nature of Advertising. Some of the most impressive perfor-
mances among self-regulatory systems are found in advertising on account of
two factors. First, advertising is highly visible (by purpose) as well as name-
able, so that its failings are readily detectable and traceable, compared to
other improper trade practices and professional misdeeds that often remain
hidden from public view. As such, competitors, consumers, citizens at large
and law-enforcers can more readily identify and react to advertising's shortcomings. While critics point out cases of subtly misleading advertisements,
unfairness and "hidden persuasion" that may escape the average person, it
remains that there are enough expert watchdogs who can easily uncover such
cases. Consequently, the pressure on advertising practitioners and the media
to put their house in order is particularly strong, because broadly diffused and
continuous. The credibility of huge advertising expenditures, mainly by large
advertisers, but also involving large agencies and media, is at stake and vulnerable to negative public reactions as well as to market and regulatory
responses.

This situation, proper to advertising, has been conducive to the development of what Streeck and Schmitter (1985, p. 21) call "categoric goods,"
that is, benefits proper to a particular category of practitioners. The latter are
motivated by their desire for "lesser uncertainty about aggregate outcomes
and higher assurance of receiving a proportionately more 'equitable' share of
whatever is disputed (Streeck and Schmitter 1985, p. 13)." In other words,
advertising self-regulation is designed to: (1) minimize unfavorable reactions
from the Community, the Market and the State in the forms of bad image,
unbridled competition and overregulation, and (2) ensure that, at least, most
practitioners behave properly without excessive evasion by "free-riders." As
Streeck and Schmitter put it: "What associations in a corporative order strive
for is . . . *satisficing interests.* By deliberate mutual adjustment and repeated
interaction, [they] avoid the temptation to exploit momentary advantages to
the maximum and the pitfall of landing in the worst possible situation. In
short, they avoid the prisoner's dilemma through interorganizational trust
backed by . . . private interest government (Streeck and Schmitter 1985,
p. 13)."

In the case of advertising, the actual generation of such categoric goods is
greatly facilitated by a second factor, namely, the fact that some 90 percent
of advertisements rely on the print and broadcast media or on postal services
so that there is always a screen between the advertiser and the public. This
unique situation of depending on an intermediary provides a check on advertising practices through: (1) these media applying their own "self-disciplinary
standards" for acceptance, and (2) abiding by the decisions of advertising

self-regulatory bodies. (For example, Italian agencies and media have a clause in their contracts that requires acceptance of the ASR Code by advertisers.) Critics point out that this screening is imperfect; and industry itself deplores the practices of advertisers and media that overlook these standards and decisions either out of ignorance or defiance. However, as Zanot (1985) observed, each screen may be imperfect but the cumulative effect is substantial. Besides, defrauders and recalcitrants can be denounced to the authorities, who face the same problems of disciplining marginal operators.

Altogether, the facts that: (1) "significant others" have accepted to participate in the functioning of many ASR systems; (2) the awareness and acceptance of advertising self-regulation have increased in those countries where public opinion has been polled; and (3) the overall image of advertising has improved in several nations where advertising self-regulation is well developed (e.g., France and the United Kingdom) reveal that the counterintuitiveness of private-interest government, while understandable, does not fundamentally impair its ability to contribute to "social order" in advertising.

ASR's Development

This is not to argue that national advertising self-regulation, where it exists (and there are scores of countries without it), will always achieve its potential and contribute to social order, that is, produce "public goods" in the pursuit of "categoric goods." Chapter 1 and the first part of this chapter have already analyzed the conditions, motivations and precipitating circumstances related to its development and effectiveness. A few elements deserve re-emphasis, however.

The State's Role. The role of government in acknowledging and fostering advertising self-regulation is crucial, yet delicate. Its goal is clear, namely, "to put to public purposes the type of social order that associations can generate and embody (Streeck and Schmitter 1985, p. 16)." As was uniformly observed, the passage and/or threat of regulation is a necessary condition and/or a precipitator for the development of ASR systems. Beyond that observation, however, there is ample room for a variety of self-regulatory responses to government prodding. Sometimes, legal remedies are so well developed as to leave relatively little room for advertising self-regulation, as in Germany and Japan. Elsewhere, we observed the delegation of major aspects of advertising control to the self-regulatory body in the Philippines, formal enlistment of the cooperation of the ASR system in the United Kingdom and even the integration of business interests in the Swedish Consumer-Ombudsman institution.

The best public-policy solutions lie somewhere between: (1) mandating, capturing or overloading an ASR system, and (2) ignoring or opposing it. The Belgian situation has elements of the latter, thereby diminishing the legitimacy of self-regulation. While exemplary in terms of fruitful business-government cooperation, the British and Canadian experiences point to the potential danger of asking ASR systems to assume more and more tasks that become as onerous as regulation and can weaken voluntary adherence to industry norms. Governments can even demand to approve industry norms or have outside groups participate in their revision—as has been the recent case in Australia (not included in the country studies). In the United Kingdom, the recent discussion of imposing a "duty to trade fairly" and the proposal of using compliance with industry codes as evidence of fair trading reveal another pitfall of integrating self-regulation too closely into public policy.

The "User-Friendly" Imperative. Whatever the form of government support and prodding, the gist of the problem lies in maintaining what Peter Thomson (of the U.K. Advertising Standards Authority) has called "user-friendly, practitioner-based regulation (private communication)." The country studies revealed that many ASR systems have come, in varying degrees, to integrate nonindustry members in the *application* of ASR standards. However, the adoption of such standards remains an industry prerogative because it is a necessary condition for "moral adhesion" to them. The Community, the Market and the State also impose standards, but it is the "voluntary" or "self-assumed" nature of ASR standards that makes the difference.

ASR standards are not democratically developed, since large advertising practitioners dominate the supporting professional associations and provide, directly or indirectly, most of the ASR financing. For that matter, the largest ASR systems have become fairly autonomous, being independently financed in the United Kingdom and not even involving any advertising practitioner in the handling of cases, as in France and the United States (except at the appeal level in the latter's case). The challenge for the private "policy entrepreneurs (Lad 1985, p. 121)" in ASR secretariats lies precisely in keeping in step with the troops whose moral adhesion is crucial for effectiveness. *A fortiori*, governments cannot impose ASR standards or require approval for their adoption or amendment without destroying the essence of self-regulation. The same requirement applies to consumerists as self-appointed representatives of Community values. In that sense, self-regulation, however hybrid it may have become (see Chapter 1), remains and must remain "pure" in the development of its standards.

ASR's Overlap with the Law. A priori, one would expect ASR systems to limit themselves to devising and implementing standards that complement the law. In fact, there is considerable overlap between legal and industry standards in most countries. The only major exceptions were found in: (1) Brazil and Philippines, where advertising regulations are relatively underdeveloped so that self-regulation has significantly preempted the task of coping with market failures, and (2) Germany, where legal remedies against false, misleading and unfair advertising are so ample and flexible as to leave little room for self-regulation outside of matters of "taste and opinion."

This overlap assumes several forms, ranging from the application by ASR systems of legal norms (e.g., in Belgium and France) to the (partial) duplication of legal standards in the British Code of Advertising Practice. Such an overlap is necessary to the extent that a good part of the law reflects generally accepted Community standards against false, misleading and unfair advertising. The role of advertising self-regulation is, then, to "internalize" such standards and generate "moral adhesion" to them. The German case is quite revealing in this respect because the Werberat's refusal to handle cases of false and misleading advertisements, even though justifiable by the fact that there are other ample ways of coping with them, has been interpreted by some critics as evidence of not caring about major advertising problems that bother consumers. Therefore, self-regulation's *complementary* role need not be conceived of only in terms of developing and applying additional norms. While the latter exist in some countries (see next section), self-regulation's complementariness largely lies in *reinforcing* norms emanating from the Community, Market and State.

ASR and Soft Issues. Despite regular claims that advertising self-regulation can best handle matters that the law finds difficult to pursue for lack of readily discernible or enforceable standards, the country studies revealed that ASR systems are reluctant to handle a variety of cases revolving around good taste, decency and social responsibility—but so are most governmental agencies. Usually, Community standards about such issues are either only surfacing (e.g., in the case of sexism) or too heterogeneous (cf. the advertising of contraceptives).

As has often been remarked, advertising is and can only be "a mirror of society," and this remark applies equally to its self-regulation. Therefore, if people at large are uncertain or divided about issues, so will advertising practitioners be—both as "people" and as belonging to different industries more or less connected with these issues. Tobacco and feminine-hygiene advertising illustrate this dilemma as many advertisers are nonusers of these products, but are aware of strong outcries against such advertisements. Yet, they are simultaneously conscious of the principle that "the freedom to advertise legal products is indivisible" and of the danger of any ban spreading to other products found to be harmful by one pressure group or another (fatty products, sugared cereals, liquor, etc.). Under such circumstances, it is unrealistic to expect the advertising industry to become a house divided unto itself, and to enact bans against controversial products. Beyond possibly imposing stricter standards of truth and accuracy about such products and issuing various reports on these subjects, self-regulation has to defer such "societal-choice" (*choix de société*) issues to other forms of social control (Community-based boycotts, Market-based refusals to buy, and State-based regulations) and/or to the self-discipline of the media, which are better able to decide what their audiences will accept (e.g., contraceptive ads in *Playboy* magazine).

ASR's Privateness. Chapter 2 discussed the rationale for allowing outsiders to participate in ASR activities as a way of obtaining legitimacy and expertise; and practically all ASR systems incorporate outsiders to some degree. It remains that self-regulation has to retain a significant element of "inside" and "behind-the-scene" intervention removed from public view and from outside participation. For that matter, many ASR cases are settled through private communications that are not disclosed.

These situations and requirements are related to the "user-friendly" argument as well as to the difficulty of precisely encoding industry norms (Boisot 1986). Besides the open-and-shut cases of clear-cut and even bad-faith violations of legal and industry standards, there are many borderline cases of truth, accuracy and fairness as well as matters of taste, decency and opinion, that require fine interpretations of the norms, and that justify approaching the advertiser discreetly as well as using "friendly persuasion" ("asking power") rather than a heavy "enforcement" approach at the advising and complaint-handling stages. As one U.S. self-regulatory official put it: "The NAD/NARB is like a little FTC, but one relying on peer pressure and, ultimately, media cooperation without any heavy-handedness." Conversely, the Italian Jury, composed entirely of outsiders, has been criticized by advertisers for its occasional insensitivity to their viewpoints.

This discreet approach, while the only effective one within industry, is bound to be misinterpreted on the outside as token behavior in the public interest and as ineffective wrist-slapping of offenders. This is a shortcoming intrinsic to private-interest government:

The price for [deliberate mutual adjustment and repeated interaction to achieve satisficing interests] is a lengthy deliberation process and a series of second-best compromised solutions which are often difficult to justify on aesthetic or normative grounds. . . . Usually, deliberations are kept informal and secretive in an effort to insulate them as much as possible from outside pressures and from dissidents within the associational ranks. The "weighting" of influences and the consequent calculation of proportional justice or equity involve often arbitrary standards and mysterious processes . . . These elements of citizen unaccountability and inequality—combined with the unavoidably compromised nature of the decisions made—can create a serious "legitimacy deficit" and expose corporate-associative structures to normative challenges by proponents of the competing orders of Community, Market and State (Streeck and Schmitter 1985, pp. 13–14).

This natural situation, as was argued before, militates against giving true parity to nonindustry members in ASR bodies. In some fundamental sense, the industry has to remain in control, however hybrid the ASR system may have become; and some of its deliberations have to remain secret, because the industry itself is divided and/or needs time to develop consensus about new standards. (It is interesting to observe in this context that competitor complaints are usually handled without outside participation unless some consumer interest is at stake.)

Besides, as Neelankavil and Stridsberg have commented: "The consumerists have confronted [ASR bodies] with demands that they take positions *publicly* on matters they were organized to settle *privately* among themselves (Neelankavil and Stridsberg 1980, p. 32; emphasis added)." This is an unrealistic demand on the part of consumerists to the extent that private-interest government has to remain fundamentally "private" to be effective even though this privateness limits its very effectiveness in terms of external credibility. Even when outsiders participate in the implementation of ASR standards, they are expected to act as "loyal" (cf. Hirschman [1970]) individuals rather than as spokesmen or spies for outside groups (the Canadian case is very revealing in this regard). Taking public positions about controversial practices (e.g., comparison advertising in France) and issues (e.g., tobacco advertising in Canada) is a dangerous exercise, which ASR bodies generally avoid and leave to advertising and industry associations. When they do handle such controversial issues as advertising to children and feminine-hygiene advertising, they limit themselves to implementing consensual standards, rather than address the core issue of the social suitability of such advertising. Addressing questions concerning the usefulness of advertising, its volume, its correspondence with societal values and related matters is outside the role of ASR bodies in any case.

Altogether, much more goes on in ASR bodies than is revealed by their reports and the relatively low number of cases publicly disclosed; and, by its very nature, self-regulation has to remain "private" and cannot be the proper arena for the deliberation and ultimate resolution of controversial issues between advertising and its publics—something better left to professional, industry and capstone advertising associations.

Outside Participation. Notwithstanding the arguments in favor of "pure" self-regulation, there is always some outside participation in its structure and/or functioning. It is really more a matter of "how much" and "in what role" (cf. Neelankavil and Stridsberg [1980, p. 19]).

The quantity of outsiders is relatively immaterial if their participation is significant and credible; and their varying proportions in the countries studied simply reflect various environmental factors as well as positive experience with outside participation (see Chapter 2 for further discussion of this point). The roles of outsiders center on credibility and expertise, but they do not extend to the fundamental questioning of advertising or to the formal elaboration of ASR standards, which has to remain an industry prerogative in order to generate moral adhesion to "user-friendly, practitioner-based regulation." Performing such roles effectively requires outsiders that are truly "independent" yet can become "loyal" members of the ASR system—clearly a requirement fraught with many ambiguities. Finding, keeping and motivating such outsiders is not an easy task; and one can even question whether those currently selected by ASR bodies truly offer a meaningful representation of the public (see Chapter 2).

However, "formal" outsiders constitute only part of "outside participation in advertising self-regulation." As was seen in practically all the country studies, ASR bodies and their supporting associations engage in repeated "side relations" with government officials, consumerists, experts, etc., who thus become "silent partners" of advertising self-regulation. Last but not least, consumer complaints provide constant "outside" inputs and feedbacks about advertising behavior and ASR effectiveness. Consequently, one can conclude that outside participation is present everywhere and definitely benefits ASR performance even though the advertising industry retains control of the ASR system—for that matter, wants and needs to retain control in order to remain a true and effective "private government." It is interesting to observe that more "corporatist" ASR systems, as in Brazil and the Philippines, are even less receptive to outside participation.

Negotiated Codes. In the light of these factors, the development of advertising codes truly "negotiated" with governments and/or consumerist organizations remains problematic. Either they simply represent the application to a particular sector (e.g., toys or appliances) of norms already accepted by business at large so that no novel obligations have really been assumed, or they amount to "legal" (contractual) obligations alien to the concept of "private government." (The British debate about a legal "duty to trade fairly," with voluntary codes serving as evidence of what constitutes "fair trading," is very illuminating in this regard.)

In this context, the analogy with the "collective conventions" drawn between labor and management is a tenuous one. First, these two parties are "private" while government is not. Second, labor unions can be considered to be representative of their membership to the extent that employees choose to join or not to join a particular union; elect the officials who negotiate labor contracts; and even ratify labor contracts. No such democratically based representative standing can be granted to consumerist organizations even in countries like Belgium and France, which formally recognize them (Goldstein's comments in Chapter 2 are particularly relevant in this respect). Third, labor contracts involve some definite quid-pro-quo in the form of "labor peace" and even concessions, while consumerist organizations do not really deliver anything in exchange in the form of specific commitments and obligations—in legal terms, there is no reciprocal "consideration" coming from the consumerist side.

This does not mean that advertising organizations cannot consult with governments and consumer organizations and ultimately adopt new norms on the basis of such consultations, which may even be "forced" upon them (cf. the chapters on Canada and the United Kingdom, and Nestlé's infant-formula case). However, one is moving outside the realm of self-regulation as a form of private-interest government when the resulting standards are not truly developed and internalized by the advertising industry but are somehow imposed upon it. Thus, the government-imposed control bodies that supervise the broadcast media in many countries cannot be considered as true exercises in self-regulation, even though their codes have involved the participation of various business interests.

Overall Evolution. Although this study has made numerous references to the evolution of ASR systems in the country chapters, it is not historical in the sense of focusing on that evolution. Yet, it is apparent from this research and other publications that the *scope* of advertising self-regulation tends to move from: (1) settling competitor complaints through and within advertiser and agency associations, to (2) handling consumer and general-public concerns through a national tripartite (advertiser-agency-media) system. Its contributions also vary in relations to the development of regulation—ranging from ASR systems that fill in for very weak consumer-protection legislation (e.g., in Brazil and the Philippines) to those that parallel developed regulatory systems (e.g., in Canada, France, the United Kingdom and the United States). In the latter case, ASR systems have to handle progressively more complex complaints and issues, although the need remains to socialize industry newcomers and even old-timers about "good advertising behavior."

The True Purpose of Advertising Self-Regulation

The dominant criticisms of advertising self-regulation are that: (1) relatively few cases are handled by ASR bodies in proportion to the number of advertisements and the true extent of advertising failures; (2) relatively little publicity is given to advertising self-regulation in many countries; (3) many ASR decisions come "too late" after the infringing advertisement has been discontinued, and (4) ASR penalties are relatively mild, except for denial of access to the major media. They are valid if one conceives of self-regulation as a "consumer-redress" mechanism, but they must be muted if one understands that the main purpose of advertising self-regulation is *to improve and internalize higher advertising standards*—something that can be done even on the basis of few significant cases, late decisions and apparently mild penalties. In this second perspective, advertising self-regulation is not primarily about the systematic invitation, collection and handling of complaints. Here, Armstrong and Ozanne's (1983) comment that self-regulation represents more an exercise in "advertiser advocacy" than in "consumer advocacy" (see the chapter on the United States) assumes a new meaning, namely, that it is much more concerned about improving advertising behavior on an industry-wide basis than in satisfying individual complaining consumers, even though these two goals are obviously compatible and related.

This purpose of advertising self-regulation—namely, to improve advertising behavior both in the industry's and the public interest—is bound to be misinterpreted as a token public-relations gesture designed to placate critics, to fend off the threat of regulation, etc.; yet, in view of its "private-interest government" nature, this is the true purpose that distinguishes self-regulation from other forms of social control. The use of coercion and punishment is exclusively a state function (Feldman 1976, p. 261), although one that can be delegated to industry in a corporatist scheme; while dominant Community values as well as Market pressures regularly circumscribe the effectiveness of advertising techniques. Advertising self-regulation cannot, therefore, be the only arbiter of norms and sanctions but can only complement other social-control mechanisms in a "user-friendly" manner. It is a form of "soft law" (Hondius 1984) precisely because: (1) it has only "asking power" rather than subpoena power in dealing with offenders, and (2) it relies almost entirely on peer pressure (including that of the media) and publicity, rather than on harsh penalties of the judiciary type.

Sweden provides a good illustration of this situation because its Consumer-

Ombudsman (KO) system represents a unique blend of regulation and self-regulation. The KO is not ready to pursue every valid complaint, but is much more interested in the improvement of the commercial standards embodied in guidelines negotiated with the relevant industries. These guidelines are not binding as a matter of law, although they can be used in the Market Court as evidence of what constitutes "good practice" (cf. the British discussion of "a duty to trade fairly" on the basis of industry codes, in the United Kingdom chapter). Only about 1 percent of consumer complaints connected with some violation of the Swedish Marketing Practices Act find their way to the Market Court—mostly to clarify some principles that will give industry groundrules for future activities (Business International 1980, p. I.62).

In this perspective, advertising self-regulation generally promotes higher standards—which is not the same as the highest standards, for sure. As one ASR leader put it: "Self-regulatory bodies won't eat their parents"—meaning that they have to work "from the inside" rather than sit in judgment on advertising practitioners. This is essentially an educational and "consciousness-raising" task, which, although backed by some effective sanctions (e.g., publicity and recommendations to the media to deny access), has to be performed in a "satisficing" rather than "maximizing" or "optimizing" manner (Streeck and Schmitter 1985, pp. 9 and 13). In this context, Wyckham's (1987) observation that self-regulation works best in the case of ads that result from poor management practices, a lack of quality control of advertising copy, inappropriate behavior of employees and consumer misperceptions rather than from management intention to mislead is particularly perceptive. The really "bad apples" are best left to government agencies.

Still, advertising self-regulation is really more proactive than reactive in that it is more concerned with *future* behavior than with correcting past errors—as is evidenced by the misunderstanding connected with how "fast" self-regulation should be. If redress and discipline were the main goals, great speed would be essential; while *deliberate speed* is sufficient for educational and consciousness-raising purposes.

Finally, self-regulation links the "public good" with "categoric [industry] goods," but with the former subordinated to the latter. As one ASR leader put it: "We have to operate in the public interest in order to protect business interests"—not the other way around. As such, it will always suffer in comparison to the Community and the State, whose public-interest goals are presumably more disinterested; while, like the Market, the institution of Private-interest Government will always look suspect, unless one is convinced that "private vices" can contribute to "public virtue."

The advertising industry values complaints to the extent that they represent some sort of a "random sample" of what bothers consumers and competitors. It also prefers to be the first line of recourse (together with complaints directly addressed to advertisers and/or the media) for complainants in lieu of suits, denunciations to the authorities and exposés in consumerist publications and programs. However, too many complaints not only overburden underfinanced ASR systems, but they also trivialize the complaining process by generating cases that fall outside of their self-assigned mission. Besides, many complaints are repetitive, either dealing with the same improper ad or with similar ones. Like enforcement agencies and the judiciary, ASR bodies cannot handle all infractions or discipline all violators, but must mainly rely on the lesson-giving, precedent-setting and deterrent effects of their relatively few decisions.

Even the monitoring of advertisements by ASR bodies, in order to detect violations that may not be revealed by complaints, has to be limited. It makes sense to obtain a broader or more focused sample of cases by systematically checking some media, industries and practices—particularly, new or problematic ones. However, the role of monitoring cannot simply be one of catching more violators in a law-enforcement or raiding perspective. Instead, its true roles are to spread and improve advertising standards by reaching more advertising practitioners—particularly, small or new media and advertisers that have not yet been socialized into the self-regulatory system.

Altogether, the true purpose of advertising self-regulation is more moral/ethical that disciplinary—almost in the spirit of one of Confucius' analects: "Lead the people with governmental measures and regulate them by law and punishment, and they will avoid wrong-doing but have no sense of honor or shame. Lead them by virtue and regulate them by the rules of propriety, and they will have a sense of shame and, moreover, set themselves right." A more recent comment corroborates Confucius' recommendation: "The Founding Fathers created a system in which private vice would be transformed into public virtue. Two hundred years later, we face the challenge of modifying that prescription in the hope that U.S. businesses will do unto themselves in lieu of the government doing unto them (Grumbly 1982, p. 118)."

The Bounds of Advertising Self-Regulation

Previous analyses and conclusions have already revealed that advertising self-regulation is neither a panacea nor a substitute for other forms of social control. Its scope is limited, its reach is incomplete and its methods are only partially effective. Even to realize its limited potential, various factors must be present.

The conclusion reached about Dutch advertising self-regulation in the pharmaceutical sector appears to be generally applicable: "Only when there is a collective interest in self-regulation, a highly developed interest association with sufficient resources to enforce a self-regulatory system, and when the issue at stake is not too closely linked to the public interest, does self-regulation seem possible (de Vroom 1985, p. 147)." The various country studies of advertising self-regulation have revealed that many economic, political, social and cultural elements are needed for it to appear, develop and fructify. Even within the advertising industry, it depends fundamentally on individual self-discipline (see Chapter 1), capstone-organization support and media cooperation.

Certain advertising practitioners will always remain impervious to its admonitions and penalties; and various forms of advertising are even excluded from its scope. Thus, private individuals placing personal ads and politicians launching advertising campaigns cannot be considered as "members of the advertising industry," because they are not "tradesmen" or "firms" in the legal sense of these terms.[3] ASR bodies also decline to handle complaints about "advocacy/ controversy" advertisements (e.g., against certain government policies) by firms or industries because they are in the realm of "opinion," which is protected by various national and international covenants about human rights, including freedom of expression in the marketplace of ideas.

As was argued before, the very nature of private-interest government prevents self-regulation from handling certain problems or from handling them in a manner satisfactory to its critics in terms of speed, publicity and harsh penalization. Even the inclusion of outsiders in its functioning is not sufficient to eliminate such shortcomings. Although advertising self-regulation cannot cope effectively with every market failure (Harris and Carman 1983), one can echo Daniel Oliver, U.S. Federal Trade Commission chairman, who observed that: "The marketplace doesn't have to work perfectly to work better than government. It is our job, before we regulate commercial advertising, to weigh the promise of the marketplace against the promise of regulation ("The New FTC," 1987, p. 10)." Similarly, advertising self-regulation does not have to work perfectly or even better than the Community, the Market and the State to be accepted as a natural and often effective form of social control over advertising behavior.

Recommendations

Many students, critics and supporters of advertising self-regulation have advanced various recommendations for its further improvement. There is no denying that some ASR systems are more developed and effective than others, and that even the most advanced ones need to keep evolving in the light of new problems and opportunities even if perfection is impossible. However, our knowledge of advertising self-regulation's operations and environments remains too limited to warrant fully defensible suggestions for their development and improvement around the world. Most academic recommendations have fallen on deaf ears, as far as can be observed. This lack of evident response probably reflects the fact that most criticisms and suggestions for reform have failed to truly understand the nature and limits of advertising self-regulation. However, this study has focused on understanding the conditions, motivations and precipitating circumstances affecting the creation, operation and effectiveness of ASR systems and of outside participation in them; therefore, very few recommendations will be advanced here.

As far as research is concerned, several topics have hardly been studied, as became painfully evident when conducting this project.

1. How do advertising practitioners feel about self-regulation—particularly those who have been investigated by ASR bodies? In other words, how "user friendly" is it actually or perceived to be?
2. To what extent are advertising practitioners in firms, agencies and media familiar with ASR standards, and to what extent have they internalized them? (The current research of professors E. J. Zanot and R.G. Wyckham deals with this topic.)
3. What has been the experience of those "outsiders" who serve on ASR complaint-handling bodies? What is their view of their roles and contributions; and how have they reconciled "independence" and "loyalty?"
4. What makes for effective leadership in private-interest governments, particularly on the part of the key members of ASR secretariats? (Cf. Streeck and Schmitter [1985, pp. 12 and 19]; and Lad [1985.])
5. Under what conditions do advertisers choose to use self-regulatory vs. market (e.g., countercampaigns) and regulatory (e.g., denouncing and suing) remedies when faced with breaches of good advertising behavior by their competitors?[4] (Similar studies have been made of consumer complaining behavior—cf. Moyer and Banks [1977].)
6. What ASR mechanisms will be most appropriate to handle complaints relating to cross-border advertising through international editions, satellite broadcasting, foreign direct-mail solicitations, etc. (cf. Baudot [1986])?

As far as policy is concerned, only one recommendation will be made, namely, that temporary exchanges of personnel be regularly made between ASR bodies, government agencies, advertising firms and even consumerist organizations so that the other modes of "social control" may be better understood by each one of them. (This is beginning to be done in France and the United Kingdom.)

Firmly convinced by now of the social usefulness of advertising self-regulation, this researcher can only wish that the conditions, motivations and precipitators needed for its further development, with or without significant outside participation, will become operational in more countries, since it exists only in some forty countries and is well developed in fewer than twenty—not enough by far for a natural contributor to social order.

NOTES

1. The rating of "1" was chosen instead of "0" to indicate minor importance because the conditions, motivations and precipitating circumstances tested here are practically always present to some degree, although their impact varies.

2. An analysis by Roger Pereira of the development of the Indian ASR system illustrates the need for a capstone organization, and the difficulties encountered in pulling various associations together (in Boddewyn 1986, pp. 92–97).

3. It is worth noting that consumerist organizations and publications rarely comment about personal ads for used cars, apartments, etc., although many of them would not meet the test of "truth and accuracy in advertising."

4. Several alternatives are available to competitors: (1) ignore the matter; (2) try to counter the false advertising through their own advertising; (3) call the competitor and ask that the advertisement be stopped; (4) complain to a private industry self-regulatory

body; (5) complain to a government regulatory agency, either at the state or federal level; and/or (6) file a lawsuit against the competitor. From: P.M. Hyman. "Alternatives to Government Regulation." Speech before the Food and Drug Law Institute, Washington, D.C.: December 11, 1984.

References (Parts I and III)

"ACA Newsletter" [Association of Canadian Advertisers]. 1423 (July 11, 1985): 3.

Advertising Standards Authority [ASA]. *Annual Reports*. London: various dates.

———. "Law Enforcement." *ASA Case Report 66* (London: October 8, 1980), pp. 1–2.

Armstrong, G. M., and J. L. Ozanne. "An Evaluation of NAD/NARB Purpose and Performance." *Journal of Advertising*, 12, no. 3 (1983): 15–26.

Astley, W. G., and C. J. Fombrun. "Collective Strategy: Social Ecology of Organizational Environments." *Academy of Management Review* 8, no. 4 (1983): 576–87.

Bardach, Eugene, and R. A. Kagan. *Going by the Book: The Problem of Regulatory Unreasonableness*. Philadelphia, Penn.: Temple University Press, 1982.

Barksdale, H. C. et al. "A Cross-National Survey of Consumer Attitudes towards Marketing Practices, Consumerism and Government Regulations." *Columbia Journal of World Business* 17, no. 2 (Summer 1982): 71–86

Baudot, B. S. "Advertising: A Case for International Regulation?" Unpublished Ph.D. dissertation; Medford, Mass.: Fletcher School of Law and Diplomacy, 1986.

Beauchamp, T. L., and N. E. Bowie, eds. *Ethical Theory and Business*. Englewood Cliffs, N.J.: Prentice-Hall, 1979.

Blakeney, Michael. "Advertising Self-Regulation under Scrutiny in Australia." *Journal of Consumer Policy* 9, no. 2 (June 1986): 181–90.

Boddewyn, J. J. "Advertising Regulation: Fiddling with the FTC while the World Burns." *Business Horizons* 28, no. 3 (May-June 1985): 32–40.

———. "Advertising Regulation in the 1980s: The Underlying Global Forces." *Journal of Marketing* (Winter 1982): 27–35.

———. *Advertising Self Regulation: 16 Advanced Systems*. New York: International Advertising Association, 1986.

———. *Belgian Public Policy Toward Retailing Since 1789*. East Lansing, Mich.: Division of Research, Graduate School of Business Administration, Michigan State University, 1971.

————. "Theories of Foreign Direct Investment and Divestment: A Classificatory Note." *Management International Review* 25, no. 1 (1985): 57–65.

Boddewyn, J. J., and Katherin Marton. *Comparison Advertising: A Worldwide Study.* New York: Hastings House, 1978.

Boisot, M. H. "Markets and Hierarchies in a Cultural Perspective." *Organization Studies* 7, no. 2 (1986): 135–58.

Bourgoignie, Thierry. "The Need to Reformulate Consumer Protection Policy." *Journal of Consumer Policy* 7, no. 2 (June 1984): 307–21.

Brandmair, Lothar. *Die freiwillige Selbstkontrolle der Werbung* [The Voluntary Self-Control of Advertising]. Cologne, Germany: Carl Heymans Verlag, 1978.

Buell, V. P. *The British Approach to Improving Advertising Standards and Practice; A Comparison with the United States Experience.* Amherst, Mass.: Business Publication Services, School of Business Administration, University of Massachusetts, 1977.

Bureau de Vérification de la Publicité [BVP]. *Rôle et Devenir de l'Autodiscipline dans la Société Française* [Role and Future of Self-Regulation in French Society]. Paris, 1985.

Burleton, Eric. "The Self-Regulation of Advertising in Europe." *[International] Journal of Advertising* 1, no. 4 (1982): 333–44.

Business International. *Europe's Consumer Movement.* New York: 1980.

Carman, J. M., and R. G. Harris. "Public Regulation of Marketing Activity, Part III." *Journal of Macromarketing* 6, no. 1, (Spring 1986): 51–64.

Caretta, A. A. "Is the FTC Abdicating Some of Its Power to Associations?" *Association Management* 20, no. 6 (June 1968): 13–16.

Cranston, Ross. *Consumers and the Law.* London: Weidenfeld and Nicolson, 1984.

Dachler, H. P., and Bernhard Wilpert. "Conceptual Dimensions and Boundaries of Participation in Organizations: A Critical Evaluation." *Administrative Science Quarterly* 23 (March 1978): 1–39.

Darvall, L. W., "Self-Regulation of Advertising and the Consumer Interest." *Australian Business Law Review* 8, no. 5, (October 1980): 309–20.

de Vroom, Bert. "Quality Regulation in the Dutch Pharmaceutical Industry: Conditions for Private Regulation by Business Interest Associations." In *Private Interest Government*, edited by Wolfgang Streeck and Ph.C. Schmitter. London and Beverly Hills, Calif.: Sage, 1985, pp. 128–49.

European Advertising Tripartite [EAT]. *"Self-Regulation and Codes of Practice; A Discussion Paper."* Brussels, Belgium, April 1983.

European Communities' [EC] Council of Ministers. "Council Resolution on a Second Programme [1981–1985] of the European Economic Community for a Consumer Protection and Information Policy." *Official Journal of the European Communities* (June 3, 1981): C133/1–12.

European Consumer Law Group [ECLG]. "Non-Legislative Means of Consumer Protection." *Journal of Consumer Policy* 6, no. 2 (1983): 209–24.

Feldman, L. P. *Consumer Protection: Problems and Prospects.* New York: West Publishing, 1976.

Garvin, D. A. "Can Industry Self-Regulation Work?" *California Management Review* 25, no. 4 (Summer 1983): 37–52.

Glaser, B. G., and A. A. Strauss. *The Discovery of Grounded Theory: Strategies for Qualitative Research.* New York: Aldine, 1967.

Goldstein, Jonah. "Public Interest Groups and Public Policy: The Case of the Consumers' Association of Canada." *Canadian Journal of Sociology* 12, no. 1 (March 1979): 137–55.

Grumbly, T. P. "Self-Regulation: Private Vice and Public Virtue Revisited." In *Social Regulation: Strategies for Reform*, edited by Eugene Bardach, and R. A. Kagan. San Francisco, Calif.: Institute for Contemporary Studies, 1982, pp. 93–118.

Gupta, A. K., and L. J. Lad. "Industry Self-Regulation: An Economic, Organizational and Political Analysis." *Academy of Management Review* 8, no. 3 (1983): 416–25.

Harris, R. G., and J. M. Carman. "Public Regulation of Marketing Activity: Institutional Typologies of Market Failure." *Journal of Macromarketing* 3, no. 1 (Spring 1983): 49–58.

Hirschman, A. O. *Exit, Voice and Loyalty.* Cambridge, Mass.: Harvard University Press, 1970.

Hofstede, Geert. *Culture's Consequences.* Beverly Hills, Calif.: Sage, 1980.

Hondius, E. H. "Non-legislative Means of Consumer Protection: The Dutch Perspective." *Journal of Consumer Policy* 7 (1984): 137–56.

Hunt, H. K., and R. L. Day, eds. *Refining Concepts and Measures of Consumer Satisfaction and Complaining Behavior.* Bloomington, Ind.: Division of Research, School of Business, Indiana University, 1980.

International Chamber of Commerce [ICC]. *International Code of Advertising Practice*, Paris: 1973 and 1987.

————. "Law and Self-Regulation; A Study Comparing Government Regulation and Self-regulation as Means of Consumer Protection." Paris: ICC Commission on Marketing, Advertising and Distribution, March 1984 (Document No. 240/166).

————. *Marketing: Discipline for Freedom.* Paris: 1978.

Jones, T. T., and J. F. Pickering. *Self-Regulation in Advertising: A Review.* London: Advertising Association, 1985.

King, C. D., and Mark van de Vall. *Models of Industrial Democracy.* New York: Norton, 1978.

Koopman, Joop. "New Developments in Government Consumer Policy: A Challenge for Consumer Organizations." *Journal of Consumer Policy* 9, no. 3 (1986): 269–86.

LaBarbera, P. A. "Advertising Self-Regulation: An Evaluation." *MSU Business Topics* 28, no. 3 (Summer 1980): 55–63.

————. "Analyzing and Advancing the State of the Art of Advertising Self-Regulation." *Journal of Advertising* 9, no. 4 (1980b): 27–38.

————. "The Antitrust Shadow Over Advertising Self-Regulation." *Current Issues and Research in Advertising.* Ann Arbor, Mich.: University of Michigan Press, 1981, 57–70.

————. "The Diffusion of Trade Association Advertising Self-Regulation." *Journal of Marketing* 47 (Winter 1983): 58–67.

————. "Toward the Theoretical Development of Advertising Self-Regulation." *Proceedings of the Second Annual Theory Conference* (Phoenix, Ariz). Chicago, Ill.: American Marketing Association, 1980c, pp. 129–32.

Lad, L. J. "Policy-Making between Business and Government: A Conceptual Synthesis of Industry Self-Regulation and a Case Study Analysis of the Direct Selling

Association Code of Conduct.'' Unpublished DBA dissertation, Boston University. Ann Arbor, Mich.: University Microfilms International, 1985.

Lazer, William, and Priscilla LaBarbera. "Business and Self-Regulation." In *Public Policy Issues in Marketing*, edited by O. C. Ferrell and Raymond LaGarce. Lexington, Mass.: Lexington Books, 1975, pp. 105–51.

Levin, H. J. "The Limits of Self-Regulation." *Columbia Law Review* 57, no. 4 (April 1967): 603–44.

Maitland, Ian. "The Limits of Business Self-Regulation." *California Management Review* 27, no. 3 (Spring 1985): 132–47.

McConnell, Grant. *Private Power and American Democracy*. New York: Knopf, 1966.

Miracle, G. E., and T. R. Nevett. *Voluntary Regulation of Advertising: A Comparative Analysis of the United Kingdom and the United States*. Lexington, Mass.: Lexington Books, 1987.

Mitchell, Jeremy. "Government-Approved Codes of Practice: A New Approach to Reducing Friction between Business and Consumers." *Journal of Consumer Policy* 1, no. 2 (1978): 144–58.

Moe, T. M. "Toward a Broader View of Interest Groups." *Journal of Politics* 43, no. 2 (May 1981): 531–43.

Molnar, J. J. "Comparative Organizational Properties and Interorganizational Interdependence." *Sociology and Social Research* 63, no. 1 (October 1978): 24–48.

Moyer, M. S. "Public Participation in Making Marketing Policies: A Canadian Experiment." *The Business Quarterly* [Western Ontario], (Winter 1979): 63–72.

Moyer, M. S., and J. C. Banks. "Industry Self-Regulation: Some Lessons from the Canadian Advertising Industry." In *Problems in Canadian Marketing*, edited by D.N. Thompson. Chicago, Ill.: American Marketing Association, 1977, 185–202.

Nadel, M. V. *The Politics of Consumer Protection*. Indianapolis, Ind.: Bobbs-Merrill, 1971.

Neelankavil, J. P., and A. B. Stridsberg. *Advertising Self-Regulation: A Global Perspective*. New York: Hastings House, 1980.

"The New FTC: Steady as She Goes: An Interview with Chairman Dan Oliver." *American Advertising*, 3, no. 3 (January 1987): 9–11.

Ogilvy & Mather. "Advertiser to Consumer: How Am I Doing?" *Listening Post* 61 (April 1985).

Olander, Folke, and Hakan Lindhoff. "Consumer Action Research: A Review of the Consumerism Literature and Suggestions for New Directions in Research." *Social Science Information* 14, no. 6 (1975): 147–84.

Opinion Research Corporation. *Implementation and Enforcement of Codes of Ethics in Corporations and Associations; A Report Prepared for the Ethics Resource Center*. Princeton, N.J.: August 1980.

Pennings, J. M. "Strategically Interdependent Organizations." In *Handbook of Organizational Design*, vol. 1, edited by P. C. Nystrom, and W. H. Starbuck. New York: Oxford University Press, 1981, pp. 433–55.

Pickering, J. F., and D. C. Cousins. *The Economic Implications of Codes of Practice*. Manchester, England: University of Manchester Institute of Science and Technology, Department of Management Sciences, July 1980.

Preston, I. L. "A Review of the Literature on Advertising Regulation." In *Current Issues and Research in Advertising*. Ann Arbor, Mich.: Division of Research, Graduate School of Business Administration, University of Michigan, 1983, pp. 1–37.

Provan, K. G. "The Federation as an Interorganizational Linkage Network." *Academy of Management Review* 8, no. 1 (1983): 79–89.

Rijkens, Rein, and G. E. Miracle. *European Regulation of Advertising*. Amsterdam and New York: North-Holland, 1986.

Rosden, G. E., and P. E. Rosden. *The Law of Advertising*. New York: Matthew Bender, 1982.

Schmitter, P. C. "Still the Century of Corporatism?" *Review of Politics* 36 (1974): 85–131.

Scrivener, Christiane. *Rôle, Responsabilité et Avenir de la Publicité* [Role, Responsibility and Future of Advertising]. Paris: Documentation Française, 1979.

Stigler, George. "The Theory of Economic Regulation." *Bell Journal of Economics* 2, no. 1 (1971): 2–31.

Streek, Wolfgang, and Schmitter, P. C. "Community, Market, State— and Associations? The Prospective Contribution of Interest Governance to Social Order." In *Private Interest Government: Beyond Market and State*, edited by Wolfgang Streeck, and Ph. C. Schmitter. London and Beverly Hills, Calif.: Sage, 1985, pp. 1–29.

Stridsberg, A. B. *Progress in Effective Advertising Self-Regulation*. New York: International Advertising Association, 1976.

Stumpf, S. A.; Zand, D. E.; and R. D. Freedman. "Designing Groups for Judgmental Decisions." *Academy of Management Review* 4, no. 4 (October 1979): 589–600.

Thain, G. T. et al. "Report of Survey of Public Members of Wisconsin Agencies, and Advocacy of a Public-Membership Requirement for Bodies Subject to the Proposed Rule; Before the Federal Trade Commission; Hearings on Proposed Standards and Certification Rule." Milwaukee, Wis.: Center for Public Representation and Center for Consumer Affairs, 1979.

Thomas, Richard. "Codes of Practice in the United Kingdom and the Consumer Interest." *Journal of Consumer Policy* 7, no. 2 (June 1984): 198–202.

Thompson, Fred, and L. R. Jones. *Regulatory Policy and Practices: Regulating Better and Regulating Less*. New York: Praeger, 1982.

Thomson, Peter. "Self-Regulation: Some Observations." Mimeographed. London: Advertising Standards Authority, 1983.

United Nations, Economic and Social Council. *Guidelines for Consumer Protection*. New York: 1985.

Venables, Tony. "European Codes: A Red Herring." *Journal of Consumer Policy* 7, no. 2 (June 1984): 296–300.

Vogel, David. "Promoting Pluralism: The Politics of the Public Interest Movement." Mimeographed. Berkeley, Calif.: School of Business Administration, University of California, 1979. Another version of this paper is: "The Public-Interest Movement and the American Reform Tradition." *Political Science Quarterly* 95, no. 4 (Winter 1980–1981): 607–27.

Weiss, Dimitri, and Yves Chirouze. *Le Consommérisme*. Paris: Sirey, 1984.

Wyckham, R. G. "Industry and Government Advertising Regulation: An Analysis of Relative Efficiency and Effectiveness." *Canadian Journal of Administrative Sciences* 4 no. 1, (March 1987): 31–51.

Yuchtman, Ephraim, and S. E. Seashore. "A System Resource Approach to Organizational Effectiveness." *American Sociological Review* 32, no. 6 (December 1967): 891–903.

Zanot, E. J. "The National Advertising Review Board: Premise, Precedents and Performance.'' Unpublished doctoral dissertation, Ann Arbor, Mich.: University Microfilms International, 1977.

———. ''The National Advertising Review Board: 1971–1976.'' *Journalism Monographs* 59 (February 1979): 1–46.

———. ''Unseen but Effective Advertising Regulation: The Clearance Process.'' *Journal of Advertising* 14, no. 4 (1985): 44 ff.

Index

About the Author

J.J. BODDEWYN is Professor of Marketing and International Business as well as Coordinator of the International Business Program at the Baruch College of the City University of New York. He is the editor of *International Studies of Management and Organization* and also serves on the editorial review board of many leading journals. Among his many books are *Comparison Advertising: A Worldwide Study*, *Public Policy Toward Retailing*, *Multinational Government Relations*, *International Divestment*, *Comparative Management and Marketing*, and *International Business-Government Communications*. His numerous articles have been published in such distinguished journals as the *Academy of Management Journal*, *Journal of Marketing*, *Journal of Consumer Policy*, *Journal of Consumer Affairs*, *Journal of International Business Studies*, and *Journal of Marketing Research*. He was elected Fellow of the Academy of Management, the Academy of International Business, and the International Academy of Management.